Manga
and
Philosophy

Fullmetal Metaphysician

Imagine a world without Superman, Captain America or Wonder Woman. Instead, the fate of humanity rests with the likes of Black Jack, Princess Nausicaä and the Elric Brothers. Rather than heroes who fight crime in costumes that hide secret identities . . .

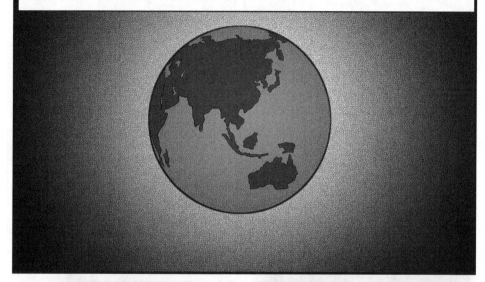

three magical sisters sent from a parallel universe rescue endangered species;

. . . a disillusioned teenager writes the names of criminals in a black notebook with devastating consequences;

These are just a few of the worlds manga help us imagine.

and a violent assassin changes his ways to become a wanderer who protects the people of Japan.

They just happen to believe that many of the people throughout history that we call philosophers would have found a lot of interesting things to think about if they had read manga too.

Manga and Philosophy is about those worlds. The writers and artists in this book love - and love talking about - manga.

In Japan, manga are also called "komikku."

The manga of this book are a perfect example of how philosophical ideas are around us all the time

and those ideas can be fun and entertaining.

This is part of the reason we love talking about the manga we're reading with our friends.

Manga are most commonly thought of as Japanese comics and printed cartoons, particularly those styles and forms that developed around the time of World War II.

"Manga-ka" is the Japanese word for comic artist or cartoonist.

One of the best-known manga-ka, Tezuka Osamu, is sometimes called the "God of Manga."

In the USA, people often think of comics as being for kids. But in Japan, nearly everyone reads manga, no matter how old or young they are. In fact, manga are sometimes classified by who they're written for:

But manga are part of a larger artistic tradition in Japan that began centuries ago.

shōjo for girls 10 to 18 years old,

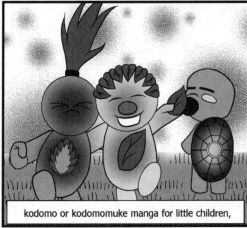

kodomo or kodomomuke manga for little children,

shōnen for boys,

josei for young women

But even older people read them.

and seinen for men 18 to 30.

Regardless of who the manga are written for, there can be many different genres: romance, science fiction, history, drama, comedy, fantasy, mystery, horror, sports, adventure . . . just to name a few.

You've probably figured out that traditional manga are read right to left, top to bottom. That's just one example of how manga can make us aware of our assumptions and give us new ways to think about . . .

. . . well, about everything!

Art is simply another word for life, and one of the common goals of art, across all cultures, is the aim for a higher truth.

"Philosophy" comes from the Greek word that means "love of wisdom," and manga-ka and philosophers have a lot in common. Piero Scaruffi, who's a poet and cognitive scientist (!) among other interests, has said that:

Ideas that excited people nearly 4,000 years ago still excite us today, and find new expression in modern art forms like manga.

Swissnex
San Francisco
2007

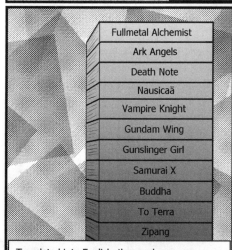

Fullmetal Alchemist

Ark Angels

Death Note

Nausicaä

Vampire Knight

Gundam Wing

Gunslinger Girl

Samurai X

Buddha

To Terra

Zipang

Translated into English, the word *manga* means something like "whimsical pictures." Sure, reading manga can be a lot of fun and seem full of whimsy, but it can also say a lot about what it means . . .

The otaku who wrote this book will help us think about manga in new ways as well.

... to be in relationships with others,

... to be alive,

... to be human.

... to be a part of society, to experience the world around us,

Now that you know a bit more about this book in your hands, flip it over and start reading like a Westerner would.

In other words, manga allow us to imagine people, places and situations that can speak to our emotions and our thoughts.

Kids ... Animals ...
and Women with Attitude

*U*nlike Spike, we *love* kids, animals, women (and men) with attitude, and we especially appreciate the people who so generously gave of their time and attention to help make this book a better reality.

Amada Rosas illustrated our dividers, title page, and manga introduction through a combination of traditional drawing and MangaStudio software. Shane Arbogast created the coordinated covers for this book and *Anime and Philosophy: Wide Eyed Wonder* (2010). Rich Meher, Asher Dunkelman, Nami Unm, Ayako Kato, Erika Harada, Maiko Tomita, Maimi Hirano & Jason Goulah, Karen Kawashima, Trisha Muro, Chikako Ozawa-De Silva, John & Ritzu Shultz, Niall Hartnett, Makiko Hori, and Ken Pletcher suggested (and reviewed) our Japanese translations for the book's sections. *Tezuka* was easy, since that's his name. A little tougher were finding titles for the other sections, like *Ketsuekigata* (which literally means "blood type" for our discussion of several different types of manga), *Kazoku* for those writing about family relationships in manga, *Nimensei* for the two chapters about *Death Note, Zen No Michi* for the section about what it takes to be a good person, *Hamon* for the chapters about manga's influence, and *Furoku* for our supplemental materials, like contributor bios, bibliography, and index. We met this great group of Japanese speakers through Ann Alter, Carol Beck, Lott Hill, Daniele Wilmouth, Bryan Barker, Ernie Constantino, Dan Dinello, Josephina Gasca, Cheryl Graeff, and Sue Mroz.

Editorial Director David Ramsay Steele and Series Editor George Reisch provided feedback, proofreading, insights, and ideas throughout the process, as did Andrew Dowd, Louis Melançon, Ada Palmer, Deborah Shamoon, Cari Callis, Hal Shipman, Sara Livingston, Joan McGrath, and Tristan Tamplin.

Thanks to Caity Birmingham, Laurel Parker, Sharon Evans, Nicole Hollander, Shelley Ferguson, KJ Mathieson, Magali Rennes, Tracy Ullman, Namita Wiggers, Johanna Draper Carlson, LeRon James Harrison, Jef Burnham, Laura Miller, Aaron Vanek, Ron Falzone, and Matt Thorn for their support and suggestions. And to the 'Bou (Steven, Laura, Joe, Jori, Jeni, Kari, Jen, Cassie, Stephanie, Megan, and Dillon) as well as our colleagues at Columbia College and Yonsei University.

We would particularly like to thank the publishers who make it possible for us to read manga and whose series are discussed in this book: ADV Manga, Dark Horse Comics, Del Ray Manga, Digital Manga Publishing, Kodansha, Last Gasp Publishers, Marvel Comics, Mixx Entertainment, Ponent Mon, San Val, Shōjo Beat Manga, Shueisha, Tanoshimi, Tezuka Productions, Tokuma Shoten, TokyoPop, Vertical, and VIZ Media. Any excerpts are reproduced for purposes of intellectual commentary and all rights are retained by the individual copyright holders.

Thanks to Masaomi Kanzaki and Masahiko Nakahira (*Street Fighter*), Yu Watase (*Fushigi Yūgi*), Kōsuke Fujishima (*Oh My Goddess!*) and Keiko Nobumoto, Hajime Yatate, Yutaka Nanten, Cain Kuga (*Cowboy BeBop*) for the titles of our *furoku*. We also appreciate the insights June Madeley has been compiling from her research at <http://v8nu74s71s31g374r7ssn017uloss3c1vr3s.unbf.ca/~jmadeley/Manga_research.htm>.

You will find additional *furoku* in our companion volume, *Anime and Philosophy: Wide Eyed Wonder*, including a glossary of manga- and anime-related terms under the heading "Subtitles."

We hope you enjoyed reading our introduction and acknowledgments in authentic manga "back-to-front" style, but the rest of the book is laid out in the Western tradition of "front-to-back." Before you turn this book over to start reading from the other end ...

Joe would like to thank Margo for introducing him to anime and manga, and Victor for actually giving him manga rather than throwing it out (like his mom did with his comics, but that's okay, Mom).

Adam would like to offer an extra special thanks to his brother Joe for introducing him to this stuff in the first place:

"You were right again. This one's for you."

WAIT!

Before you start reading, flip this book over.

Why, you ask?

As with traditional manga, you have to flip this book over to start. That's where you'll find our introduction—*Fullmetal Metaphysician*—written as manga.

If you're new to manga, read the introduction from right to left, top to bottom, like this:

Confused? Don't worry.

Just flip the book over, and you'll see how fun and easy it is. If you've read manga before, you already know.

If you're in a hurry to read *about* manga, then go ahead and turn this page to dive right into chapters about *Nausicaä, Vampire Knight, Samurai X, Phoenix, Death Note, Gundam Wing, Gunslinger Girl,* and all the other great manga we've written about.

Be sure to check out our companion volume, *Anime and Philosophy: Wide Eyed Wonder,* as well.

Whether you're a true otaku or whether this is your introduction to Japanese comics, we hope you have as much fun reading as we had writing.

Manga
and
Philosophy

Popular Culture and Philosophy®
Series Editor: George A. Reisch

For full details of all Popular Culture and Philosophy® books, visit www.opencourtbooks.com.

POPULAR CULTURE AND PHILOSOPHY®

MANGA
AND PHILOSOPHY

Edited by
Josef Steiff
and
Adam Barkman

FULLMETAL
METAPHYSICIAN

OPEN COURT
CHICAGO AND LA SALLE, ILLINOIS

Volume 52 in the series, Popular Culture and Philosophy®,
edited by George A. Reisch

To order books from Open Court, call toll-free 1-800-815-2280, or visit our website at www.opencourtbooks.com.

Open Court Publishing Company is a division of Carus Publishing Company.

Printed and bound in the United States of America.

Library of Congress Cataloging-in-Publication Data

Manga and philosophy: fullmetal metaphysician / edited by Josef Steiff and Adam Barkman.
         p. cm. -- (Popular culture and philosophy ; v. 52)
         Includes bibliographical references and index.
         ISBN 978-0-8126-9679-0 (trade pbk. : alk. paper)
         1. Comic books, strips, etc.--Japan--History and criticism 2. Comic books, strips, etc.--Japan--Moral and ethical aspects. I. Steiff, Josef. II. Barkman, Adam.
      PN6790.J3M36 2010
      741.5'6952--dc22
                                  2010016759

Contents

FUROKU

TEZUKA

1

You Need a System to Play Black Jack

TRISTAN D. TAMPLIN

A recklessly driven sports car careens down a European sidewalk, narrowly missing several pedestrians—though a newsstand proves less evasive—before violently crashing headlong into a telephone pole. The accident is catastrophic, and the young driver's injuries are very grave.

Fortunately for him, his father is a "famous tycoon" who will pay any price to ensure that his son's life is saved. The hospital that he has been rushed to is, however, not quite up to the task. Indeed, no doctor is willing to guarantee success in such a seemingly hopeless case—no doctor, that is, aside from an extraordinarily gifted physician from Japan, a "surgical genius" known only as Black Jack.

Even though Black Jack is confident that he can save the tycoon's son, he can only do so by replacing those body parts that are beyond remedy. To save this patient, another must sacrifice his body. For a man possessing both vast wealth and great power, while lacking any moral squeamishness about putting them to their most effective use, this proves to be an entirely soluble problem. A young tailor who had barely escaped injury in the accident is accused of being its cause. After having him arrested, the father buys off the judge and the other witnesses and by the end of the day (literally!) an innocent young man is convicted and sentenced to death. At which point it is simply a matter of providing those needful parts of the condemned tailor's body to the tycoon's good-for-nothing son. And, just as Black Jack promised, the subsequent operation is a complete success. Well, sort of, anyway.

It was clear all along, clear even to the father, that Black Jack had some strong reservations about this case. And despite the blatant illegality involved, his reservations are not pragmatic—after all, Black Jack practices without a license and, as such, already operates in the shadowy periphery of the medical community. No, Black Jack's reservations are entirely moral in nature—he objects to the sacrifice of a worthy life to an unworthy recipient. But he performs

the operation anyway and is paid handsomely upon its successful outcome. More precisely, he performs an operation, though not the one the tycoon had in mind. Rather than saving the tycoon's son by replacing his damaged parts with those from the tailor, Black Jack merely operates on the face of the tailor to make him look like the tycoon's son.

Once recovered, the tailor immediately returns to his own mother and together they escape to "some foreign country" using money that Black Jack gave him. Hooray! The enigmatic doctor has performed yet another miracle with his scalpel.

Raising the Stakes

From this very first chapter ("Is There a Doctor?" 1973) we begin to see the sorts of significant themes and issues that will be in play throughout the series. The stories told in *Black Jack* always involve high stakes, and not just because they tend to be about matters of life and death. This "peerless medical drama" persistently grapples with foundational issues in medical ethics as well as wider questions of social justice, from informed consent to access to care and distribution of limited resources.

The Black Jack series looks at these issues from the perspective of a very singular doctor, one who is driven by principles that are not always readily apparent, and this allows us to see these troubling issues in a new and unusual light. And the narrative framework has a decidedly personal edge that makes it all the more penetrating.

Black Jack was written and illustrated by renowned manga artist Osamu Tezuka, who received his MD from Osaka University in 1946 and passed the exam to become a practicing physician in 1952. A year later he chose instead to devote himself to his artistic endeavors. By the time Tezuka began work on *Black Jack*, the Japanese health care system, in a process that began in the late 1920s, had evolved to provide relative equality of access through a mandatory universal health care insurance program. But what makes thinking about *Black Jack* a useful way to consider medical issues of moral import is not merely that it takes up the perspective of a divinely skilled doctor, nor the fact this perspective is sharpened by the added weight of personal experience and social history. What's truly significant about Black Jack is not that he's a doctor, but that he's a pariah.

While we know right from the outset that Black Jack doesn't have a license to practice medicine, it's never explicitly revealed why this is the case. Surely it is not from lack of skill or an inability to pass a required exam. Nor is it ever implied that he had a license at one time that was either revoked or renounced. We know that his motivation to pursue a career in medicine was sound (he greatly admired his mentor and savior, Dr. Jotaro Honma), we know that he was

successful at medical school (from flashbacks, as in the chapter "Confluence"), and we know that his private practice is legendary. So why is he unlicensed and generally reviled by the medical community?

The only reasonable answer—made all the more so by its confluence with Tezuka's own life—is that Black Jack has *chosen* to pursue his career outside of the established medical system and without the sanction of its institutions. The basis of that choice is far less clear than the fact of it, and the vagueness of Black Jack's position is in many ways the underlying narrative force of the series. But we can begin to come to grips with at least aspects of that choice by observing the ways in which he navigates the rather disparate relationships that his position as a pariah involves him in. Chief among these are his dealings with the medical community and its institutions on the one hand, and his patients on the other. While the former are characterized by a consistent and thorough antagonism, the later are, on the whole, ambiguous in important ways. By paying close attention to these interactions, we can begin to get a sense of the principles that guide his everyday normative choices, as well as the more essential choice to become a pariah.

But these same observations also point to the conclusion that when the stakes are raised sufficiently high enough—say, from the evaluation of a single doctor to the examination of an entire system of healthcare—a set of principles might not be enough. To play for those stakes requires a more comprehensive normative framework. We're going to need a system.

Reading the Players

It hardly seems surprising that Black Jack has chosen to pursue his work outside the purview of the established medical community when we witness the disregard that he frequently displays toward it. And while his disdain is occasionally directed at other doctors—typically those who doubt his abilities or who are too unsure of their own—it's most commonly leveled at hospital managers and administrators. In their roles as the representatives and agents of medical institutions, they must suffer the brunt of Black Jack's antagonism because the true source of his hostility cannot be confronted in any other way. Black Jack's withdrawal from the medical community seems to stem from a deep dissatisfaction not with its members, but with its institutions. He takes up his position on the outside as a result of his alienation from the health care system itself. Although the system itself is not something that can be engaged directly, Black Jack is no Don Quixote ineffectually jousting with windmills. What allows Black Jack to assert his position is that he brings something to the table that all the other players value highly—his extraordinary skill. And what allows him to maintain that position is that he is pragmatic (and perhaps cynical) enough to leverage his skill effectively. Despite the disapproval he

obviously feels toward patients and institutions alike, he does not seek to extract a promise of reform in exchange for his services. No, Black Jack seeks to extract money, lots and lots of money.

A recurrent theme in *Black Jack* is that even though hospitals possess vital resources on a massive scale, they are often oriented in ways that serve as an impediment to treatment and quality health care. We'll pick this point up later, but these shortcomings typically manifest themselves in terms of issues of distribution rather than access (not surprisingly, given that the health care system in Japan at the time provided universal coverage). The issue is not so much that patients aren't being treated, but that they aren't being treated as well as they could be. This is expressed in a variety of ways, including concern about the mechanization of care and a tendency toward over-specialization.

In *U 18 Knew* an entirely automated medical center is held hostage by the super-computer that handles every aspect of its day-to-day operation, from clinical to administrative. After its encounter with Black Jack it is, ironically, the computer itself that realizes "it takes a human to treat a human." In *Assembly Line Care* Black Jack argues that an efficiently run, low-cost hospital is losing patients because it has failed to grasp that "patients want one doctor to stick with them from beginning to end" rather than be passed from one specialist to another during the course of their treatment. We often observe the ways in which hospital bureaucracy and politics can impede treatment, impediments that Black Jack himself is easily able to avoid because of his position as a pariah. If the hospital is getting in the way of providing the best treatment, then it's best to get out of the hospital.

The fact that Black Jack doesn't have a license to practice medicine rarely stands in the way of his actually doing so. His amazing skill seems to completely circumvent one of the most significant institutional controls in the healthcare system. Their need of his skill offers a more meaningful sanction than his willingness to submit to their authority ever could. Everyone is aware of his illegitimate status yet it ultimately doesn't seem to matter. His skill always outweighs his lack of credentials; their need always trumps their rules. Even in those rare instances when the fact that he has no license is actually taken seriously, it doesn't amount to anything of consequence.

In *To Each His Own*, Black Jack is under scrutiny by some regulatory agency when a serious accident occurs just outside. The hospital doesn't have enough doctors to cope with the emergency, so he offers to help in exchange for the charges against him being dropped. The official, of course, readily agrees. In *Helping Each Other* a hospital director stubbornly refuses Black Jack access to a patient because he doesn't have a medical license. So Black Jack simply approaches the owner and buys the hospital. In cash. What can be gleaned from these interactions is a clear assessment of the relative value of what the

parties bring to the table. Hospitals offer resources and access to treatment that, as vital as they are, are ultimately of instrumental value only. What is of necessity is the ability to treat. A skilled doctor is indispensable to the healthcare system, and if we lose sight of this fact, Black Jack will surely bring it to our attention.

In contrast to his rather uniformly disdainful attitude toward institutions, Black Jack's dealings with his patients are somewhat surprisingly fraught with ambiguity. On one level, his stance on traditional questions of medical ethics seems inconsistent. For instance, he often blatantly (and sometimes spectacularly) disregards his patient's right to informed consent. In addition to the secret face transplant already described, he has also shot a patient in the course of treatment (*The Face Sore*), and retained and eventually brought to life the unformed twin of another (*Teratoid Cystoma*) without either's consent. This lack of regard for the autonomy of his patients is not particularly noteworthy—the concept of informed consent has only gained prominence in the last several decades, and was virtually nonexistent in Japan at the time. What is noteworthy is the degree to which he does inform his patients, including cases where it was exceedingly uncommon practice to do so (in *Confluence,* he frankly discusses a cancer patient's prognosis with her).

On another, perhaps deeper level, it is unclear if Black Jack is motivated primarily by concern for his patients or by his own egoism. While there's no doubt that he is thoroughly driven to treat his patients successfully, and is willing to go to any length to "cure" them, exactly why he is so committed is far more dubious. In *The First Storm of Spring* a cornea transplant he performed fails to cure his patient and, despite her obvious distress, he responds as if he is more aggrieved by his "disgrace" than she is by the persistence of her symptoms. But Black Jack is not entirely oblivious to the dangers of hubris. In *Sometimes Like Pearls* he learns from his mentor that "to crave control over life and death is sheer arrogance," while in *Needle* he is reminded that treatment of the human body isn't always subject to reason. He is, however, a rather unwilling student in such matters and tends to chafe against these lessons.

Part of the reason that Black Jack struggles to take the lessons of hubris to heart is that his belief in the indispensable value of his skill is constantly reinforced. Institutions will ignore their own rules to retain his services, and patients and hospitals alike are more than willing to pay his astounding fees. Indeed, at times those fees seem both arbitrary and cruel, as if charging for his services is in some way punitive. On more than one occasion he demands a fee that he knows will require that his patient sacrifice everything for his services, and he seems entirely unashamed that he might be "the greediest man ever." And yet in other cases he charges nothing, and will even suffer great personal risk or financial cost in the course of treatment.

I don't believe that it can be plausibly argued that there is any sort of demonstrable consistency in Black Jack's ethics or his fees, nor would I expect Black Jack to be particularly troubled by this lack. But even if his actions are somewhat inconsistent they are certainly not incoherent, and there does seem to be a fairly strong underlying principle at work here, though it is never made entirely explicit. That principle is simply that good health is immensely, incalculably valuable. Acknowledging this fairly innocuous principle immediately affords us a better understanding of certain features of Black Jack's relationships. If good health is immensely valuable, then the ability to restore it is similarly valuable. This helps to explain not just the extent of his fees, but also, and more importantly, his attitudes toward charging them. Sometimes his patients need to be reminded about just how valuable good health is; sometimes they need to be made aware that they've got their priorities all wrong. The principle also has significant implications for Black Jack's dealings with institutions. Hospitals, medical centers, research laboratories and regulatory agencies are, quite obviously, not people. They cannot be healthy or unhealthy in any non-metaphorical sense and, as such, are incapable of appropriately valuing good health. At best, they value health in terms of money; at worst, they value money instead of health. But, in any case, this divergence over the fundamental value of good health goes a long way toward explaining why Black Jack is a pariah of the medical community.

The Need for a System

The principle that good health is intrinsically and significantly valuable provides Black Jack with a potent source of motivation as he navigates his relationships with both patients and institutions, but it can only provide normative guidance in a very general sense. It gives him a certain basic moral orientation, but effectively little else. And while that principle is not comprehensive enough to ensure that his actions and choices are ethically consistent, it seems to work well enough for him, by and large. His behavior may sometimes be morally vague, and his reasoning might occasionally be inscrutable, but he does manage to get along quite adequately. He may be disappointed from time to time, but he is not unhappy. He is successful enough and respected enough that he never wants for patients. He is not infrequently heroic. His career certainly must be regarded as a success by the standards, if not the auspices, of the medical community.

Adherence to a normative principle about the value of health likely had very little to do with this success *per se*, but it had almost everything to do with the way that success was achieved. It was this simple principle that led Black Jack to become a pariah. If good health is incredibly valuable, and if the institutions

that constitute the health care system do not adequately recognize this value, then the promotion of good health is best pursued outside that system. Put another way, measured against perhaps the most significant normative standard in Black Jack's life the health-care system was found lacking, so he rejected it.

The conscientious application of a normative principle to Black Jack's life led him to fundamentally change its course—because he valued good health so highly he chose to be a pariah of the medical community. Well and good for Black Jack, but what if our concern is the healthcare system itself? A single principle may have been a sufficient basis for one man to evaluate his life and lead him to reform it, but what impact would that same principle have if we applied it to an entire community? We might be able to draw some fairly broad, though not entirely unhelpful conclusions, but likely little else. We might recognize the overall inadequacy of the system (we don't have as much good health as we could), or uncover certain institutional conflicts that undermine the maximization of good health (efficiency and profit, for instance). We might be able to milk a few more conclusions like these out of our principle, but after we've identified all the shortcomings, failings, and inconsistencies that we're able to, well then what? If we care about having a health-care system at all, then we can't simply do what Black Jack did and abandon it for greener pastures. However potent and meaningful it may be, our normative principle seems ill equipped for the task at hand. The problem seems to be one of scope—if one principle works for a man, then we're probably going to need a whole set of them to reform a system.

Oddly enough, this was more or less the functional directive given to the Ethics Working Group of the Clinton White House Health Care Task Force in 1993. They were charged to write a "preamble" to legislation that did not yet exist, drawing on broad traditional values in American culture, in the hope that this would provide "a useful framework for focusing discussion on morally sensitive and controversial choice points in the design of a health care system" (Norman Daniels, "Principles for National Health Care Reform," *Hastings Center Report*, 24: 3, p. 8). While the group more or less succeeded in carrying out its charge, the impact on the subsequent legislative attempts at health-care reform was, to put it mildly, not as hoped. They were able to agree on a set of midlevel principles and values and use them to specify desirable features of health care reform, but there was no such agreement on what sort of ethical theory might provide deeper, more systematic support for those values and principles. This, it turned out, was incredibly significant. Norman Daniels, a Harvard Ethics Professor who served on the group, described the problem this way:

> By seeking agreement on principles and values without agreement on underlying theory, we paid a price. No one reform proposal can fully comply with all the

principles and values, since all feasible proposals will involve different trade-offs among them. A body of systematic theory could have provided more guidance about which kinds of trades are more acceptable by providing grounds for claims about priority among the principles. ("Principles for National Health Care Reform," p. 8)

A set of principles, even a set of principles chosen from within a single tradition of values and selected specifically for the purpose, was unable to provide sufficient guidance to reform the healthcare system. What's necessary is a comprehensive normative framework that will allow us to relate and prioritize those principles and values that are relevant to the context of healthcare. It's going to take a system to reform the system.

Dividing Up the Pot

Easy enough to say, but what is actually involved in applying a comprehensive normative framework to the healthcare system? At root, it involves orienting our evaluation along a normative dimension rather than a pragmatic one. Certain practical considerations will of course be relevant, but they are not, initially at least, our primary focus. The basic idea is that we will use a system of values and principles to choose among available, which is to say, possible, arrangements of our health-care institutions.

If the normative system we adopt requires institutional arrangements that are simply not possible (such as; everyone should have everything they want), then we must reject the system. To avoid such errors and ensure that the normative framework we adopt isn't a non-starter, we might seek to include certain very general facts into our deliberations at the outset. Facts such as the relative scarcity of resources and the lack of a shared conception of the good (often referred to as value pluralism) are often employed in this manner. We'll also need to clarify just what it is that we want our normative framework to do. In the present case, let's assume that we want our value system to frame answers to at least these two fundamental questions:

1. Who should have access to health care?

2. How should health-care resources be distributed?

These are precisely the sorts of questions that fall under the purview of theories of distributive justice. To get a feel for the scope of available theories of distributive justice, we can focus on two examples that will give us very different answers to our two questions—Libertarianism and Egalitarianism.

Libertarian principles do not seek to achieve some desired distributive pattern regarded as just. Rather than proposing that any particular distributive outcome is just, Libertarians instead describe the sorts of acquisitions or exchanges that are themselves just. As such, the justice of a given distribution lies not in the distribution itself, but in the process by which it was achieved. Robert Nozick is perhaps the most well known contemporary advocate of this sort of Libertarianism, and in *Anarchy, State, and Utopia* he advances the view that "a distribution is just if everyone is entitled to the holdings they possess under the distribution" (p. 151).

This sort of Entitlement Theory, which can trace its roots to John Locke, puts great emphasis on the role of the market in ensuring a just distribution. The market plays that role not as a means to some pattern, but insofar as the transactions it permits satisfy the conditions of just exchange described by the principles. If these conditions for exchange are adhered to, then whatever distribution results is thereby just. Under such a theory, health-care reform would take the shape of making sure that the relevant market forces were operating freely and fairly, which would in turn guarantee that everyone who was entitled to health care had access to it. So a Libertarian would answer the question of access in terms of entitlement, and the question of distribution in terms of principles of just acquisition and transfer.

An Egalitarian, on the other hand, would give a very different answer to the first question: everyone should have access to healthcare. There is no similarly succinct answer to the second question, however, and the responses will diverge amongst the various strands of this sort of theory. Strict Egalitarianism would say that every person should have the same level of health care. If each person is owed equal moral respect, requiring that material resources be equally distributed is the best way to realize that ideal.

However, the idea of giving everyone an equal amount of health-care resources seems significantly flawed. A healthy eighteen-year-old certainly doesn't need the same level of medical care as an eighty-year-old diabetic. And even if we attempted to normalize the health-care resources we distribute over a lifetime, the core problem remains—people have irreducibly different medical needs, and as long as we assume finite resources, then a surplus of unneeded medical care is wasteful. Because it tends to lead to just these sorts of problematic results, several alternatives to the principle of strict equality have been developed.

One such alternative formulation, proposed by John Rawls, is the Difference Principle. Its moral inspiration is fundamentally the same as that for strict equality—equal respect for persons. But the Difference Principle allows for unequal distributions under certain conditions. Most notably for our purposes, social and economic inequalities are permissible so long as "they are

to be to the greatest benefit of the least advantaged members of society" (John Rawls, *Political Liberalism*, p. 6). Put another way, inequality can be justified, but only if can be shown that those who are worst off—the poor, the disabled, the chronically ill, and so on—will benefit the most from the unequal distribution. While this principle might be used to justify some of Black Jack's actions, the method of reasoning that Rawls used to derive it has important, and somewhat surprising, implications for healthcare reform.

Getting a Fair Deal

One of the reasons that Rawls's *Theory of Justice* is widely regarded as one of the most significant philosophic works of the last several decades is the theoretic structure he developed for thinking about matters of social justice, the central element of which is the idea of the original position. The original position is a hypothetical situation in which individuals are to choose the principles of justice that will govern their society. Rawls seeks to describe the original position in such a way that we would regard it as "fundamentally fair," so that by imagining ourselves to be participants in that situation we thereby take up an unbiased point of view. The core idea is that if we subject our reasoning about matters of justice to the conditions imposed by the original position, it will ensure that the principles we chose will be as widely acceptable as possible.

Rawls originally described his view as "justice as fairness," since the essential point is that fair conditions of choice yield the most appropriate conception of justice. The features of the original position are intended to guarantee the fairness of the outcome, and two of its most prominent features are primary social goods and the veil of ignorance. Primary social goods are what the parties in the original position are choosing how to distribute. They are all-purpose social means to a wide variety of rational life plans, so that individuals should want them no matter what their conception of the good happens to be. No matter what kind of life I may want to pursue, having an adequate share of primary social goods will help me to do so. The veil of ignorance is employed to remove bias from the original position. To ensure that the choice that the parties make is fair, they are deprived of all sorts of specific information about themselves and their society. Without any particular knowledge of themselves or their circumstances, the parties much choose principles of justice that would be acceptable to anyone. According to Rawls, reasoning from behind the veil of ignorance ensures that the parties in the original position will select principles that will distribute the primary social goods in a way that each of them will regard as fair, no matter who they turn out to be once the veil is lifted.

Rawls argues that the parties in the original position will select two principles of justice. The first is a principle of equality, and the second involves the Difference Principle, which permits inequality but only when it is most beneficial to the least well-off members of society. Part of the rationale for the Difference Principle is that the parties will adopt a "maximin" strategy when making their choice. The aim of this strategy is to ensure that worst-case scenario is as good as possible. Because the primary social goods are so important, because the stakes are so high, Rawls argues that the parties will take a rather cautious approach and play it safe with how they distribute those goods. They will hedge their bets a bit by seeking to maximize their minimum prospects and will select distributive principles whose worst outcome leaves them better off than the worst outcome of all other alternatives.

And herein lies the relevance of the idea of the original position for thinking about justice in the health care system. For health care is just the sort of all-purpose means to any rational life plan that would have it count as a primary social good. And the maximin strategy seems extremely compelling in the case of healthcare. After all, guarding against the worst-case is precisely the motivation for health insurance (and why lack of coverage is such a significant concern in the United States). Having no share of health care resources is a truly abysmal worst case, no matter whom I might turn out to be once the veil of ignorance is removed.

Playing by the Rules

Even though he possesses nearly divine surgical skills, Black Jack is not particularly well regarded. His legendary skills may earn him grudging respect and high demand for his services, but he is always viewed with suspicion. And it's not just because he's a pariah. Nearly all heroes are pariahs—but very few of them charge astronomical fees for their services.

Black Jack might be generally unloved because he charges those high fees, but is he unjust to do so? According to the Difference Principle, economic inequalities are permissible so long as they benefit the least advantaged members of society. Charging the fees that he does creates economic inequality, most narrowly, between Black Jack and everyone else. And if we think about doctors in general, then the inequality becomes more widespread. To justify this unequal distribution of wealth, we would need to show that it somehow improves the condition of the least well-off.

One of the arguments against Strict Equality is that it provides no incentive for the exceptionally skilled to fully utilize their talents. If my exceptional performance yields no additional benefit for me, then what's the point of

performing exceptionally? This becomes a problem once we recognize that exceptional performance benefits society as a whole. So we need some sort of motivation to encourage innovation and effort, motivation that is lacking when resources are always equally distributed—hence the Difference Principle.

If we don't allow people like Black Jack to receive some additional benefit for providing their services, then they might not bother to provide those services or, more worryingly, they might not cultivate them in the first place. It's not hard to imagine that some people would be put off of the idea of going to medical school if they knew that it wouldn't make them any better off materially than if they just went to work in a coffee shop. And if people stop going to medical school, then we're all going to be a whole lot worse off. So, while the extent of his fees might occasionally be morally suspect, the mere fact that he charges them is entirely justifiable according to our theory.

We suggested that the reason that Black Jack charges the fees that he does is because of the value he places on good health and the derivative value of the ability to restore it. And it's this same assessment of value that led him to become a pariah of the medical community. One way of explaining his concern is to say that the institutions of that community, because they don't properly value good health, contribute to an unjust distribution of medical resources. But even if we share Black Jack's concern, it doesn't provide us with any insight into how to redress that injustice.

The whole point of finding a comprehensive system of justice was to cope with exactly this issue, and if the system we've borrowed from Rawls is going to pay off, here is where it must do so. And, in at least one way, it does indeed give us what we're looking for. The interests and values of health-care institutions—hospitals, insurance organizations, research labs, medical centers, pharmaceutical companies, and all the rest—are simply *not relevant* to reasoning about social justice.

The most appropriate principles of justice are those that would be chosen by the parties in the Original Position, the conditions of which ensure the fairness of the outcome. By selecting principles from behind the Veil of Ignorance, we ensure that our choice is unbiased and reflects equal respect for all persons. No matter who we turn out to be once the Veil is lifted, we'll get a fair share of the primary social goods. But here's the thing—we're not going to turn out to be a hospital, or an insurance company, once the Veil is lifted. Even if the Veil does not preclude us knowing about such institutions, no one in the original position will reason from their point of view.

In thinking about the Original Position, we're attempting to model the reasoning of free and equal moral persons. That reasoning will certainly impact our social institutions, but it does not include those institutions in the choice process itself. If it even makes sense to frame the question, "What

principles of justice would a pharmaceutical company chose to well-order its social institutions?" the answer would be morally irrelevant because institutions like pharmaceutical companies simply have no standing in the Original Position.

It might seem far-fetched to suggest that the interests of health-care institutions are irrelevant when thinking about healthcare reform. Indeed, if we consider the current legislative debate in the United States, the idea that we ought simply to *ignore* the insurance and drug companies seems fairly preposterous. But remember that the motivation for Black Jack's rejection of the health-care system was value-based, and we approached the question of health-care reform from that same perspective. In asking the question "How should health-care resources be distributed?" we framed the issue of health-care reform as a moral rather than a pragmatic issue.

This re-framing of the issue would have a profound impact on the current debate. Another member of the Clinton administration's Ethics Working Group, William F. May, put it this way:

> A major reform of our health care system will rank as the most comprehensive piece of social legislation since the establishment of the social security system. We cannot engage in so grand an undertaking without being clear about its moral foundations. ("The Ethical Foundations of Health Care Reform," p. 573)

The stakes are indeed high, and the risks are magnified if we're unsure about the basis of our wager. To have any reasonable hope of a payoff, since blind luck surely won't help us here, we're going to need a rational system to guide us. That's something you can learn from *Black Jack*.

2

"You, God of Manga, Are Cruel!"

ADA PALMER

Remember that you are an actor in a play, which is as the playwright wants it to be: short if he wants it short, long if he wants it long. If he wants you to play a beggar, play even this part skillfully.... What is yours is to play the assigned part well. But to choose it belongs to someone else.

—EPICTETUS, *Handbook of Stoicism*

It's the end of the future. The Phoenix, avatar and guardian of creation, chooses three humans to survive the extermination of all life on Earth: the weak romantic Yamanobei, who wants only to surrender to the nostalgic embrace of his alien lover; the cold enforcer Rock, who will carry out any order, no matter how ruthless, except the call to war; the selfless sage Saruta, who has sacrificed his long life on the altar of science in search of the secret to restoring Earth's lost vitality. Two will die, alone and failed along with their world. The Phoenix will transform the third into the immortal father of a new Earth and a new human race. She chooses Yamanobei. Even he screams, "Why me?"

It's 1976. A young doctor is diagnosed with the same terminal cancer which claimed the lives of his entire family. His life's dream has been to cure at least a few patients, to strike back at the cruel disease before it claims him too. He struggles through his first operation, dying on his feet in his effort to save a single life. This young man is also Yamanobei, and his lifelong wish to be a preserver of life was granted by the Phoenix in a cosmic choice which here at last makes sense. It doesn't make sense in *Phoenix* "Future" (1967), nor anywhere in the twelve stories of the *Phoenix* series, where dozens of other characters, noble and wicked, quest desperately for the immortality the Phoenix offers, yet she finds none worthy. The story of Dr. Yamanobei appears in *Black Jack* "Tenacity" (1976), a completely different series written nine years after the decision it explains.

Young Dr. Yamanobei begs Dr. Tezuka to let him work, in *Black Jack* "Tenacity," 1976;
© Tezuka Productions and Vertical, Inc.

Osamu Tezuka, "God of Manga," was one of the most prolific authors
in history. He founded dozens of major new manga genres and transformed
dozens more. His first published work, *New Treasure Island* (1946) introduced
the so-called "cinematic" art style, discarding the flat, stage-like structure
which had dominated earlier manga and introducing zooms, close-ups, vistas,
reflections, motion blurs and many other techniques borrowed from the silver
screen which vastly expanded the visual repertoire of ink and paper. He created
the first Japanese animated television series *Astro Boy* (1963), and with it the
alliance between manga and animation in Japan, which so dominates both
industries.

These contributions are already enough to earn him the title "God of
Manga." Add to them his political work promoting environmentalism, pacifism,
racial and religious tolerance, and international cooperation in the development
of technology and medicine, work which countless of today's top Japanese
scientists, doctors and politicians have cited as their inspiration.

Still, the direct and easily-measurable impact of prominent works like *Astro
Boy* (begun in 1952) and even his magnum opus *Phoenix* (1954–1957 and
1967–1988) are not the six-hundred-pound gorilla. Osamu Tezuka left us more
than seven hundred series, including 150,000 pages of manga and more than
seventy animated works. Only when this corpus is read together as a synthetic

whole does the truly unique work of Tezuka the philosopher emerge from that of Tezuka the activist and Tezuka the founder of modern manga and animation.

Prayer and Punishment

Analyzing seven hundred separate stories together isn't as impossible as it sounds, since Tezuka provides a key for reading them: *Phoenix*. Each of the thirteen stories of the *Phoenix* series is a separate saga set at a completely different point in time: the dawn of civilization, the extinction of the human race, the foundation of ancient Japan, the collapse of humanity's great space empire, stories alternating between past and future but drawing ever closer to the present, like a pendulum running out of force. The story isn't linear because the causality isn't linear. It's dominated by a karmic cycle of crime, reincarnation, and punishment which operates irrespective of linear time.

Saruta, the series's central figure, demonstrates its structure. In A.D. 2557 the young space explorer Saruta commits infanticide and is cursed by the Phoenix to eternal punishment, to wander forever through space, ugly and spurned by all around him (*Phoenix*, Volume 3, "Space," 1969). In A.D. 240 Saruta lives out this punishment as a long-suffering general (Volume 1, "Dawn," 1967), then again in A.D. 720 as a mass-murdering outcast (Volume 5, "Karma," 1969–70), in 1468

Saruta is cursed by the Phoenix for his crimes, in *Phoenix* "Space," 1969; © 2003 Tezuka Productions and VIZ Media.

Saruta discovers the beauty of life, p. 356 of *Phoenix* "Karma," 1969-70; © 2004 Tezuka Productions and VIZ Media.

as a callous, diseased warlord (Volume 9, "Strange Beings"), in 1980 as a cloning researcher (Volume 10 "Life"), over and over until Dr. Saruta of "Future" watches Earth die around him in A.D. 3404.

Saruta's punishment feels cruel and unusual. Why should he suffer eternally for a single crime, particularly when many characters around him, and even Saruta himself, commit much worse crimes frequently throughout the series?

Let's take a narrower example, Akanemaru, the gifted sculptor and Saruta's rival and enemy in *Phoenix* "Karma." Akanemaru quests to create a sculpture of the Phoenix, and succeeds thanks to a vision in which he remembers seeing her in a different reincarnation when he was a bird. After being corrupted by jealousy and court politics into committing his own share of atrocities, including having his artistic rival's arm cut off, destroying his ability to sculpt, Akanemaru sees the Phoenix again as he lies dying, and begs her for a chance to carve her once more. She answers that his fate is sealed: he will never again be reincarnated as a human. Like the rival he had dismembered, he will never again have human hands with which to create art.

This too seems cruel and unusual, but as we remember Akanemaru's bird reincarnation, which we now realize lies three reincarnations in the future from his life as a sculptor, we recall that the young bird and his mother are both horrified at the thought that he might ever be a horrible human. The Phoenix's decision that Akanemaru should have no more human lives is for the sculptor a cruel but fitting punishment, but for the bird it grants his and his mother's wish that he never become a terrible human. The wish made in one lifetime is granted in another, where it serves as punishment.

Looking again at Saruta now, we see that his punishment too is the answer to a prayer. Dr. Saruta of "Future" longs to understand the secrets of life. This understanding he receives in "Karma" through his long suffering, and the Phoenix even grants him visions of his other reincarnations, revealing his far future crime and punishment, and with it the true, interconnected nature of life. Saruta's lives in other *Phoenix* chapters guide him toward even more aspects of the secrets he seeks, secrets too complex for any one lifetime to achieve them all. Without many centuries of isolated wandering, without many deaths each of which brings a new discovery, Saruta would never approach the understanding he desires. His sentence, to wander forever ugly and alone, grants his prayer.

Wise and Cruel Law

Saruta's wise and cruel fate isn't limited to *Phoenix.* We see him again in *Rainbow Parakeet* as another ugly and doomed philosopher, Cyrano de Bergerac (1981). We see him again in *Black Jack* as Dr. Honma, who dies in disgrace, rejected by the medical community but content with his own discoveries about the nature of life which he shares with his pupil Black Jack. The law of *Phoenix,* which governs the interconnected web of life, also governs the interconnected web of the larger Tezuka corpus.

Keeping Saruta's many lives in mind, when we see Yamanobei reborn in *Black Jack* we can now read it as another chapter of *Phoenix,* looking for the conjunction of prayer and punishment. In "Tenacity," our young Dr. Yamanobei wished fiercely for a chance to live on and create life. In *Phoenix* "Future," Yamanobei is a useless, backwards-looking, nostalgic romantic, a man without tenacity, content to watch Earth and the human race wither away around him. By making him the immortal creator of new life, the Phoenix at once grants the prayer of the tenacious doctor and punishes the lethargy of his far-future counterpart.

Two separate Tezuka series combine to answer Yamanobei's "Why me?" Fourteen together answer "Why not Saruta?" So why not Rock, who fights so tenaciously to survive? Because in 1975 his activities as a terrorist leader claimed many innocent lives (*Black Jack* "Rats in a Sewer"); in 1970 he raped and exploited an innocent girl (*Alabaster*); in 1951 he turned his back on mankind, choosing to save himself instead of the human race (*Nextworld*); and in spring of 1967, months before Tezuka began to write Phoenix "Future," Rock tried to destroy human civilization and even murder Osamu Tezuka himself (*Vampires*). Tezuka referred to his re-use of characters as the "Star System," describing the characters as actors whom he would cast repeatedly in different roles. Rock Holmes (sometimes Roc, Roku or Makube Rokuro) is one of the system's superstars, appearing in more than seventy stories written

over forty years. He is even the tycoon's reckless son whom Black Jack left to
die in "Is There a Doctor?", and the doctor's ostensibly callous choice seems
newly wise when we read of Rock's past and future crimes. Just as with Saruta,
the more widely we seek Rock among Tezuka's seven hundred series, the more
we understand what complex prayers and crimes his repeated fate rewards and
punishes, and the clearer it becomes that the Phoenix's law remains consistent
in all Tezuka's works.

Consistent but still cruel. Ignorance is a large part of what makes the
Phoenix's law hard to accept. Akanemaru, Yamanobei, Saruta and even Rock
suffer in punishment for crimes they do not remember committing. They die
believing that their prayers have gone unanswered, receiving their desires only in
different incarnations which do not want them. Their rewards and punishments
may be just, but from their perspectives within each lifetime it still seems cruel
and arbitrary. It stings, particularly in the case of Saruta, who suffers so much in
service of understanding but is never permitted to have complete understanding
at any one time, so his suffering is never truly rewarded.

To understand why this ignorance stings so, and to understand the larger
commentary on fate which Tezuka is constructing, we must look even beyond
Tezuka's corpus to the older philosophical models for understanding the
relationship between Fate, Justice and ignorance at work behind the narrative
and the reader's reaction to it. I say *models*, plural, because there are two
separate understandings of Fate at work when we read Tezuka's corpus: the
Buddhist model, which is the primary tradition influencing Tezuka himself,
and the separate European philosophical tradition. We know Buddhism is
at the center of Tezuka's universe, not only from his language of karma and
reincarnation, but from *Buddha,* the companion piece to *Phoenix,* a biography
of Siddhartha populated with Tezuka's recurring stars, including Saruta himself.
Here Saruta appears as a cult leader still trying to understand and manipulate
science and nature, but then gives up his theories to follow the teachings of
one being in Tezuka's universe who understands the Phoenix even more than
Saruta himself: the Buddha. The European model of Fate, on the other hand,
is less present in Tezuka's mind, but is a powerful filter affecting Westerners'
perceptions as we read. This makes it an important factor in understanding
how and why the mind of the average European or American reader rebels at
the Phoenix's justice, and how that rebellion differs from Tezuka's own equally
powerful internal criticism of the same system.

Stoicism: the Buddhism of the West

The Western counterpart to Buddhism is Stoicism, the Hellenistic school which
gave us Zeno of Citium, Chrysippus, Seneca, Epictetus, Marcus Aurelius and,

eventually, modern iterations like that of Spinoza. So similar are Buddhism and Stoicism in many fundamentals of moral and psychological theory that, on first comparison, it can be difficult to believe that they developed independently. This makes Stoicism a perfect tool, both for explaining many Buddhist concepts to Western audiences, and for highlighting those elements of Buddhism which are uniquely Eastern, since where Buddhism and Stoicism differ so too do many larger philosophical trends of both traditions. Stoicism had a large impact on many later Western philosophies and religions, Christianity especially, both through its circulation in the Roman world and its revival in the Renaissance. Buddhism has many sects and variations, some of which are more and others less in line with Stoic doctrine, but many of those most common, and most central to the specific form of Buddhism which influenced Tezuka, are also most Stoic.

All Life Is Sacred

What do Buddhism and Stoicism have in common? First and foremost, the conviction that the universe is one interconnected, sacred whole. Stoics are monists, believing the entire universe is one contiguous object, in contrast with dualists who believe in separate material and immaterial realities (Plato and Descartes), or the Stoics' old rivals the Epicureans, who believe that the universe is made of an infinite number of separate parts called atoms. A monist universe admits no separate self and other, I and you. The apparent differences between I and you or stone and air are merely differences in qualities, as stripes on a shirt may be blue or white but remain one substance. Tezuka's vivid images of the web of all being blurring into one interconnected whole, depicted in the Enlightenment scenes in *Buddha* and *Phoenix,* are equally fitting illustrations of the concept. The Stoics arrived at this physical model largely in order to answer fundamental questions of time and motion, like Zeno of Elea's Paradoxes[1] (for example, Achilles need not overtake the tortoise at all if Achilles and tortoise are in fact one object which simply chooses to manifest Achilles-ness in one place and tortoise-ness in another). Since the Stoic universe is one being, attributes possessed by any section of it are therefore possessed by all, so if any one thing is alive, sentient or sacred, so is the whole. "All life is sacred," the recurring message of both *Buddha* and *Phoenix,* was reached by Saruta through suffering, but by Zeno of Citium, through argument and reflection.

---

[1] Zeno of Elea (c. 490–c.430 B.C.) lived before Socrates and was a follower of Parmenides. His Paradoxes are famous, but he is not the same Zeno who founded the Stoic school we've been talking about -- that's Zeno of Citium (334-262 B.C.).

While the Stoics destroy the Self-Other distinction using physics, Buddhism uses reincarnation. Before the formation of Buddhism, the Hindu traditions which influenced it so strongly already included monist and dualist veins, the monist arguing there is no true separation between the soul and the immanent divine Brahman. Buddhism maintained this concept of a unity of divinity and life, as well as the same concept of an eternal, reincarnating soul. If any two living beings may be reincarnations of one another then all living things must be considered, not only equal to, but potentially identical with the most precious loved one and, often more precious, the self. While stones and water, dust and sun are also part of the sacred universe, life, the living universe of interconnected, reincarnated souls, is the central miracle. The conviction that this universal chain of life is also sacred is justified in part by the infinite beauty of creation, but more so by the experiential descriptions of Buddha and other sages who have glimpsed the sacred unity of life through meditation and other approaches to Enlightenment. Additionally, if Buddha was able to achieve Enlightenment and, through it, sacredness, and Buddha was originally just another soul in the cycle of reincarnation, then, as Saruta discovered through his sufferings in *Phoenix* "Karma," even the lowest insect has the potential to achieve divine Buddhahood. Thus, all life is sacred.

Surrender of Self

Saruta, and Buddha, as Tezuka shows us in *Phoenix* and *Buddha*, achieve their wisdom partly through suffering but also through meditation. Stoicism, like Buddhism, promotes meditation as a method of achieving true understanding of this universal unity, and insists that the sage who can truly grasp the enormity of universal oneness is rare indeed. Just as divine powers are attributed to Buddhas and bodhisattvas, Diogenes Laertius and other late antique accounts frequently describe Stoic and Platonic sages as separating their souls from their bodies and achieving miraculous affects, including clairvoyance, prophecy, the ability to cast charms and curses (a form of ancient magic called Theurgy), and a death-like physical state including the cessation of aging. Epictetus tells us that Heraclitus and Diogenes of Athens, the philosophers who most successfully threw away the trappings of civilization, are deservedly called gods. Had he read Tezuka's biography, he would certainly have added Buddha to his list.

This focus on the utility of meditation is part of the traditions' shared focus on surrender of self as an indispensible step to achieving happiness and wisdom. In both traditions, the sage is one who is able to let go of worldly concerns, self-interest and eventually self-defense and even self-identity, recognizing himself as a tiny part of an infinite whole. Legend tells us that the true Stoic sage wouldn't scream even when being baked to death in the infamous Bull of

Phalaris, because he cares not about his own body but only about the universe as a whole, which doesn't suffer when one small piece of it's destroyed. The recommendations against grief and anger repeated by Epictetus, Seneca, and Marcus Aurelius are reiterations of the fundamental thesis that you should not be any more upset by your own sufferings than by damage to any stripe in the universal cloth. Seneca even discusses the readiness of the philosopher to calmly lose an arm (letter 24), while Epictetus describes that everything, goods, a child, the body, life itself, should be considered no more than something leant to you by nature, or offered at a banquet where you are no more than a guest. We see the same in "Karma," where worldly Akanemaru is consumed with rage and despair when he loses use of a limb, while the sage Saruta suffers the same yet weeps for joy at the beauty of life.

In the Eastern tradition, self-inflicted physical trials practiced by some Buddhist sects and many other Indian ascetic traditions, most importantly by the hermits young Siddhartha encountered and responded to, used physical mortification of the flesh to force the mind to set aside concern for the body, and with it the material world. Self-inflicted pain here was partly intended as self-punishment for sin, penance for karmic guilt much as flagellation served as penance in medieval Christianity, but it was equally a method to force the separation of mind from body, a technique resorted to by those who could not achieve such separation it through meditation alone, as Buddha did. A nobler form of self-surrender than self-inflicted pain is self-sacrifice, the sage who is able to calmly give up not only his self-interest but his self in service of others. Tezuka opens and closes *Buddha* with the story of the noble rabbit who, having no gift to give the great sage, sacrifices its body to feed him. No creature understands better the law of Nature—that all things are born and all things die.

The thesis that separation of the mind from the flesh enables the unification of mind and universe is another central element of both Stoic and Buddhist traditions. Enlightenment, the ultimate goal in the Buddhist tradition, is achieved by separating mind from body and eroding the division between self and other. Only after this erosion can the mind assume a universal perspective, seeing life from all directions at once and so understanding the true nature of the cycle of life and death. Tezuka depicts this dissolution of the self as a web-like network of interconnected life forms, an image which appears in subtly different forms in his depiction of Siddhartha's enlightenment in *Buddha*, in Saruta's near-enlightenment in *Phoenix* "Karma," in Yamanobei's elevation to immortality in *Phoenix* "Future" and at several other moments of death or near-enlightenment throughout the Tezuka corpus.

The Stoic version we may visualize similarly, as the collection of qualities which seems to be a separate individual merges with the rest of the universe

around it, like a spot of concentrated color which diffuses to instead become a subtle tint coloring the whole fabric. Perfection and with it happiness, in the form of the cessation of suffering and worry, is achieved through the union of I with all. The visuals are similar, but they are not identical. Just as the web-like network of fate, reincarnation, and relationships depicted by Tezuka isn't quite the same as the infinite unity of the Stoic monist universe, so the structure of Tezuka's karmic Fate is not the same as the structure expected by a mind raised in the Stoic-influenced European tradition.

Providence Versus Karma

The critical difference lies in the contrast between Stoic Providence and Buddhist Karma. In one sense the two are very similar. Both traditions believe that the infinite, divine, interconnected, living universe contains a universal Justice, perfect but beyond human comprehension. All events within the system are predetermined for all time. All suffering has a cause, but the cause is inscrutable. The individual living within the system can no more hope to understand the reason for his suffering than a fingertip can understand why it keeps being pricked by the seamstress's needle. Yet, while in both systems the reason for man's suffering remains inscrutable, the inscrutable reason is, in the two separate traditions, fundamentally different.

Theodicy, the question of the existence of evil in the universe and whether it disproves the possibility of a universal Good or a benevolent God, is one of the oldest concerns of Western philosophy, and Stoicism engaged in it very directly. The Stoics were one of the first sects to argue that the universe is fundamentally good. No evil exists within the Stoic universe, and any evil which seems to exist is an illusion created by limited perspective. If you lose, it's because it was better that someone else won. If a child dies, he would've either committed wicked deeds or suffered a terrible fate had he survived. Zeus, the gods, God, Fate are all guiding people toward good ends, and the wise and happy man is the one who accepts their guidance and has faith that all evils are for the greater good. These types of examples are common in later Christian discussions of Divine Providence, and indeed Stoic Providence was borrowed and expanded by later philosophers throughout the Christian Middle Ages, the Renaissance, up through Leibniz's famous formulation that everything happens for the best in this best of all possible worlds.

In the Buddhist karmic tradition, suffering isn't a necessary evil to bring about a good end, but a balancing of the scales, which Tezuka phrases as punishment. There is no perceptible good consequence of the suffering of Dr. Yamanobei and his cancer-stricken loved ones; he saves one life and dies. There is no perceptible good consequence of Akanemaru's suffering: he helps

others, hurts others, creates art, destroys art, and dies without any clear net good outcome. There is certainly no perceptible good consequence of Rock's suffering: in his many reincarnations he destroys countless others then dies himself, paying for his crimes and committing more, over and over, forever. Saruta's suffering does help him achieve his partial Enlightenment, but that is an internal, intellectual consequence, where traditional Western Providence demands a real-world good consequence: saving a life, raising a child, founding an empire. *Phoenix* "Future" itself is the ultimate proof. In a providential system, if the human race were exterminated it would be so that a new, better race could follow it. Tezuka makes it very clear that his humanity is replaced by a new, identical human race, just as wicked and prone to violence, ignorance, nostalgia, and self-destruction as the original.

"Future" is far from the only Tezuka story to end with genocide. In *Birdman Anthology* (1971–1973), *Norman* (1968), *Vampires* (1966–1969), even *Apollo's Song* (1970) inter-species violence stops only with the effective extermination of one race. In *Nextworld* (1951), *Adventures of Rock* (1952–1954), *Zero Men* (1959–1960) and *Wonder Three* (1965–1966) only the forced separation of species onto separate planets ends the warfare, and that only after massive casualties. In real-world stories like *Ayako* (1972–1973), *MW* (1976–1978) and *Adolf* (1983–1985) postponement of genocide is the happiest outcome. *Astro Boy* itself is fundamentally a story of racial conflict between humans and robots, and even here violence never stops flaring, and the boy hero himself frequently fails to prevent the extermination of friends, groups, even entire nations, robot and human. Suffering may make men and races wiser, but it doesn't make them morally better.

Life After Life

Reincarnation lies at the heart of this difference. Buddhist souls have many lives, many opportunities to interact with the universe, and many lifetimes whose actions must be balanced. Stoic souls have only one. At death, the Stoic soul merges with the universe, instantly gaining the universal perspective which allows it to see the ultimate good structure which underlies all the apparent evils of this world. Enlightenment is automatic. The individual is completely dissolved at death, leaving only the universe, good and happy.

Buddhism doesn't think the dissolution of the self is so easy. A soul must undergo numerous reincarnations, gradually moving away from worldly concerns, until it becomes liberated enough to surrender itself and achieve Enlightenment. Various Buddhist sub-sects, such as some forms of Pure Land Buddhism, posit the existence of one or more heavenly celestial realms beyond the material world into which souls who have come closer to Enlightenment can

be reborn, especially with the help of various Buddhas and bodhisattvas. Still, both these and those forms of Buddhism which focus on the existence of good interceding figures like the Goddess of Mercy don't make the argument that all evil leads to good, and maintain that true Buddha-like Enlightenment is a higher state than individual existence in the celestial realm. The noblest self-sacrifice of a bodhisattva is its choice to refrain from dissolving itself into unity with life and to remain an individual in order to aid others. This isn't the Buddhism Tezuka shows us. The Phoenix is no Goddess of Mercy, and the primary celestial heaven he depicts is that of *Princess Knight* (1954–1968), overtly modeled on the Christian heaven, and disrupted by the mischief of the imperfect angel Tink.

The greatest disruptor in the Tezuka universe is *Unico* (1976–1979), the enchanted unicorn born with the ability to magically make all living things happy and, in some versions, to solve any problem, making any situation good. The gods, here modeled loosely on the Greek pantheon, immediately condemn Unico to death, declaring that no living thing should have such power. The universe isn't designed for living beings to be happy, nor for their problems to be solved and turned toward good: such power is a disruption that must be purged.

In *Unico* as in *Princess Knight* the technicalities of the metaphysics differ from those of *Phoenix* and *Buddha*, having one pseudo-Christian god or many pseudo-Greek gods instead of the Buddhist Brahma or the Phoenix herself, but the moral metaphysics remains the same. Good is not the goal. In *MW* and *Ode to Kirihito* (1970–1971), the Tezuka series which deal most seriously with Christianity, Tezuka treats Christian ideas of sin, sexuality, spirituality, personal development, and damnation but doesn't touch on Providence, divine intervention or the concept of an ultimate Good. Tezuka's Christian God, if he exists (which is never proved or disproved in the stories), tests and torments his faithful, but doesn't assist or protect them. No ultimate metaphysical Good exists even in the non-Buddhist corners of Tezuka's cosmos.

Historically, the concept of absolute Good exists only in the minority of philosophies and religions. In its formative years Buddhism's strongest influences were the various Hindu traditions, as well as Daoism, Zen and, in Japan, Shinto, none of which have any model of dominant, universal Goodness. In the early European philosophical tradition there existed many schools which similarly lacked the belief that the universe is fundamentally Good, notably Stoicism's rivals, Epicureanism, Skepticism, Cynicism, Pythagoreanism, and Manichaeism. Those schools which did have absolute Good—Platonism, Aristotelianism, Neo-Platonism and, of course, Stoicism—eventually became dominant in Europe, largely through being absorbed into the later Christian tradition.

Unlike the Stoics, the Platonists and Neo-Platonists (as well as the earlier Pythagoreans and other Hellenic and Hellenistic mystery cults) believed in

reincarnation. Platonic souls originally existed in a divine (celestial) realm, but fell into physical forms by being drawn into Earthly concerns, and can, though repeated reincarnations as philosophers, gradually train their minds upward toward the celestial and, ultimately, break the cycle of reincarnation. This may at first sound identical with Buddhism, but Platonic reincarnation still insists that the universe is fundamentally governed by the Good from which all things emanate and to which all things return. The soul's fall is unfortunate but, once he breaks free of the Cave and learns to contemplate the Good, the philosopher can achieve true, perfect happiness and goodness, and discover the fundamentally good nature of all around him. Not so for Tezuka's souls. Even the Buddha's Enlightenment as Tezuka portrays doesn't lead to perfect happiness or uncover any moral or consolation beyond the revelation that all life is sacred. There is no light at the end of the tunnel except life itself.

Unacceptable

The providential worldview, adapted from Stoicism, reached the modern peak of its dominance in the early eighteenth century thanks to Gottfried Leibniz. It was destroyed by Voltaire, who countered the argument that all evils happen for a greater good simply by depicting the horrors and suffering of the world with such vividness that the reader of *Zadig, Candide,* or the *Poem on the Lisbon Earthquake* can no longer forgive or trust a God or Fate which would be so cruel. Voltaire and his reader reject the idea that any Good can necessitate the unimaginable suffering of those crushed to death by earthquakes, the vast wastage of endless, pointless warfare, or the intellectual suffering of those who must watch their loved ones die without hope of ever understanding why. The Angel of Providence, who forbids Voltaire's hero Zadig to question why death and disaster are necessary for the greater Good, asks too much.

Tezuka's universe reads to us like Voltaire's. Here too innocents are exterminated by earthquakes and volcanoes, pointless warfare cycles on generation after generation, and loved ones die for no comprehensible purpose. Rarely, if ever, does the Phoenix deign to show souls why they must suffer what they suffer, and when she does, they usually rage at her, as Zadig does at his angel. European philosophy trains the reader to expect these types of examples to be in dialogue with a concept of Providence. They aren't. We search instinctively for the greater Good we expect the author to be attacking or defending. It isn't there. Because the palette of suffering and questioning which Tezuka presents seems so familiar, it's easy to mistake it for the providential world of Leibniz and the Stoics. If we do so, Tezuka's universe seems infinitely more unforgivable than Leibniz's because his destruction doesn't produce any change, any progress, any greater good. Tezuka doesn't expect it to. Tezuka's Fate serves

Justice, not Good. If Tezuka's characters continue to rage against this Fate, it's not for the same reason that Western philosophy trains us to expect.

Rebellion

Sharaku of *The Three-Eyed One* (1974–1978) is probably the most stereotypical manga character in the whole Tezuka corpus. He is a fourteen-year-old, uniform-wearing schoolboy, teased by his peers, harassed by bullies, with a hopeless crush on the beautiful class tomboy, but when the seal on his mystic third eye is broken, he gains supernatural powers which send him on grand adventures in exciting, exotic lands. Now for the Tezuka touch: Sharaku is the last of the ancient race of Three-Eyed Ones. His ancestors ruled the Earth before the advent of humanity, but were fated to perish, just as humanity is in turn fated to be exterminated and replaced in the great cosmic cycle of birth and destruction governed by the Phoenix. The Three-Eyed ones had the power to see through multiple cycles of reincarnation and foresee their own destruction, and Sharaku's survival. The directive their great king left for his last descendent: exterminate all life that follows us. Wipe out the humans. Wipe out any new race that tries to follow them. Make the Earth a barren wasteland forever, one on which not even Yamanobei and the Phoenix could create new life. Make the planet Earth a monumental tomb, a testament to the cruelty of the Fate which wiped us out, so throughout the infinite and cruel cycle of time the injustice of our deaths can never be forgotten. This isn't the mandate of a hero. This is the mandate of a rebel in a universe that knows there is no Good. This is the mandate of a character whose author realizes that the Justice of the law that all things are born and all things must die is unacceptable. The one race that is capable of seeing past and future incarnations, of understanding the larger structure underlying life, rejects it.

Sharaku fulfils every escapist fantasy of the un-athletic student who daydreams about using magic powers to get back at school bullies, as we know Tezuka himself daydreamed as he was himself bullied in childhood due to his weak physique and the unruly, wavy hair which later inspired Astro's iconic spikes. We must then read Sharaku in part as an alter-ego for Tezuka, specifically for the young, pre-war Tezuka who had already tasted the petty cruelty of humanity in childhood and already fantasized about payback. This makes the Three-Eyed race's mandate of rebellion against Fate an even clearer reflection of Tezuka's own discomfort with the cruel justice of the karmic universe as he understands it.

In *Buddha,* Sharaku, with his third eye and powers sealed away, appears in the role of the childlike prophet-sage Assaji. Assaji, one of Siddhartha's first

five adherents, is one of many figures in the Buddha narrative whose character Tezuka transforms radically as he ties the story into his "Star System." Tezuka's Assaji is an infallible prophet, yet rather than use his prophecies for gain or even for good he shares them only when asked, and then so casually that he seems unaware of their import. He seems so infantile, and so unaware of the larger philosophical questions raised by his abilities, it's hard to read him as anything but mentally retarded despite his great wisdom. This is typical of the sealed form of Sharaku, who even in the Three-Eyed One behaves so foolishly that it's hard to read the removal of his third-eye powers as anything short of a lobotomy. Yet Assaji is presented as a sage. Indeed, he is the most enlightened creature we see apart from Buddha himself, as demonstrated by his death. Assaji sacrifices his own body to feed a pack of starving wolves, literally living the parable of the self-sacrificing rabbit that frames the *Buddha* narrative. What's more, he knows this will happen, having prophesied it long before, yet walks calmly to his death. Those who watch are filled with awe and horror.

It's easy to compare Assaji here to the Stoic stories of Cato and even Socrates, wise men who went calmly to their deaths armored in philosophical conviction. Assaji isn't such a man. Voltaire's attacks on Providence also left us the *Story of a Good Brahmin*. A good, wise, wealthy, educated Brahmin lives in misery, tormented by the fundamental questions of life, the soul, evil and the nature of divinity, which all his studies cannot answer, while on the same street there lives a mentally retarded woman who lives in perfect happiness, unable to understand the questions that torment the philosopher. The wise man says that he realizes he would be happy if he were as stupid as his neighbor, yet he has no desire to attain such happiness. Voltaire concludes that, though men value happiness, they value reason more.

Sharaku is both imbecile and Brahmin: with his powers free he is a super-genius who knows more of the universe than anyone and so makes war on Fate; with his powers sealed he is an imbecile, content to play with toddlers in his sandbox and, as Assaji, to accept the precepts of self-sacrifice that Buddhism prescribes. Assaji isn't a sage like Cato or Socrates, so convinced by philosophical argument that they are confident death holds no pain. Tezuka's choice to cast Sharaku as Assaji is an overt statement that Assaji's perfect surrender is only enabled by the fact that his higher faculties, his intellectual self, his rebellious self, have been sealed away.

If Voltaire concludes that man prefers reason to happiness, Tezuka argues that surrender of reason, along with surrender of self, is necessary for the kind of Enlightenment presented in the fable of the rabbit. The fact that humans don't have their intelligence sealed away, that they can understand Fate and are driven like Sharaku to rage against it, dooms them to suffering. Yet this suffering is deserved, since in rebelling, men, like Sharaku, do great evil, and thereby deserve

the punishment they experience. Does Tezuka think we should reject Reason and choose to be the happy imbecile Assaji rather than the evil genius Sharaku? Does he advocate lobotomizing his own alter-ego? Here we must turn from the alter-ego of childhood to that of adulthood.

The Hands of God

Black Jack is a special star within Tezuka's system. He's the genius maverick surgeon so famous and popular in Japan that, if Astro Boy is the Japanese Superman, Black Jack is certainly his darker and more human counterpart, Batman. He is also Tezuka's most overt alter-ego. Osamu Tezuka was himself a medical doctor but never practiced, partly because he was drawn to drawing, but partly because of his intense frustration with the corruption he saw in the Japanese medical establishment. Black Jack is the doctor-ideal, strong enough to turn his back on law and license, using his genius to heal the sick and to teach his patients the true value of life by asking his wise but cruel question: "How much would you pay to stay alive?" Answer: anything. Life is sacred. Nothing can replace it. Nothing can restore it. Nothing can equal it, except another life.

Black Jack stories repeat the lesson that nothing is worth giving up one's life, not failure, not love, not patriotism—nothing except saving the life of another. Not even Enlightenment. Black Jack frequently sees wise, sage-like mentors die for their wisdom and doesn't accept it, fighting death to the end, and never relinquishing his anger when he fails. His nemesis, Dr. Kiriko, is a euthanasia specialist, advocating the belief that sometimes suffering is so great that death is the better choice. Black Jack cannot accept this. In "Two Dark Doctors" (1957), a paralyzed mother asks Kiriko to kill her while her children ask Black Jack to try to save her. The two dark doctors make a bet: if Black Jack can save her, he wins; if he can't, Kiriko wins. In the end, Black Jack ends her paralysis but she and her children are all killed in a car accident on the way home from the hospital. No one is saved. As Kiriko laughs, a devastated Black Jack swears to continue to fight back. He does so, and frequently succeeds, but just as frequently death claims his patients just after recovery, or worse, as he stands on the verge of discovering a cure.

Black Jack is described as "the Surgeon with the Hands of God," able to perform medical miracles no other doctor can aspire to, to cure the incurable, achieve the impossible, change Fate. Except that he can't change Fate. Despite his superhuman abilities, despite the "Hands of God," which clearly set him up as a rival to the Divine Plan, in story after story, Tezuka repeats the painful lesson that even Black Jack cannot save everyone. He comes too late; the poison is too fast; the victims are too many; the patient is murdered just

YOU,
SO-CALLED
GOD!
YOU ARE
CRUEL!!

Dr. Black Jack protests the death of Professor Togakushi (Saruta), in *Black Jack* "Shrinking," 1974; © Tezuka Productions and Vertical, Inc.

as the operation ends. Black Jack himself never fails, his operations are perfect, but arbitrary factors claim his patients, arbitrary Fate. On very rare occasions, the condition is simply incurable, as in "Like a Pearl," where Black Jack struggles to use the "Hands of God" to save the teacher who gave them to him, Dr. Honma, the *Black Jack* incarnation of Saruta. Dr. Honma, may receive a portion of enlightenment from his wretched ignominy, but that is little comfort to his pupil Black Jack, who watches his beloved mentor live in disgrace on his operating table.

Like Sharaku, Black Jack lives on filled with rage at the cruelty of Fate. Yet, if it's Black Jack's intelligence which fills him with this rage, it's that same intelligence which lets him fight back, in his case by curing, helping others, and teaching others to value life as it should be valued. The triumphant stories in which we see Black Jack save and transform lives are certainly proof that Tezuka doesn't think it would be better if Black Jack were the lobotomized but happy Assaji. Indeed, in *Phoenix* "Nostalgia" Tezuka even shows us another Black Jack, a drunken gang leader who has given up on rebellion, one of few reincarnations in the Tezuka corpus which leaves the reader with a distinct feeling of wrongness: that's not Black Jack. What, then, is Black Jack? In this context, he is Tezuka's statement that intelligence, while it may make one unhappy, is still preferable to ignorant happiness if the rebellion that intelligence stimulates is a rebellion which heals instead of harming, one which

quests, as Saruta always does, to create life—in other words, if the rebellion is science.

In "Shrinking" (1974) Black Jack struggles to save one Professor Togakushi, whom we can recognize as a young version of Saruta. Black Jack finds the solution too late, returning in time to hear Togakushi's dying conclusion: he says he is ready to die, and that he believes the epidemic which claimed him is part of a larger plan, a warning from God that all living things need to share their resources. Once again Saruta receives a piece of enlightenment from his suffering. Black Jack, Tezuka's alter-ego, doesn't, and ends yet another story screaming at the heavens: "You, so-called God, are cruel!" Of course this so-called God—the power who created his "Hands of God" and also controls the Fate which so often strikes down his patients—is Tezuka.

Actor and Playwright

"Remember," Epictetus reminds us, "you are an actor in a play, which is as the playwright wants it to be. . . . What is yours is to play the assigned part well. But to choose it belongs to someone else." Here too Stoicism matches Tezuka's universe almost too well. The playwright, the one who controls the Star System that determines, is Tezuka himself.

Tezuka appeared as a character in his own manga, not just through alter-egos, like Black Jack, but as himself. This began with *Son-goku the Monkey* (1952–1959) where, when the characters proved too weak, Tezuka entered his own drawing to defeat the pencil villains with his eraser. Over time his visits to his own universe became more serious. In *Black Jack* "Baby Blues" (1974), when Tezuka has Black Jack say something so insulting that it provokes a woman into slapping him, Tezuka substitutes himself for Black Jack in the slapping panel, literally taking the punishment for dialogue he put in his hero's mouth. In *Black Jack* "Tenacity" he appears as young Yamanobei's attending physician, literally telling the dying hero and the audience of the doom he has himself scripted for his actor. In *Rainbow Parakeet* (1981–1983) Tezuka's cruelty is so excessive that his star literally stands up on the paper as it sits on Tezuka's desk and threatens to knock over the inkwell, preferring to destroy his universe and himself (just as the Three-Eyed Ones desired), rather than to continue suffering at Tezuka's hands.

In *Paper Fortress* (1974) Tezuka barely survives the firebombing of Osaka, watching corpses burn in horror as the world around him goes up in flames. *Paper Fortress* is autobiography, depicting Tezuka's real life experiences during World War II, but it's a familiar sight, one he inflicted on many of his stars, over and over in many reincarnations. The cruel fate of Tezuka's universe is neither thought experiment, nor a simple vehicle for drama. It's the world he

Young Tezuka witnesses the firebombing of Osaka, in *Paper Fortress*, 1974; © Tezuka Productions.

experienced. *Phoenix* takes place in Earth history, the past sections depicting real incidents from Japanese history, the future ones real possibilities Tezuka imagined, as the pendulum swung ever closer to his own lifetime, to the event which drove so much of his writing and his political activism: the War. The God of Manga is cruel because he perceives his God to be cruel too. He doesn't like it, can't accept it, as Black Jack and Sharaku can't accept it, but, having experienced it first-hand, he nonetheless believes it. The world is filled with suffering. It's not Good. It might be Just, but if so it's a justice which does not hesitate to exterminate individuals, nations, and species in service of its cycle. This justice is not sufficient consolation. *Buddha* almost is.

In *Buddha,* Tezuka places himself among the followers who listen as Siddhartha preaches. His stars join him: Sharaku, Saruta, even Rock. This is their opportunity to share the Buddha's teachings, to learn to accept the suffering in the world around them. They still suffer. Rock still commits great crimes and dies for them, as always, but this time at least Buddha helps him accept his suffering, accept the cruel nature of the Fate that governs him and the Will behind it. Out of more than seventy incarnations, only two versions of Rock are able to accept their deaths calmly like this, achieving the acceptance and surrender of self which is supposed to make sages, Buddhist and stoic, almost divine. *Buddha* is one instance. *Black Jack* "Imprint" (1978) is the other, and here Rock is able to accept death thanks to lifelong friendship with Black Jack himself.

In the end of *Buddha*, as Siddhartha feels his own death approaching, he describes himself as a doctor of the soul, even appearing drawn as Black Jack for

IN OTHER
WORDS, I'M
A DOCTOR.

The Buddha depicted as Dr. Black Jack, in *Buddha*,
1972-82; © Tezuka Productions and Vertical, Inc.

a single panel. The connection is clear. Both the sage and the maverick doctor spend their lives teaching others to value life. Buddha is able to accept the cruel design of Fate and preach acceptance. Black Jack is unable to surrender and screams rebellious curses at Fate and the Divine Will behind it. Both understand that, whether or not there is an unknowable karmic Justice behind the structure Fate has in store, that Justice isn't enough. Life itself is the value, the infinite web of which sage and doctor know they are a part. Tezuka knows it as well. As long as the web continues, as long as his stars continue to appear, to play their roles well in the different lives in which he casts them, the play is worthwhile even if filled with suffering. So for fiction, so too for reality.

Like the doctors of soul and body, Tezuka spent his life teaching others to value life. All his political agendas, environmentalism, pacifism, medical reform, tolerance, technologies he hoped would aid mankind and someday take him to the stars, supported this one value. These are not the values of a providential system, in which lives are tools in service of a higher Good. They are not the values of dominant Western philosophy, which chooses Reason over Happiness, since for Tezuka Reason is preferable only when the rage against Fate, which intelligence inevitably generates, is channeled in service of life. These are also not values of karmic Justice, wherein Fate serves the balance between crime and punishment. They are the values of Tezuka's own system, a Buddhism in which the goal isn't to leave the cycle of reincarnation through Enlightenment, but to live, live more, and teach and help others to live.

The more life, the more lifetimes, the richer and more beautiful the fabric of this universe becomes. The best goal, pursued by the sage Saruta, by tenacious Dr. Yamanobei, and by Tezuka's ego-ideal Black Jack, is to create more life. Tezuka pursued this too, not through medicine in his case but by spreading these values through hundreds of stories to millions of readers. Like Providence and Karma, the "God of Manga" is cruel when we try to understand his work from one lifetime alone. Taken by themselves, the vast majority of his seven hundred works are, like *Phoenix* "Future," tragedies. Read together they are a triumph, the triumph of life.

3

Imagination Rising

BRUCE SHERIDAN

*O*ur planet is dying, a devastated surface of swamps and withered grass.

Below ground, white-collar workers spill out of office buildings into the claustrophobic crush of giant escalators that shuttle them throughout the crowded sectors of Yamato, while Masato and Tamami cavort in the Pacific surf near Diamond Head.

Masato is disappointed that there is no life in the ocean and longs for at least a jellyfish to brush against. Tamami has only a vague idea of what a jellyfish looks like but tries to conjure one up for her master anyway, with less than satisfactory results. She promises to study harder next time so that she has memories strong enough to generate more accurate simulations.

Tamami and Masato collapse on the sand of Waikiki, as it was a thousand years earlier and declare their infinite happiness together—until a loud alarm evaporates the illusion to reveal their stark underground Yamato apartment.

All along they have been aware of the illusion; they know that what they are experiencing is not real.

Theses images from *Phoenix* "Future" form an extraordinary opening even by the standards of manga, not because of the action, which is minimal, but because manga master Osamu Tezuka manages in such a compressed way to evoke complex characters, portray their physical context, and declare thematic currents that will ebb and flow for 287 pages. He does this by demonstrating his own imaginative powers and by invoking the imagination as a central story element and narrative mechanism.

He also stimulates the imagination of the reader by what he leaves out: Tezuka provides just enough for the story and characters to be set up in a comprehensible manner yet the reader must work hard mentally to lay enough of a foundation for the story.

In 1949 the British philosopher Gilbert Ryle published his famous and influential work *The Concept of Mind*—a book that was widely interpreted as denying the very existence of human imagination. Five years after that, the

Phoenix series was begun, an opus of self-contained yet linked stories that Tezuka was still working on at the time of his death thirty-five years later. *Phoenix* investigates creation, mortality, and morality via the universal story of a bird that cyclically perishes and is reborn.

Tezuka chose to move back and forth in time, so the order of publishing does not reflect the chronology of the story: the conclusion comes in the second volume of the twelve published *Phoenix* "Future," and opens a door to important questions about the imagination and what it means to be human.

Ashes

Even the dullest comics are imaginative. Without the human imagination, drawn images would never come to life at all. But what is this "imagination" that is so essential to comics?

We use the concepts of "imagine" and "imagination" in different ways. We mean different things when we say

1. **Imagine a skier in full flight.**

2. **Imagine a unicorn eating the grass.**

3. **Imagine having no political opinions.**

In the first case we can generate a mental image of a skier, perhaps a skier we have actually seen. In the second we can mentally "see" a creature that has never existed. And in the third we are not really seeing an image at all. So what is imagination? If you're puzzled, you're not alone: philosophers through the ages have been vexed by the imagination and what it does—or does not do.

In the twentieth century, both psychologists and philosophers started to view the imagination with suspicion. The imagination cannot be measured or quantified. Does it really exist at all, and if so, does it do very much? Many psychologists, eager to be objective and scientific, embraced behaviorism: explaining human action in terms of observable behavior, especially the ways in which behavior could be modified by learning. Maybe there is no human imagination, or if there is, it has no effect on human action.

At the same time, many philosophers were attracted by materialism: whatever goes on in the mind must be something going on in the brain. But the brain consists of physical particles, and—so materialist philosophers assumed—physical particles cannot act; they can only react to forces acting upon them. In *The Concept of Mind*, Ryle coined the derisory phrase "ghost in

the machine" to refer to the notion that there is something purely mental and non-physical going on inside our heads. According to Ryle, there is no distinct realm of the mind, no ghost inside the machine of the human body. When we talk about imagination, we're really just talking about human behavior.

These ideas exerted a powerful sway and imagination seemed to be killed off, perhaps reduced to ashes. However, like the Phoenix, imagination has lately risen from the ashes of Ryle's philosophical furnace and is once again a subject for serious inquiry as something much more than mere behavior. Today imagination has once more become a respectable topic for study by both psychologists and philosophers.

Phoenix

Phoenix "Future" begins early in the fourth millennium A.D. The surface of the Earth is dying, and humankind has retreated underground to five autonomous capital cities called Yourk, Lengud, Pinking, Ralais, and Yamato, each of which is run by a supercomputer.

Space patrolman Masato Yamanobe lives in Yamato with Tamami, an alien Moopie life-form that can be molded to suit its owner's desires (at the beginning of the story she's a beautiful young woman) and is capable of inducing a dreamlike state in humans with effects similar to those that result from swallowing psychotropic drugs. Moopies provide direct access to imagining in a world so lacking in vibrancy and spontaneity that imagination is absent from everyday existence. Largely because the authorities believe that vivid imagining in the general population is potentially dangerous, Moopies have been banned as human companions and are scheduled to be destroyed.

Masato is instructed by his boss Roc (a.k.a. Rock Holmes, who in many ways exemplifies in *Phoenix* "Future" the absence of the ability to imagine) to kill Tamami but can't bring himself to do it. Masato and Tamami flee Yamato for the devastated surface, where they take refuge in the artificial dome of an old scientist named Dr. Saruta. Saruta is obsessed with creating new life and repopulating the planet and is so buffeted by a ceaseless, unconstrained imagination that he is just as unstable and potentially dangerous as Roc. Masato and Tamami are trapped between Roc and Dr. Saruta, exemplars of the risks of insufficient and overactive imagination respectively.

Masato doesn't know that prior to his arrival Dr. Saruta was visited by the Phoenix, a mysterious bird claiming to be the "flesh and blood of the Earth" (p. 51). The Phoenix warned Dr. Saruta of the imminent arrival of "the one person who can save the Earth" (p. 53).

As a result of Roc's pursuit of Masato, the two supercomputers that run Yamato and Lengud declare war on each other. The remaining three cities are

drawn in and the citizens of all five perish in simultaneous nuclear explosions. These supercomputers are analytical machines that can generate millions of possible scenarios but each scenario is discrete and distinct from the others. This is not how human minds function. The challenge for human beings is that every desire and belief can potentially influence whatever comes to mind, which is the source of Masato's predicament: his professional success would logically be enhanced by killing Tamami, just as Roc (on behalf of Yamato's computer leader) instructed, but his emotions won't permit it.

Tezuka does give the supercomputers emotional responses—they are by turns resentful, jealous, and angry—but these are false emotions because intelligence (in the sense of computing power) cannot compensate for imagination, which is organic and creative. The output of imagination is more than the sum of the inputs whereas computers merely make extremely efficient use of their input. Even when the chess supercomputer *Deep Blue* beats a grandmaster, it does so using sheer computing power to produce millions of answers in response to "if-then" steps without resort to desire, belief, or intuition.

The computer wins mainly by accurately calculating huge numbers of variations, something quite different from what a human chess player does, with his intuitive feel for the possibilities in a chess position. There's a long science-fiction tradition of computers that possess human personalities and mental states, such as Hal in *2001: A Space Odyssey*, but machines like this are purely fictional, just like unicorns and flying dragons.

Only the few inhabitants of artificial domes on the surface survive the nuclear war, amongst them Masato, Tamami, Roc (a last minute escapee), and Dr. Saruta, who hopes to use the essence of Tamami in his experiments aimed at creating life. This would result in her death, and Masato refuses to allow it.

The Phoenix visits Masato, tells him he has been chosen to found a new race of humans, and renders him immortal. Soon, all around Masato have perished, and he lives a solitary existence struggling with loneliness and despair and hoping for the rebirth predicted by the Phoenix.

Eventually Masato tries to synthesize life in the style of Dr. Saruta, but fails. He finds a sea and waits millennia for life to evolve. A slug life-form ascends and develops laws, a moral code, and methane gas-powered vehicles. Against Masato's advice the slugs splinter into two disagreeable factions (black and white) and overreach until they are extinct.

After billions of years humans "re-evolve." Masato is disappointed—he had hoped for a new kind of human—but the Phoenix returns and equates Masato's own pure, essential form (he no longer has a physical body) with being God. Masato enters the Phoenix and becomes part of the Cosmos within which he encounters the essence of Tamami and they recognize each other. The Phoenix

watches over humanity and becomes known to all cultures in numerous stories that tell of the reincarnating, immortal bird.

Being Human

The Moopie Tamami generates worlds she and Masato can inhabit from memories that have no direct connection to her own experiences, which means she functions more like a machine than a human being (her resemblance to the latter is a visual trick). Her memories are the result of study, not direct sensory interaction with the elements she deploys such as the Pacific Ocean rolling onto Waikiki Beach, although her memories may result from sensory interactions with representations of the real world. Tamami's creations are not just odd thoughts but are themselves close to complete worlds that can be physically occupied by other beings.

Tezuka doesn't merely introduce this fantastic idea for momentary entertainment: he makes it central to the story and tracks the implications and consequences in ways that touch on several philosophical fields from metaphysics to ethics. What value would a reality so easily and safely generated have? What is the essence of existence? Is being human merely a material matter or is there more to it? What's memory when it has no connection to direct experience?

The relationship between mental function and physical experience fascinates philosophers and most definitions of memory assume that it arises from some experience. If a memory turns out not to be directly connected to experience, we're inclined to stop saying we are remembering and admit that we are imagining or hallucinating or have been deceived. In other words, in everyday use there seems to be a sharp distinction between memory and imagination.

The issue of whether or not we have mental images (and equivalent mental aliases for our other senses) has complicated philosophical considerations of imagination for centuries. Plato conceived of the imagination as part of conscious thought, particularly in relationship to the acquisition of knowledge, but his student Aristotle saw it more from a metaphysical perspective, located between perception and judgment, with an emphasis on sensation (or physical experience).

The Stoic philosophers believed the imagination affords active mental editing, a way to generate novel content through addition and recombination. Via our senses we can perceive a man and a horse but not a centaur, however the imagination can combine our perceptions of [man] and [horse] to produce a new category – centaur – which is mentally available to us even though it has never been directly perceived. This is a very important step because it introduces

an aspect of the imagination we tend to take for granted today: creativity—
producing a result that is more than the sum of the parts.

After the Stoics it was natural to link imagination with artistic production.
Roman orators were thought to be the source of something novel and original,
using their imaginations in an act of mental creativity to generate an artwork
and make it available in the minds of their audiences. The difference is that
the content did not necessarily depend on the receivers' prior perceptions in
the way that our having the thought "centaur" relies on having the prior direct
perceptions of its components "man" and "horse." Thus, artistic creativity was
seen as rooted in the productivity of imagination and similar to divine creativity,
which is supposedly unconstrained by prior existence: gods can create ex nihilo
(or "out of nothing").

Eighteenth-century Romantics emphasized this analogy between artistic
and divine creativity, equating the artist's imagination with the creative powers
of nature or God. Although Romantics generally polarized reason and feeling
to the extent that the former was seen as the enemy of the latter (a belief many
people still hold today), Samuel Taylor Coleridge took the view that the
imagination unites reason and feeling (he used the term "intellectual intuition"),
an approach supported by twenty-first-century cognitive scientists who make
compelling arguments that rational and imaginative mental processes draw
from and may even depend on each other.

David Hume (1711–1776) argued that all mental activity, including both
memory and imagination, is derived from perception. Hume distinguished
imagination and memory on the basis that memory is merely *re*generative (it
recreates experience) whereas imagination is generative in virtue of its capacity
to generate products not previously experienced, albeit from pieces that have
been experienced. Hume's first step was to collect together externally derived
"sensations" and internally arising "feelings" in the category of "impressions."
He then argued that all ideas (or thoughts) are copied from impressions via
either memory or imagination.

Thoughts arising from the memory are closely related to impressions
derived from prior experience. For example, my thought about an L train ride
to work will coincide with sense impressions of that actual experience. On the
other hand, the imagination can freely use both sense impressions and internal
feelings, and so is capable of forming new ideas that, taken as whole, do not
necessarily coincide with any specific prior experience.

Hume gave the example of a golden mountain. This is something we have
not seen or otherwise experienced, but we have assembled it from elements
we have experienced. We have seen gold and we have seen mountains, so we
are able to construct the idea of a golden mountain. Hume concluded that
all the creative power of the mind "amounts to no more than the faculty of

compounding, transposing, augmenting, or diminishing the materials afforded to us by the senses and experience."

Although this theory of Hume's is close to common sense, recent research in psychology suggests that it is mistaken. Imagination is involved in remembering, and even in perceiving. A memory is not something stored intact, as an impression of something we experienced in the past. A memory is created afresh every time it is recalled. Remembering something is an exercise of the imagination. That is why it is so easy, as Elizabeth Loftus and other researchers have shown, to implant false memories in people.

Osamu Tezuka appears to be especially interested in where creation gets its raw materials from, the legitimacy of those sources, and just how memory and imagination contribute to creative processes. Dr. Saruta can only try to force new life from the old pieces he has at hand (which includes the Moopie Tamami), and even Masato in his penultimate form as a man-god entity fails to "create" life that can transcend old human weaknesses. It seems that the ability to create something out of nothing is a minimum requirement for gods; something the universal, endless essence of the Phoenix possesses and makes accessible to individuals and societies prepared to sublimate their selfish impulses.

When Masato can't bring himself to kill Tamami he says "I've been cold-hearted for a long time . . . a machine like Roc. You've finally made me think like a human" (p. 25). Just eight pages later, when all their options for escape appear exhausted, and Tamami can only think about comforting Masato, he says "This is not the time and place for Moopie games Tamami" (p. 33). Tamami's powers have afforded the closest thing to human experience possible in this world but those powers are not themselves what it is to be human. And when things get really serious, even Masato, the beneficiary of these psychotropic adventures, admits their childish character. They are not substantive but merely a distraction in an intolerable world. Worse still, the Moopie experience is unreliable and that undermines any sense of authenticity. On page 102 Tamami, while constrained in one of Dr. Saruta's life support tubes, tries to take Masato on a Moopie trip to nineteenth-century Venice. Masato doesn't feel a thing, and the trip fails.

This Way Lies Madness

When we first meet Dr. Saruta a number of organisms he synthesized are doing well in life-support tubes, including "human" creatures such as Bradbury, who is desperate to have direct experience: "I am tired of living in this tube. . . . The more books I read the more I want to experience the real world" (p. 39). Bradbury is sentient but has even less direct connection to the physical world

than Tamami. He crams as much indirect "experience"—intellectually acquired information—into his mind as possible but gains no satisfaction. It's not just what we know that's important but also how we come to know it. Bradbury appears to have the mental capacity to imagine, but if this is the case, he is as anti-Humean as Tamami is: a creature whose imaginings are entirely constructed without resort to direct experience.

Although Hume was mistaken in thinking that ideas or thoughts are simply impressions of experience, it would be equally wrong to suppose that imagination alone, without making contact with reality through experience, could construct its own reality.

Saruta warns that the world is not the way the books describe anymore, reminds Bradbury that he is a synthetic life form and not a real human, and predicts that he will perish outside of the tube. Bradbury won't listen: "Not me. I am human. . . . Just once I want to go out in the world like a real human being" (p. 41). Bradbury knows the truth, and he knows he will perish, but he has hope—a brand of faith—that is not entirely dependent on his knowledge. For Bradbury, one single direct experience of the real world is worth the likely price. Maybe, just maybe, things will turn out other than the way our knowledge indicates the outcome has to be.

We humans are not natural fatalists: we're inclined to believe that our desires and actions make a difference, whatever the odds, and we find it very difficult to comprehend our own non-existence. Anything that helps us survive is an advantage, so believing in an improbable yet desirable outcome could be useful. If we're wrong, we're no worse off—we die either way—but if our false belief affords new strength or merely keeps us alive long enough for circumstances to change, we can win against the odds. It makes sense that Bradbury *believes* in his need for direct experience even though he *knows* it will kill him. A computer could know the way he knows but it could not believe the way he believes. Belief locates Bradbury nearer the "human" end of the spectrum just as emotions give the replicants in the film *Blade Runner* a plausible claim to being more "human" than the desensitized people who created and exploit them.

Dr. Saruta releases Bradbury, who at first is okay but soon begins to disintegrate. Bradbury calls out to his "father" for help but his pleas are futile. Dr. Saruta can't help his creation and has to watch as Bradbury loses his physical form and expires. Both the narrative structure and visual presentation style are used by Tezuka to emphasize the sense that Bradbury is like mankind calling out to God for salvation, but Saruta isn't God, and when the chips are down, Bradbury isn't human. We can imagine all we want but just conjuring things up and believing in them doesn't make them real.

Tezuka makes us aware of the benefits and limitations of the Moopies' ability to create experience mentally. The illusion of the Moopie dream isn't the

problem, but it cannot deliver the real, and it cannot sustain. The imagination is a powerful tool, but there is a gap between the imagined and the existent that cannot be bridged by desire: wishing does not make the imagined real.

The Saruta-Bradbury scene also raises what we might call the Frankenstein Problem: a monster is always a monster no matter how it came about or how it feels and it is doomed by its unnaturalness (in this story as in Shelley's *Frankenstein*, anything not created naturally is a monster). Life is not defined at the individual or even the species level but is integrated and extended. The term Tezuka uses for this totality of life is "the cosmos," which is symbolized by the Phoenix although not limited to the bird's physical form. Saruta's intellect and his obsessive personality are the source of his creativity, but he does not have the full range of sensitivity required to balance his expansive imagination. The result is an unnatural "monster" that cannot survive.

Overreaching

Dr. Saruta is himself playing God without the appropriate authority, and everything about the way he is drawn and behaves signals "mad—or at least deluded—scientist." He could be Einstein, but if he doesn't know the limits of his powers—his intellect—he's doomed just like the brilliant student Faust, a story with direct parallels to the biblical fall of Lucifer. At the same time, inculcating a prohibition against overreaching as a fundamental principle of a state-sanctioned religion is an excellent way to keep political power in the family—dissenters would call it courageous ambition.

At root this conflict involves imagination and existence. Anybody can imagine being God or the king. Does the ability to imagine those positions alone justify enforcing that status for oneself? In *Phoenix* "Future," imagining is an essential human faculty that has atrophied and become distorted to the point that it is either impotent (as in Moopie-driven dreaming) or unhealthy (Dr. Saruta's omnipotent inclinations).

Saruta beseeches God to teach him the meaning of life (p. 47) but is unanswered, although he is not without self-awareness: "Everything I created was weak and died the moment it was exposed to outside air. . . . Perhaps man is not meant to imitate God. But I'm determined to create life, life that will survive forever" (p. 105). Dr. Saruta has respectable qualities and good intentions. He's dedicated to humanity's survival and takes seriously the Phoenix's prophecy about the savior who will come. But Saruta's fatal flaw is that he cannot accept that the creation of life is beyond his powers even while acknowledging that he is doing an unnatural thing. When Masato and Tamami arrive, Saruta gives them refuge, and they find him interesting and reasonable—he may also be their only

hope for survival. However, the doctor's eccentricities are gradually revealed and are a warning of just how malevolent scientific fundamentalism can be.

The problem is not science itself but the nature of Dr. Saruta, who seeks only to confirm his prior beliefs and never looks for evidence that might contradict his own theories, as any good scientist would. Robita, Dr. Saruta's robot assistant, reveals information that calls his master's integrity into question when he talks to Masato about how ugly Saruta is—physical ugliness is a sign of spiritual ugliness in "Future." Numerous surgeries failed to improve his looks, and all his life he was "scorned by women and neglected by his mother . . . so he created countless robot wives, lovers and daughters . . ." (p. 74).

Train Your Imagination

Tezuka illuminates the slippery slope on which we stand when gratification trumps moral considerations. Masato isn't an evil person but that doesn't stop him from using Tamami (who is effectively a living drug) to have desirable albeit fake experiences because the world's not the way he wants it to be. Masato says he loves Tamami, but it's unclear if his feelings are substantively different from the kind of love a user would have for a euphoric drug, especially one that comes in the guise of an attractive, idealized woman.

This calls to mind the twenty-first-century phenomenon of 2-D lovers that has arisen within otaku manga fan culture. Although probably coincidental, Tamami as drawn by Osamu Tezuka half a century ago is very similar to many of these 2-D lovers, who can look prepubescent yet sexually inviting. A high proportion of otaku with a 2-D lover are men over thirty who either can't find (or in fewer cases wouldn't want) a relationship with a real person. Toru Honda, an experienced 2-D lover and leading commentator on the phenomenon, has said "As long as you train your imagination, a 2-D relationship is much more passionate than a 3-D one."

I doubt this development would surprise Osamu Tezuka: he knew what the human imagination is capable of, including its ability to substitute for reality. What he probably didn't know is that the brain's biochemistry makes few fine-grained distinctions related to the origins of stimuli. It's at least plausible that at a biochemical level a successful Moopie dream could be as real as, well, reality.

We never know what Masato would do if Tamami were eternally available to him, because he loses access to her Moopie dreams once the Phoenix has shown him his destiny. The essences of Masato and Tamami are reunited at the end of the story but then there is no need for fake dreaming; it has been replaced by the direct mingling of Masato and Tamami's essences (or souls) as they are dissolved within the infinite and eternal cosmos symbolized by the Phoenix.

There is something troubling about this picture of nirvana. Tezuka seems to want to have it both ways: a dissolution of the individual in a great oneness yet enough remnants of the individual consciousness and identity to register the pleasure of that condition. This may be a wonderful state to be in but it denies fundamental—plausibly definitional—human characteristics for the first part while depending on them for the second. It's as if *not* being consciously aware as an individual would constitute a failure, although this could be a problem of how to convey a story from the inside when there are no individual minds left to make reports. If that's the case, the author keeps Masato just sufficiently differentiated within the Phoenix to convey what has happened.

Using the Imagination to Simulate Other Minds

Although Tezuka seems confused about how to relate distinct human identities to an essential singularity that creates and subsumes all things, he does appear to have anticipated one of the aspects of the imagination that today places it at the center of interactions between individuals and within social groups and makes it a legitimate subject for philosophical inquiry: the rise of so-called simulation theories.

A central mental capacity that human beings (and maybe only human beings) have is the ability to draw on their own mental processes to evaluate and understand the actions of others. According to one theory known as simulation theory, humans predict, explain, and evaluate the behavior of their con-specifics by running in their own minds (not necessarily consciously) processes that, if followed through, are likely to yield similar behaviors. Although this theory is still controversial, it has been strengthened by the discovery of mirror neurons, nerve cells that fire in the brain both when we take an action ourselves and when we see another person take the same action.

When Masato and Tamami are fleeing Roc and his patrolmen after Masato's refusal to kill his Moopie girlfriend, they seek refuge in a rundown back street hotel (p. 29). As the fugitives follow a sleazy hotel clerk up the stairs to their room, a television broadcast booms out information about the authorities' pursuit, and the game is up. The clerk says he will do nothing if Masato gives him the Moopie, and Masato knocks him to the ground. After Masato and Tamami flee, the clerk calls the authorities. In this short sequence both parties are trying to figure out the other's thoughts, motivations, and likely actions. Masato knows—and we know—what the clerk will do once he hears the broadcast; that "other mind" is predictable to him and us.

Much later in the story, this characteristic is expanded and confronted more directly. Dr. Saruta commands Robita to prepare his rocket so he can

escape the doomed laboratory. The robot is suspicious and probes further until Saruta reveals he intends to take Tamami with him because "the future of the Earth depends on my research and if anything should happen to her. . . ." Robita accuses Saruta of lying: "my computer registers that your heart and mind are in conflict. . . . I have served you for over sixty years and I know you better than anyone else. . . . You are in love with Tamami but refuse to admit it saying instead that she is for your research."

Here we have a robot—really a specialized computer—that has lived so long with Dr. Saruta it can detect his motivations and intentions in the same way human beings understand each other. The two supercomputers that ran the cities Yamato and Legnud never interacted psychologically with humans or each other and were only able to run logic-based algorithms. Even though they could feel emotion (they were easily angered) they could not think in what-if terms and that failure to imagine multiple possibilities meant they were doomed to enact the output of their calculations, which resulted in mutual destruction.

Robita has developed in the way that human children do. First comes the concept of what a mind is, which is followed by an understanding that other people have minds similar to but distinct from one's own (human children typically make that leap between the ages of three and four). This developmentally acquired "theory of mind" and acceptance of "other minds" underpins psychological simulations and empathy, which in turn support social interactions. Tezuka's genius is to expose such a fundamental human characteristic, first superficially in the human-to-human interaction between Masato and the clerk, then more deeply in the revelatory scene between Dr. Saruta and Robita.

The Ability to Imagine Is a Necessary but not a Sufficient Condition for Humanity

By two-thirds of the way through "Future," Masato is the only living creature on the Earth, and he is soon reduced to a non-physical essence (without losing self-awareness, as noted above). When given a preview of this situation by the Phoenix, Masato was terrified: "I'll be the only one alive but what happiness is there? What will I have to live for?" (p. 164). Although depressed by this, Masato has no choice and lives for billions of years. His hope is that a new kind of human will emerge, but in the end the new man is the same as the old one. Masato has in a certain sense become God, but even he cannot create a completely new human being.

Some drastic and arbitrary change would make us a different creature. As humans, we have to get wherever we are going by choosing. Good or bad,

the choices we make individually and collectively define us: we rationalize, we believe, we hope, we doubt, we feel empathy (or not), we act compassionately (or not). In other words, we're human and none of these things are possible without imagination, although imagining alone isn't enough: we need the full mental symphony.

Osamu Tezuka understood that to be human is to be both rational *and* emotional; only machines and aliens could be one *or* the other. All the human characters in "Future" use and integrate both intuition and reason via their ability to imagine, with results that range from very bad to wonderful. The supercomputer overlords of Yamato and Legnud can't use intuition to make decisions and solve problems (they have emotions but can't integrate them with logical reasoning). The result is a disastrous total dependence on mathematical logic: they are computers, and all they can do is compute. At the other end of the continuum, Tamami, for all her charms, has only feelings, and we never see her use reason to determine how to act. Tamami's inability to be rational renders her helpless outside the false dream world she creates for her master, and her existence is always in the hands of someone else.

If Tezuka were alive today he would probably take a great deal of interest in the discoveries of contemporary cognitive scientists like Ruth Byrne, who calls the imagination "one of the last uncharted terrains of the mind" and holds that rational thought and imagining are interdependent: "Rational thought has turned out to be more imaginative than cognitive scientists previously supposed" and "imaginative thought is more rational than scientists imagined" (*The Rational Imagination,* p. xi). Tezuka did not have at his disposal tools like fMRI (functional magnetic resonance imaging) that can record changes in a brain while its mind imagines. Simply by combining his own imagination with his considerable storytelling and artistic abilities, and, most importantly, by trusting in and inviting the imaginative participation of his audience, Tezuka articulated the powers and limitations of this fundamental human capacity.

Art that remains relevant over a long period of time transcends the sources available at its creation, often because in some way the artist both expresses and challenges what it is to be human. *Phoenix* "Future" is a great work of art and also a philosophical work, in the sense that it advances our thinking about existence, knowledge, and moral responsibility. Imagine that!

KETSUEKIGATA

4

Why Are There So Few Superhero Manga?

Andrew Terjesen

Walk into your average American comic book shop and you'll be struck by the relative homogeneity of the titles: rows upon rows of the latest comics featuring iconic characters like Superman, Batman, Spider-Man, and Wolverine. If you frequent some place that sells manga you can be overwhelmed by the diversity of genres available. Consequently, you'd expect the superhero genre to make up a smaller portion of the manga market, but still, the number of manga that can be said to fall within the superhero genre is even smaller than that. Superheroes are almost non-existent in manga (given how many stories are serialized in the Japanese market).

Despite the dominance of the superhero genre in America, you can still find a regular output of a few titles that are firmly embedded in other genres: crime comics like *100 Bullets* or fantasy comics like *Fables* and *Sandman*. And yet there isn't even this kind of small but steady stream of superhero manga in Japan.

The popularity of superheroes in America and their relative unpopularity in Japan has to be seen in terms of market demand—superheroes sell in the US and they don't in Japan. To be fair, until the 1970s, comic book racks had a fair amount of diversity in their genres with humor , horror, science fiction adventures, sword and sorcery, romance, and detective thrillers being published by the "Big Two" (Marvel and DC). Although, it's hard to find exact figures, some people have claimed that the best-selling comics today (not including manga translations) are Archie comics! However, the rise of dedicated comic book shops in the late 70s certainly created the perception that comics were all about superheroes.

In any case there's no question that superheroes are vastly more popular in the US than in Japan. There must be some underlying reason why a certain genre of story is so very popular in one culture and so very unpopular in another. Given the subject matter of the superhero genre, it seems that the difference is a result of differing perspectives on ethics in the two cultures.

Who Is a Superhero?

Before going any further, I should be clear about my terminology. After all, how can I claim there are so few superhero manga if it's not clear what I mean by "superhero." It would be very difficult to come up with one set of conditions that all superheroes would meet, but if we reflect on some superheroes we might be able to get a sense of what they have in common—what philosophers would call the "family resemblance" of the term "superhero."

Let's look at some prime examples: Superman, Batman, Spider-Man, the Fantastic Four, and the X-Men. All of these characters seem to be extraordinary humans (in one way or another, even if it's just being super-rich and super-obsessed) who have fashioned an alter ego for themselves that they use when they fight for what is right. I use the term "alter ego" and not "secret identity," because not all superheroes keep their identities secret (most famously, the Fantastic Four and some of the X-Men like Beast). But even if their civilian identities are not a secret, when they're fighting for justice they adopt a persona with a codename and usually a colorful costume.

The definition of "superhero" I've given is inspired by Peter Coogan's book *Superhero: The Secret Origin of a Genre* (MonkeyBrain Books, 2006). According to Coogan, the core of the superhero genre is the following three features: a hero with a prosocial and unselfish mission, powers, and an identity defined by a codename and a costume. Coogan thinks that the last of the three is the most important. So, Luke Skywalker has elements of all three, but he's more properly thought of as a science-fiction hero because his identity is not tied up in a certain visual presentation. On the other hand, a character called Jedi Knight who wears a distinctive black uniform would be a better candidate for a superhero. The case of Luke Skywalker also illustrates another condition that Coogan puts on being a superhero, in order to be a superhero on his definition, the character cannot fit into any other established genre. A borderline case like Luke Skywalker is settled when it becomes clear that he can fit neatly into another genre.

Coogan admits that his definition retains a certain ambiguity, because borderline cases like Luke Skywalker and pulp heroes like The Shadow do exist. Moreover, several "traditional" superheroes seem to be on the fence as well. Why isn't a technological hero like Iron Man considered a science-fiction story like *Cannon God Exaxxion* or *Astro Boy*? Why are the X-Men superheroes, but the mutants of *Akira* are not? And why is Thor a superhero instead of a mythological character?

The answer to these questions has two parts. First of all, in explaining borderline cases (like the Hulk) Coogan appealed to other genre elements than the core three, for example, the presence of supervillains and a sidekick. The idea seems to be that since genres are like families, the more additional

features a character has that tie him or her to traditional superhero stories (as opposed to features that tie you to science fiction or horror stories) then the more confidently we can say that character is a superhero. I think this is what Coogan means by "cannot be easily placed into another genre" (p. 40). For example, the characters of *Dragon Ball* have elements of the superhero genre, but the motivations of the characters are not as close to a Batman or a Spider-Man story as they are to the martial arts and tournament stories. Plus, the stories have elements such as elaborately named moves that also tie them more closely to the martial arts genre.

The second part of the answer has to do with the fact that this is a definition of superhero in terms of genre. There is a reason why this chapter is entitled "Why Are There So Few Superhero Manga?" as opposed to "Why Are There So Few Japanese Superheroes?" Depending on how one tells the story, a character can move towards a different genre. Most obviously, the mythological figures like Thor became superheroes when their stories were told with lots of the conventions of the superhero genre (and more than the core three).

In recent years, some writers have tried to shift the genres of their characters, so that Iron Man has become more of a science-fiction hero and Daredevil was really a ninja in the 1980s. Marvel Comics has even recently created a line of comics called "Marvel Noir" that tells stories in the noir genre using Marvel characters. These stories are not superhero stories even if they feature characters who are usually thought of as superheroes. Similarly, I think magical girl manga like *Sailor Moon* contain characters that could be written as superheroes, but almost always the story is focused on elements of other genres like fantasy and romance. So, when I refer to someone as a superhero, what I really mean is that they are a character who usually appears in stories that usually follow a certain set of story-telling conventions. However, those conventions are not etched in stone (otherwise it would not be possible to innovate a genre).

Even with these restrictions, we can find some well-known manga that feature superheroes—Cyborg 009, Skull Man, 8-Man, Devilman, Shadow Lady, and Zetman.[1] There are also adaptations of American superheroes into manga publications, notably Batman, Spider-Man, Spawn, Witchblade, and even a

---

[1] Since I want to focus on manga storytelling, I will not discuss superheroes that began in anime or live-action television and were adapted to manga. However, superheroes are far more popular in *tokusatsu* (live-action television series known for their special effects and extravagant costumes) and anime. Those media are the source of most of the really obvious Japanese superheroes (Ultraman, Kamen Rider, Kikaider, and all the Sentai series which were adapted as the *Mighty Morphin Power Rangers* in America). It's a question why those media were more successful with the superhero genre than manga. My suspicion is that part of the reason is that they were much more obviously aimed at children, something I'll return to later.

short-lived Hulk manga.[2] So it's not that people in Japan don't read superhero stories at all, but they are an incredibly small fraction of what is published. Given the way the market works in Japan, one would not expect superheroes to dominate the publications like they do in the US; but it is surprising that there is so little demand (most of the titles I've listed were short-lived).

In the book *Comic Book Nation* (Johns Hopkins University Press, 2003), Bradford Wright argues that superheroes in America became popular in the late 1930s because they were an embodiment of the New Deal mentality. Many others have made similar arguments connecting the rise of superheroes in America to various historical events like the Great Depression and World War II and trying to connect their periodic resurgence to things like the Kennedy presidency and the 9/11 attacks. But we could find similar events in Japanese history without finding a rise in the popularity of superheroes, so it is not the events alone that made superheroes popular.

There's something in the way that Americans (and possibly Westerners in general) think about ethics that is different from how the Japanese think about ethics. As a result, American comics readers have been far more receptive to superhero stories than their Japanese counterparts.

With Great Power Does NOT Come Any Greater Responsibility

A good place to start in discussing the differences between Japanese and Western ethics is the treatment of Spider-Man in manga. Spider-Man was adapted twice by Japanese mangaka and in both cases a central element of Spider-Man's backstory is omitted. Although he has an Aunt May, there is no Uncle Ben and, consequently, no death he could have prevented if he only acted more responsibly. In the original Spider-Man story (*Amazing Fantasy #15*), the death of Uncle Ben prompts Peter Parker's realization that "With great power comes great responsibility." For the next forty-plus years, that mantra has been the defining characteristic of Spider-Man's battle against criminals. And yet in two separate adaptations, that aspect of his origin is never touched upon.

The reason for this is probably that the motivation for being ethical that makes sense in the West does not have the same resonance in Japan. For at least the last two hundred years, Western ethics has been dominated by a

---

[2] There was also an adaptation of the X-Men, but it was not a reinterpretation for Japanese audiences. It simply retold episodes of the animated series from the 1990s that happened to be on the air in Japan at the time it was serialized. As a result, it does not offer much insight into how a Japanese ethical framework might shape a superhero story.

debate between two distinct camps. On the one side, there are the Utilitarians, the most famous being John Stuart Mill (1806–1873), who argued for the Greatest Happiness Principle. According to the Utilitarians, an action is right if it produces the greatest amount of happiness for the greatest number of people. On the other side are the Kantians, named after Immanuel Kant (1724–1804). Although Kant phrased his moral principle, known as the Categorical Imperative, in a number of ways; the gist is that we should always act in such a way that our intentions reflect our duties, no matter what the consequences will be of doing so. Even if killing just one person would mean infinite bliss for the rest of the universe, the Categorical Imperative would forbid doing so because the intention is to treat someone as a tool we can use to ensure our happiness. That goes against our duty to respect the life and freedom of every human being.

These two are not the only ethical principles one might find invoked in a moral discussion, but they have defined a lot of the debate over the last two centuries. And they share some interesting similarities. For example, both camps reduce ethics to an abstract principle that applies to everyone equally.

In the case of Stan Lee and Steve Ditko's Spider-Man, the death of Uncle Ben demonstrated a principle to a young Peter Parker. The principle was that he should prevent all unjust actions because they cause harm to somebody. Every crime victim is someone's "Uncle Ben." Knowing how awful it felt to lose his Uncle Ben, Peter does not want to be responsible for anyone else experiencing that pain. Spider-Man's mission is never-ending, as it seems impossible to conceive of a world in which no one is treated unjustly. And there are lots of superheroes, like Superman and Wonder Woman, who are not motivated by a personal tragedy. They simply decided to use their abilities to further certain moral principles that they deemed important.

Most Japanese superheroes have a specific enemy and, therefore, a limited mission. Although the characters of *Cyborg 009* are fighting for world peace, the main obstacle in the first two runs of the series was the Black Ghost and his organization of war profiteers. The implication is that once they defeat the Black Ghost, they will have completed their mission. Still, the cyborgs did fight for world peace and so their missions did not end after defeating the Black Ghost (though a number of fans consider the series to have ended at that point). However, their later adventures also involve combating specific threats to world peace (mostly aliens). More commonly though, Japanese superheroes are fighting against someone who has wronged them and are seeking retribution, such as in the *Skull Man* manga. Japanese ethics has difficulty justifying a mission that requires the superhero to go above and beyond the call in the name of an abstract principle like justice. *Cyborg 009* and *8-Man* are the exceptions rather than the rule for Japanese superheroes. Why is that?

The Importance of Connection in Japanese Ethics

Japanese ethics is the result of blending philosophical influences from Confucianism, Buddhism, and Shintoism. They have become so thoroughly enmeshed in the Japanese ethical framework that it is sometimes hard to trace an idea back to a particular philosophical influence. However, one of the major ideas of Confucianism is the emphasis on social relationships in determining our moral responsibilities. This is in stark contrast to Western ethics where our relationships are often seen as governed by abstract and impersonal principles.

This is not to suggest that Confucianism allows personal relationships to always trump principles. Among the Confucian virtues are *li* (which includes proper ritual observance) and *yi* (which is usually translated as "righteousness"). In the Confucian text *Mengzi*, there are stories where the underlying message is that there are some things that no good person should ever do even if their superior commands it.

What's really different about Confucianism is that it treats our relationships as the source of some of our moral values. In the *Analects*, Confucius (around 551–479 B.C.E.) is reported to say "'Once the roots are firmly established, the Way will grow'. Might we not say that filial piety and respect for elders constitute the root of Goodness?" (*Analects*, Hackett, 2003, Book 1, Section 2). Our familial relationships are seen as the model of our other moral relationships and the source of our ideas about right and wrong. The second most important Confucian (after Confucius himself) is the philosopher Mengzi, often called 'Mencius' in the West (around 372–289 B.C.E.) who summarized the idea in the following way: "Treating one's parents as parents is benevolence. Revering one's elders is righteousness. There is nothing else to do but extend these to the world" (*Mengzi*, Hackett, 2008, 7A15). Western ethics (especially based on Kant or Mill) does not treat our relationships with family and friends as the place where we find our notions of right and wrong. Instead they claim their principles come from an impartial approach to morality.

A very good example of this difference in approach is how superheroes become involved. Look at the prototypical superhero Spider-Man. In the Marvel Comics, Spider-Man can be found patrolling on a regular basis and stopping the crimes he stumbles across (which fits with the idea that he is driven to do everything he can to prevent tragedy from befalling someone else). In the 1970s Spider-Man manga (written and drawn by Ryoichi Ikegami, who would go on to do the art for *Mai the Psychic Girl, Sanctuary*, and *Crying Freeman*), Yu Komori is usually drawn into events by his relationships.[3] He embarks on his first adventure, fighting the criminal Electro, because he thinks the reward

---

[3] Marvel Comics reprinted some of these stories, but not all, as *Spider-Man: The Manga* which ran for thirty-one issues.

money will help his Aunt and his friend Rumi find her brother. It turns out her brother is Electro, so the connections in that adventure were pretty deep. The Lizard kidnaps Yu's friend in front of him. Mysterio impersonates Spider-Man in order to portray him as a criminal, which forces Yu to take action to protect Spider-Man's name. Or Yu stops an "evil" Spider-Man who got his powers from a blood transfusion with Yu's blood. Very rarely in the manga does Yu simply run around as Spider-Man and fight evil.

From a Confucian perspective, our social roles dictate our moral obligations. When Confucius is asked about governing in the *Analects*, he replies "Let the lord be a true lord, the ministers true ministers, the fathers true fathers, and the sons true sons" (Book 12, Section 11). A more literal translation of this passage would be "lord lord, minister minister, father father, son son." In other words, the obligations of a lord are defined by their being someone's lord (the addition of "true" in the translation drives this home).

The idea that our moral life is defined by a set of basic relationships is a central part of Confucianism and it is an influence we can see in the Japanese superhero. If Yu has an Uncle Ben who had been killed by a robber, then he would have been obligated to seek justice (maybe even revenge) with that robber. Once he caught the robber though, he would no longer have any reason to take the law into his own hands. In a Japanese context, the death of Uncle Ben would be the impetus of one story, while in the American context, it is the source of a moral lesson that leads Peter Parker to become a full-time superhero.

In the classic cases of tragedy-driven superheroes (Batman and Spider-Man) the criminal is pretty generic. These criminals seem to be stand-ins for crime in general and the crimes (at least in the initial origin stories) are pretty random. One debate among Batman writers is whether Batman should ever catch the person who killed his parents (depending on the story, he has or hasn't). Some writers think it's very important that he still have the unsolved death of his parents to keep him motivated, which suggests a view of moral action that is more in line with the Confucian perspective.

Good evidence of the importance of family relationships in dictating our moral responsibilities can be found in one of the Japanese manga involving Batman. After discovering he has a mutant gene, Governor Warner decides to accelerate his mutation in order to help humanity—since they don't know if the mutant race will be malevolent or helpful, he can be the case study. Even if he's a danger to humanity, one mutant would be containable and other potential mutants could be operated on before it's too late. In justifying his actions, the Governor refers to "a duty, to myself, to humanity."[4] But right before the

---

[4] This and several other Batman manga stories can be found in *Bat-Manga!: The Secret History of Batman in Japan* (Pantheon, 2008) edited by Chip Kidd, manga translations by Anne Ishii.

Governor is about to be mutated, it is discovered that he has a daughter. At that point, the doctor says "You didn't tell me you had a family. I urge you to reconsider. Allow me to perform the brain operation and end all of this, please. You have a responsibility."

The Governor's familial relationships change the nature of his moral obligations in the minds of the doctor and Batman. In fact, when he refuses to stop the mutation process, the Governor appeals to his responsibility to humanity and says that it trumps his responsibility to himself or his daughter. Given the tragic outcome, the Governor's decision to ignore the moral obligations of his social roles seems to make him the "villain" in the story.

The Batman manga were very loose adaptations of American comic stories for a Japanese audience. In the original version of the mutant story in *Batman* 165, there is no statement by the Governor that he is doing this because he has a duty (either to himself or humanity). In fact, the idea that allowing himself to mutate might be beneficial for humankind is proposed by one of the doctors in the American version. The most startling difference is that in the American comics, the Governor does not have a daughter. It is as if he would not be a human being in the manga if he was not related to somebody. And it is the relationship with his daughter in the manga that explains the subtle clues he leaves that tell Batman how to defeat him. As presented in the Japanese version, the connection to his daughter is the good part of the Governor that still exists inside the cold and detached mutant he has become. In the American version, he also gives those clues, but it seems less clear why the transformed mutant would act that way.

No One's a Moral Failure Who Has Friends

It's not just family that matters, friends are important too. The closest superhero manga come to promoting a specific moral principle is in their repeated pronouncements that friendship and working together are the keys to success. It's not the same as the Greatest Happiness Principle or Categorical Imperative, because it is not an abstract and impersonal principle. It's very vague, but it is an important moral ideal in Japanese manga.

In *Spider-Man J*, which was a more recent adaptation of the Spider-Man character for Japanese audiences, the importance of friends is driven home repeatedly. When Spider-Man J encounters the ninja Elektra, he teaches her the value of making friends when they try to stop an evil ninja from getting his hands on a mysterious scroll that is rumored to have the power to destroy all your enemies. The villain is able to get his hands on the scroll, but what he finds is the following statement: "if all the people in the world became friends, there would be no enemies. This indeed is the greatest of all secrets" (*Spider-*

Man J: Japanese Knights, Marvel 2008). In another adventure, Spider-Man J encounters a rebellious Human Torch, who declares that "Teammates never let you show your true potential" (*Spider-Man J: Japanese Daze*, 2009). The Human Torch learns his lesson when the Fantastic Four and Spider-Man J face off against Doctor Doom. They defeat Doom because, according to Reed Richards, "Friendship is the greatest source of power."

Part of the value of friendship is inspirational. If I see my friend taking on the bad guy, I will be inspired to do my best to do the same. Seeing how Spider-Man J never gave up against Dr. Doom, the Human Torch gives it his all to defeat Doom. But friendship is more than just about encouraging each other to the right thing. Friendship is important in Japanese ethics because those social relationships define who we are. This is something we sometimes say in the West, but we don't mean it the way the Japanese do. The Japanese have a very different conception of the self than the individualistic West. In Confucianism, the self is a network of relationships. Who Spider-Man J *is*, is the nephew of Aunt May, the crime-fighting partner of Detective Flynn, the friend of Mary Jane and so on.

In addition, the Buddhist and Shinto traditions that influence Japanese ethics view the self as something that is interpenetrated by our relationships. There's no clear separation between me and my family because of our shared interests, goals, and experiences.[5] The Japanese philosopher Tetsuro Watsuji (1889–1960) argued in his book *Rinrigaku: Ethics of Japan* (SUNY Press, 1996) that ethics was the study of *ningen*, a Japanese word that is usually translated as "human being," but Watsuji said should be understood to include the "betweenness" of human beings. In other words, their relationships to each other.

Even saying things like "I'm a human being" reveals important relationships that define who we are. Human beings are creatures that share a similarity with other creatures called human beings. They are not the same as lions. We can also be defined by our relationships to other species, such as human beings being superior to animals. At the end of another *Bat-Manga!* adaptation entitled "Professor Gorilla's Revenge," Batman tells Robin: "As humans, we have a great responsibility to treat animals with kindness and compassion." This is not the ending of the original story in *Detective Comics* #339. In the Japanese

---

[5] This distinction between Western and Japanese ethics is sharpest if we focus on the traditions of Kant and Mill that have dominated public moral discourse in the West for the last two centuries. If you go further back to figures like Aristotle and Plato, the differences are less pronounced. Even today, there are cultural and religious traditions that derive moral obligations from one's role as a sibling or a parent. Until very recently, the way we articulated moral concerns in public (which would greatly influence the presentation of ethical ideas in American comics) has followed the dominant tradition that de-emphasized family and social roles.

version our relationship to other animals is appealed to, to justify a certain moral way of life. And if we have a relationship to animals that leads us to treat them a certain way, you can bet that every human being has a relationship to strangers—because they both share membership in the human species—that will tell them how to act towards each other. As a fellow human, they can't let another human be harmed in their presence. This connection though is not so strong that Yu Komori will go patrolling as Spider-Man in order find as many strangers in need as possible.

The Danger of Being More than Human

Another interesting aspect of the 1970s Spider-Man manga is that he spends relatively little time in costume compared to his Western counterpart. For much of the manga (at least the eight out of thirteen stories printed in the US), Yu is uncomfortable with his spider-powers and spends much of the time avoiding their use. He's not alone. Many Japanese superheroes seem uncomfortable with their abilities and seem to be just as much a threat as the villains they fight.

You might be tempted to conclude that the reason for this is that a superhero stands out from everyone else and therefore challenges the collectivism of Japanese culture. While there's some underlying truth to this (as we'll see), it's not very accurate to think of the difference between Western and Japanese ethics as simply a difference between individualism and collectivism. Collectivism implies that Japanese ethics requires people to sacrifice their individual identities for the sake of a common good. The problem with this way of looking at things is that it assumes that the Japanese share the Western notion of what makes us persons.

In the West, we tend to think of persons as individuals first, which means removing them from their social context. In viewing people this way, we see all individuals as equal and interchangeable. Our conception of what it means to be a moral person is based on this view of personhood. This is why we tend to emphasize impartiality and see morality as something that comes before our social relationships. In Japan, the self is not something that can be understood apart from its social context. A person's identity is created by putting them into relationships with family, friends, co-workers and even strangers.

The problem with superhumans is that they are not a part of the social relationships that everyone else in their community is a part of. As a different species, superhumans are not related to the average person as an equal and consequently they do not have the same moral responsibilities to human beings or even to their human families. Maybe they are different enough from us that they have no moral responsibilities to humans (just as most people would

think that we have no moral responsibilities to insects). When he becomes a mutant, Governor Warner is no longer a part of the human species. Batman recognizes this when he tells the Governor's daughter, "He begged me to kill him, in order to spare humanity. I couldn't bring myself to do it. But it's all changed now. That monster is not your father. He's a savage creature bent on wiping out mankind." When the Governor attains mutant status, he loses his relationships to humanity and his daughter, which changes Batman's moral responsibilities. He kills the Governor (whereas in the American comic he only knocks him unconscious, because Batman in the West does not kill under any circumstances).

In Ikegami's Spider-Man, we see Yu constantly wrestling with the idea that he is unique among all human beings. Any time he finds someone who is superhuman, like Electro, the "evil" Spider-Man and the "Winter Woman," he gets involved with these characters in the hopes of finding someone he can become connected to. Spider-Man sees his powers as making him into a monster because they detach him from humanity. The only way to cope is to repeatedly reach out to other super-powered beings in the hopes of forming a new moral community.

These relationships do not come or go whenever we feel like it. This explains why so few Japanese superheroes have secret identities. Batman's a crime-fighter, but his alter ego is a playboy and dandy, in order to keep people from figuring out who he is. But this means separating out his responsibilities and relationships as Batman and Bruce Wayne, which is not possible from a Japanese perspective. It's no surprise then that in Kia Asamiya's recent Batman manga, *Batman: Child of Dreams* (2003), there's a scene where Bruce Wayne has Alfred drive him towards the screams of a woman. Alfred asks him if he'll be needing his uniform, he rebuffs Alfred stating that "Bruce Wayne is still a concerned citizen." In order to give some justification to his actions as Batman, it needs to be clear that his actions are derived from a particular relationship to all humans that Bruce Wayne feels even when he isn't wearing a batsuit.

Who's the Bad Guy?

The lack of connection to his fellow humans seems to leave Ikegami's Spider-Man morally paralyzed. Moral ambiguity is much more at home in Japanese ethics than it is in Western ethics. Much of this is probably derived from the Shintoist influences on Japanese ethics. It is difficult to talk precisely about Shinto beliefs because Shinto was not formalized until after the introduction of other religious traditions into Japan. Even then, Shinto practices and beliefs were not the same throughout Japan. The object of worship and reverence in the Shinto tradition is *kami*.

As described by Robert Carter, "kami means something more like the mystery, superior quality, and the awesome . . . immanent in the world, rather than transcendent and separate from the world except for specific interventions in its history" (*Encounter with Enlightenment: A Study of Japanese Ethics*, SUNY Press, 2000, p. 40). Kami can be thought of as spiritual essences that can be found in things in the world, like mountains or people. There is not a sharp distinction between what is and isn't kami, so there is a sense in which the spiritual essence is continuous with the natural world (as opposed to being apart from it as usually depicted in Western religions). In contrast to the Western idea that the divine is all-good or all-pure, kami are a mixture of elements that are both good and evil. Or more precisely, as a divine force, kami can produce effects that we deem to be bad and effects that we deem to be good. The kami themselves transcend the distinction between good and evil and Shinto teaches one to respect the interrelationship between (what we think of as) good and evil. For example, growth sometimes requires the destruction of what came before.

In the one instance of a superhero manga created by a Westerner (Stan Lee, the co-creator of Spider-Man and most of the rest of the iconic Marvel superheroes) for a Japanese audience we find evidence of the different attitudes toward good and evil. The manga *Ultimo* (available in English through Viz Media) features two robots, one who is supposedly pure good (Ultimo) and one who is supposedly pure evil (Vice). Superhero comics in the West (at least for most of their existence) were built on the idea that superhero conflicts were battles between good and evil. Since Japanese ethics has trouble with the idea that there is such a thing as "pure evil," it's not surprising that superhero stories would not have a wide audience. The simplistic nature of Western superheroes would alienate Japanese readers. It's no coincidence that the superheroes who have had some success in Japan tend to be morally complex.

Even Ultimo shows the Japanese influence as the creator of Ultimo (clearly modeled after Stan Lee and called "Dunstan") is confronted by a chivalrous thief. Dunstan seems to represent the Western party line that good and evil are distinct when he tells the thief that the thief's actions can't be good under any conditions. The thief responds by saying to Dunstan, "Are you an idiot? In this world, there was never anything 'ultimate', 'good', or 'evil' to begin with. All that is nothing more than your own stupidity."

The fact that the thief has many admirable traits reflects the mixture of good and evil in all people. Similarly, Ultimo does things that are good, but also seems to have an evil streak insofar as his actions can produce damaging results. According to the comic, Dunstan created Ultimo and Vice in order to have a final battle between good and evil to see which was stronger. However, both creations must be paired with a master until they learn the difference

between good and evil. After almost a thousand years, they still need masters, so it does not look as if they will learn the difference any time soon. Plus, Dunstan eventually built many other robots to reflect other emotional states. So, it's no longer a battle between good and evil, but instead it has become a competition between a variety of different human emotions and attitudes to see which is strongest. (I often wonder how much of these later developments were Stan Lee's doing or the work of his Japanese collaborators as the series progressed.)

Who Are the Good Guys?

Just as Japanese villains are not all bad, Japanese superheroes do not appear to be all good. In two different superhero manga, *Shadow Lady* and *Zetman*, the focus is on a character who fits the definition of superhero except their mission is not obviously prosocial and selfless. Shadow Lady uses her magic eye shadow to be a cat burglar, but in the course of the series she starts catching criminals and fighting evil demons. Jin (who can become the even more powerful ZET) demands payment for rescuing people and hires himself out for gangfights, but when he comes across situations where someone is being bullied or threatened, he steps in with his superstrength. Neither character is the kind of solid citizen we associate with Superman or even Batman.

Both of these manga feature supporting characters who are self-styled superheroes.[6] Shadow Lady is opposed by Spark Girl, who wants to capture and reveal her secret identity. However, Spark Girl's attempts to capture Shadow Lady only end up endangering bystanders. In *Zetman*, Kouga Amagi is a wealthy heir to a major corporation who wants to be a superhero like he used to watch on television. His attempts to be the hero are incredibly ineffectual as he not only lacks the powers needed to fight injustice, but he also lacks sound judgment. His one act of heroism that the public is aware of (saving a mother and her children from a fire) was really something Jin did. Kouga was actually going to leave the unconscious mother for dead because he didn't think it was possible to save them all.

Kouga's desire to be a superhero is openly mocked in the series as a childish fantasy. A very intriguing subplot in *Zetman* revolves around a mysterious antagonist issuing a series of bizarre challenges to Kouga. These challenges were designed to undermine Kouga's conception of a superhero as a certain kind of person who fights evil. The point is to teach Kouga the lesson that being

---

[6] The parallels in the manga stories are not surprising when you consider that they were both created by the same mangaka, Masakazu Katsura, who is probably more well-known for the manga *I"s* and *Video Girl Ai*.

someone who fights for justice means sacrificing family and friends and making cold calculations to increase one's chance of success. When Kouga learns that his father is behind unethical experiments that created super-powered beings like Zet, he refuses to help take his father down because it would be wrong to act against his father. Kouga's antagonist responds by telling him that he will soon get rid that attitude, if he wants to be someone who fights for justice.

In his pursuit of "justice," Kouga fashions for himself a superhero identity based on the cartoon he idolized. In contrast to this, the sympathetic Jin has little interest in becoming Zet and using his power, except insofar as it would help him to protect the people who are important to him. It makes it clear though that he does not want to help just anyone in need. This seems to be a condemnation of the sort of superhero who abandons the importance of relationships in the pursuit of some abstract ideal of justice which (according to Kouga's antagonist is simply a matter of individual preference because there is no clear standard of good and evil). In other words, almost every American comic book superhero.

Will There Be Fewer Superhero Comics in the West, Too?

In the back of your mind, you have probably been thinking that it's wrong to couch this comparison in terms of Western versus Japanese ethics. After all, other Western countries, like Belgium, Britain, France, Canada, Mexico, Spain and Italy, put out a fair number of comic books of their own and most of them don't feature superheroes.

Well, even though they don't have many superheroes, those countries have all produced superheroes that have had some longevity. Plus, in most of those countries, American superhero comics (especially Marvel) have sold decently. So, even though superheroes are not homegrown in other Western countries, the superhero story is still well-received compared to Japan. (And while the examples given in this chapter might suggest that the superhero genre has a respectable history in Japan, it should be borne in mind that percentage-wise the number of superhero stories in Japanese manga is still pretty small.) The reason for this, I would argue, is that those countries do share a cultural history with America that means they are more receptive to the traditional superhero who dedicates his life to fighting injustice.

At the beginning of the twentieth century though, there was a growing dissatisfaction in the West with universalistic, absolutist ethics. The postmodern movement (which had greater traction in Europe than in America) questioned whether ethics could exist at all. In American comics, the result has been a rise in 'anti-heroes'. Characters like the Punisher and Spawn are not really good people that we can model our lives after. They have much more specific

missions and their motivations tend to be selfish. And "old school" heroes like Batman, Spider-Man, and Superman are being portrayed as more flawed and more willing to do what they have to in order to stop murderous villains. They're confronted with moral dilemmas that do not seem to have an easy resolution and they occasionally kill people pre-emptively (as Wonder Woman did a few years ago). On the flipside, villains are becoming more sympathetic. Many of these early developments in the 1980s can be traced to people who were heavily influenced by Japanese manga—for example, Frank Miller whose runs on *Daredevil* and *The Dark Knight Returns* really got the ball rolling for grim and gritty comics.

Postmodernism and its accompanying moral relativism does not dominate American conceptions of morality, which is probably why those anti-heroes exist alongside more traditional, I-have-a-code-against-killing superheroes. Still, more comic-book creators are experimenting with genres other than the superhero or challenging the traditional notions of superheroism. In light of this, it's tempting to think that American comics and manga are moving towards a shared moral sensibility. However, just because they might contain similar ideas, that does not mean that they have the same moral framework. A postmodern rejection of the superhero still presumes that morality is understood as a set of abstract principles and the failure to find such principles is what leads to the postmodern take on morality. The Japanese rejection of the superhero is not a rejection of moral standards in their entirety, but rather a rejection of one particular conception of morality.

Japanese ethics still has resources to construct a moral theory, albeit one deeply rooted in social roles and relationships with the understanding that good and bad must be understood in relation to each other. But this doesn't annihilate the distinction between good and evil, it just makes it more complex than in the traditional superhero story. The Japanese heroes are found in other genres like fantasy and science fiction. The ethical framework of Japan is not compatible with the ethical framework that seems inseparable from the traditional superhero story. That's why Superman, the first and most paradigmatic American superhero, has probably never been adapted into manga (there are rumors, but I have yet to see proof which means that if it did exist it was an incredibly short run). The alien superhero who becomes a symbol of impartial morality does not fit with the tradition of Japanese ethics. At best, traditional superheroes have to be reinterpreted to fit that ethical framework, as we have seen with the examples of Spider-Man and Batman.

In considering why comics in the USA and Japan are different, there may be a cautionary tale here for the creators of American comics. American comics are flirting with the anti-hero and the very flawed hero in all genres. At first, this might seem to be equivalent to the moral complexity of Japanese heroes,

but it ignores the fact that Japanese superheroes are a critique of one kind of ethical framework and that there are other ethical ideals being modeled in the various genres of manga.[7] Western comics seem to be tearing down one idea of morality without offering anything substantial to take its place (probably because we are so used to seeing morality in only one way). That's a very dangerous road to take, and as we can see from Japanese manga it is not the only road open to us. Other ethical traditions offer us alternative ways to think about what it means to be a good person.

One reason there may be so many superhero stories in American comics is that those of us in the Western ethical tradition have an almost singular conception of what it means to act morally. For the same reason, the lack of a regular supply of superhero stories in manga could be attributed to the Japanese tradition's dissatisfaction with the ethical ideal that the American superhero represents. It's also quite likely that the incredible diversity of stories in manga could be a function of the much more complicated ideas about morality in the Japanese tradition which not only allow for a wider range of kinds of heroes, but also demands that the full range be explored so that a Japanese reader can develop their capacity for mature ethical reflection.

---

[7] We also shouldn't ignore that the critique is being made in manga that are targeted at older audiences. Japanese children are still getting a steady stream of superheroes, fighting for an abstract principle like justice, on their television sets. So, even the Japanese with a different ethical framework recognize the need to start with a simpler approach to ethical ideals before exploring the complexities of morality.

5

Should Athena Really Wear Pink?

ADAM BARKMAN

*K*aesong, in North Korea, with its empty streets and boarded up shops, was like something out of a zombie movie. Exploring that desolation, I happened upon a small shop selling such things as the North's own brand of imitation *Coca-Cola*, stamps with Kim Jung Il's face on them, and, of all things, a *manhwa*—the Korean word for manga—containing some very impressive art; indeed, to my utter surprise, the images in this North Korean *manhwa*, a retelling of a famous Korean myth, filled me with a deep yearning for something quite inexplicable.

As I thought about my reaction, I began to realize that certain genres of manga—specifically manga having to do with mythology—have been stirring in me these kinds of feelings ever since I could remember. I discovered that it didn't matter whether the culture producing the manga was largely atheistic, like North Korea, Shintō-Buddhist, like Japan, or Christian, like the USA: manga dealing with mythological themes produced anywhere and by any type of believer or nonbeliever seemed to be capable of awakening in me spiritual longing or what Plato calls spiritual *eros*—the love that sends the soul searching for Ultimate Reality. This Ultimate Reality, according to Plato, is the World of the Forms but we can envision it as a non-sectarian name for God Himself, insofar as he is the being who contains the fullness of every perfection, such as rationality, morality, universality, joy, and love.

Now from all of these insights and others, I was able to formulate my own philosophy of myth, which goes something like this: myths could have either historical or non-historical roots yet some of them could also be thought of as embodying, in a universal, though concrete, non-metaphorical way, certain supra-rational facts—facts that don't contradict reason but can't be deduced by reason—or our limited ability to reason—either.

We don't know for sure whether the myths about the dying and rising gods, such Osiris, Ishtar, Baal, Persephone, Mithra, and the Maize God, are based on historically true events or not. However, certain aspects of these myths may be true descriptions pictures of Ultimate Reality. There are three reasons for this.

First, *nothing* about a dying and rising god *contradicts reason*, unlike the myths about the Mesopotamian gods creating human beings to be their slaves, which is likely a false description of Ultimate Reality since, as Plato argues, the more divine a being is the more moral he or she will almost certainly be.

Second, these myths are *universal*, meaning that they are found in nearly every culture, though, of course, every culture dresses the universal myth in its own particular cultural trappings. However, just because such myths are found in nearly every culture, it doesn't follow that every culture's take on these myths is an equally true description of Ultimate Reality and hence equally capable of exciting spiritual longing. Just as the much newer myth of the dying and rising Mithra is more moving than that of the older myth of Ishtar, so too we might find that a Japanese retelling of a myth is actually better than the original— even if both are still universal.

Third, myth is different from both metaphor and extended metaphor or allegory, which rationally reduce one concept to another in order to produce some doctrine, such as that God is like the Sun because both God and the Sun are life-giving. Myth, as I see it, is concrete, meaning that its images or situations describe something that is true about Ultimate Reality yet at the same time it is not easy, as it is with metaphor or allegory, to say what the "meaning" of it is; so instead of speaking about "the dying and rising god myth," I should simply describe the individual, concrete myths, which are universal but which provide people with a supra-rational sense about Ultimate Reality, which in turn excites spiritual longing in many precisely by being irreducible to our limited categories and concepts.

Unlike Plato and the Stoics, who reduce myths to metaphors, Freud, who associates myths with childhood trauma, Carl Jung and Joseph Campbell, who see myths as embodying universal, though not necessarily true-to-Ultimate-Reality archetypes, I see myths as irreducible and important descriptions of Ultimate Reality.

Prometheus and Pandora

Although myths don't always speak in a unified voice, Prometheus, an immortal Titan and sometimes ally to the Olympian gods, is usually credited with creating the first man, who enjoyed a carefree life like Adam in the Garden of Eden. However, because of the perceived faults of man, Zeus, the chief Olympian god, determined to destroy him; indeed, one of the ways that Zeus thought to destroy man was by ordering the creation of the first woman, Pandora, who was made beautiful (by Aphrodite) and treacherous (by Hermes) and who, like Eve and the fruit, brought sorrow to man by opening a jar containing all the miseries of the world. Nevertheless, Zeus's attempts to

destroy man were thwarted by Prometheus, who gave man technology—that is, fire—to survive.

Both the Prometheus and Pandora myths are likely rooted in some common historical event (which, as with all myths, has been embellished over time). However, Prometheus—the divine creator and savior of man—could also represent some mysterious, supra-rational fact about Ultimate Reality; for instance, a Christian could say that Prometheus is a Christ-type or a myth preparing us to understand God's creation and redemption of man, while a Mahayana Buddhist could see the savior aspect of Prometheus as a Maitreya or Future Buddha-type.

In manga, both Prometheus and Pandora are mentioned, or alluded to, many times.

In *Saint Tail*, Meimi and Asuka Jr. go to Pandora's Fortunetelling to ask the evil Maju about their future. Given the miseries of Pandora, it comes as no surprise that Maju ends up tricking Meimi into revealing her identity as Saint Tail. Or again, in *Pandora Hearts*, Oscar Bezarius is lured to a hidden tomb by a musical watch, which, upon being opened, releases an evil female spirit who swears she will kill Oscar; nevertheless, while this is clearly a reference to the Pandora myth, the actual word "Pandora" is used to describe a group of the country's national security division that is actually trying to find the "Abyss"— an evil underworld. While neither of these series do anything particularly interesting (for better or for worse) with the Pandora myth, this is not true of the Prometheus myth.

The four volumes of the manga *Appleseed* all carry subtitles with reference to Prometheus: *The Promethean Challenge*, *Prometheus Unbound*, *The Scales of Prometheus*, and *The Prometheus Balance*. If one were only to watch the anime, one would never be aware of this Promethean element since Prometheus is never explicitly mentioned throughout. Yet, Prometheus is vital to understanding this series and another series, *Chrno Crusade*.

In *Chrno Crusade*, the focus is largely on the idea of rebellion against the gods. This idea is implemented by merging Prometheus and Satan together into an angel named Pandemonium, who, out of hatred for God, gave knowledge of the divine image to humans. In all likelihood, the creators of *Chrno Crusade* were not aware of the Promethean element in their manga; nevertheless, it shows up via one of its chief influences, John Milton's *Paradise Lost*, which explicitly links Prometheus and Satan, a connection which itself may be based on some more ancient historical event. Because Ultimate Reality is perfectly moral and the closer one gets to it, the more moral one will be, the gods should be seen as more moral than all others, and so rebellion against them should be seen as impiety, which is not in accordance with Ultimate Reality. *Chrno Crusade* fails to improve upon the Greek original, which rightly concentrates

most of its attention on what I believe are the supra-rational elements: the divine creation and defence of man depicted in a concrete story.

In *Appleseed* the focus is not on rebellion against tyrannical gods, but rather on rebellion against an apparently tyrannical utopia called Olympus, whose leaders, mostly bioroids or manufactured, emotionless humans, bear the names of the Greek gods, such as Athena, Nike, Hades, and Uranus. *Appleseed*'s genius lies in its unique blending of the Prometheus myth with Plato's *Republic*. As the story goes, the Elder bioroids, who, in the mythology, correspond to the highest Olympian gods and in Plato's *Republic*, the guardians, are plotting to sterilize and eventually wipe out the human race, which is perceived to be too controlled by its emotions; however, Deunan Knute, the daughter of the man whose DNA was used to create the bioroids (meaning that she is related to the bioroids), thwarts the Elders' plan and, like Prometheus, saves the human race from extinction. Setting aside the fact that *Appleseed* misunderstands a few of Plato's ideas—for instance, Plato was never opposed to emotion itself, only emotion as it overrules reason—*Appleseed* is very successful as a Japanese retelling of the Greek myth since it feels fresh and awe-inspiring while at the same time preserving the key idea of the divine savior of man (that is, Deunan, the savior of the human race, is related to the bioroids, who are the equivalent of the gods here).

Homer (No, the Other One)

The writings of Homer are a major source of Greek mythology and as such have inspired many Japanese manga writers. The *Odyssey* in particular has been influential.

The *Odyssey* picks up just after the Greeks triumphed over the Trojans in the Trojan War and were setting sail to return home. Odysseus, the protagonist of the *Odyssey*, is one such Greek; however, through some misfortune, Odysseus and his men arrive on an island ruled by the evil Cyclops Polyphemus, who is a son of the sea god Poseidon. Odysseus and his men manage to blind Polyphemus and escape from the island. Nonetheless, the blinding of Polyphemus makes Odysseus hateful to Poseidon, who sends a torrent of misadventures Odysseus's way.

After sailing for some time, Odysseus meets with the witch-goddess Circe, who causes all but Odysseus to turn into swine as a result of eating magical food; Odysseus himself escapes from this fate by taking a drug given to him by the god Hermes (who was ultimately acting at the request of Odysseus's patron goddess, Athena). Because Odysseus resists Circe's charms, she falls in love with him and allows him to leave her island. Following this, Odysseus goes to the underworld or the land of Hades, where he learns that his wife, Penelope, is

constantly being harassed by bunch of greedy suitors. Subsequently, Odysseus becomes even more desperate to return home, yet is shipwrecked again and again, until he eventually washes ashore on another island where he is aided by a young woman named Nausicaä. Eventually, sympathizers on the island help Odysseus return to his home in Greece, where he, disguised as an old beggar, wins Penelope's challenge that whosoever can string the bow of Odysseus is worthy to be her husband. Following his victory, Odysseus reveals his identity and together with his son, Telemachus, overthrows the evil suitors.

At least parts of this myth are grounded in historical events, either directly, such as with the Trojan War, or indirectly, such as with a few events that it borrowed from the Mesopotamian *Epic of Gilgamesh*, which itself borrowed from more ancient historical events. But more importantly, certain elements of the *Odyssey*, like the disguised Odysseus stringing the majestic bow and thus revealing his true identity as the rightful king, wonderfully capture a mysterious, supra-rational fact which more than a few people have found to be a source of spiritual longing. Of course, to speak of the "return of the king myth" is, as I said, to reduce myth to metaphor or motif, and so we are better off thinking of Odysseus's return as J.R.R. Tolkien, a devout Christian, thought of Aragorn: Aragorn's rise from a nameless ranger to the true king of Gondor mythically or concretely reflects (though is never reducible to) Jesus's humble life on Earth before his future return in majesty and power.

Many different manga series pick up on themes in Homer or the *Odyssey*, such as the demonic sirens in *Devilman*, Achilles's Spring in *Big Wars*, and Nausicaä, the heroine of *Nausicaä of the Valley of the Wind*, who helps restore the lost harmony between man and nature. Yet only *Ulysses 31* really goes beyond mere allusions.

Ulysses 31 follows the adventures of a man named Ulysses—the Roman rendering of Odysseus—as he, piloting his spaceship the Odyssey from the planet of Troy, rescues his son, Telemachus, from a giant mechanical Cyclops, created by the god Poseidon. By rebelling against Poseidon, Ulysses "defies the will of Zeus," thus making himself an enemy of all the gods (not even Athena will help him).

And so Ulysses's crew is cursed with endless sleep until he can reach the Kingdom of Hades, whereat his crew will be restored. All along, Ulysses is referred to as "the plaything of the gods" since like his namesake he has to overcome countless challenges thrown at him, such as fending off Circe's charms, only to have her fall in love with him because she, like he, "will never submit to the gods;" almost being tricked by Mecurius (the god Mercury or Hermes) into stealing the jewel of the titan Atlas, who holds the universe in its place; having a strange encounter with his original Greek counterpart, who he helps, without any bloodshed, defeat the suitors who are after Penelope; and

enduring the underworld itself, wherein Zeus reluctantly keeps his promise to restore Ulysses's men back to their waking state.

As one can see, *Ulysses 31* is only partially true to the original *Odyssey*. Nevertheless, there are a number of events which fail to improve upon, and a number which do improve upon, the original. For instance, by making all the gods evil and by making Ulysses a kind of secular humanist hero who defies them with passion, the mythical aura of the series is very nearly dispelled; it would have been better to make at the very least some of the gods good, thus allowing for concrete depictions of the divine good to permeate the series. Or again, when Ulysses goes back in time to meet his counterpart, this event fails as myth since the revealing of the true king is diminished by the presence of the future Ulysses's cheesy robot sidekick, Nono, and the fact that the blood of the evil, upstart suitors is not spilt; in other words, true myth is not rated G.

Among examples of improvement over the original myth, the vastness of outer space is a wonderful choice for the setting of the interactions between the gods and man since such a setting brilliantly depicts the infinite, mysterious nature of Ultimate Reality; indeed, when I saw Atlas standing on his ice comet upholding the luminous universe, it was impossible to suppress spiritual longing. Or again, transforming Circe into a sorceress-librarian set on acquiring all possible knowledge in her Tower of Babel-like library is an ingenious mixture of Greek and Hebrew mythology, the result of which is a deep mythical resonance which sparks the curiosity and spiritual desire people have for the unknown and sublime.

Athena and Co.

Many Greek gods and goddess appear in Japanese manga. Aphrodite, the goddess of love, is a central figure in *Wedding Peach*; Zeus is the arch-villain of *Ulysses 31*; Poseidon is a robot in *Babel II*; Gaia, the Earth goddess, is a computer in *Appleseed* and the totality of all spirits in *Final Fantasy: The Spirits Within*; the demigod Hercules is a summoned spirit in *Fate/Stay Night*; Apollo, the god of prophecy and the arts, appears in *Apollo's Song* and his attempted rape of Daphne is alluded to in *The Shamanic Princess*; and Hades, the god of the dead, is a villain in countless series, such as *Arion* and *Kamichama Kirin*.

But Athena, the daughter of Zeus, goddess of war, and one of the twelve Olympian gods, is probably the most famous Greek deity in manga. She appears not only in *Appleseed*, *Ulysses 31*, and *Kamichama Karin* (where she is a thirteen-year-old who wears only pink), but also, and much more importantly, in the hugely popular series *Saint Seiya*.

Saint Seiya largely centers around five "saints" who wear battle cloths representing particular constellations, such as Taurus or Leo, and who have

the ability to tap into cosmic power or "Cosmo," much like a Daoist master who achieves his superhuman power or *De* by tapping into the infinite *Dao*. These saints, however, are called "saints" because they are supposed to be the protectors of the goddess Athena, who has been reborn as a Japanese woman named Saori Kido.

Needless to say, *Saint Seiya* isn't always faithful to its Greek source material. First, the word "saint" is a Christian, not a pagan, word, and it refers to a follower, not a protector, of God. Second, *Saint Seiya* employs a number of Buddhist misreadings of Greek mythology. In the Greek tradition, gods and goddesses are immortal, implying both that they don't need to be reborn and that their power is qualitatively different from that of mortals; however, in the Buddhist tradition, gods and goddesses are simply long-living mortals, meaning both that the gods and man are equally trapped in *Samsara* or the illusionary cycle of death and rebirth, and that the gods and man are not absolutely different in regard to power; thus it makes sense, from a Buddhist perspective, for *Saint Seiya* to talk about Athena being reborn or the saints being able to defeat a god like Poseidon ("Humans can expand their strength beyond imagination," Athena tells Saint Seiya, "You can even create miracles that exceed the powers of the gods!")

Nevertheless, true to the mythology, *Saint Seiya* does show Athena to be opposed to Poseidon. Yet even here there's a discrepancy, for in the mythology Athena competes with the Sea God for the patronship of Athens, while in the manga, Athena and her saints fight for justice and world peace, which are being disrupted by the evil Poseidon.

And here we have another interesting difference between the Greek source material and the Japanese manga: although in the mythology the Greek gods and goddesses aren't particularly moral and are certainly nothing like the perfection of moral goodness, in *Saint Seiya*, clear ideas of right and wrong are anachronistically applied to the gods and goddesses, with Athena being a morally good figure and Poseidon, and later Hades, being morally evil. Although the historian in me doesn't approve, the ethicist and, especially the mythologist in me, thinks this to be an improvement, for when we see Athena holding high her golden staff, flanked by her battle-weary saints in an epic battle to save the world from total destruction, Ultimate Reality is touched and spiritual longing follows. Thus, while being far from a true depiction of the original Greek account, *Saint Seiya* is a triumph of reinterpreted myth.

Atlantis and the Philosophers

The supposed lost continent and kingdom of Atlantis was first mentioned by Plato in his twin dialogues the *Timeaus* and *Critias*. According to these

dialogues, the ancient Egyptians possessed records mentioning a place called Atlantis or the Kingdom of Atlas, which was named after its first king, Atlas, a son of Poseidon (and not the titan who holds the world on his shoulders). As the myth goes, Atlantis was a powerful, technologically advanced kingdom that invaded and conquered much of Europe and Africa around 10,000 B.C.; however, due to some terrible misfortune, Atlantis was completed destroyed by a massive earthquake, which sent the entire continent to the bottom of the sea.

Although it's possible that the myth of Atlantis is based on some real historical place and event, far more important is the spiritual longing that is awakened by this myth; indeed, the countless New Age movements that make reference to the Lost Continent prove the allure. And part of what makes Atlantis so appealing as myth is that it represents the lost secrets of antiquity; that is, it represents something extremely important made obscure by distant time.

Atlantis is often mentioned in manga. Yet surprisingly, more than being the subject of manga, such as in *Saint Seiya* and *The Undersea Encounter*, the myth of Atlantis functions best when only the name "Atlantis" is dropped. Thus, in *Cross*, when "the secret runes of Atlantis" are mentioned in the same breathe as the mystical symbols of the ancient Hebrews, the taste of some deep, distant, obscure reality—Ultimate Reality—is fleetingly enjoyed.

Furthermore, part of what makes the Atlantis myth so intriguing is precisely the fact that it's mentioned by such an important figure as Plato. Indeed, Plato the ancient philosopher and mythmaker himself has a mythical aura around his very person. For instance, the mere title of the manga *Socrates in Love* conjures up images of our now-familiar Platonic doctrine of spiritual *eros* or the claim, which is itself told as a myth in the dialogue *Phaedrus,* that by loving any beautiful thing in this world, we can, if we properly understand it, come to see that all such loves are copies of some perfect Beauty, the contemplation of which is what we once possessed in a previous life but which can be regained through proper knowledge and effort:

> This then is the fourth type of madness, which befalls when a man, reminded of the true beauty by the sight of beauty on earth, grows his wings and endeavors to fly upward, but in vain, exposing himself to the reproach of insanity because like a bird he fixes his gaze on the heights to the neglect of things below; and the conclusion to which our whole discourse points is that in itself and in its origin that is the best of all forms of divine possession, both for the subject himself and for his associate, and it is when he is touched with this madness that the man whose love is aroused by beauty in others is called a lover. As I have said, every human soul by its very nature has beheld true being—otherwise it would not have entered into the creature we call man—but it is not every soul that finds it easy to use its present experience as a means of recollecting the world of reality. (Plato, *Phaedrus*, lines 249–250)

This philosophical doctrine, which is itself told as a myth, permeates a number of other manga in various forms. However, the results are mixed. On the one hand, in *Big Wars*, when the gods do possess or "subvert" a human, the human is not sent longing for Ultimate Reality but rather he or she becomes an uncontrolled sex addict—which of course keeps this manga on a far too human level to be much good as myth. Or again, in the *Platonic Chain*, the stretch of total reality—from the highest to lowest—is alluded to, but when put in the context of manmade computers and the vast reaches of the internet, it fails to inspire as myth.

On the other hand, *Hermes: Winds of Love*, written by Ryuho Okawa, the founder of the cult The Institute for Research in Human Happiness, is surprisingly an excellent semi-Platonic, pseudo-Buddhist retelling of the Theseus and Minotaur myth. For instance, we get such Platonic remarks as "You don't seem to understand that Heaven is the real world and the world on Earth is just a reflection." Or again, the myths surrounding Plato and his teachings are superbly explored in *Reign: The Conqueror*, which adds a mythical layer to the history of Alexander the Great by portraying Alexander as a man capable of discovering and possessing the "Platohedron" or the secrets to the universe, which Plato himself had discovered and had hidden from the narrow, practical, anti-mythical Aristotle.

Goddess for a Girlfriend—Fantasy or Myth?

While Greek mythology is the most famous of the European mythologies, Norse mythology is the second most famous and appears nearly as often in Japanese manga. One of the best known Norse topics in manga is that of the brave and beautiful semi-goddesses, the valkyries, who carry the souls of courageous warriors to Odin's table in Valhalla, and the three goddesses of human fate, the Norns: Urd, Verdandi and Skuld. Nevertheless, in Japanese manga, both the valkyries and the norns are given the magical girl treatment, the results of which are mixed.

Some of these reinterpreted myths are nothing more than boyhood fantasies about slave-like girlfriends; C. S. Lewis calls the creation of such stories "Egotistical Castle-Building" since the idea is, among other things, for the male reader to project himself onto the protagonist who is surrounded by two-dimensional, fantasy women.[1] On the other hand, some of these reinterpreted myths have genuine mythical elements that hint at Ultimate Reality; in these, the idea is not for the reader to project himself into the story but rather to observe the myth, take in its essence and feel the weight of glory.

---

[1] C. S. Lewis, *An Experiment in Criticism* (Cambridge University Press, 1999), p. 52.

The valkyries are mentioned in a number of manga, including *Macross II*, where the principle space fighter-mecha-Gerwalk is called the Valkyrie, and *Valkyrie Chronicle*, where a brave *shōjo* joins the military to protect her village. Yet for our purposes, the most important manga having to do with valkyries is *UFO Ultramaiden Valkyrie*.

UFO Ultramaiden Valkyrie tells the tale of a young princess of Valhalla named Valkyrie whose spaceship crashes into a Japanese bathhouse run by a teenaged boy named Kazuto. Because Valkyrie's ship nearly kills the young man, the princess gives him half her soul in order to keep him alive; however, as a result of this soul-draining procedure, Valkyrie becomes an elementary school girl who can only, temporarily, return to her original, powerful, voluptuous self when she kisses Kazuto.

While for the most part this series is a clear example of Egotistical Castle-Building in the manner of *Ranma ½* and *Tenchi Muyo!* two things need to be qualified. First, in Norse mythology, valkyries *do* often fall in love with, and marry, mortals; hence, *UFO Ultramaiden Valkyrie* isn't a clear misappropriation of its Norse source material. And second, romantic love itself *can*, if properly understood and portrayed, become mythical in the sense of pointing to a larger, more profound fact, namely that Ultimate Reality seems to be the source of infinite Happiness and Love; thus, the idea of Valkyrie and Kazuto having "one soul and two hearts" does rightly strike us and strike us deep.

As for the norns, they are mentioned in a few manga series, including *The Mythical Detective Loki Ragnarok* (where they uncharacteristically enter the human world to try to subvert Fate), and, of course, *Oh My Goddess!* which demands a little more attention.

On the surface *Oh My Goddess!* seems to be another instance of Egotistical Castle-Building: one day a sophomore loser with a golden heart, Keiichi Morisato, dials the wrong telephone number and, by the will of "Yggdrasil" (a supercomputer, named after the Norse tree that connects all reality), reaches "the goddess hotline," where the beautiful goddess Belldandy (that is, the norn Verdandi) magically appears to him and fulfills his deepest wish, which is for her to remain with him forever. We must remember that *Oh My Goddess!* is supposed to be a romantic-comedy—and it succeeds greatly at this thanks to the appearance of the two other norns: Urd and Skuld. Nevertheless, the series does reach mythical status on a few occasions.

One such occasion is when the series blends Norse mythology with Shintō-Buddhism. For example, when Belldandy first appears to Keiichi, she enters through a mirror, which is one of the three sacred objects in Shintoism. Furthermore, Keiichi and Belldandy take up residence in a rundown Buddhist temple, surrounded by pink cherry blossoms—the flower that best represents Japanese Buddhism insofar as cherry blossoms, like life, bloom beautifully for a moment, but then fade to insubstantiality. The result of linking these

symbols of Shintō-Buddhism with Norse mythology is a moving reminder that "the world is *kami*-filled," [2] which is to say that it is filled with rays of Ultimate Reality—rays which need to be chased upward to their Source.

Another occasion where *Oh My Goddess!* equals or improves on its Norse sources is in regard to Fate. According to Norse mythology, Fate—whose will is discerned by the Norns—is supreme; even the gods are bound by it. The very idea of Fate as the Absolute Unchanging Will is mythically stirring, but *Oh My Goddess!* one-ups this notion by replacing Fate with Destiny. That is, whereas Fate is absolute and unchanging, Destiny, in *Oh My Goddess!* refers to the best possible plan that Ultimate Reality has for individuals; however, because people like Keiichi have free wills they can still choose whether or not to follow the best possible path for themselves. Hence, a Divine Plan coupled with free agency within a vast universe is mythically more powerful—and hence more spiritually stirring—than mere unchanging Fate.

Ragnarök: A Laughing Matter?

No theme in Norse mythology, or perhaps in any mythology, is more memorable and moving than that of Ragnarök or "the final battle of the gods." Part of the reason why this theme is so mythically powerful is because of the Norse understanding of Fate. But even more than this is the fact that despite being fully aware that most of the gods will be killed in the final battle between the gods and the giants, the gods, led by Odin and his son Thor, accept this Fate and still press on, determined to show unmatched valour in combat. While it's anachronistic to say that the gods are "good" and the giants, led by Loki, are "evil," the gods do seem to be more ethically upright than, say, their Greek counterparts, and Loki and giants can at times be clearly evil—indeed, Loki, desiring to be the ruler of Asgard, the home of the gods, waits until Odin takes his "Odin Sleep" and then instigates Ragnarök.

A number of manga deal with the theme of Ragnarök: *The Mythical Detective Loki Ragnarök*, *My Cat Loki*, *Angel Sanctuary*, *Sword of the Dark One*, *Ragnarök Guy*, *UFO Ultramaiden Valkyrie*, *Ragnarök*, *Oh My Goddess!* and *Saint Seiya*. However, none of these manga come close to the mythical unveiling of Ultimate Reality that we get in the original Norse myths. While at first this might seem to be a dead-end for us, finding why these series fail as myth is important to an understanding of myth.

First, most of these series are comedies, and while this doesn't in itself guarantee that mythical status won't be reached (that is, comedies might have some serious moments), it does show that a light-hearted approach to the most

---

[2] Thomas Kasulis, *Shinto: The Way Home* (University of Hawai'i Press, 2004), p. 17.

serious of mythical themes is not just ineffective in touching Ultimate Reality, but actually feels *blasphemous*: if we can laugh at this theme, it demonstrates that our stock responses both to the divine and moral goodness are malfunctioning, for sacred awe is the only proper attitude to the courageous gods marching off to their doom.

Second, most of these manga series actually support Loki over and against the gods. For instance, *The Mythical Detective Loki Ragnarök* (and *Angel Sanctuary* in its own Norse-Christian way) portrays Odin as an unjust tyrant and Loki as a freedom-loving hero. While one may be able to appreciate the myth of a righteous war waged in the highest realms, I think this reversal of the original Norse mythology is a devolution since the more divine, or the closer a person is to Ultimate Reality, the more ethical he or she should be.

Through a Glass Darkly

Spiritual longing is best stirred by myth, which itself reflects something true, though obscure, about Ultimate Reality. And while myth can come in many forms—movies, songs, pictures and so on—an important, underestimated source of myth is Japanese manga.

Because there's just so much mythology in manga, I have only looked at European mythology as it appears in manga. And while I wanted to show how true the Japanese were to their source material, I also—more importantly—wanted to explain how the manga myths improve, or fail to improve, on their originals. In this way, I agree with Susan Napier, who writes in *From Impressionism to Anime* that Japanese manga allows its American fans to "leave home" for a little while "to discover aspects of home at a different location" (p. 190). However, the aspects of home such people discover are often, at least in the case of manga myths, of a Home seen through a glass darkly.

6

Re-Staging World War II

CARL H. SOBOCINSKI

Manga and anime have long had a strong place in Japanese popular culture, and a fair number of them address historical topics, either as part of the setting, or sometimes as major themes in themselves. So they often give present-day Japanese perspectives on Japanese society during the Pacific War (which is what the Pacific theater of World War II is often called in East Asia).

Popular culture can exert a strong influence on our perceptions of history. While comic strips, films, and television programs are usually created simply for entertainment, they frequently use historic references as part of their settings, which often illustrate popular concepts of history. They can also shape people's perceptions of history, and sometimes even create powerful myths which historians often expend much classroom time and effort to dispel. Such difficulties often appear when history is revised, or historic facts are distorted, in order to satisfy popular preconceptions of how someone might like it to appear.

Conjecture about alternative endings for historical events is a fine practice, and can actually be useful. The late Professor Carl G. Gustavson of Ohio University was fond of putting speculative, hypothetical questions on his history tests. One particularly memorable question, from a Soviet History class in 1983, asked the students to describe what would happen during the following ten years. Professor Gustavson had some fun, but his speculative questions were a teaching tool, and illustrate an important concept of history: it is first necessary to understand what actually did happen in order to construct a plausible argument for how it might have happened differently. Thus, ethical historic speculation, and its cousin, historical revisionism, remain subject to the same constraints as all proper history: any interpretation of history must be based on the most accurate and reliable facts available.

Historical facts, in their ideal states, are objective and neutral. But, unlike the exact precision of mathematics, historical facts are not always certain. New facts are sometimes discovered, which often question the validity of previously

accepted facts. The historian's cultural background may limit his perception of the facts, or may lead him to ignore facts which do not fit well into his frame of reference.

The difficulties of factual accuracy and prejudiced interpretations can become a problem when popular entertainment, such as manga and anime, use historical events as their settings. Factually based, authentic stories should maintain a higher standard of accuracy, but the authors and producers of fictional or semi-fictional stories are not bound by the constraints of strict historical accuracy, and can take advantage of this freedom to delve into more speculative and hypothetical concepts. But problems can emerge when facts are ignored, altered, or simply imagined in order to conform to some ideological or social standard.

When manga and anime stories contain World War II references, Japan's devastating defeat is a recurring theme. Defeated peoples tend to re-interpret major events or insert fantastic speculation into their histories in order to rationalize their losses, or to gratify their yearning for victory. Japan shares this tendency with many other lost causes. For example, after the American Civil War many southerners fantasized about re-fighting the war, hoping for a different result. This theme reappeared in American popular culture during the 1960s via the DC Comic Book series *Haunted Tank*, in which the ghost of Confederate cavalry commander Jeb Stuart haunts an American World War II M-3 tank (nicknamed the "Stuart" tank) . . . the ghost of a defeated commander helping modern mechanized "cavalry" to eventual victory.

The tremendous cost of the war, including the widespread destruction of Japanese cities, has exerted a huge force on Japanese thinking in the decades since 1945. Manga and anime have become a rich source of social and moral commentary on Japan's actions in the war, the ideologies which supported it, and the war's effects on families and individuals. The longing for a different outcome has also led to speculations about how the war might have unfolded differently.

Cosmoship Yamato

Some of these concepts appear in the animated science fiction series *Space Battleship Yamato*, set in the year 2199. Best known as a televised anime program, it actually appeared simultaneously in manga form, under the slightly altered title, *Cosmoship Yamato*. Published in the 1970s, its scenario is reminiscent of H.G. Wells and many motion pictures.

An advanced alien race is bent on destroying Earth. *Cosmoship Yamato* begins with humanity on the edge of destruction when another, more friendly alien race gives Earth the technology to fight back. Armed with this advanced technology,

Earth's survivors raise the wreckage of World War II Japanese battleship *Yamato*, sunk in 1945, and re-fit it with advanced engines and weaponry. Converted to a spaceship, *Yamato* then embarks on a 148,000-light-year voyage to the friendly advanced civilization which can give Earth the technology and weapons sufficient to defeat its invaders and re-create the planet to support human life.

This plot is very basic, and in itself not at all unique. But having been produced in Japan less than thirty years after the end of the Pacific War (still a living memory to many Japanese), and featuring the one-time pride of the Imperial Japanese Navy, *Cosmoship Yamato* provides many opportunities to examine the Japanese perspective of the war and to re-visit many of the controversial issues of that time.

The story's opening scenes delve into this immediately. As spaceships of the "Earth Defense Force" (recalling postwar Japan's Self-Defense Forces) face overwhelming odds, the fleet commander orders the ships to withdraw. One ship's captain refuses, saying that it's his duty to "fight and die," claiming he will be "too ashamed to face the dead" otherwise. As his ship is destroyed, the fleet commander says that such sacrifice is futile, that it is better to retreat and "put up with the shame of today" in hope of a better future. "That's how a man should be," he concludes.

This brief scene is actually a poignant criticism of Japanese military policies during the Pacific War. As Japanese forces began meeting a series of defeats after 1943, they became notorious for their tendency to fight to the last man, literally. However clichéd it may sound, their motto may well have been "victory or death." Many accounts tell of refusal to surrender or even evacuate a hopeless position. One Japanese soldier in the Philippines, Hiroo Onoda, remained hidden until 1974, believing that Japan was still fighting. He did not surrender until his commanding officer, who survived the war, personally ordered him to stand down.

Few Japanese soldiers were taken prisoner, capture being regarded as unendurably shameful. There were even cases of captured Japanese soldiers being forced to kill themselves after having escaped and made it back to their own lines. (By contrast, any American soldier who achieved this was greatly honored.) Conversely, this attitude toward surrender and capture led to the brutal treatment of American and allied soldiers held prisoner by the Japanese. (Director Akira Kurosawa criticized such policies in his classic movie *Seven Samurai*, when one of the samurai berates the farmers for mistreating a captured bandit.) There were horrific examples of mass suicide, even amongst civilian Japanese populations, as happened when American forces captured the Japanese island of Saipan in 1944. Thus, when *Cosmoship Yamato* portrays such instances of futile self sacrifice and impetuous courage, it actually makes a strong condemnation of the Japanese military during the Pacific War.

It seems unlikely that the publishers of this series deliberately intended to re-examine the morality of the Pacific War. Most likely they were simply attempting to give their characters plausible principles and motivations, with which their audience could identify. But, however unintentionally, they succeeded in presenting many themes and concepts which invite incisive moral commentary.

The actual, historic *Yamato* appears in a flashback sequence early in the series. The war was in its final months, and Japan had no hope of victory. Regardless, *Yamato* was sent with a small task force, against a much larger American force, with insufficient fuel even to return home. This portrayal of the IJN *Yamato*'s destruction is historically accurate, though somewhat flattering. The ship's sacrifice is portrayed as both heroic and futile. Emphasizing this heroic self-image, the anime version of these events concludes with an American navy pilot saluting the doomed *Yamato* as it vanishes into the ocean, a very implausible incident, considering the severe nationalistic animosities of the time.

Such scenes echo the futility which appears at a later point, when Captain Okita condemns useless sacrifice. But one important idea that the overall series examines, which is absent from the historical flashback, is the concept of a just war. Views of what makes a war just certainly vary, and many pacifists deny that any war can be just. But one of the first to propose a theory of just war, the Christian philosopher-theologian St. Augustine, listed the essential criteria for a just war: the prevention of destruction of the victims of aggression; the absence of any viable alternative to war; reasonable belief that fighting an aggressor has a chance for success; and the limitation of destruction. If the concept of a just war is valid, then *Cosmoship Yamato*'s fictional struggle against a technologically superior alien race bent on destroying Earth, with no quarter or terms even considered, certainly qualifies.

This raises many ethical questions about the use of historical settings in fictional stories, and in particular, the wish fulfillment that historic revisionism often engenders. Is this an admission that the Japanese were not justified in waging war in the Pacific and in China? The historical *Yamato* is a symbol of national pride.[1] Would its resurrection, replete with powerful, unstoppable weapons rendering it invincible (as the historical *Yamato* was supposed to have been), fighting a just war, serve to redeem Japan's sins of aggression?

One particularly striking theme of *Cosmoship Yamato* is its commentary on weapons of mass destruction. The attacks against Earth by the hostile alien forces are portrayed exactly like nuclear explosions, and the resultant

---

[1] In the 1980s, the Tamiya company of Japan produced an accurate scale model of the historic Yamato, whose instructions were replete with many proud statements of the ship's size and power.

radiation is destroying all life on the planet. But the resurrected spaceship *Yamato* also has a very destructive weapon, called the "wave motion gun." The first time it is used against an enemy outpost, *Yamato* destroys an entire moon. Its crew is horrified, and questions whether such destruction was necessary. The Captain attempts to make some moral comments, but is actually a bit ambiguous, concluding that "we must think very carefully before we use it." This is striking, considering that Japan is the only nation that has ever been attacked with nuclear weapons. The story does not condemn such horrifying destruction outright. Reflecting some of the principles of a just war, it gives the qualification that such a weapon must be used with great restraint, instead of being totally eliminated as irredeemably immoral.

Barefoot Gen

While *Cosmoship Yamato* addresses nuclear weapons as one of many themes, other manga make them the central focus. One such example appears in *Barefoot Gen*. Originally a manga series, and later a feature-length anime, *Barefoot Gen* is the story of a young Japanese boy, Gen Nakaoka, during the final days of the war, and his experiences after the nuclear bombing of Hiroshima. The story is semi-autobiographical, as its creator, Keiji Nakazawa, was a Hiroshima survivor, and had earlier published a factual account of his experiences. Nakazawa clearly based the character Gen on himself.

In many ways *Barefoot Gen* is a standard story of a family struggling to survive during the final months of the war, very similar to the acclaimed anime feature *Grave of the Fireflies*. It also shares some commonality with *Cosmoship Yamato*, in that both series were originally published during the mid-1970s. Such perspectives are quite common. Frequently, catastrophic historical events do not receive major critical attention in popular media until years or decades after their conclusions. One thinks of films such as *All Quiet on the Western Front*, first produced in 1930, or *Full Metal Jacket* from 1987, which addresses US Marines in Vietnam. As such, both *Cosmoship Yamato* and *Barefoot Gen* view the war from the perspective of some thirty years, still within living memory but nonetheless affected by the intervening decades.

One major distinction between *Cosmoship Yamato* and *Barefoot Gen* is their perspectives on war. Although Gen's father Daikichi Nakaoka is killed early in the series, his pacifist views become an important underlying theme for the entire series. At one point he suggests that the war began as little more than another form of class oppression, with nationalistic propaganda enticing the lower classes to fight wars to enrich their overlords. Also, Daikichi makes many statements condemning war in general. "Traitors, cowards . . . these words mean nothing to me," he announces to his sons as they desperately search for

food. One particularly striking scene portrays a Japanese teenager marching off for military service, to the loud acclaim of his neighbors. Gen and his brother are initially impressed, but their father bluntly condemns this, announcing that it "takes more courage not to fight than to fight, to not want to kill, when all around you are calling for blood. That's real courage," he concludes. One striking scene, appearing in the manga version but absent from the anime, shows a policeman beating Daikichi for his anti-war remarks.

Such convictions deny any concept of a just war, and from his perspective, it is difficult to challenge him. *Barefoot Gen* portrays war itself as the enemy. Though it does not praise the United States for defeating Japanese militarism, and certainly regards the nuclear bombs as irredeemably immoral, the US military appears largely as an impersonal force. Gen's daily struggles are simply for survival, and Japan's dictatorial government receives the brunt of condemnation for having started the war.

Gen's mother Kimie makes this quite clear when Hirohito announced Japan's surrender. While some of her neighbors are distraught, Kimie is enraged that they didn't surrender sooner to avoid the destruction that Japanese persistence brought.

Much of this may be the dramatic setting of the series, in that Gen and his family simply had more contact with Japanese authorities than American. But the pacifist message in *Barefoot Gen* could well have originated from a postwar re-examination of Japan's role in the war. According to Japanese historian Saburo Ienaga's *The Pacific War*, public antiwar statements during the war were "unthinkable" (p. 109). However, he does say that some of the Japanese population opposed the war. In particular, Ienaga portrays farmers as the most likely opponents of Japan's militarist system.

In that *Barefoot Gen*'s main characters were a family of farmers, Nakazawa's antiwar statements could well have been a common sentiment amongst that class. But this does not discount the possibility that *Barefoot Gen*'s popularity during the 1970s might have found fertile soil in the Japanese public's re-examination of their nation's role in perpetuating the war. Saburo Ienaga provides some evidence to support this, emphasizing that Japan's newfound freedoms in the postwar era would ensure "a passionate and committed defense of pacifism" (p. 244).

Barefoot Gen, as its less optimistic counterpart *Grave of the Fireflies,* portrays the war almost entirely from a child's perspective. The anime *Rail of the Star* also follows this device. This 1997 film focuses on a Japanese family in occupied Korea, near the Soviet Border. The entire story is from daughter Chitose Kobayashi's perspective, and there is a strong emphasis on her innocence and ignorance in the face of Japanese imperial policies during the 1930s and 1940s.

Chitose's family had been in Korea for some time (exactly how long is not specified), but her father is an executive in a Japanese-owned coal mining company. As such, the family has a comfortable life, with a large house, plenty of food, and a Korean servant. The story portrays the family as the distant war gradually affects their lives and increases their hardships. Eventually the coal mine ceases operations, they lose their home, and dismiss their Korean servant. Finally, they flee southward in retreat from Soviet occupation forces. Young Chitose notes that they are following the stars to guide them to the south, which she describes as a "railway in the sky," hence the feature's title.

Unlike *Barefoot* Gen, *Rail of the Star* does not directly criticize Japanese imperialism. Rather, such instances appear through the innocent eyes of Chitose, who has no understanding of the circumstances. In one striking scene, she witnesses several Japanese boys beating a young Korean for refusing to adopt a Japanese name. Chitose helps the Korean after his assailants depart, and she is genuinely confused when he explains the different pronunciations of his name, in Japanese and Korean, despite being written in the same characters. Toward the war's end, Chitose is equally baffled when this Korean boy heads to the wild to join up with patriotic Korean guerillas. Her confusion is magnified when she realizes that this Korean, with whom she was friendly, may well end up fighting her recently conscripted father. Finally, when Japan's surrender is announced, she is bewildered by the contrast between her family's depressed spirits and the exuberant Korean celebrations.

Rail of the Star assumes that the viewer will have some knowledge of the historical circumstances in order to understand the implications of these scenes, unlike *Barefoot Gen*, whose moral stance is unmistakable.

Examining the war from children's perspectives is an effective technique to emphasize the war's horror and destructiveness, without directly portraying the actions of the Japanese military, or delving deeply into Japan's aggressive policies which initially triggered the war. In fact, such things are rarely mentioned. *Grave of the Fireflies* and *Barefoot Gen* make little direct mention of such acts, and *Rail of the Star* only hints at them weakly in the context of occupied Korea. This may be an example of the Japanese reluctance to acknowledge the atrocities committed during the war, or perhaps the publishers and producers of these features avoided such subjects for fear that their intended audiences would avoid their films.

Zipang

Many of these acclaimed manga and anime stories approach the war in a historical, factual fashion, with little hypothetical speculation. Even *Cosmoship Yamato*, despite being science fiction fantasy, does not speculate on how the

war might have developed differently. A great exception is the series *Zipang*,[2] which combines science fiction with factual historic settings and people.

The basic premise of *Zipang* is the popular science-fiction device of time travel. The Japanese Maritime Self-Defense Force ship *Murai*, a new, modern Aegis-class guided missile cruiser, is mysteriously transported back in time to 1942. The ship's name itself is symbolic, meaning "future" in Japanese. In some ways *Zipang* is reminiscent of the 1980 America motion picture *The Final Countdown*, which has the aircraft carrier USS *Nimitz* transported to December 6th, 1941. But, unlike the lame conclusion of *The Final Countdown*, which sees *Nimitz* returning to the future before taking any action at Pearl Harbor, *Murai* remains in the past, and is drawn into the conflict.

Pervading the entire story is the concept of just war. In the very first scenes, a journalist is interviewing one of *Murai*'s officers about the role of Japan's modern military. Commander Kadamatsu Yosuke, *Murai*'s second-in-command, affirms modern Japan's principle of a military for defense only, but concludes that if ordered, he and other servicemen would fight. En route to a joint exercise with the US Navy, *Murai* encounters a mysterious phenomenon and loses all contact with the US or Japanese navies. In a dramatic scene, *Murai*'s crew realizes that it has traveled back in time when it sights the Imperial Japanese Navy battleship *Yamato,* just as the battle of Midway is beginning to unfold. *Murai*'s Captain Umezu thus faces many decisions fraught with moral uncertainty.

As his desire is to return to the twenty-first century, Umezu is reluctant to do anything which might change history. But, as captain of *Murai*, he has a responsibility to protect his ship and crew. Furthermore, as a Japanese officer well versed in naval history, he is reluctant to stand by and watch his country fight on pointlessly to the massive destruction it will experience by 1945. In this environment, all decisions are uncertain, and ethically correct actions seem impossible to determine.

A popular concept of science-fiction time travel is that "you can't change history" (hence the lame conclusion of *The Final Countdown*). But, *Murai* had already changed history, albeit in a small way, simply by traveling to 1942. And, the possibility remained that the ship's crew might change history more drastically. Had Captain Umezu made the maintenance of history his priority, he should have scuttled his ship over the Mariana Trench to the loss of hands.

Other moral questions emerge. To whom does the crew of *Murai* owe its allegiance? Captain Umezu and his crew have repudiated Imperial Japan's

---

[2] The title *Zipang* is based on an old name for Japan, Cipangu, a word Marco Polo used in his memoir, based on an old Cantonese word. The Portuguese adopted this word when they came to China in the sixteenth century, and the name Cipangu became the basis for the name "Japan" in many European languages.

aggressive policies, yet in 1942 the US military is about to begin its long counter-offensive which will destroy the Imperial Japanese Navy, along with much of Japan itself. Should he accept imperial Japan's authority and use *Murai*'s advanced technology to ensure a Japanese victory? Conversely, if Captain Umezu makes his priority the protection his crew and the avoidance of altering history, he must ignore imperial authority and remain hidden. Or, should he act independently and use *Murai*'s advanced weaponry to hasten the end of the war, without victors, and prevent the deaths of millions? But, his country's defeat in 1945 did eliminate Japanese imperialism and set the foundations for a prosperous Japan which would eventually produce the very *Murai* itself, which must remain unchanged if *Murai* should ever return to the twenty-first century. There seems no possibility of an ethically correct path. Rather than find the perfect solution in this moral quagmire, Captain Umezu focuses on the present, making the preservation of life, of both his crew and others, his highest priority.

But, even this humanitarian approach changes history when *Murai* rescues a downed Japanese pilot of 1942, Lieutenant Commander Kusaka. Some research in *Murai*'s library revealed that Kusaka originally perished at sea. Subsequently, Commander Kusaka managed to learn the true origin of *Murai*. Also, Captain Umezu finds that he cannot ignore Kusaka, as Murai needs someone from 1942 to assist in getting essential supplies such as food and fuel. Initially, Kusaka is dismayed when he learns that Japan will surrender in 1945, but as he learns more about *Murai*'s sophistication, he resolves to use its advanced weaponry to alter the course of the war. He envisions a new Japan, abandoning its imperial aggression, avoiding destruction and surrender, but nonetheless dominating East Asia. He names his hypothetical nation *Zipang*, hence the name of the series.

The reputed ruthless savagery of the Japanese forces also comes under attack, as Captain Umezu consistently tries to limit his use of force. When sighted by an American submarine, he uses *Murai*'s advanced features to protect his crew, but refrains from destroying the submarine, which he could easily have achieved. When Captain Umezu decides that deadly force is unavoidable, it is with great regret, and with all effort to limit its destructiveness.

Zipang's portrayals of the historic Japanese admiral Isoroku Yamamoto provide particularly striking opportunities to comment on the war. In one scene, Yamamoto condemns the pointless sacrifices which badly depleted the ranks of the Japanese military. Historically, this is plausible, in that Yamamoto was one of the more progressively-minded amongst Japanese officers, who had never harbored great hopes for a Japanese victory.

Pervading the dialogue of many characters in *Zipang* is a desire to avoid a disastrous defeat and massive destruction, while simultaneously

strengthening Japan and building the foundations of its postwar prosperity. The author's choice to include several scenes of Admiral Yamamoto, who remains a respected historical figure, provides a focus on which to fantasize about alternate histories. If Yamamoto had been able to exert some restraint on Japan's imperialist policies, could they have avoided an unwinnable war? If, in 1942, the admiral could have had access to *Murai's* power, would he have been able to force the United States into a negotiated peace? Such desires reveal a longing that Japan might have avoided destruction and surrender, had it followed more enlightened policies and had enough power to enact them.

Although *Zipang* displays a certain amount of Japanese patriotism, it does not avoid the dark realities of imperial Japan's dictatorship. When *Murai* calls at Singapore to re-fuel, the crew sees the subjugation of the local peoples under Japanese rule. Later, Lieutenant Commander Kusaka, the pilot spared the death that history originally dealt him, encounters the *kempei-tai*, imperial Japan's secret police. Thus, *Zipang* stands in a unique position. While patriotically Japanese, it criticizes imperialist expansion, but also disavows the clear pacifism of *Barefoot Gen*. And, like *Cosmoship Yamato*, *Zipang* creates many opportunities to condemn aggressive war and brutal policies. Its use of accurate historical settings makes such statements more poignant, and creates fertile ground for speculation and longing for an alternate end to the Pacific War.

The Future of History

Manga and anime, which form only a specific segment of popular culture, are generally not intended to re-write history in any formal, academic sense. Their main purpose is entertainment. But they must illustrate the values, thoughts, and aspirations of a society in order to cultivate any kind of audience. Also the historic events of their settings must be portrayed with some degree of accuracy to retain a plausible environment for the development of their characters. The interaction and development of a story's characters usually provide the greatest appeal for an audience. Hopefully, the actual historical facts, so far as they can be verified, will not be altered or falsified in order to pursue any parochial interests.

So popular culture retains a significant interest for the historian. True-to-life, realistic dramas such as *Barefoot Gen* and *Rail of the Star* can create settings to examine various perspectives and criticisms of historic events and national policies, which add to the drama of these stories and give the historian some views of how the Japanese view their own history. In the case of science fiction, freed from the constraints of realistic drama, such media as manga and anime can create forums from which to delve into regret for ill-conceived policies and

desires for the re-creation of history. Average people, particularly the youthful devotees of these media, frequently acquire most of their images and concepts of history solely from films, television, and of course, manga and anime. Thus, the influence of these media is an important part of how our understanding of history is shaped, requiring historians to actively engage in these media in order to better understand popular concepts (and misconceptions) about historic periods and events but more importantly, to help readers judge them accurately.

7

Living Happily Never After in Women's Manga

JONATHAN CLEMENTS

On the publication's cover, a woman in a threadbare, dirty yellow smock sniffs back the tears. On her back, a squalling infant screams for attention. She doesn't even meet the reader's gaze, but plaintively whispers, downcast: *"Won't somebody help me . . . ?"* In letters the size of her head, the magazine's title yells out in angry red: *Gokinjo no Warui Uwasa*, "Bad Gossip of Your Neighborhood."

Comics aimed at adult women are one of the newest niches in the manga market, first appearing in the 1980s. Amid a flurry of foreign interest in Japanese comics for boys, college-age young men, and teenage girls, manga for adult women remain tantalisingly unknown to many manga researchers, despite a Japanese study of the gender issues arising in them (Miya Erino's 1993 book, *Ladies' Comic no Joseigaku: Dare ga Sodateru, Naze Teishaku shita? [Gender Studies in Ladies' Comics: Who Raises (the children), and Why So?]*).

> These magazines targeted adult women—college students, office workers, and housewives—and by 1993 there were reportedly 57 of them, with a combined circulation of over 120 million. Some magazines today focus on nonsexual areas such as marriage and child-raising or mystery stories, but most include so much erotic material that *redikomi* [ladies' comics] has almost become a synonym for racy reading material for women. (Frederik Schodt, *Dreamland Japan: Writings on Modern Manga*, p. 124)

But much of what is written about "ladies' comics" dates from just after the peak of the Japanese economy in 1990. The "racy" material Schodt noticed twenty years ago is still prevalent, although arguably over-represented in attention abroad. Foreign critics often seem fixated on transgressive subsets of Japanese women's erotica, such as the bondage and "boys' love" niches. In fact, it is easy to find "plain vanilla" erotica: heterosexual, consensual sex, for

example as the prime focus of the *For Mrs* spin-off *Ren'ai Cherry Pink*, aimed at happily married young mothers in their thirties.

Kinko Ito, a Japanese researcher based in America, published several articles on manga in the early twenty-first century, including "Japanese Ladies' Comics as Agents of Socialization: The Lessons They Teach," a summary of the twelve "messages" of socialization she discerned in a sampling of contemporary women's publications. Otherwise, much of the scholarly coverage of women's manga is contained or implied within discussion of Japanese comics for teenage girls. The only women's manga to have achieved any measure of Anglophone fame is *In the Light*, a title originally serialised in *For Mrs* magazine and with a subject matter, raising an autistic child, that is not typical in the women's manga world.

To some degree, the very success and marketability of the women's manga market *within* Japan has hampered the attention it receives abroad. Manga aimed at teenagers are often adapted into anime, with a far greater likelihood of reaching the west, and result in a type of synergy as translation of one leads to translation of the other. Women's comics, however, usually with real-world settings and contemporary themes, are easily adapted into live-action TV dramas, gaining greater domestic exposure but eluding the anime connection that inspires so much western research. Hence, for example, one of the true superstars of the last two decades of women's manga, Fumi Saimon, whose work has been adapted into primetime TV serials such as *Tokyo Love Story*, *Unmarried Family*, and *Asunaro Confessions*, remains largely unread in American manga fandom, and by association, scholarship.

Unlike other sectors of the manga world, Japanese women's comics have yet to be strip-mined by foreign publishers, and hence are largely impenetrable to researchers without knowledge of Japanese. Moreover, unlike the multi-part epics of many teen or male-oriented serials, the women's manga market often relies on *yomikiri*—"one-shot stories" that disappear without a trace by the following month. As the cover lines clumsily promise on *Harlequin* magazine, which has been adapting foreign romance novels into manga for the last decade: "All stories *yomikiri*, and with happy-endism." However, this compact nature also reduces the chance of such stories enduring in compilation reprint volumes and reaching a readership beyond the original consumers in magazine form.

The Birth of Women's Manga

Comics for women in Japan have a contradictory origin story. It was, after all, a woman who wrote the best-known comic strip in post-war Japan, the story of a homemaker in Tokyo: Machiko Hasegawa's *Sazae-san*, which ran from 1946

to 1974. But *Sazae-san* is often excluded from official accounts, variously for being too much of an old-fashioned strip cartoon, or for running in a newspaper instead of a dedicated manga magazine. Both it and its creator are, for example, oddly absent from Osamu Takeuchi's *Encyclopedia of Contemporary Manga 1945–2005* (2006), and yet, in chronicling the tribulations of a calculatedly average housewife, *Sazae-san* was surely a pioneer in Japanese women's comics.

For the history of manga aimed specifically at women (*josei*) rather than girls (*shōjo*) in the postwar market, the accepted orthodoxy instead favors a progression from comics for girls, created largely by men in the 1950s and 1960s, through comics for girls created largely by women in the 1970s, and the subsequent development of a market of comics by women, *for* women in the 1980s, when both readers and creators had sufficiently matured.

The first generation of post-war girls' comics was largely a matter of male authorship, with creators such as Osamu Tezuka and Mitsuteru Yokoyama laying the foundations of archetype and stereotype for the girls' genre. A generation later, female artists co-opted the field that had been established in their name. In particular, the Year 24 Group, named for their common birthdates around Shōwa 24 (1949), produced the artists who would transform girls' comics in the 1970s— such as Keiko Takemiya, Riyoko Ikeda, or Moto Hagio. Jason Thompson's *Manga: The Complete Guide* notes several early failed experiments in manga for women, including *Funny* (1964), and *Josei Comic Papillon* (1974) (p. 171). Thompson also cites the still-running *Petit* (1977) as a women's comic, although the Japanese Magazine Publishers Association files *Petit* as a comic for teenage *girls*, not adult women. Today, the Japanese Magazine Publishers Association recognises manga for women as a category of its own, offering a snapshot of popular titles in the women's comic sector.

The JMPA listing excerpted on the next page is instructive, but not comprehensive—it's limited to publishers who are members of the JMPA. It does not specify the publishing cycles, and hence a weekly with a seemingly low print-run can, theoretically, outstrip the annual sales for a monthly or bimonthly periodical that at first appears to be more profitable. The relative size of the women's category is not immediately apparent, as we must go to the other categories to gain a frame of comparison. The list excludes comics for *girls*, such as *Ciao*, which sells more copies each month than the *women's* top five combined. It also excludes, of course, amateur publications—a vibrant, thriving community that often subverts the norms of the mainstream. Meanwhile, it includes *Cookie* and *Kiss*, which are arguably aspirational magazines for older teenage girls rather than genuinely adult women—pandering, here, to a publisher's desire to attract advertisers in a particular sector, rather than a true reflection of the majority readership. Most notably for foreign analysts, the JMPA counts copies *printed*, a radical difference from most other nations'

Best-selling Japanese Comic Magazines for Women in 2009

TITLE	PUBLISHER	#PRINTED/Issue
You	Shūeisha	179,542
Be Love	Kōdansha	173,125
Cookie	Shūeisha	165,000
Chorus	Shūeisha	150,417
Elegance Life	Akita Shoten	150,000
For Mrs	Akita Shoten	150,000
Ren'ai Kosho Pastel	Ōzora	150,000
Kiss	Kōdansha	145,542
The Dessert	Kōdansha	115,167
Office You	Shūeisha	111,667
Petit Comic	Shōgakukan	106,167
Dessert	Kōdansha	93,417
Harmony Romance	Ōzora	80,000
Young Love Comic Aya	Ōzora	80,000
Betsu Fre 2009	Kōdansha	73,000
Gokinjo no Warui Uwasa	Ōzora	70,000
Silky	Hakusensha	60,334
Comic Beeslog Kun	Enterbrain	50,000
Shiawase-na Kekkon	Ōzora	50,000
Melody	Hakusensha	46,567
Feel Young	Shōdensha	42,542
Saiko no Ai to Kando	Ōzora	40,000
Hontō ni Kowai Yomeshū	Ōzora	40,000
Ciel	Kadokawa	27,584
Comic Aqua	Okura	25,000

Source: Japanese Magazine Publishers Association

<www.j-magazine.or.jp>.

audit bureaus of circulation, which count copies *sold*. We might then assume that twenty-five to thirty percent of these official print-runs are unread before recycling.

The titles on the JMPA list reflect typical market segmentation. It's difficult to imagine that the woman who reads *Shiawase-na Kekkon* (*Happy Marriage*) is also a regular purchaser of *Hontō ni Kowai Yomeshū* (*Truly*

Scary Brides and Mothers-in-law). Or perhaps she is, but a simple descriptive design such as this can only report the figures, it can't determine whether such stories are a mirror to a reader's personal reality, or an escape from it. In many of the stories under review, the reader's horizon of expectation seems contingent on her marital status. Hence, the notion of the "implied reader" is open to debate—in terms of reader-response criticism, we face the prospect of multiple subjectivities.

Comic for Your Life: *You* Magazine

The figures on the JMPA list are dominated by the *You* franchise, which pioneered women's comics in the 1980s, and remains a powerful influence on the field—most titles are conceived in either imitation of it, or reaction to it. The golden age of women's manga publishing, in fact of all Japanese publishing, was the asset price "Bubble" era, from approximately 1986 to 1990, during which the *You* franchise rode the rising graph of affluence, quick to capitalise on a burgeoning sector within Japanese consumer culture: the young, cash-rich white-collar workers known as Office Ladies.

But intriguingly, just as some magazines for early-teen girls pretend that they are actually aimed at older teenagers, some of these new manga were *about* Office Ladies, but not *for* them. Ito ("Japanese Ladies' Comics") suggests that many readers of women's manga are either homemakers or workers in the "pink-collar sector"—in conservatively feminised professions such as nurses, kindergarten teachers, or store clerks. This is far removed from the glamorous, jet-setting white-collar occupations portrayed within many women's manga, particularly the so-called *katakana* jobs such as journalism, design and broadcasting, so highbrow and exotic that the very terms for them are written not in Japanese but in English (Jonathan Clements and Motoko Tamamuro, *The Dorama Encyclopedia: A Guide to Japanese TV Drama Since 1953*, p. xxv).

Whether manga for Office Ladies were read *by* Office Ladies or not, the entire sector began to suffer from changing economic conditions. As the yuppie aesthetic slumped with the economy, the position of the male-dominated media moved from condescension to envy. The term Parasite Single began to take over, for a young woman who still lived with her parents but held down an office job, taking home a good salary every month and with nothing to spend it on but herself.

Regardless of public envy or admiration, women in their twenties with a disposable income were targeted by the publisher Shūeisha with *Lady's Comic You* in 1982, two years after initial market tests. It was followed a year later by *Office You*, with a more urbane, secretarial stance. In 1986, the franchise split again. *You* aged with its original readership, while a new "little sister" *Young*

You scooped up a new sector of women in their early twenties. In 1988 there was *Mystery You* and *Bridal You*, then *You-all* in 1990. In 1991, with economic collapse looming, those readers who were not reading about office life, or detective stories, or marriage, were exhorted to go out and enjoy themselves in *After Five You*.

In 1993, the original magazine went from monthly to twice-monthly, although the Bubble had already burst, leading to a decade-long recession caused by over-inflated Tokyo real estate prices. Many of the spin-offs were soon cancelled, but the original magazine clung to its readership, gaining the subtitle "Comic for Your Life"—a life seemingly torn between the empty freedoms of singledom or the fulfilling chains of motherhood, and meditations upon this dualistic dilemma.

Whereas comics for men usually vary within a publication by *topic*—a sports manga, a detective story, a cop series—those for women appear to vary by *marital status*—something for the single girl, something for the happily married woman, something for the divorcee. Meanwhile, there remains the possibility that the signifiers for the readership are similarly fragmented. In her essay on "Japanese Ladies' Comics," Ito talks about the "vicarious experiences" of taking revenge on evil mothers-in-law, but perhaps there are also "vicarious torments," in which the misadventures of an unhappily married, put-upon heroine are interpreted by a readership of singletons as a different form of entertainment—an unexpected "implied reader."

Christmas Cake

We might be forgiven for assuming that female manga consumers spontaneously combusted in their mid-twenties, reaching a deadline like something out of *Logan's Run*, and suddenly disappearing from the market. The infamously cruel epithet "Christmas cake" took its name from a cream-heavy sponge confection with a limited sell-by date. Due to media-defined trends and the necessities of timing sales to coincide with demand, such cakes usually went on sale in the week before Christmas Eve—a date that has, in modern Japan, become accepted as a night for lovers, and for shy Japanese boys to pop the question. Due, once again, to both popular myth and the prosaic realities of shelving and food storage, such Christmas cakes were deemed "unsellable after the twenty-fifth."

Was there a manga market for women who had passed their twenty-fifth birthday? *You* magazine's editors certainly expected to retain a few stragglers into their thirties. If life for twenty-somethings really were a dichotomy between Mrs or Miss, *You* magazine offers stories for each, with different meanings.

You is one of only seven women's manga magazines included in the JMPA's full online statistical survey. According to the JMPA, *You's* readership in 2009 was 100 percent female, 73.9 percent married, and 37 percent homemakers. Only 1.3 percent of *You* readers have no children at all, while 52.1 percent have two. Over two-thirds of the readership of *You* magazine are over thirty—30.3 percent are aged over 36. Considering the length of time that *You* has been publishing, we might speculate on the implied presence of a glass ceiling in manga magazine development. The *You* brand is still classed as a "young adult" comic in the JMPA figures, but has vastly more readers over 36 than its rival *For Mrs* magazine, which is openly aimed at older women. Each issue of the "young adult" magazine *You* is read by more than fifty thousand women over 36. *For Mrs*, supposedly for "adult" women without the mitigating "young" qualification, is only read by twelve thousand women over 36.

Such statistics suggest that *You* continues to attract a diverse readership, requiring an editorial awareness of a fragmented audience—an understanding that the single lives of those readers looking for romance and adventure are already leavened by others who have paired up, married and become mothers. There seems to be understandably scant appeal for a reader of *You* to be identified by self or publisher as "not young." Instead of creating magazines openly for women in their forties, the manga market instead allows them to linger in the bracket for women ten years their junior, and, it seems, secretly aims some of its stories at this hidden, bonus readership sector. Part of the strategy for older readers lies in denying they are no longer "young." Instead, they are invited to consume the misadventures of younger protagonists in a knowing, voyeuristic manner—as implied readers whose response to the everyday lives of twenty-somethings is defamiliarized. Thus, for some readers, stories in *You* are a reflection of how things are, and for others, a speculation about how things could have been.

You's past highlights have included self-explanatory high-concept titles such as *Nurse Station*, *Happy Trouble Wedding*, and *I Am a Mother*. Its biggest title in the years 2000–2007 was Kozueko Morimoto's *Gokusen*, about the granddaughter of a mafia boss who tries to stay straight by becoming a teacher at an all-boys high school. *Gokusen* was an uncharacteristic title for a "ladies" comic, but it was caught up in the dual influence of *The Sopranos* (broadcast in Japan in 1999 as *Aishū no Mafia—Sorrowful Mafia*) and *GTO* (a similar manga, but aimed at young men).

Not That Bad

Opening the May 2008 issue of *You* magazine, the stories themselves give us a further glimpse of reader interests. Stories of marital woe can be vicarious entertainment or cautionary tales for people without spouses (a quarter of *You's* readers), or slices of life for couples. In *Steel Lady* by Kaoru Fukuya, Ineko, a thirty-five-year-old woman, volunteers to teach a class of difficult fourth-graders. No Mafia connections here—instead the story concentrates on Ineko's relationship not only with her pupils, but also with their parents. One pushy mother is tough on her daughter, hot-housing her to get her through the exams and into the right secondary school, but blissfully unaware that in the process she has turned her little girl into an overbearing, self-obsessed bully, who pushes the other kids around. Another child is disruptive in class, but Ineko has trouble telling his single parent because the father is a charming cameraman with designer stubble.

Steel Lady challenges the perceptions of its readers, asking which is the "correct" assessment of these broadly drawn characters. Is the pushy mother bad? Is the handsome, appealing father really good? This dilemma plays straight to the heart of the twelve "Lessons and Messages" outlined by Kinko Ito in her analysis of women's manga, particularly Ito #5: "Do not assume anything. It could be in your head. Try to make an accurate assessment."

Conversely, the tribulations of a single existence are presented either as horror stories for those who no longer have to date, or slices of life for those that still do.

In the one-shot story, *God of the Bookshelf* by Kasumi Fukazawa, we can see these two worlds contending for the reader's attention. "There is nothing beautiful around me," sighs its nameless heroine, a pretty but lonely divorcee. Her life is an endless repetition of mundane drudgery; her young daughter pays her no attention, and she continually bats away the affectionate mewling of the family cat. The message, however, is not one of romantic redemption or love with the postman. Instead, it is a simple nudge towards redefining one's priorities—realizing that the growing daughter and the pestering cat are just

two of many truly beautiful things already in our heroine's life. The distinctly pessimist message is not one of escape, but of acceptance. Ito #11: "Always appreciate those who are in your life. They are special people. We are all inter-related and interdependent."

Across the Sea at Dawn, by Mutsumi Tsukumo is another juxtaposition of two very different lifestyles. The leading characters are Misuzu and Hanako, girls born in 1860s Japan, at the beginning of the modern era. Misuzu is a traditional Japanese girl, demure, kimono-clad, and obedient to her parents. But Hanako is free-spirited and independent, and scandalously walks out on her family to live with an Englishman, Henry Jefferson. Jefferson, of course, is a dashing, handsome industrialist, ever attentive to his Japanese fiancée. Misuzu, meanwhile, is plunged into a loveless marriage with a gruff and bullying older man. Three years on, and the childhood friends suddenly find their worlds changing. Unhappy though Misuzu might be, at least she "knows her place" in the Japanese world. Henry is called away to his sick father's bedside in England, while Hanako frets that she will be cast aside and forgotten like a new Madame Butterfly, particularly if Henry makes a rash promise to his dying father to marry a nice English girl. But if Hanako travels to distant, exotic England with Henry, will she ever see Japan again?

Across the Sea at Dawn never misses the chance to ogle nice frocks and sumptuous kimonos, luxuriating in the differences between the life, possessions, and expectations of these two Japanese women. In other words, it artfully conveys some of the cultural confusion felt in Japan at the time, all dressed up in a tale of Victorian romance. One wonders about the deeper message behind *Across the Sea at Dawn*. It can't possibly be a tale fashioned around Ito #9: "Your happiness counts. Get out of your bad marriage." Instead, it seems like a variation of Ito #1: "Your case is not that special." The heroines endure their hardship as a means of reminding readers that however bad their modern problems may be, life and opportunities in other times was far worse.

After You: Manga Magazines for Housewives

Figures from any audit bureau of circulation lose their reliability once out of the best-selling sector. The reason is universal—magazines setting advertising rates want to prove high sales; they are more reluctant to discuss sales if their readership is lower than expected. Magazines with lower circulations prefer not to be audited at all—their sole saving grace is if they can offer a "closed circle of consumption": in marketing terms, a captive audience that can be targeted for specific niche concerns.

One of the most powerful niches in the women's manga world is the genre of pets. There is but a single manga magazine for hamster-fanciers, a single

manga publication for dog-lovers, but an astounding eleven manga magazines in today's Japan dedicated solely to cats, including *Neko Bunch*, *Nekopara[dise]*, and *Manga Neko Shippo* (*Manga Cat's Tail*). Strangely, none of them predate the year 2000, and nine of them only began publishing in 2006, a generation after the debut of *You* magazine. *Neko no Akubi* (*A Cat's Stretch/Yawn*) is one of the class of 2006, commencing as a bimonthly, before speeding up to a monthly schedule in 2008, with advertising content that suggests its readership is primarily single women in their thirties and forties, who are, or at least are ready to believe they are, fifteen kilos overweight.

Another subset of women's manga magazines, aimed at the married woman, is distinguished by the keyword "Truly," stamped in smaller print above the main logo, implying that some or all of the contents are real-world reportage. This has become a discernable brand for the publisher Bunka-sha, in titles such as *Hontō ni atta Onna no Hito Jinsei Drama* (*Woman's Life Drama that Truly Happened*), *Hontō ni atta Waraeru Hanashi* (*Funny Stories that Truly Happened*), *Hontō ni atta Shufu no Taiken* (*Wives' Experiences that Truly Happened*), and *Hontō ni atta Josei Drama* (*Women's Drama that Truly Happened*). Elsewhere, its use can be subversively adverbial; while a casual glance might suggest that the same publisher's *Hontō ni Nakeru Hanashi* magazine means *True Tales to Make You Weep*, this is cunning editorial misdirection. The title is better translated as *Tales that Will Truly Make You Weep*. Similarly, in a device relatively common in Japanese prose fiction, proper nouns in these manga are often identified by anonymous single letters, ("Town N in P Prefecture") as if innocent real-life victims need to be shielded from identification.

In the case of *Gokinjo no Warui Uwasa* (*Bad Gossip from Your Neighborhood*—hereafter, *Neighborhood Gossip*, specifically the October 2009 issue), published by Ōzora Shuppan, the sense of real-life reportage is implied less by the title than by the reader response form. Although these reply coupons are standard issue with all Japanese magazines, the one in *Neighborhood Gossip* includes large sections for personal reminiscences and tall tales, suggesting, even to the vast majority of readers who do not habitually return such surveys, that a significant proportion of the magazine is based on such confessions from others.

Coping Strategies

The attitude of *Neighborhood Gossip*, a thick, five-hundred-page magazine, is reflected in its ads for diet pills, miracle cures, and phone lines, and competition prizes including a nightlight, a Nintendō Wii, a toy ATM for the kids, and supermarket vouchers. It prints, according to the JMPA, seventy

thousand copies every two months and is loaded with *yomikiri* "one-shot" stories designed to remind the reader that no matter how bad her life might be, someone else has got it worse. In her "Lessons and Messages" of women's manga, Kinko Ito identifies a number of coping strategies for readers such as, for example, Ito #1: "Do not dwell on your misfortune or a bad situation. (Almost all Japanese women have similar experiences. Your case is not that special)." *Neighborhood Gossip* seems designed to make Ito's first lesson come to life.

The magazine is distinguished by a note of glum acceptance throughout, with many stories suggesting that the winners in life's lottery are those who are quiet, forgiving, and indulgent of men's idiocies and peccadilloes. Self-identification appears to be part of the appeal. In writing the synopses, it's often difficult to work out what people's names are. This is because the heroines often seem deliberately anonymous, seemingly to aid the reader in placing herself in the characters' shoes.

Parts of *Neighborhood Gossip* rail against the fairy-tale idea of marriage as a happy ending. Far from it, is the message—instead people's troubles are only just beginning, and far from escaping from one's own family problems, one is instead trapped with one's spouse's. In Yuki Madoka's *Sotsukon*, illness strikes a family member and forces everyone to rethink their priorities. The title is a coinage based on the Japanese words for Graduation and Marriage; the message is that our housewife heroine hasn't really taken on her new role until she has looked hardship in the face and stared it down. Ito #2: "Help is always available. Do not get stuck in the situation. Talk to people."

In *Trouble Election* by Yōko Nagaya, the father-in-law is the problem. A wife and her husband are feeling the pinch in Tokyo after the birth of their young son, and are invited to move out into the sticks where the husband's father, Takeshi, has strong connections. In a country with an aging population,

many of whom only have a single adult child to care for them, the issues of in-laws is a hot topic. In-law appeasement stories are a whole subset of cruel entertainment in Japan, and this is no exception, as Takeshi proves to be a bullying, hectoring ogre, who calls the heroine lazy because she is still in bed at five in the morning. Author Nagaya adds spice to what would otherwise be a misery memoir by throwing an interesting new element: the father-in-law has decided to run for office. This now drags the heroine into his political campaign—she's obliged to help him pass out leaflets, even though she knows that in private he is an awful, overbearing tyrant. Even worse, the rival candidate is a good-hearted local housewife, whom Takeshi ridicules from the hustings. In a victory for democracy, the heroine and the rest of the village get their revenge the modern way, by simply casting their votes. This neatly encapsulates both Ito #3: "Cut off your big ego and pride that makes you suffer. You win by losing," alongside Ito #10 "Be assertive where necessary." But the neat ending rather avoids the broader question—what happens the next day at Takeshi's kitchen table?

Nor does *Neighbourhood Gossip* look kindly at shortcuts, particularly illegal ones. In *Path to Shoplifting*, by Saori Kirino, a harassed housewife is pestered by her children, caught short at the supermarket, and incensed to find her husband coming home every night with a bag full of beers. When a part-time job proves to hardly make a scrap of difference, she turns to a life of crime, stuffing occasional items into her handbag, and surreptitiously putting discount labels on full-price goods. It all ends in tears, firstly when she is caught, and then when she discovers that her young son has learned from her how to be a thief.

There's another cautionary tale in *Ice World* by Mariko Sakurai, contrasting two women's approaches to staying healthy. One exercises and eats well, the other pops vitamin pills and has a good time. Healthy eating, it also turns out, won't just stop you turning into a drug-addicted harridan, it will also contribute towards a fragrant home, as we discover in *The Trouble with My Husband's Body Odor*, by Reiko Kawashima. Reading like an extended Persil commercial, it features a housewife hitting the books as she tries to solve the problem of her sweaty husband. I was half expecting her to discover the same odour suspiciously lingering on her cordial neighbor's bedsheets, but it was not to be. Instead, she learns why armpits smell, complete with cutaway biology diagrams.

A similar, didactic content is imparted in *Good Air* by Paseri Aona, which grapples with her mother-in-law's heavy nicotine habit. Complete with cutaway images of lungs, it also offers the readers an irresistible opportunity. Since they are statistically less likely to be smokers than their husbands' unreformed mothers, it gives them the moral high ground—the chance to make a Confucian argument: that they are forbidding their mother-in-law from smoking indoors out of a filial concern for her long-term health. In all such cases, from shoplifting to armpits to smoking, there is an emphasis on taking charge of one's own life. Or rather, Ito #12: "Grow up and become an adult."

Conversely, other stories in *Neighborhood Gossip* depict single life as an unremitting hell, from which the married reader is fortunate to have escaped. In *Honeyed Whispers* by the pseudonymous "Okashimaya", a gullible lady is lured into a host club and charmed by a group of handsome, debonair, attentive men, only to be landed with the bill for their feigned interest. Similarly, *Aren't You Alone?* by Lynch Ito is a cunning tale of *Schadenfreude*, inverting the tropes of *Sex and the City* to give the readers a good laugh at the expense of single women. Its leading lady is Mio, an attractive thirty-something who is still in the dating game, but realizing that men are not treating her with former levels of devotion. Dates are postponed, cancelled or otherwise ruined, and she begins to notice that *"even the plain girls"* at the office are getting hitched. Eventually, Mio is the last office lady left on the shelf—she realises that she has missed her chance, and goes mad in a knife-wielding hysterical meltdown. The denouement is bitterly cruel, and leaves an innocent woman dead on the pavement, while her would-be fiancé clutches an engagement ring in a restaurant and looks at his watch!

Kitchen sink drama might be the aim of *Neighborhood Gossip*, but it cannot resist the temptations of such Grand Guignol. The October 2009 issue of *Neighbourhood Gossip* comes with a bonus hundred-page mini magazine called *Truly Terrifying Tales of Women's Revenge*. This contains three stories, the most interesting of which is *Forbidden Visage* by Takako Hashimoto, in which a housewife's life is turned upside down by her overworked husband's suicide. The distraught widow begins a rebound relationship with her late husband's work colleague Akio, unaware that Akio was the dastardly employee who caused all the killer stress in the first place. She soon finds out the hard way when Akio turns into a widow-beater. A year later, the couple argue about whether or not the widow's new child is Akio's or her late husband's. Cue magic-realist cutaways as the tormented Akio is haunted by images of the man whose death he caused, reborn before his eyes in the form of his own son. It's an odd story, not the least because it is hardly terrifying, and not all that vengeful, but there is a compelling twist. Akio is stuck *in loco parentis* with his enemy's offspring for the next 20 years—longer than some "life" sentences. He has to pay for him, care for him, and put up with the sight of him every day. In that regard, there is the subtle suggestion that parenthood itself is a hellish torment, which many readers of *Neighbourhood Gossip* are currently enduring.

Surviving Suburbia

Neighborhood Gossip might be glum and terror-struck, but it continually re-assures its readers that they are better off than the hapless heroines. Its great rival is the magazine *Neighborhood Scandal* (*Gokinjo Scandal*) which takes an oddly contrapuntal approach to its cover design. Whereas the front of *Neighborhood Gossip* unfailingly presents a scene of spousal turmoil, *Neighborhood Scandal* puts

a fluffy animal on its covers. This is strangely misleading—a sweet puppy, kitten or rabbit, belying the contents of crime, anguish and shame.

Neighborhood Scandal's statistics claim a 99 percent female readership, of which the greater proportion is in its thirties and forties. 77 percent of the readers give their occupation as "housewife." Every month, the publisher Takeshobo claims to print 160,000 copies, and as with *Neighborhood Gossip*, the reader response form is equipped for story suggestions, including an entire sheet of blank, lined paper. The stories themselves, however, often

have a hectoring, didactic tone, as if the magazine intends itself to be a means of surviving suburbia, imparting vital knowledge to help readers negotiate the pitfalls of modern living.

In the June 2009 issue, "Misato" writes *Grass of Misfortune* about a divorced mother-of-three, Makiko Sugimoto, who celebrates her eldest son Kazuki landing a job straight out of high school. But trouble soon arises when Makiko runs into her loathsome ex-husband, a dapper man in a sports car who breezes back into her life six years after he left her for his bargirl mistress. Even as Kazuki tries to enter the adult world, he is forced to confront his dark shadow: his drug-dealing bad-boy half-brother, Yuya. As Kazuki's behaviour becomes increasingly more erratic, Makiko turns to the Internet to help her work out what's wrong. Kazuki's wearing sunglasses indoors, he's moody . . . and with a start, Makiko realises that her son has turned to drugs. The police smile on Kazuki because it is a first offense, the feckless relatives are swept aside, and Kazuki is soon going to college, not quite out there in the tough real world, but saved from a shameful decline.

Dream Wish, by Natsuki Mio, is another dire warning to the fretful mothers of Japan. This time, it deals with a boy called Dago (a bad start), whose loneliness as a child and constant appeals for attention put him on a collision course with the music business. He overcomes teenage rejection, copies his rock idols, and ends up as a pop star, although he worries about how to tell his

grandma that he is gay. Eventually, he plucks up the courage and she shrugs her shoulders in mild disinterest—a fascinating non-reaction, as it suggests that since neither Dago nor his grandmother are bothered, the "scandal" is not Dago's homosexuality, but in his belief that anyone would despise him for it. If that is that case, far from slapping readers in the face with the promised shocks, the magazine is gently trying to educate them.

In the significantly racier *Dream of Deception* by Naru Komaki, Sayaka believes herself to be the sole love of Kosugi, an up-and-coming sumo wrestler who says he sees a future for them both. In fact, he's just using her for rough and perfunctory sex after his big matches, and she only starts to suspect when he makes a booty call on her cellphone and inadvertently calls her by someone else's name. Before long, Sayaka discovers that exclusivity is not the only lie she's been hearing from Kosugi, who has left a trail of crooked deals and broken hearts behind him since high school. Watching the news of his corruption scandal unfold on a giant public TV screen, she resolves to make better choices in men. Meanwhile, the reader is expected to count her blessings—at least when things go wrong in the mundane world, the dirty laundry isn't washed on the national news. This is something of a departure from Ito's "Lessons and Messages", but only in the sense that Ito's sample from 2003 does not tackle pre-marital sexual mores. Ito #6 says: "Married men are not good for you. The wife always wins." Kosugi is not married, but might as well be for all the impact that Sayaka makes on his morals and his heart. But there are no winners here, only survivors.

And yet, despite the torrid storylines, the artwork is remarkably staid. *Neighborhood Scandal* is drawn very much in the no-nonsense fashion of other magazines for the older female reader, with the emphasis on faces and two-shots. It's the clash of wills and personalities that concerns *Neighborhood Scandal*'s creators, and background detail is often noticeably lacking.

One recurring artistic device is the cellphone, which not only affirms the notion that the story is from our era (and not merely republished from decades earlier), but also as a narrative device. Panels depicting phone screens can supply large amounts of data and backstory, and speed up the storytelling process with what amounts to simple blocks of word-processed text. Lost signals, misdirected mails and unwise public confessions also form a vital part of many stories. In *Family Standing Tall* by Momo Urito, the phone serves a different purpose, with a daughter's boorish texting at the dinner table irritating her mother more than usual. The cellphone here is a symptom, not a cause—the father's being posted away to a new town, and everyone in the family is suppressing their worries about the consequences this may have. This includes Harry the family dog, who acts up when Dad is not around, even to the extent on urinating on the family's shoes in the entrance hall! Harry

returns to normal when Dad's company moves back home, and any "scandal" that may have arisen is swiftly forgotten. *Family Standing Tall* hence cunningly (albeit oddly) allegorises fears of marital breakdown, with the misbehavior of a pet standing in for the unspoken anguish of a suburban family. Ito #4: "Always try your best to understand others. Put yourself in their shoes and see from their perspective."

No Longer Familiar

Presumably at some point in the previous 161 issues, *Neighborhood Scandal* exhausted all the usual suburban trials, since it does now seem to rely on lurid and somewhat unlikely tales of stalking and murder. Beyond the dog's dirty protest, the drama gets progressively nastier in this issue. In *I Want to Peep* by Maya Akashi, a nosy neighbour becomes all too intrigued by the comings and goings of the tousle-haired beauty Miss Hazuki at number 305. When she sees Hazuki coming home with a handsome gentleman, she can't help sneaking a look through the spyhole, but sees very little. Yet she is sure that she can hear something being chopped up, and she is convinced that she sees the lady from 305 in a bloodstained dress. Has Miss Hazuki *murdered* her boyfriend? And if she has, how can we report it unless we admit we've been snooping? In fact, Mrs Hazuki has indeed *accidentally* killed her boyfriend, and a friendly sugar daddy at the police department has helped her clear up the mess. When our nosey neighbour goes to report the crime, she runs into indifferent and then obstructive police, who decide to frame her for the crime. Ito #5: "Do not assume anything. It could just be in your head. Try to make an accurate assessment."

Destroyed? by Akiko Miyazaki appears to take its lead, once again, from *Sex and the City*, positing four femme fatales having a great time in Korea while the local currency is weak. Creator Miyazaki is even found on the contents page exhorting her readers to do the same, and to take advantage of the exchange rate of the Korean currency: "The *won's* really low!" she trills. "Let's go now!" Although presumably Miyazaki is not hoping to run into similar problems on her own holiday of a lifetime, as her four girlfriends encounter an old flame with a creeping flesh disease, a woman with disfiguringly botched plastic surgery, and a knife-wielding mother who beheads unsuitable boyfriends. Ito's Lesson #8, "Don't be afraid of taking new steps," is open to debate here. Perhaps "new steps" are best taken at home, and not in the apparently dangerous otherworld of Korea.

Bonds is the name of the latest story in *Neighborhood Scandal*'s best ongoing series, which runs under the cumbersome umbrella title of *Case Files of Mail Medium Mina Saeki*. These manga stories by Riura Tanahara are based on

the "real-life" adventures of Mina Saeki, an online tarot reader, astrologer, and palmist, who includes her biography and website details. In this episode, she recounts the story of Keiko Ishizuka, a young wife who complains that her live-in brother-in-law is making inappropriate advances. It's not all that clear how the Mail Medium helps her, as she does not prevent Keiko getting disturbed in the bath, felt up at dinner, or ultimately abducted. In fact, as the twist ending reveals, it is not Keiko who has been emailing Mystic Mina at all, but Keiko's mother, who is somehow led by the tarot readings to arrive on her bike in the nick of time to save Keiko. Although by that time, Keiko has already saved herself by smacking her assailant into a tree. Eventually, Mystic Mina performs a reading for the real Keiko, and reveals that Keiko has a bright future ahead of her as a wife and mother.

After hundreds of pages of escapism and gossip, Mina's advertorial manga reaches right off the page with an exhortation to seek her supernatural aid. Coming at the end of the June 2009 issue of *Neighborhood Scandal*, it's a fitting, shocking finale to the whole affair. Unexpectedly and inadvertently, with its suggestion that a stranger with a pack of cards can help protect readers from rapists, the story of Mystic Mina proves to be the most scandalous thing of all in a magazine that is already knee-deep in outrage. It's strange to see it in a genre that places so much emphasis on life lessons and personal growth.

Women's manga magazines present a captivating look at some of the issues and anxieties facing women in Japan. The transient nature of the *yomikiri* stories often makes them difficult to trace after initial publication, but also offers multiple opportunities to examine the timely cares and concerns of a large sector of Japanese readers. Statistics suggest a readership sector that conceals an entire generation of older readers, smuggling themselves in to witness the aspirations and mythologies of younger women, often subverting the original narratives to draw new meaning from them. The magazines themselves function as agents of socialization and education, employing fictional devices to confront contemporary issues more often seen in factual articles. The result is a fascinating, defamiliarized perspective on Japanese suburbia, fraught with urban myths, cautionary tales and strategies for long-term survival.

8

Dirty Pictures

NANCY KANG

*T*he first syllable of the Japanese word *manga* is "man-," a potent coincidence because boys and men were historically the first audience to access and consume Japanese comics. *Shōnen* manga targeted young boys and teens with the mighty, often politicized exploits of such characters as Osamu Tezuka's sci-fi hero *Astro Boy*, while *seinen* manga focused on the diverse interests of adult males, typically aged eighteen to thirty.

Manga historians like Frederik L. Schodt (*Manga! Manga! The World of Japanese Comics*, Collins Design, 1986) and Paul Gravett (*Manga: Sixty Years of Japanese Comics*, Kodansha, 2004) are also quick to acknowledge the role of girls' and women's comics (*shōjo* and *josei*, respectively) in the post–World War II era. The work of the Fabulous 49ers, a group of women *mangakas* born in 1949, swelled the rising currents of manga as a versatile medium with the capacity to integrate historical realism and escapist fantasy. Yet the centrality of the male gaze cannot be ignored when we turn to erotic manga, often referred to collectively as *18-kin* ("prohibited to age eighteen or below"), *seijin* (adult manga—although not all adult manga is pornographic), or *hentai* (abbreviated as "H" or *ecchi*, a more slang term meaning "perverted" or "degenerate").

Sex has never been divorced from the Japanese cultural consciousness given that it is a nation with a large population concentrated in a small area; public and private spaces are often pushed uncomfortably close to one another (not unlike passengers in the subway), but often in a paradoxical way. It may be unspectacular to purchase smutty items like rape-themed porn or used panties (in tune with the *bura-sera* fascination with schoolgirls) from a vending machine, but such openness would find a stark contrast in the desire for modesty, humility, and discretion that simultaneously permeates the culture. In such a place where tradition and modernity collide, the multiple facets of human experience, from the sacred to the profane, have to co-exist as well. These realities are important for readers of erotic manga, including *lolicon*, which is a genre that depicts children in an overtly or covertly sexual

way. Readers may convince themselves that these little girls are sexually mature and hence, sexually available. At the same time, we have to remember that lolicon deals with pictures, not real bodies.

Young and Innocent?

When the still frames of manga morph into the moving pictures of its companion genre *anime*, we might as well call this process "(man)imation" in the same spirit of the word-play that started the discussion. The sexually-interested male gaze remains the target of images ranging from the explicitly pornographic to the playfully suggestive.

In the first category, we find such graphically rendered acts as consensual sex, rape, BDSM (bondage/discipline; dominance/submission; sadism/masochism), inter-species couplings, and fantasy hook-ups with demons, gods, or other supernatural beings. In the second, we peer at modest panty and cleavage shots, winking "wardrobe malfunctions," clumsy and hilariously messy sexual experiments, subtly eroticized puppy love, and desire that lingers for years, often unrequited. Satisfying the largely—but not exclusively—heterosexual reader requires a careful combination of at least three key ingredients: feminine beauty, the pairing of power and vulnerability, and danger. Vladimir Nabokov's novel *Lolita* (1955), the literary basis for the lolicon phenomenon, has all three in abundance.

Literary historians of manga usually situate its origins in the nineteenth century with the *ukiyo-e* woodblock prints of Katsushika Hokusai (1760–1849). One of his most famous works, *Tako to ama* (variously named "Dream of the Fisherman's Wife" or "Girl Diver and Octopi," among other translations), depicts a naked woman being orally pleasured by two very awake, highly dexterous, and tentacled sea-males. Here, we have a combination of understated but obvious sexuality combined with light humor, perhaps a nod to a tradition of caricature found in *shunga*, or "spring pictures."

Shunga's light-hearted eroticism dates back to the Edo Period (1603–1868), where we may find well-attired, squinting women accompanied by enthusiastic men (endowed with massive, sword-sized penises) coupling amid mundane scenes of daily life. Like manga, shunga featured sex as a nothing scandalous or show-stopping; indeed, there were no great religious or moral taboos associated with these images, and their subject matter was democratic enough to include a range of couplings, including people from different age groups as well as sexual orientations. Artists were relatively free to create what they saw as most fitting to the tastes of the time without fear of grand-scale censorship or social repercussions. These Japanese may have leaned toward the conservative, but they were not prudes.

The Butterfly Effect

Erotica has not always been flashy, cheap, and gratuitous; it can also be a highly political, satirical, and complex form of social coding meant to illustrate the intimate fantasies of ordinary people. When Commodore Matthew Perry helped to "open up" Japan in 1854 to greater Western influence both in terms of trade-goods and cultural exposure, erotic prints had to compete with other forms of visual media such as racy photography for the audience's fickle interest. In turn, non-Asian countries, especially the United States and England, became fascinated with "things Japanese," one term for which was *Japonica*. This was an exotic-sounding equivalent, say, of a word like *Chinoiserie*, which meant "things Chinese" that were palatable to the outsider's tastes.

We witnessed the collision of the erotic and the exotic in such fictional characters as the iconic Madame Butterfly. Based on Frenchman Pierre Loti's novella *Madame Chrysanthème* (1887) and American lawyer John Luther Long's subsequent short story "Madame Butterfly" (1898), the character is a very young geisha who falls for an older, morally questionable foreigner and eventually kills herself out of love for him. The pathos is supposed to be thrilling. Loosely based on actual individuals but now well-known to the extent of being called an archetype of Asian and Asian American femininity, Madame Butterfly underscores the asymmetry of power between the male West and female East, capitalizing on the difference for symbolic effect.

In many ways, this cultural amplification and fetishization of Butterfly is twisted. Her life represents a sacrifice to a purity of love that Westerners can appreciate precisely *because* it is not theirs to make. Italian composer Giacomo Puccini's *Madama Butterfly* (1904), also based on the same mythology, remains one of the most famous and frequently performed operas in North America today. There's nothing pornographic about Butterfly's character or her demise, but her story is based on the assumption of vast cultural and gender differences, which are what fuel the sexual tension in the pairing. This tension, a direct result of gender, age-related, and apparent cultural inequalities, can be intensely erotic, as is often the case in lolicon manga.

Few readers will recognize how much the non-Asian in the Madame Butterfly archetype (here, the white man, Pinkerton) is supposed to represent the self-assured masculine ideal and the Asian woman (in this case, Butterfly, or Cio-Cio San) the submissive, fragile, self-sacrificing, child-like woman. What if we were to place the reader of lolicon in the first position as the powerful man, the symbolic, free-spirited, careless rogue-reader who can "love 'em and leave 'em" without one bit of remorse? He does so because he can, and this capacity to choose is intensely gratifying to the ego. What she feels is of little consequence because his pleasure is paramount; she exists to serve him.

Obviously, feminist thinkers would argue this is an inherently flawed understanding of a reciprocal heterosexual relationship. It is actually the final adjective, "child-like," that requires the bulk of our critical attention because lolicon focuses on the sexualized child as the object of desire, simultaneously unattainable and yet so easily conquered. The problem with erotic lolicon is one that runs parallel to Butterfly's: the female subjects are voiceless, maybe not in a literal sense (mute or dumb), but in a figurative sense (unequal objects rather than equal subjects). If we, recalling Aristotle's meditation on literary theory in *Poetics,* understand art as a reflection of reality, then seeing a human child in the position of a virtual one should not be too much of a conceptual stretch. That possibility is what makes lolicon potentially dangerous: the blurring of the line between fantasy and morally acceptable reality.

The above analogy should not be read in a starkly literal way, as suggesting that all readers of lolicon are non-Asians or morally bankrupt like Pinkerton, or that the child characters in lolicon are able to have the same capacity for feeling that we ascribe to the Butterfly character. These little girls are, after all, bound to the page and not fully human. Even a female contemporary of Long's, Winnifred Eaton (a half-Chinese who adopted a Japanese pseudonym, Onoto Watanna) capitalized on the infantile, playful, essentially "kidult" (kid + adult) mystique of the young Asian female. Her narrative response to the Madame Butterfly stereotype in *A Japanese Nightingale* (1901) offers a heroine that is small, playful, winsome, and downright cute. Although a woman, she retains her capacity to be child-like, a quality that carries a lot of weight in youth-obsessed Japan. Yet this character is also, at least by initial appearances, scheming, greedy, eager to marry the first foreigner that comes around, and a naughty brat. She also talks English like the worst ESL student ever. Obviously, buying in to the cult of youth is nothing new in Japan or elsewhere; an obsessive relationship to being, looking, or feeling young offers us all the more reason to examine ubiquitous themes in visual culture more critically.

The sexy Asian girl-woman has been contested by such works as David Henry Hwang's Tony Award–winning drama *M. Butterfly* (1988), so it is not that people are *unaware* of the stereotype or the truth that representations matter. It is still important for readers of manga to understand the complex collision of constructed sexual identities and how they can influence the way we approach art philosophically as a reflection of life. Lolicon girls, while not *racially* Asian or *ethnically* Japanese (although they can be) come from a non-Western cultural base. Their genesis is from a "foreign" cultural matrix, especially in the eyes of non-Japanese consumers.

Women and girls of Asian descent, however far removed they are from the genre or the media industry as a whole, still bear the burden of being stereotypically associated with sex, either as sexually-knowing in a special "Asian way," as eager-to-please prostitutes, submissive housewives, mail-order brides, kinky masseuses, super-sexed-freak girlfriends, or any number of

occupations or cultural positions construed as sexually-charged. The point is thus to draw a cultural parallel between Asian women being depicted as child-like (regression), and lolicon hentai's depiction of little girls as adult-like (acceleration). Sex is the catalyst in both equations.

The Loli-Pop(ular)

Manga is a transnational phenomenon, a non-Western medium welcomed and enjoyed by Westerners, so it has long ceased to be just Japanese. In the digital age, more and more global readers are aware of lolicon and have become *otaku*, or full-fledged (sometimes crazy, socially-disconnected, basement-dwelling) fans of it, as well as of anime and related graphic novels. Philosopher Noël Carroll classifies manga and anime as "mass art": they cater to a large, mixed audience, take advantage of an industrial and market-driven society, and are easily accessible (that is, cheap and available, unless of course they've been blacklisted, banned, or burnt).

We could say the same thing about sex in many of the cultures and markets that are now twinkling constellations in the erotic manga cosmos. A person only has to stroll into a well-stocked comics store, specialty emporium, or online bookseller to have access to any number of racy titles. While the hard-core material tends to be self-published (*dojinshi*), the less explicit versions may appear in obscure to better-known men's and boys' manga publications like *Morning, Afternoon, Big Comic*, and the *Young* series. What the mass culture of consumption and conversely, the consumption of mass culture tell us is that sex, bodies that have sex, and comic books depicting sex are interdependent and consubstantial; all are commodities to be bought, sold, and consumed.

There are still some readers who subscribe to the high culture–low culture divide and look down upon mass art as crass art. We would be hard pressed to find a title like *Anal Water* or *Princess 69* on a "Great Books" reading list. Comics still have trouble shaking the long-held reputation—at least in America—as the renegade medium enjoyed by consummate time-wasters, social loafers, and bad kids.

Philosopher and social critic Theodor Adorno viewed popular genres in this negative light, arguing that they are self-perpetuating cultural artifacts that reflect their time and place but lack the depth of insight that more genuine art has to offer. He was speaking in abstract terms, not specifically about manga. Products of mass culture, by this token, are deficient when it comes to encouraging imaginative engagement and real social change in their readers. They are the intellectual equivalent of junk food; it may taste good, but it doesn't help the eater's health in any way beyond the relatively short satisfaction of the meal. In the long term, such food, especially in large quantities and without healthy variation, may prove harmful.

This "prolonged harm" hypothesis is exactly the rhetoric that anti-manga (and anti-lolicon) critics use when attacking the medium as potentially addictive, morally questionable, and quite simply, devoid of artistic merit. While these critics may have a point, we should ask who has the right to determine whether looking at stimulating material is harmful, why it is harmful, and what measures should be taken to ensure compliance against such "harm." This is the problem of moral guardianship that arises with any censorship debate.

Does manga have the same artistic purpose that drives great literature and other visual arts like painting or sculpture? The answer is "probably not." We usually read or consider these latter forms as part of a quest to create memorable, lasting, original, and provocative impressions of the human condition. Erotic manga—including lolicon—has instant gratification as its central objective. What feels good *is* good, to put the hedonistic (that is, pleasure-loving) agenda into clearest focus. In his "Preface to *Lolita*," novelist Vladimir Nabokov insisted that there was no moral principle that he wanted to impress upon readers; he wished instead for them to be enchanted by the text, just as Humbert Humbert, the main character and clever pedophile, was by his elusive child-lover, Lolita.

A medium like lolicon alone (or combined as loli-hentai) can potentially be insightful and useful (for places above the neck rather than merely below the waist) because there are usually characters, plotlines, and narrative devices to complement the straight-up sex. The art can be appreciated for its own sake as well, being somewhere on a continuum of richly nuanced to downright outrageous and fun (usually the space for tentacles and slaughterhouse bondage gore). Because the fan base has evolved to be so large and varied, so too are the media and its messages.

Beyond aesthetic concerns, critics cannot deny that manga and anime porn are big sellers, especially outside of Japan where the stereotype of the Land of the Rising Sun as a sex-saturated, depraved little island country still exists (and often to its benefit). Membership in the Nippon Wannabe Club usually carries with it a necessary membership fee, which can be used to ensure the longevity of the institution and its representative arts. Observers of manga will know that most hard-core porn is not published—if even—by major houses due to regulations against obscenity. We might recall the landmark trial of artist Suwa Yuuji and the publisher of the super-hot *Misshitsu*, or *The Honey Room*, for crossing the line of acceptable smut. Also, explicit manga is always under the moral surveillance of watchdog groups, from parent organizations to the anonymous reader who has the capacity to complain, at least in Japan, to the Youth Policy Unit, among other regulatory bodies which concern themselves with popular media. The edgiest material tends to be published by smaller presses often funded by the artists themselves, and may have more of

an underground life than one amongst the so-called moral majority. Healthy profits alone must reveal *something* about the success of a medium so difficult to grasp through juiceless generalizations about "content versus form." Save that for the textbooks.

Not all readers want to spend their downtime engaged in the serious study of the classics like the Bible or Plato's *Republic*. There's nothing wrong with doing so, of course, as reading comprehension, historical competency, critical thinking, and complex writing skills have to be picked up from somewhere. But with the increasing digitalization of books, newspapers, and magazines, even regular publishers of print media are feeling a greater pressure to attract and sustain readers during fluctuating economic times. While not impossible, it might take a special kind of sex-pervert to become aroused by the epic similes of Homer. The texts that have earned accolades as worthwhile comics and graphic novels (for example, Art Spiegelman's Pulitzer Prize-winning *Maus I* and *II*) tend to be meditations on serious world events, quite a leap from the narrower lolicon lens that focuses, say, on the under- or over-developed chest of a horny ten-year-old tween. (The accompanying saying might be, "Not too big for *certain* kinds of toys, and not too young for *certain* kinds of boys!") Coffee-table books about the art of Michelangelo and Picasso are not sequential art, so there is a lack of flow and development, and the aesthetic bliss derived from them may be more cerebral than sensual. Speaking of hot spilled liquids, "happy endings" are usually not that abstract either.

If readers do not expect lolicon to be the source of profound truths and result in powerful social revolutions, they will likely be less critical of the genre's somewhat predictable failure to generate these results. This debate travels to the very heart of what we consider to be "good" art, which is a subjective measure at best. "Good" art is determined through critical consensus, through awards and recognition, and through debate in the court of public opinion. That does not mean, however, that communities of readers should blindly accept all forms of media as equally integral and ignore the potential consequences of thinking in terms of "good" and "bad." These categories are so reductive that they do not mean much anyhow. This is the same ethos that perhaps governs the very existence of sex in manga. What is less important than the actual *presence* of sex is the *reaction*—short-term or long-term, major or minor—that the audience has to it. The consequences for readers, in other words, are more important than authorial intentions.

If we accept that as humans, we are capable of learning truths through non-truths (loosely defined, this means "made-up" material such as visual art, music, and literature), and that imitation is central to the learning process, then we should certainly attune ourselves to the way people understand manga as an art form and potential vehicle of truth. At the same time, even though a person

may be exposed to horrific images defined as art (for instance, cornea-searing cruelty or vomit-inducing ultra-violence), there is nothing that automatically predisposes that person to go forth and dogmatically replicate what she or he has just witnessed.

Adult readers have *agency*, or the capacity to act as they see fit. On the other hand, exposure to so-called fine art does not automatically make a person moral. Being an informed consumer of art, whether it is wildly imaginative or firmly grounded in the complexities and limitations of our time, requires the will to evaluate, prioritize, praise, criticize, and above all, ask questions about what we encounter. Readers should keep these imperatives in mind when approaching a controversial domain like lolicon.

Sex and Candy

Neither the lyrics nor the original video for the Academy Award-winning rap group Three 6 Mafia's 2008 song "Lolli, Lolli (Pop That Body)" features young girls, but they do praise attractive females, and the "lollipop" here is obviously not just a piece of shiny candy perched invitingly on top of a hard stick. From rapper Lil Wayne's undulating hit "Lollipop" to alternative crooner Mika's jingle of the same name, lollipops are intimately suggestive of two concepts that relate to lolicon: sex (through the suggestive acts of sucking and licking, especially by an eager little mouth), and childhood (a time when candy does not translate into worries about costly dental work, diabetes, and size XXL).

Sweets are easily available, come in a variety of flavors, offer a quick sugar fix, and are not worth very much, presumably a comment on the young subjects of loli-hentai. The nexus of sex and candy brings us to the parallel scenario of projecting adult themes onto juvenile content. The effect is shocking to some, subversive and daring for others, as when adult boutiques sell plush toys (like bears, dogs, monkeys with red hearts and floppy dolls) engaged in outrageously risqué positions, often with distorted and anthropomorphic (human-like) body parts. This mating of sensuality and smut with innocence and purity enacts the cognitive dissonance posed by the raunchier forms of the genre.

The LOL factor in lolicon runs from minor to major: simply put, it features very young people—kids, such as toddlers and even babies—in a sexualized way, whether explicitly or implicitly. The representations, while not deliberately funny in many instances, may register to some readers as patently absurd, even a form of social parody. Many cannot imagine getting turned on by a toddler in a falling-off sundress or string bikini worthy of a paper doll kit. Humor can certainly defuse sexual tension, enlivening and diversifying most dramatic scenarios, but it can also trivialize what is supposed to be taken

seriously. By the same token, proponents of lolicon can argue that because the medium can be as light-hearted and bubble-brained as some of the children depicted, critics should climb down from their moral mountaintops and acknowledge that not all art needs to adhere to the Classical ideal of *dulce et utile* (that is, to be "sweet and useful," entertaining and educational). These fans, in other words, just want their candy, no matter how personally or socially decaying the consequences.

Lolita's Literary Genesis

A novel written by a Russian-born American academic, *Lolita*'s main premise is to explore the forbidden passion of a middle-aged European man named Humbert Humbert for a pre-teen American girl, Dolores Haze (nicknamed Lolita, Lo, and Dolly, among others).

The book is fiction and written in a dense, lyrical style, almost the opposite of manga, which is so digestible to readers because of its continuous image flow and verbal sparseness. Lolita's original name, Dolores, comes from the Spanish word for pain and suffering, *dolor*. She does cause considerable pain to her older suitor (what we might call her "Loli-Pop," since Humbert does masquerade as her father to the outside world). She does not go about inflicting pain in a deliberate way, however. Her admirer's pain is largely self-generated, a concept of mind resulting from his seeing Lolita as the reincarnation of a lost childhood love, Annabel Leigh. This naming is a clever reference to Edgar Allan Poe's iconic poem "Annabel Lee." Both Annabels die young, and the men they leave behind suffer through years of mourning and turbulent, unresolved melancholia for what could have been.

Humbert's fetish is Lolita's youth, but his understanding of it is not a desire to corrupt innocence so much as to explore the nature of that innocence and toy with its very corruptibility. So in essence, there's a lot of philosophical and existential depth to the plot; it is not the simple story of an aged opportunist wanting to "score." Humbert uses Lolita to re-establish a more potent understanding of his own psychological needs. It's about ego-gratification and the re-collection of things past. Ironically, he accomplishes this not by denying the body but by embracing it—rather, hers.

Lolita was a book published during the mid-twentieth century, a time remembered in the West as much for its post-war exuberance (the time of the baby boom) and sexual self-consciousness (with the release of the Kinsey Reports) as for its rising Cold War anxieties about invasion, indoctrination, and loss of control. The text has proven its longevity with a global audience. It is not so much the character of Lolita herself that spurs the fascination, but rather the eroticized difference in power between the much-older, cosmopolitan male

and a weaker, less worldly, and unprotected female. It's a dated and patriarchal archetype.

Besides lolicon manga and anime, Nabokov's book has inspired a number of spin-off cultural movements in Japan and abroad, including Lolita-inspired fashion (Goth-loli, *ama-* or "sweet"-loli, punk-loli, Orientalist-inspired *wa-* and *qi*-loli), Lolita cosplay (performance art), and other "sexy little girl" motifs in personal grooming, music, movies, games, books, fan clubs, and websites. There have been at least two major Hollywood film versions of the text, one by Stanley Kubrick in 1962, and one by Adrian Lyne in 1997. Much of the continuing faddishness has to do with an obsession with youth and youth culture that transcends national borders. Sometimes, older men who date much younger women are accused of having a "Lolita complex" or of being "pedos" or "perves," even though their dates may not be minors at all. Although there are variations depending on culture, May-December romances remain scandalous exactly because of the age and power differentials. Cultural commentators like such pairings because they appear so easily explained, which is definitely a false assumption.

An alternative spelling of lolicon is *lolicom*, an abbreviation for the aforementioned Lolita Complex. This condition has a Japan-specific psychopathology; these are men who have a fixation with young females (shōjo) and the culture of girlhood. Lolicon is a type of comic that is not so much *for* kids as *about* kids. Critics acknowledge that sometimes, the desire of the lolicon reader is not so much sexual—the desire to possess, conquer, and consume—as it is ontological, or based on "being-ness." They want to imitate and appropriate youthfulness through youth; these fans would rather *become* the little girls than merely behold or, for that matter, be caught holding them.

Regardless of national affiliation, readers with Lolita complexes may harbor a strong ambivalence toward young females. Fixation is not always about unchecked admiration; intense hatred and fear may also play a major role. Being able to have and control images of young girls in vulnerable positions can be strategic because it underscores personal power, especially when the individual is adult and male.

Licking the *Loli*

Because manga is obviously manufactured and not a documentary medium like photography which can aim for the true-to-life transmission of experience, the realism factor is always already in question. Seeing a child under ten with lactation-worthy breasts, splayed legs, suggestively open mouth, obvious camel toe (engorged or otherwise pronounced genital lips), and hyper-developed buttocks may leave some adult readers downright disgusted. Others may be

deeply confused, embarrassed, aroused, or even cynically delighted that sex has penetrated even the "sacred" zone of childhood.

Lolicon is a kind of reception-dependent manga, which means that it has the capacity to invite a wide spectrum of responses from its correspondingly diverse readership. In that sense, detached cultural observers as well as avid fans will agree that it is useful, if merely as a nimble provocateur. It combines the easily-digested mainstream with the palate punch of the counter-cultural. Although it may not be tasteful to some, especially its more spicy variants, lolicon cannot be accused of blandness.

If one generalization can be made about lolicon readers, it is that they thrive on fantasy. Perhaps this is true about manga more generally, that it seeks to erect dream worlds, but worlds that are not so outrageously different from our own to be unimaginable. Similarly, Nabokov's Humbert is well aware of his privileged position in the world as a cultured man with a rigorous, dexterous imagination. He has the means to make his dreams materialize. He does not hide his complex fixation with Lolita from us because the text is written as a parody of a lover's (as well as a murderer's) confession. Persuasion and presentation—in novels, through words; in manga, through words and images—are what mediate truths. Although he does reveal his soul, stirring up our sympathies, his narration is wildly unreliable. He admits that what we receive from him may not be the actual truth at all. This uncertainty forces us not to take him too seriously, destabilizing our assumption that passionate narration is an eventual portal to genuine and lasting feelings.

Such a skeptical approach is vital to the text because Humbert tells us Lolita is not the docile child—innocent, clueless, and vulnerable—that popular audiences assume is the distilled character of prepubescent little girls. We bear witness to how he attempts to manipulate our reading of her victimization. In Nabokov's conception, as conveyed through Humbert's controlling "I," she is a "nymphet." This word is not just a reference to her young age or an allusion to Greek mythology, where a nymph is a kind of lesser goddess from an earthly element like trees or the sea who attends to a higher power. Instead, a nymphet is a part of a romanticized landscape, a zone of enchantment; she is not even human, but rather a kind of "demoniac" being, a miniature temptress. In contrast to those mythological characters that are granted eternal life without eternal youth, she will "never grow up," remaining a "girl-child" in Humbert's willful imagination. If she's so powerful, why can't she fight him off?

The parallel between Lolita's character and those in lolicon is that they are supposed to be understood as fictions, moving fragments of impossible dreams. To quote Nabokov's text, they exist on an "intangible island of entranced time (p. 17)," therefore remaining "out of reach, with no possibility of attainment" by the seeker (p. 264). This literary context helps those

unhealthily obsessed with lolicon kids to understand that fantasies have only limited reach in the real world. Where zealous fans run into trouble is when they, like Humbert, becoming unwilling to accept limitation. Lolicon love is meant to be fundamentally fleeting; it's not about forever, it's about right now.

The Lo-Down

Some readers may infer that the Japanese approach to under-age obscenity in the media is lax. If that is not the case, they reason, why does lolicon hentai even exist? Portraying the country's publishing practices as an amoral free-for-all would be misinformed. Article 175 of the Japanese penal code prohibits the production and distribution of obscene material, and manga has been privy to a long tradition of print censorship involving, among other more passive tactics, obscuring genitalia and euphemizing sex acts through metaphor and other figurative devices. Such camouflage methods as blurring body parts and strategic substitution with phallic objects (curved swords, long vegetables, darkness and blank spaces) trace the wide arc of the public's attitude toward overt sexuality. Manga artists who generate hard-core smut are subject to fines as well as possible jail time. So there are public safety measures in place to regulate lolicon.

One problem that characterizes controversial genres like lolicon is the inability—or for some stubborn haters, a deep-seated unwillingness—to recognize that it is not uniform, trans-historical, and unchanging. Just as we would be doing a disservice to literature by arguing that all works of a particular genre (for instance, travel writing or romance novels) follow the same plotlines, conventions, and characters, casting lolicon as a homogeneous pool of pedophilic pleasure would be near-sighted at best and inaccurate at worst.

Skimming the online *Baka Manga Updates* for lolicon will yield multiple titles and descriptions, many of which focus on effect (comedy, horror, sci-fi) or a particular target audience rather than straight-up bang-a-longs. Skimming for recent titles offers an embarrassment of choices. Beside such transparently raunchy titles as *Her and My First Sexual Experience* are the more innocuous-sounding *Having Ice Cream Outside,* which is probably less family-friendly on the inside; *Ase Moe!* which incorporates *shotacon* (similar to lolicon but focusing on little boys); *Love Is Blind,* whose proverbial tone seems fit for a Valentine's Day card; and *Milky Twins,* which may suggest a Dairy Bureau ad campaign before any threesomes with a toothsome twosome.

Because of its prodigious popularity, lolicon fans have the luxury of choosing from a spectrum of topics, themes, and characters. Thinking about manga's longevity as both industry and as expressive medium, such supply-and-demand dynamics would be expected. What was found in *Manga Burikko,*

a loli-hentai publication during the early 1980s, would be dated and stale by contemporary standards. Fans of the longer-running rival magazine *Lemon People*, instrumental in buoying up the genre to the height of its popularity last century, were certainly not reading formula fiction for close to two decades. Beyond sexuality, some depictions appear deeply ambiguous, even morally conflicted, about their fetishization of juvenilia and the wholesale valorization of children's "cuteness" in general.

For instance, *Kodomo no Jikan*, originally serialized in the weekly *Comic High* magazine, challenges readers to reconsider their assumptions about intergenerational attraction and adult responsibility. Translated literally, Kaworu Watashiya's title means "Time for Children" or "A Child's Time." By extension, it could also be read as "A Child/Children's Quality Time." The irony of this latter version, with its positive, almost commemorative connotations, is stark. The plot's central premise is the reversal of expectations about sexual initiative-taking. It features a young man, Daisuke Aoki, who finds a job teaching elementary school. One of his third-grade students, Rin Kokonoe, develops a mad crush on him and pursues him relentlessly. Her sexual precocity is unnerving, as are her attention-seeking antics. Daisuke finds himself troubled by her almost predatory persistence; his feelings range from exasperation to protective tenderness. Rin's aggressive behavior does not emasculate her male quarry as much as force him into the traditionally female position of being the pursued rather than the pursuer.

The narrative tension lies in his task of ascertaining his position professionally, emotionally, and then morally. Is he the concerned authority figure and surrogate parent, or is he a sexual free agent, able to choose between what feels good and what feels right? The power disparity, combined with the erotics of instruction, add to the attraction-repulsion dynamics of the pairing. If the spirit and flesh are willing—at least in Rin's case—why not indulge? That is the question.

The series's proposed English title, *Nymphet*, alludes to Nabokov's text on a level beyond the older male–younger female partnership. Rin embodies the demonic version of Lolita with a vengeance, as well as going one step further by being even younger than Nabokov's Dolores. Controversy over the premise of the attraction and its cultural implications (since schools and teachers are supposed to be safe places and safe faces, respectively), extinguished plans to translate and distribute the series in North America. In some ways, this decision by well-known American manga publisher Seven Seas Entertainment was unfortunate because the series could have catalyzed meaningful discussion. *Kodomo* could have prompted English-speaking audiences to evaluate popular art's role in generating both spectacle and scandal, and how these relate to the classroom as a microcosm of civil society.

One of the most well-known examples of this tabooed scenario is Mary Kay Letourneau (now Mary Kay Fualaau), an American elementary school teacher who pursued, conceived children with, and eventually married her student despite having to go to prison for statutory rape. Her infamous story is synonymous with inappropriate student-teacher relationships, just as the sensationalized life and death of JonBenét Ramsey, a child beauty pageant winner found murdered in 1996, spurred a series of debates about how quickly children—especially little girls—should grow up. The gender dynamics of *Kodomo* (pursuing female student) and Letourneau (pursuing female teacher) remind us that art and life are intimately entwined.

LOL: Law, Order, Lolicon

For censors, child welfare advocates, and concerned citizens (usually parents and victim's rights groups), explicit lolicon is not only ridiculous, it is objectionable because it *reinforces* rather than contests a prematurely sexualized persona for children. In America, where childhood, adolescence, and adulthood are carefully delineated (by biological changes like puberty, social achievements like school graduations, and ceremonial milestones like earning the right to drink and vote), this accelerated aging of youngsters into coy sex-objects can appear downright perverse.

Some adults admit discomfort even at the sight of their young children cavorting naked in the house or the backyard paddle-pool, a hair-trigger sensitivity that may be the result of moral panic. Novels like Tom Perrotta's *Little Children* (2004) include characters stigmatized for inappropriate behavior towards children, asking us whether someone convicted of indecent exposure in the presence of a child is as guilty of perversion as someone who commits rape or murder of a child or another older human being.

Although it cannot claim the same Puritanical origins as America, Japan is not without its reverence for moral instruction and the vigilant safeguarding of children. Aside from a well-known emphasis on filiality (being a good son or daughter) and a vigorous education, concerted efforts have been made to vet lolicon for objectionable content. As the *ComiPress Manga News and Information* website reported in June 2007, the municipal government of Kyoto Prefecture issued a list of thirteen loli-hentai titles it found to be "harmful." Quoting the *Kyoto Shimbun* newspaper, among the titles censured by the Commission on the Health and Growth of Youths were (in their original translation): *Youjo no Yuuwaku* (*Temptation of the Little Girls*), *Shōjo Club* (*Young Girls' Club*), *Rabumirukushawaa* (*LoveMilkShower*), *Youchi*

Utage (*Pedophile's Banquet II*), *Seifuku de Ijimete* (*Rape Me in My School Uniform*), and *Chisetsu na Ana* (*Childlike Hole*).[1]

Adults found to be in possession of child pornography and who engage in sex or sex traffic with minors are held legally accountable in many countries. Declaring lolicon hentai to be "kiddie porn" without careful examination may be ill-advised. Definitions such as this require considerable aesthetic, ethical, and legal debate, especially because in many cases, the power lies in suggestion rather than the actual exposure of any flesh. As well, the subjects of lolicon are fragments of the mangaka's artistic imagination, not actual children who can be victimized. As such, lolicon hentai can seem a temporary oasis for some consumers because the legal apparatus is not as strict compared to other visual media like video porn or nude photography. That being said, the medium is hardly a private island.

Supporters of more explicit loli-hentai allege that these forms are the perfect alternative indulgence and a kind of liberating (if not entirely satisfying) hyper-reality that deters abusers from acting on their impulses. The moral issue then is how much the *medium* contributes to the actual choice by child molesters to perpetrate such crimes. There is no surefire way to ascertain the relationship between exposure to suggestive art and immoral (or moral) action, especially when the art may merely *expose* the contours of human experience rather than actively encourage or discourage imitation. Notwithstanding concerned citizens' groups, the question of how seriously to take lolicon and its portrayal of children lies largely within the ideological purview of the individual. It may be the interpretive communities—groups of like-minded or dissenting thinkers—that can actually effect the most change one way or the other.

The Lost and the Foundling

Lolicon hentai and related forms of erotic manga offer a range of visually stimulating portals by which adults, male and female, can claim and transform what was formerly cordoned off as juvenile space. Fundamentally, these manga make the adult childish and the childish adult, resulting in numerous questions about the boundaries that exist (or should exist) on the use of minors in "artistically rendered" sexual expression. Unlike the demonic nymphet Lolita who dies, symbolically, at the age of eighteen (hence, upon reaching adulthood), children exposed to the sexual predilections of adults will someday

---

[1] "Kyoto Police Identifies 13 Loli Manga as 'Harmful Books'," *ComiPress Manga News and Information* (6th June, 2007), <http://comipress.com/news/2007/06/18/2139>.

grow up to become adults themselves. They will then have to negotiate their own sexual identities and moral codes. This is a far cry from art that might be deemed prurient, socially demeaning, and devoid of cultural worth in the eyes of its critics. That is why the racier versions of loli-hentai are often accompanied by a disclaimer that no minors were involved in or harmed by the production of the work. Is this enough though? And enough for whom?

Feminist critics will point out that we do not hear Lolita's story from her own mouth or pen, nor are we able, for the most part, to access the perspectives of the children in loli-hentai. It does not matter that these kids are two dimensional and fake; silencing the subject is a politically-informed choice that is disempowering and can be deeply misogynistic (displaying a hatred or distrust of females). Some impressionable readers may assume that pliant, docile, and silent subjects are imitations of real life girls and women. What's more, unless we are working in the postmodern mode of irony and self-conscious meta-analysis, constructed entities are hard-pressed to "observe their observers" and comment on them accordingly. Not every reader of lolicon—from otaku fiend to curious dabbler—is willing to listen to a lecture about the potential dangers of reading what is in front of them. As with cigarettes, some consumers simply ignore the warning labels. Intellectualizing fun, in other words, kills the mood.

Feminist philosophers may still find redeeming qualities in lolicon, although this is less likely in the erotic variants. When little girls emerge as pockets of wonder, magic, and enchantment in a mundane world, they are not degraded so much as upgraded, elevated to almost divine status. It's possible to construe such children as saviors or angels, repositories of hope and promise amid dark and fallen times. This scenario is particularly suggestive when the objects of salvation are men, and not eunuchs or aged monks for that matter. Sometimes they are bishōnen, or "beautiful boys" and otherworldly men who challenge the parameters of traditional heterosexual masculinity. In some ways, they too are transcendental in their endowments, a rich complement to lolicon's angels and demons. Corollary arguments, however, may be cleverly self-serving. They allege that sexual contact—or any contact—with the goddess-child is a form of worship, and that there is no harm intended when it is done under the auspices of sincere devotion. Engaging the "help" of these children, thus, is not only symbiotic and healthy, but also a necessary rite of passage, both for the child and the supplicant adult. Whatever the level of passionate sophistry used to argue this platform ("I am engaging in little-girl worship for self-improvement"), it is easy to see where a less spiritually-invested and more earthbound individual might find a rhetorical "in."

As one such devotee, what Humbert feels for Lolita cannot be defined as mere perversion or infatuation spurred by loneliness. The two characters exist

in a more complex matrix of emotions: honest admiration, intense nostalgia, sexual fervour, paternalistic concern, and irrational idealism. *Lolita* is very much a text about exploring the historical moment as much as exploring these characters' roles in it. Likewise, manga is a deeply nuanced, polyvalent forum for examining the sexualized child. As a medium for popular consumption, lolicon masks and distorts the moral conundrum of pairing an adult and a child as sexual partners. Is it against nature, or is it a heavenly match of complementary opposites? When children are left to fend for themselves in a vacuum of unchecked adult desire, there is little chance of the power dynamics being reversed. In other words, the pairing is a "sure thing" for the adult, whether as a character or as reader-voyeur. This asymmetry creates problems when some lolicon fans refuse to accept that fantasy lives and real lives are not often—if ever—interchangeable.

Complex art, whether primarily verbal (as with literature) or visual (as with manga), tends to ensure its own longevity by continually eliciting responses. Lolicon's audacity compels us to confront and evaluate our sexual mores, or what we deem to be acceptable practices, attitudes, and assumptions about our intimate lives. Whether erotic lolicon and other varieties of manga are praised or condemned, the intoxicating combination of words and pictures will continuously demand an open and insatiable philosophical mind.

9

No Man Could Love Her More

ELIZABETH BIRMINGHAM

Several years ago, as a reader new to shōjo manga, I began Kaori Yuki's *Angel Sanctuary* with the expectations of a western reader of young adult novels. I assumed this was a teen-goth "problem" story when the blurb at the back of Volume 1 introduced the hero, Setsuna, by asking, "Why is Setsuna so mixed up? Despite his attempts to be noble, he'll fight anyone anytime; he ignores authority; and he harbors feelings for his sister that can only be described as 'incestuous.'"

Perhaps it was the use of scare quotes around the word 'incestuous', but I assumed the publishers meant something else. I guessed this was a story about a teen boy who was confused and not appropriately identifying his feelings of love for his sister.

No.

Within the first chapter of the first volume, Kaori makes it very clear that Setsuna Mudo, the hero of this twenty-volume series, loves his sister, Sara. But he's also in love with her. And he wants to have sex with her, something he thinks about in that obsessive way teen boys think about sex. Because Setsuna is not only the protagonist, but is nearly always the point-of-view character in most of the scenes he occupies, the reader realizes quickly how much he wants his sister. After he saves her from a threatening situation and carries Sara's seemingly unconscious body to her bed, he kisses her, she allows herself to be kissed, and their religious mother, as a witness, vows to keep them apart to save Sara's soul. (She has already washed her hands of her son, as irredeemable.)

He *Really* Loves His Sister . . .

By the end of the first volume, Sara also declares her love for her brother (in the presence of their horrified mother); Setsuna denies he feels love for his sister, suggesting instead that he "was getting really horny" and wanted to "get some

from my little sister. I mean, you were right there." But the reader sees his thoughts as he speaks. He is thinking, "All I have to do is say the exact opposite of how I feel."

As the first volume draws to a close, their mother comforts the anguished Sara, telling her she will meet an appropriate man with whom she could truly fall in love and be happy, but the reader knows Setsuna's thoughts about his mother's claim: "You'll never find a man who loves her more than me." Setsuna's love for Sara, and we assume hers for him, though we are never privy to her thoughts, represents a love that is true, pure, mutual, and willing to defy all social and parental convention.

The incestuous relationship Kaori sets up as a dyad between Sara and her brother Setsuna is played out as a more complex triad in Matsuri Hino's gothic *Vampire Knight*. *Vampire Knight*, a far more mainstream and popular title, is easily available in the US, at major bookstores and serialized in *Shōjo Beat*.

. . . And Yuki Loves Her Brothers

The series tells the story of Yuki Cross, the fifteen-year-old amnesiac protagonist and point-of-view character of the ongoing manga series, who is raised with an adoptive brother, Zero Kiryu, by the headmaster of Cross Academy. The school is home to a surprising social experiment: a day-class of humans shares the campus with a night-class of vampires in an effort to prove that the co-existence of the two groups is possible.

The leader of the night-class is pure blood vampire Kaname Kuran, a beautiful older boy who is the object of Yuki's infatuation. He's also the boy who saved her life when a vampire attacked her ten years before. In the course of the series, it's revealed that Kaname is also Yuki's brother, and that her parents (who were also brother and sister), conceived her to be Kaname's wife. (The reader is told this incest is common practice among pure blood vampires, because marrying a sibling assures the purity of the next generation.) In the world of *Vampire Knight*, Yuki's love interests are both "brothers."

While *Angel Sanctuary* tells its readers very clearly and in the first volume that Setsuna felt so certain he must not be Sara's real sibling that he checks birth records to confirm their kinship (and has it confirmed), *Vampire Knight*'s incest flirts with the reader a bit more. Zero is *like* a brother (but he is not, biologically); Kaname is *like* a crush. But he's a brother. (And then again, maybe he's not, biologically, on a technicality of resurrection and reincarnation.)

Masami Toku argues that "Shōjo manga is said to be a mirror of Japanese girls' and women's desires and expectations" ("Shōjo Manga! Girls' Comics!," p. 30). The huge number of examples of these incest stories in love-themed manga for adolescent girls suggests that the incestuous sibling relationship must act as

a trope in these texts; it stands in for and represents something beyond its literal definition. Literally, incest is a powerful taboo; there is little reason to interpret real sibling incest as romantic, and it is unlikely that something as culturally distasteful as sibling incest would reflect girls' "desires and expectations." But like a mirror, shōjo manga distorts as it reflects back those desires. In many ways, the protective older brother becomes a perfect lover: he has always been there for her, has always cared for and loved his younger sister with a love reinforced by family bonds; he will not go away easily, because he is tied to the sister through the family unit.

The authors of both *Angel Sanctuary* and *Vampire Knight* use regular flashbacks to share scenes of these earlier, childhood interactions between siblings. These flashback scenes reinforce the theme that a loving childhood bond led to the current relationship.

A Universal No-No?

Incest is often claimed to be one of the few universal taboos. It's so generally reviled that for nearly a century scientists have been trying to discover a biological, sociological, or psychological explanation for incest avoidance.

Finnish sociologist Edvard Alexander Westermarck first noted that children raised together, regardless of their genetic relationship, rarely form sexual feelings for each other. The Westermarck effect, as it is called, defines this as a reverse sexual imprinting, suggesting sibling incest is rare because it defies both biological and socialized aversion. Although sibling incest is perhaps not as rare as we might think based upon the powerful taboo against it, in cases where it does exist, it is only very rarely mutual or consensual, but rather the result of power, control, and coercion in dysfunctional family dynamics, as noted by Jane Mersky Leder in "Adult Sibling Rivalry: Sibling Rivalry Often Lingers through Adulthood."

The taboo associated with incest might make its depiction seem unlikely in love stories written by women for schoolgirls. These contemporary stories, often serialized weekly in magazines for teen girls, such as the very popular *Shōjo Beat,* employ a common theme, "How love triumphs by overcoming obstacles" (Masami Toku, "Shōjo Manga! Girls' Comics! A Mirror of Girls' Dreams," *Mechademia* 2, p. 19). In Japan, shōjo manga appears to have few constraints placed on subject matter; in fact, one of the most popular sub-genres is shōnen-ai, or boy's love, stories for girls that feature romance between two boys ("Shōjo Manga! Girls' Comics!," p. 30).

Although incest stories would not be considered a sub-genre, and are rarely even discussed as sharing a theme, they are very common in shōjo manga. A 2010 call-out on the Baka-Updates Manga discussion board

generated hundreds of titles; of these titles, eighty-seven included instances of sibling incest, either as a central feature or as part of one or more subplots. The ubiquity of incest in general, and consensual sibling incest in particular, woven into the fabric of love stories for teen girls, combined with the lack of discussion or acknowledgement of the motif by any but its fans, suggests that the idea of incest is fulfilling an important fantasy role for the readers of shōjo manga.

Just Regular Siblings

In the first three volumes of *Angel Sanctuary*, each flashback shows Setsuna protecting Sara from harm or hurt. In one instance, a university student seems to be inappropriately touching the child Sara and is clearly interested in further sexual abuse; Setsuna attacks and nearly kills him (Volume 1). The story also establishes Setsuna giving Sara a toy ring in their childhood, an item she treasures. The reader understands that the ring functions as a symbol of the love vows this couple can never share publicly, and it is also the artifact that Setsuna uses to help restore Sara's memory of him at the series' end (Volume 20).

These flashback scenes mirror contemporary scenes in which Sara is threatened with sexual violence or harassed with sexual innuendo and is repeatedly saved by Setsuna's intervention. In addition, flashbacks establish the family dynamics—parents who are physically (father) or emotionally (mother) absent, from each other and the children, and children who are then separated from each other by divorce. Notice that these same factors the author establishes as present in the story are usually contributing circumstances in real cases of sibling incest or abuse ("Adult Sibling Rivalry").

Matsuri employs flashback to establish similar circumstances in *Vampire Knight*. The first volume opens with a flashback—five-year-old Yuki being attacked by a vampire when Kaname intervenes. As in many vampire stories, the vampire's desire to share blood is sexualized, and the attack on the child Yuki is eerily similar to the fondling in Sara's childhood experience; the bestial vampire, shown in close-up in a tight frame, leers, "Are you lost, little girl? May I drink your blood?" Yuki responds with a tiny, but clear, "No," before Kaname attacks and kills Yuki's attacker. Each time Matsuri uses the flashback of this scene (the next time in volume three), she offers a little more information: Yuki's terror at her attack, Kaname's kindness, Yuki beginning a new life with the kind Headmaster Cross at Cross Academy, the child Yuki coming to love her savior, Kaname, and finally realizing that Kaname is one of the vampires she so fears.

In contrast, when Matsuri illustrates Yuki's initial meeting with Zero in the first volume, Yuki is the savior. A bloody and silent child Zero is brought to

the academy, and an eleven-year-old Yuki gently bathes the pale and frightened boy. Readers discover later that Zero was orphaned in this attack by a pure blood vampire. Matsuri offers ample evidence that the vampire's unwelcome attack is like a sexual imposition. In volume three, again by means of flashback, Yuki comforts the child Zero as he claws at the healing wound on his neck, causing renewed bleeding and pain. He says, "It feels yucky. I can still feel that woman here." Later, when he discovers Kaname is a vampire, he stabs and attempts to kill him, saying, "You smell the same as that woman" (Volume 3). Yuki's childhood relationship with her two "brothers" is of being protected by one, protecting the other.

Lovers Come and Go, Brothers Are Forever

As Jane Leder suggests of siblings, "They know us in a unique way during our childhood and share a history that can bring understanding and a sense of perspective in adulthood. Friends and neighbors move away, former co-workers are forgotten, marriages break up and parents die, but our brothers and sisters remain our brothers and sisters." In each iteration of the sibling relationship in these manga, the characters demonstrate love, protection, and a notion that their relationship is forever. Even when Zero attacks Yuki, biting her too hard, and drinking too much blood, all Yuki thinks is that he has suffered alone for four years, having not shared with her—his closest confidant—that he had become a vampire when attacked those years before. She intervenes before he can kill himself in his horror and remorse at what he has done, and understands that his long hatred of vampires—his family was one of famous vampire hunters—assures that he must now hate himself.

Kaname, who knows from the beginning that he is Yuki's brother, though she (and the reader) does not know this until far into the series, responds to Zero's attack on Yuki like a lover, with an attitude of sexual jealousy toward Zero, but love for Yuki: "I can't keep my composure when my dear girl has been pierced by someone else." He repeats twice in a few pages Yuki's "dearness" to him, reaffirming his love, while he curses Zero for "robbing" her (Volume 1). Although Setsuna's relationship with Sara seems to more often place him in the protector role, at the important moment after they have run away together and consummated their relationship, Setsuna reveals that he killed Kato, and Sara promises to protect him (Volume 3).

The desire reflected in these narratives is not for an incestuous relationship, but for a mutual, caring affection, and perhaps, a complete renunciation of weighty social mores and an almost Platonic struggle for balance between human self-control and the divine madness of love, forces that govern the teen reader's lurching march toward adulthood. Both *Angel Sanctuary* and *Vampire*

Knight offer readers stories in which incest is the embodiment of the divine madness Plato suggests in *The Phaedrus* is a gift of the goddess Aphrodite—a love Plato asserts is sent to benefit both the lover and the beloved.

A Divine Form of Madness

The *Phaedrus*, Plato's dialogue between Socrates and Phaedrus, was written about 370 B.C.E. and is commonly read for Plato's insights on rhetoric, although the primary subjects of the dialogue are the soul's reincarnation and erotic love, also common elements of gothic shōjo manga. In the *Phaedrus*, Plato describes the human soul through an analogy to a "pair of winged horses and a charioteer." Human souls struggle to control a good horse and a bad horse, making driving the team a challenge as the soul struggles for a balance between the sight of beauty and self-control. The sight of beauty conjures a memory of heaven, and the radiant purity the soul experienced there. The beautiful beloved, therefore, stirs in the lover the memory of heaven, and seeing the beloved's face causes joy; separation brings intense pain and longing.

Angel Sanctuary's trippy, pseudo-Christian, surprisingly Platonic mythology of fallen angels, heavenly politics, reincarnation, a multi-layered heaven and hell with no clear good or evil, but many seemingly baseless taboos, provides a narrative backdrop for Kaori's decorative, gothic panels. The story itself is as confusing and convoluted as the mythology Plato describes in Phaedrus: characters die and return in different bodies, bodies that look identical to those of established characters house other consciousnesses, boys look like girls, women look like girls, and men are stunningly androgynous. While none of these are characteristics unfamiliar to shōjo's regular readers, they challenge the reader's understanding of who's even in a scene.

Plato writes that the soul "traverses the whole of heaven, appearing in one form and sometimes another" (*The Rhetorical Tradition*, p. 123), a central feature of the characters in *Angel Sanctuary* as they work their way through layers of heaven and hell toward the Heaven's Gate, and seeing the true face of god the creator. Toward the story's end, Sara has been "programmed" not to recognize Setsuna's form, and to see him as a dark and faceless monster. Setsuna must seem to kill Sara, an action that wholly confuses the computer-like god that struggles to manipulate and control the action of all the players: angels, humans, and demons. Only then does the dark veil hiding Setsuna's form waver and lift (Volume 20). In addition to appearing veiled to Sara, Setsuna dies on a number of occasions and must occupy other bodies, including that of Alexiel, a female angel (with a bombshell body) who rebelled against heaven and was reborn on earth as Setsuna. Sara herself occupies many different forms across the series; she dies immediately after consummating her relationship

with Setsuna (Volume 3), and he searches for her, finding her in many different "forms" in Heaven and Hell.

Setsuna perpetually attempts to find Sara through the glimpses of reality afforded by those moments the horses guiding the chariot of his soul are in balance. His struggle to find his love follows the pattern Plato describes when he asserts that when a soul is able to identify a true thing by keeping his chariot in balance long enough to glance over the rim of heaven at reality, the driver will be granted another circle around the rim, each time gaining a fuller vision of Truth, as long as the good horse and bad are controlled and in balance (*The Rhetorical Tradition*, p. 127–29).

In the end, Sara, in *Angel Sanctuary*, is not precisely a love interest. She's an ideal, ensconced in Heaven, and Setsuna's quest for her, scouring Heaven and Hell to return her to life (and maybe save the world at the same time), is more important to the plot than Sara herself. Sara symbolizes the Platonic balance between beauty and self-control. On several occasions during his quest, Setsuna spies what he believes to be Sara, and sometimes is, but he must forgo an attempt to save her for the good of the larger battle to overthrow Heaven, a battle in which he has taken the form of a winged angel and a role as "savior."

However, Plato argues that the harmonious life is lived both through self-control (or philosophy) and love and honor. Plato does not condemn the lovers who, like Sara and her brother, "in some other moment of carelessness" accomplish bliss, even if they repeat the action, and go through life "believing they have exchanged the most binding pledges of love" (*The Rhetorical Tradition*, p. 129). Moreover, Plato suggests that when these lovers "depart from the body, they are not winged, to be sure, but their wings have begun to grow, so that the madness of love brings them no small reward" (p. 129). The final panel of *Angel Sanctuary* depicts Sara and Setsuna embracing, his feathered wings fading to transparency around them both as they return to Earth, Setsuna knowing he is once again an ordinary human, in love with his sister. The text reads, "Neither god nor human, the ones born wrapped in a dazzling love. They are called angels" (Volume 20).

Platonic Love and Restraint

In *Vampire Knight*, Yuki's character offers a different embodiment of Plato's divine madness. Matsuri's gothic is European, with characters framed by arches, in vaulted crypts and dorms, adorned with Maltese crosses, wearing silk braid frogs in the shape of roses, brocade, and lace on their school uniforms. The most common visual motifs are the blood spatter, the red rose, and the Maltese cross. While *Angel Sanctuary* has a cast of hundreds, *Vampire Knight*'s smaller cast enables it to develop characters of greater complexity. Yuki is warm, open

and loving, and has loved Kaname since she can remember; he has also treated her with a notable warmth and kindness, as he is considered by his peers to be cool and aloof. Similarly, Yuki pledged her love and care to Zero nearly at their first meeting; as they have grown up, Yuki has made it clear that she will do anything to protect him.

The narrative demonstrates the purity of Yuki's love through contrasting her with her peers (boy-crazy—vampire crazy—human girls), and through her interactions with both Zero and Kaname. The manga includes several early scenes where Cross Academy's day-class students fervently clamor for a look at the night-class boys (Volume 1).

This sort of ardor for beauty, Plato suggests, is not the madness of divinely inspired love, but rather interest in pleasure and procreation. This lover's interest in beautiful bodies isn't reverential, Plato claims, but focused on "pleasure and like a beast proceeds to lust and begetting; he makes license his companion and is not afraid or ashamed to pursue pleasure in violation of nature." We see these girls in several scenes, so their inappropriate infatuation with the night-class students is repeatedly made clear. In a Valentine's-like holiday, the girls prepare and offer chocolates to the night-class students, who politely accept their gifts, but clearly view them as foolish (Volume 1).

In contrast, Yuki is portrayed as immune from that silliness; in fact, her headmaster father has made her a prefect, and her role is to keep the day and night classes from interacting. In an early scene, a night-class student, Hanabuso Aido, approaches two day-class girls on the grounds at night. Having smelled blood from a cut on Yuki's hand, he pursues the girls, who Yuki steps out to protect, though the girls make her work harder, as they don't necessarily want to be protected, saying, "He said we smelled good." Although Yuki is injured saving them, she says to Zero, "I feel sorry of them" (Volume 1). Yuki has no place in her serious make-up for girlish silliness.

In contrast, Yuki loves Kaname, but is modest, in Plato's sense of being in rational control of herself. She understands Kaname's position as a pure blood, is aware of her own humanity, and is clear that she cannot ever be with him. For example, toward the end of the first volume, when discussing her feelings for Kaname, she admits to Zero, "There's a line vampires and humans . . . can't cross." But she now knows Zero is a vampire and turns to him, "Zero, I'm sorry. I didn't mean . . ." And Yuki clearly did not mean Zero, whose status as a human-turned-vampire is similar to hers. Only Kaname would represent "pursuing pleasure in violation of nature."

In Volume 7, Yuki is even more explicit, as she tries to discover the truth of her past, realizing Kaname holds the key to her locked memories. She calls him on his consistent interest in her, saying, "No matter how hard I try to reach beyond my station, I'm not suitable for you." Despite her love for him, Yuki

is aware of their respective places in the social order and shows a consistent restraint the other human girls aren't capable of.

Girl Power

In many ways, *Vampire Knight* portrays Yuki as the level-headed charioteer, trying to keep her team in balance. Kaname's power and social standing among vampires make him seem the good horse on the right, of beauty and good breeding, wearing the white uniform of the night-class. Zero, because he is degenerating into a "level E," the bestial form humans who become vampires eventually must take, is the dark horse on the left, wearing black, difficult for Yuki to control. She regularly must tell him, "No!" or "Stop!" when he's drinking her blood. Yuki's happiness is predicated upon keeping these two brothers she loves in balance. She offers Zero her own blood to keep him alive, even though the guilt of it is devastating to him. Kaname wants to kill Zero, but won't, because he both needs Zero to protect Yuki and he knows that hurting Zero would lose him Yuki. When the vampire hunter Yagari Toga (Zero's mentor), remarks to Kaname that he must realize Yuki has given herself to Zero, he says, "But of course you realize what she's done? You must be seething with rage?" He wants to know if Kaname does nothing because he is an "honor" student. Kaname replies, "It's so I won't lose my girl" (Volume 2).

But simply keeping her team in balance will not gain Yuki the blessings "the friendship of a lover will confer upon you" (*The Rhetorical Tradition*, p. 129). It is not until Yuki is bitten by Kaname, too, and then takes Kaname's blood, that she regains her memory and gains her birthright as the full-blood princess. Because of Yuki's love for her "brother" Zero, Kaname also offers himself to Zero, so that his own pure blood will keep Zero from degenerating to a level E (Volume 7). Plato asserts that "the affection of the non-lover, which is alloyed with a moral prudence and follows mortal and parsimonious rules of conduct, will beget in the beloved soul the narrowness which the common-folk praise as virtue" (*The Rhetorical Tradition*, p. 129).

The blood-stained panels with overtones of three-way sex in the blood sharing and BDSM in Yuki's control over Zero (with weapons and a magical chain), and Kaname's ever-creepier manipulation of both Zero and Yuki, make the play with incest seem one of the least deviant things about this teen girls' series. Certainly the model of love presented in *Vampire Knight* does anything but "follow mortal and parsimonious rules of conduct."

For girls, parsimonious rules of conduct strictly inhibit the kinds of pleasures they are likely to seek and find. Anne Allison explains in *Permitted and Prohibited Desires: Mothers, Comics, and Censorship in Japan* that incest taboos help establish kinship, which in turn, generates the social exchange

of women between and among men. Because men aren't allowed to have relationships with their own sisters, they must trade them to other kinship groups, assuring that "women are the medium of an exchange conducted in terms of male authority and desire" (p. 135).

These fantasy worlds where brothers are under no obligation to trade away their sisters to strangers may defy both social taboo and Plato's articulation of a narrow moral prudence. But what they offer girls is a chance to explore desires that are truly their own because they undermine one of the earliest and most universal taboos of patriarchy by suggesting that kinship might offer girls something more than being an item of merchandise.

10

Is Al Still Ed's Brother, or Is He Already Dead?

NICOLAS MICHAUD

*I*n an amazing feat of Alchemic prowess, Edward Elric saved his brother Alphonse's life by attaching Al's soul to an empty suit of armor. Al, who was once a boy, is now a walking, talking suit of armor. Al doesn't need to eat, cannot bleed, and lacks the ability to feel sensations the way he once could. Nevertheless, he remembers his life as a child and he continues to follow his brother, learning and growing mentally as any boy would.

We wonder, though, how feasible this really is. Granted, Alchemy as depicted in *Fullmetal Alchemist* lacks any scientific grounding, but what interests me is whether this separation between soul and body, as Al experiences it, is even possible.

Does Al, after this change, remain who he once was? Is he still Alphonse Elric—Ed's little brother?

While it's highly unlikely that it will ever be possible to attach a boy's soul to a suit of armor, we seem to take it for granted that the human soul actually exists and that this soul exists separate from the body. Is this reasonable?

In assuming that the soul exists, most of us take for granted that the soul is immaterial and therefore impossible to study or examine. In the world of philosophy, though, the question of the soul's existence and interaction with the body can be considered and studied in great depth, even if the soul itself is intangible. Two famous philosophers, René Descartes and Gilbert Ryle, fall on opposite ends of the argument regarding whether or not the human soul can actually be separated from the human body.

Fullmetal Alchemist focuses a great deal on the notion of the human soul. Al is a boy's soul attached to a suit of armor, Homunculi are human-like creatures created without human souls, and human transmutation is forbidden because there is no price that can be paid that is enough to create a human soul. But where does this idea that there is a human soul come from? Why are we so certain that this soul is separate and distinct from the human body?

Descartes is in large part responsible for our common-sense notion that there must be a soul component to humans which is separable from the body. This separation between the soul and the body was one that Descartes believed to be reasonable and his idea continues to echo through to our time.

Ed seems to take it for granted, that Al's soul is a separate thing and can be moved from place to place. And he is sure that Al remains who he once was, but even Al himself isn't so sure.

Are Al's Mind and Soul One and the Same?

As we try to understand how it can be possible that Al can retain his memories and thoughts, we should bear in mind that in Descartes's argument there is no real difference between the soul and the mind. He argues that there is a mind component to every human and that this mind is immortal and exists beyond the existence of the body, so it is, in essence, what we refer to as the soul.

Descartes is what philosophers refer to as a "substance dualist." He thinks that there are two substances: a mind substance and a body substance. The mind, or soul, substance is immaterial, whilst the body substance is physical and subject to the laws of physics. As the soul is an immaterial thing, according to Descartes, it doesn't have to follow the laws of physics and does not interact in the same way that normal matter does. The world of *Fullmetal Alchemist* deals with this kind of dualism.

Al's substance-like soul can be removed from his body and attached to something else, like a suit of armor. Although this soul is immaterial, it can still be moved and dealt with as if it is an actual thing in the world. This idea that the soul is immaterial and, yet, a substance-like thing comes from Descartes. And as in the world of *Fullmetal Alchemist*, Descartes's view of the world sees the soul as the seat of the intellect. When we think of the mind, we think of the thing that houses our personalities, intellect, and memories. So if that thing is preserved, our essence is preserved, regardless of what happens to the body.

This leads immediately to a question that plagued Al's mind: if his body is gone, how can he be sure that he is the same person? This is a fundamentally difficult question in philosophy. What we are asking is, "What makes us, us?" If we follow Descartes, we can't say that it is our body, but if it is not our body, then what is it that I identify as me? For Descartes, the argument is simple: I have a clear and distinct idea of my own mind. I can imagine that mind without a body; therefore, the body and mind are separate and distinct substances. This mind, which is distinct from your body, is what makes you, you. But how can Al still be who he once was? Without a body and without a brain what makes him Ed's little brother?

I do not need to think of the body to conceive of the mind. This is different from other kinds of connected ideas. There are ideas that need other ideas in order to be thought about and, therefore, are not separate and distinct. For example: try imagining a square without borders. It seems impossible to do. The square, in order to be a square, must have boundaries and cannot be thought about without those boundaries. For this reason, a square is not separate and distinct from its boundaries. On the other hand, it's not difficult to think of the mind without the body. There doesn't seem to be anything particularly necessary about the body to conceive of the mind.

I can imagine minds switching bodies, I can imagine minds outside of bodies, and I can imagine bodies without minds. It seems then that the mind and the body are two conceptually distinct things. Although I cannot get my hands on the soul and actually remove it from the body, there's no reason to view them as stuck together. The mind does not need the body to exist as an idea.

Can Al Actually Have Memories?

But how does this mind thing exist? We view it as the seat of all that is us, but there seems to be no way to understand what about the mind makes us, us. Modern science tells us that the brain houses memories, and that those memories can be lost when there is damage to the brain. Descartes believes that we have this clear and distinct idea of our minds and thereby have significant access to it, but this is not necessarily true.

How much access do I really have to my own mind? I cannot keep myself from getting amnesia or from going senile; those things seem to be brain things. But if memories are located in the brain, what about the soul makes me, me? Al is tortured by a variant of this question. Without a brain, what reason does he have to believe that his memories are actually the same memories as were acquired by his material brain?

It's not particularly sensible to assume that our memories continue on after death. It's pretty clear that not only are our memories located in the actual material stuff of our brain, but that our personality itself is actually a brain-stuff issue. Think of cases of significant changes to the brain, like those of a chimera's—as in Nina's case. If a little girl is combined with a dog, the girl acts very differently, although, in theory, she maintains her soul. Why would she act so differently, not as intelligent, for instance? It's because significant changes in the brain can result in significant changes in personality. The fact that our personality and thoughts are impacted by what happens to our brains should be fairly obvious to us.

We can think about cases like that of the famous Phineas Gage, who sparked a great deal of discussion in the nineteenth century. He was a railroad worker who survived an iron rod being driven completely through his head. It seems that Gage was a really nice guy until he suffered brain damage. After that he was mean, ill-tempered, and just an all-around jackass. Some of his friends reported he was no longer the same person. Although details of the Gage case are controversial, this and many more recent cases do seem to show that damage to specific areas of the brain can cause dramatic changes in personality.

If I'm depressed, I take anti-depressants, which are a material thing, and they may cheer me up. If I'm hyper-active I can take medication to calm me down. So there's no question that a great deal of our personality is located in our brain. If I have a stroke, I lose memories; I can even forget how to speak. Why? Because of damage to the brain. Given this, what part of *me* is actually a non-material mind thing?

Al's concern that his memories are not actually his own is a very legitimate problem. How is it even possible that Al, without a body, is able to make new memories? It's not as if he is forming new synapse connections in the brain, which is what we do whenever we make memories! It seems Al would not be able to sense things as we do, because he does not have a body, but if memories are a brain thing, then how does he access his brain's memories or record new ones? What is it that Al is accessing when he remembers something, and what is it that he is writing upon when he creates new memories? Surely not his suit of armor! He remembers that he's Ed's brother, but where is that memory recorded?

It must be Al's mind that his memories are recorded in and it must be from his mind that his memories are accessed. Descartes is very comfortable with this idea. Descartes's realization was that the mind must exist as a separate thing that is the locus of our intellectual selves because while we can even doubt the existence of our bodies, we can never doubt the existence of our minds. This is a somewhat trippy, but honest realization. You've probably wondered if you're actually dreaming at a particular moment in which you think you're awake, or wondered if you are just a figment of imagination in the mind of God, but you have never doubted that you, as a thinking thing, exist. How could you?

As soon as you doubt your own existence, you affirm your existence through the act of doubting it. So even if you considered the most obscure possibilities in terms of doubt, you cannot doubt that you are doubting. If you're doubting, there is a "you" that is doing the doubting. Descartes's point, then, is simple: I can doubt my body, but I cannot doubt my mind. And because of this, I can conceive of my mind without my body.

This is a fine answer to Al's problem until we really push on the means by which the memories are actually recorded in Al's mind. How does his

non-material mind record memories at all? Even worse, how does his non-material mind move his very material armor body? This is the problem that Gilbert Ryle poses to Descartes. In criticizing Descartes, Ryle pushes very hard on a very problematic aspect of Descartes' philosophy—a problem Descartes himself recognized: How can a non-material anything interact with a material something?

If a soul has no matter, how does it interact with matter? Perhaps you think of the soul or mind as energy, but, remember, if it is non-material, that means it is not energy that has any material properties, so it is not like electricity, for example, because electricity can interact with physical things. So yes, Al's soul is anchored to his armor through his blood seal, but how does his soul actually push his body around? You might want to argue that I don't understand—Al's soul is actually infusing the armor in some way, and this is fine. But even if Al's armor is infused with his soul, how does that make his armor move? Your body moves because the working parts—muscles—pull on it. Material objects in the world move because material things push and pull on them. So how can non-material things move anything physical?

How Does Al's Soul Interact with His Body?

Descartes's initial answer was that the mind and the body interact through the pineal gland in the brain, in a way not so dissimilar from the way Al's soul interacts through the seal on his armor.

But how can this interaction make any sense? The pineal gland and Al's seal are physical things; so how is it possible that a non-physical thing can touch them? Touch, itself, is a physical idea that takes place in physical ways. Someone might want to argue that Al's seal is both in and out of the world; it is spiritual and physical, so the spiritual aspect of the seal interacts with his soul and the physical aspect of the seal interacts with his armor. But this only pushes the problem up one level, because then we must ask, "But how does the spiritual aspect of Al's seal interact with the physical aspect of Al's seal?" If non-material things do not follow the laws of physics, by what means can they cause things to happen in the material world of physics? Remember that when we think of our mind or soul we think of something we can never find, no matter how you cut us up. We can never, through any means, ever, touch it or see it or interact with it. (Otherwise, it would make sense to look for the soul with microscopes and other instruments, but it's usually agreed that this would be silly.) So how does the soul interact with out body? If we can't ever grasp it through any physical means, how does it push and pull on us?

Even worse for Al is the realization that the things that cause his memories are physical things. When Al sees something, hears something, or touches

something, these physical events—if impactful enough—result in him creating a memory. Now, when he had a human body, he would see something with his eyes, that information would be transferred to his brain, and his brain would record the information through a rather complex electro-chemical process. Nevertheless, it was a *physical* process that created the memory. Not only was the memory recorded by physical means, and could be lost through physical means (due to a stroke or being transmuted into a chimera, for example), but the event that caused him to record the memory was a physical event—he saw *something*. So how can his non-physical soul experience physical events? Yes, the answer might be, "Ah, because his physical body is experiencing it," but that still does not suffice, because the problem of how the soul interacts with the physical body remains.

If Al's soul is not a physical thing, how can physical events impact it, to even form memories in the first place? The answer cannot be, "Well, we just don't understand it," because this is not like a normal scientific problem where we know "it" happens, but we do not know how "it" happens. Instead, this is a cognitive problem; we realize that there is no way to make sense of how this can happen. Because we have defined the soul as non-material we have made it impossible, by definition, for it to interact with the physical world. The mind can't be touched, seen, tasted, heard, smelled, or interacted with physically at all, and so it has no way to interact with the body. We cannot create memories in it; it cannot move us, and it cannot have physical experiences. Even worse, now that we understand the brain, we are starting to understand how it is that we move, think, and record memories, without even appealing to a soul at all. In other words, when Al was a human boy we could explain how it is that his brain moves his body and causes his thoughts, but there is no reasonable way to conceive of how his mind does this now, as a suit of armor.

For this reason, Ryle believes we have made a mistake, a special kind of mistake which he calls a Category Mistake. And this is horrible news for Al. Basically, Ryle thinks we have made an error in our thinking, not because we think we have a mind, but because we treat the mind as if it is a *substance*; as if it is something that can be anchored. Things that can be attached to bodies are physical things... because they are *attached*. Ryle also offers an explanation for what the mind is without having to propose a soul-substance, but if his answer is right, Al's is already dead. Ryle argued that there is no substance "mind." Instead, he argued that the mind is basically just the function of the brain in a particular way. Yes, we can imagine brains, without minds, and so Descartes was right, the brain and mind are not the *same thing* but that does not mean that the mind does not need the brain. Ryle thinks that the mind is the result of the brain's components working together.

What Is Al's Mind if Not a Soul?

To see what Ryle means by a Category Mistake, imagine a place like Central City. Your friend has never seen a "city" before and so you show him Central City. You show him all the places in the city, the military installations, markets, homes, schools, churches, and so on. Afterwards your friend says to you, "Well, thank you for showing me the military installations, markets, homes, schools, and churches, but when are you going to show me *Central City?*"

When your friend asks this, he is making a Category Mistake. He is thinking that the City is the same kind of thing as a *building.* But when you think about it, you realize that they are not the same thing. As a matter of fact the city and the buildings can be separated from each other. Isn't it possible to have all of the buildings of the city remain standing and yet have the city no longer exist? And isn't it possible to burn all of the buildings of the city to the ground and have the city continue to exist? Yes, if the people in the city are still interacting in a way that makes it a city. The point is that what makes the city isn't the physical stuff, it is the way that the people work together, the mayor, and judges, and police, and pedestrians all working together to make a functioning city.

Granted, a city may not be the best example because you can still speak of "lost cities" that clearly have no people that are functioning in any way, and, yet, we refer to them as cities. But those are basically just dead cities. And, to make Ryle's point, if the city is "dead," does that means that its soul has gone somewhere? No, of course not! It just means that while much of the physical stuff remains—buildings, roads, landmarks—the functioning of the city has ceased. There never was a soul to the city; the city itself was just the working together of the component parts.

If Ryle is right, then the human mind is the functioning of the brain. It's not the brain, but the mind is created when the brain parts work together to create a mind. But this working together does not create a non-material substance any more than the people in a city working together create a non-material city-soul. The brain, by itself, isn't the mind, it's just a dead brain. But the mind isn't a spiritual thing that can be anchored and interacted with physically, it's a kind of concept, or functioning. "The mind" is *what we call a working brain,* in the same way that "Central City" is what we call the functioning city. But what does this mean for Al? . . . Because this seems like very bad news indeed.

Ryle is the philosopher who first uses the phrase "the ghost in the machine." He's bothered by how easily we are willing to attribute a ghost-like entity to human action. In the same way that a machine does not need a ghost to act, we don't need more than a functioning brain to act. Al is in essence, now, a ghost

in a machine. But if Ryle is right, there never was a soul substance or ghost to begin with. Al's mind was never separable from his body. Al's mind was the functioning of his brain in a certain way. When Al's brain stopped functioning in that way, Al's mind ceased to exist and so did Al. Whatever it is that moves that armor around, it can't be Al, because his mind is dependent on his brain. His memories, personality, his very self, was located in, and produced by his brain. So there's literally nothing to attach to the armor. We can't attach Al's mind to the armor any more than we could attach Central City to a new set of buildings. We can move the name from place to place, but if the functioning of Central, as Central, stops, the city ceases to exist. Yes, new buildings can be built and old ones destroyed, just like you can gain new bodily cells and lose old ones, but when the functioning itself ceases, there is no city and there is no mind.

So what is it that moves Al's armor? Certainly not Ed's little brother. Al died that fateful night. His brain ceased to function and his memories, personality, and selfhood were lost. He ceased to exist because that which made him Al—not his brain, but the functioning of his brain—ceased to exist. The armor that we think of as Al does not—and *cannot*—function anything like his brain, so it cannot even replicate the functioning of Al's brain. Whatever Ed attached to that armor is homunculic in nature . . . soulless, mindless, and not quite human.

11

Humanity Grows Up

DEBORAH SHAMOON

*E*ver since Freud, the idea that experiences of infancy and early childhood shape our adult personalities has become commonly accepted, so much so that we often look to specific events in childhood to explain our personality quirks to ourselves and others. Biology, Freud said, is destiny, and it seems we believe this too.

But what if we could alter our biology so radically that it completely changed the process of birth and development? What if biological birth were abolished and all humans were created in labs? What if we could skip childhood and adolescence and go directly from babyhood to adulthood? How would that affect the human psyche, and would that society be a paradise or a nightmare?

These are the questions that Keiko Takemiya asks in her science-fiction manga series *To Terra* (*Tera e*), which first appeared in the magazine *Monthly Manga Boys* (*Gekkan manga shōnen*) from 1977 to 1980, and appeared in English translation in 2007.

In the future society Takemiya describes, humanity has scattered into the far reaches of space, fleeing a polluted and uninhabitable Earth. Society is governed by the Superior Dominion, ruled by a computer called the Grand Mother, which controls all aspects of life. In this highly regulated, hierarchical society, humans are grown in labs, then placed with adoptive parents until they are young teens, when the memories of their childhood are erased in preparation for entry into the adult world. But this system occasionally produces a mutation: powerful psychics called the Mu. The Grand Mother orders the extermination of the Mu, but they band together and attempt to find their way back to Terra (Earth) where they believe they can live in peace.

In the opening chapter, we see the main character, Jomy Marcus Shin,[1] on the day of his passage from childhood to adulthood. The Grand Mother

---

[1] The names of the characters have been Romanized differently in the manga and the DVD subtitles, as well as on various fan websites. For instance, Jomy's middle name,

computer prepares to wipe his memory, but his latent Mu powers manifest and he fights back, determined to retain the memories of his childhood, which are how he knows who he really is. The chapter ends with Jomy joining the Mu underground resistance, destined to lead them in their battle against humans and their journey to Terra. It's easy to sympathize with Jomy's desire to hang on to his memories, but why is it so important that he remember the woman who is not his biological mother? Why is the supercomputer trying to become a substitute mother?

The Imaginary Phallus

At the heart of *To Terra* is a preoccupation with reproduction, mothers and fathers, and the trauma of the maturation process, described by Freud as the Oedipal conflict, and by Lacan in terms of desire and lack.

Jacques Lacan, who lived from 1901 to 1981, was a French psychoanalyst who began his career working with psychiatric patients in Paris in the 1920s, although he is best known for his theoretical writing and for the seminars which he began in the 1950s and continued until his death. He critiqued, revised, and expanded Freud's theories. He was not just concerned with understanding and curing psychiatric illness, but with describing how all people experience selfhood, and how our views of ourselves and the world around us take shape as we mature from infants to adults. In other words, Lacan moved psychoanalysis from medical science into the realm of philosophy.

At the basis of Freud's theories of the psyche, which Lacan drew on, is the Oedipal conflict. Freud theorized that the father's authority in the family forces the male child to form an individual identity by separating from the mother. According to this theory, infants have no sense of individuality; they think of their mothers as part of themselves. As the child matures and realizes the mother is a separate person, his desire for food and comfort from the mother takes the form of desire to possess her, sometimes expressed in sexual terms. However, the child's desire for the mother is thwarted by the father: the child fears that if he angers the father by competing for the mother's affections, he will be punished with castration, which he presumes the mother has already suffered. Eventually, rather than challenging the father for possession of the mother, the child internalizes his obedience to the father's authority and looks elsewhere to fulfill his desires.

This theory of the Oedipal conflict has been challenged. Feminist critics have pointed out that this only applies to boys; whether girls go through a

---

Maakisu, is sometimes spelled Marquis. For the sake of simplicity, I will follow the spellings used in the Vertical translation by Dawn T. Laabs.

mirror image sort of process (sometimes called the Electra complex, desiring the father and challenging the mother) or a more complex version of the Oedipal conflict is still open for debate. And while Freud claimed his theory applies universally to all cultures, that is also open to debate. For instance, Japanese psychoanalyst Heisaku Kosawa modified the Oedipal conflict according to Japanese mythology (Anne Allison, *Permitted and Prohibited Desires*, pp. 3–4). However, the Oedipal conflict has shaped the way we think about ourselves and informed the ideas behind novels and popular culture texts all over the world. So even though *To Terra* is a manga written by a woman in Japan, it still relates more clearly to this basic theory of the Oedipal conflict rather than to the feminist or Japanese critiques.

Many of Lacan's additions to Freud revolve around the basic theory of the Oedipal conflict and the fear of castration. Lacan moved the discussion of the Oedipal conflict from the literal to the symbolic. Rather than talking about the penis, he uses the term *phallus*, meaning the ideas the penis represents (such as power or the fulfillment of one's desires), not just the physical organ. The phallus is an imaginary object, a symbol of what the child wants but can never have. Part of the successful resolution of the Oedipal conflict means accepting that there are desires you can never fulfill, or that you can only partially fulfill by means of substitutes. This concept of *lack* is central to Lacan's writing. In order to form an individual Ego, we must accept this lack in others and in ourselves. Because Lacan was writing in symbolic terms, this holds true even when there is no physical father present, for instance with children raised by single mothers.

Teenage Mutants

To Terra, set in an imaginary world without biological reproduction, reflects on the importance of the relationship between parents and children. None of the characters in *To Terra* have normal childhoods, and while this gives them great power for a short time, ultimately it's not the basis for a healthy, stable society.

The leader of the Mu, Jomy Marcus Shin, is powerful because he remains in a state of arrested development: unlike the humans, he has not had his memories of childhood erased. The story begins when Jomy is fourteen, on the day before he will undergo a maturity check and memory wipe by the Grand Mother computer, then be sent to live as an adult. In this world, not only are children conceived artificially and raised by foster parents, but the children and adults live in completely separate worlds, the children on a colony planet called Ataraxia (a Greek philosophical term, indicating tranquility). After having their memories erased, teens are sent for training to other planets or to giant space ships, in preparation for humanity's eventual return to Terra.

The separation between children and adults is like Lacan's description of the maturation process, although in real life this takes place in much younger children. At the basis of Lacanian thought is the triad of the Imaginary, the Symbolic, and the Real. The Imaginary includes the unconscious, but for Lacan that is always a state that can never be accessed by adults. Freudian ideas of the unconscious or the subconscious have filtered into common usage in a simplistic way, usually meaning either dreams or daydreams, or urges that are not fully articulated (for instance, wondering if you failed to achieve a goal because you "subconsciously" didn't really want it).

But for Lacan, the Imaginary is the state of infants before they realize they are separate from the mother, before the symbolic castration that forces the formation of individual identity. Once that happens, and we gain entrance to the adult world through language, we enter what Lacan calls the Symbolic Order. Beyond both the Imaginary and the Symbolic is the Real, also a state we can never achieve, but which we attempt to describe through language. These terms may seem confusing, since in everyday speech we tend to refer to the adult world as "real" and relegate the symbolic to the world of dreams or fantasies. But Lacan is asking us to recognize that language is never more than a system of symbols, and that language in fact mediates or creates distance from that which we desire (the phallus).

Once we begin to form a separate identity, and more importantly, allow our world to be structured and ordered by the rules of language, the unconscious is lost, and we can't access it directly anymore. This is another dimension of lack, realizing that the Symbolic Order of language distances us from the phallus (the things we desire). In *To Terra*, this break with the unconscious and entrance into the symbolic world of adults plays out in teenagers rather than infants (since of course a story about teenagers is more fascinating than a story about infants).

For Jomy, the entrance into the adult world is traumatic—the Grand Mother computer threatens to erase his childhood in order to bring him into the rules and structure of adult society. If that happens, as Lacan describes, there will be no return; he will forever lack direct access to the unconscious. But at the last moment, the Mu intervene and rescue Jomy from the Grand Mother. He retains his childhood memories, and like all the Mu, resists aging. Jomy's direct access to the unconscious is represented by his eternally youthful appearance; no matter how much time passes, he still looks like a young teen. And like all the Mu, he has strong psychic powers.

However, simply retaining childhood memories is not enough to remake this distorted human society. Although he is the most powerful Mu, Jomy himself never has children. He recognizes the importance of parents and childhood, however, and encourages the Mu to begin biological reproduction. Ten babies are born, all with extremely strong psychic powers. After a particularly brutal

attack by the humans, these babies use their powers to artificially age themselves from toddlers to teens, in order to protect the Mu. They are led by Tony, the oldest and strongest of them, who was left an orphan in the attack.

Tony, however, is more a monster than a hero. He claims his powers arose from his natural birth, but his unnatural maturation cuts him off even from the other Mu. Although he looks like a teen, emotionally he is still only a baby, and has difficulty controlling his urges, particularly his anger at the humans. Skipping the maturation process and seizing adult power (the phallus, or what he thinks is the phallus) too soon leaves Tony unable to function as a self-regulating adult. Indeed, at the end of the story, his inability to obey Jomy's orders sabotages the last chance for a peaceful resolution between the Mu and the humans.

Nature versus the Law of the Father

Tony is not the only character who lacks a childhood. The main antagonist to the Mu, Keith Anyan, is an artificial being created entirely by the Grand Mother and brought to consciousness as an adult to act as her agent among the humans, although he is not aware of this himself. Engineered by the Grand Mother to be perfect, he quickly rises to an elite leadership role in human society, on board a spaceship bound for Terra, tasked with preparing humans to create a new utopia on Earth. But his perfection sets him apart from other people; he is distant and lacks compassion, and doesn't even really believe in their mission.

The truth about Keith's artificial creation is revealed by Seki Ray Shiroe, a young human with latent Mu abilities, who resists the memory wipe and retains memories of his childhood. Shiroe sacrifices his own life to delve into the computer archives and uncover proof that Keith was created by the computer, in hopes that this will undermine the Grand Mother's authority. At Shiroe's urging, Keith confronts the computer, who tells him:

> The education of children will determine Terra's fate. We're exploring all options to raise a leader who can steer Terra with a steady hand. You were inside a womb until the age of fourteen, the year of your maturity check. Your emotions weren't warped by your parents, friends, or teachers. You are our immaculate child. . . . Your duty is to use your intelligence and lack of bias to see reality more perfectly than anybody else. Your powerful intellect will make you leader of the human race. (Volume 1, p. 287)

In order to create a perfect human, the computer attempts to create an adult who has not suffered the traumas of the Oedipal conflict, or castration fears.

But Keith is far from human—in his single-minded, cold-hearted obedience to the Grand Mother's plan, he is more like Tony than the other, weaker humans.

Keith's counterpart among the Mu is Physis, a blind seer who is among the oldest of the Mu, although because she too lacks a childhood, she maintains a youthful appearance. For the first half of the story, Physis is little more than a passive mother figure for the Mu. She projects a psychic image of Terra, providing them with a goal and an object to desire, but she does not lead them in an active way, as Jomy does. Eventually we find out that Physis was also created by the Grand Mother computer in the same manner as Keith, with the intention of creating a perfect human, but she was rejected as imperfect because of her blindness. However, the computer used some of Physis's genetic material to create Keith, so in a sense, Physis is his mother.

Keith and Physis represent another facet of the Oedipal conflict, the opposing forces of natural urges and the laws of society. The word *physis* is a Greek philosophical term for nature. The character Physis represents the natural, pre-castrated state of the Imaginary. All of the Mu, because they remember their childhoods, and thereby have access to the Imaginary (the subconscious that in real life Lacan says is unknowable), are living in a state of nature. Thinking about the Oedipal conflict in symbolic terms, Lacan argues that the child must accept the authority of the father, but this is not necessarily a real father. Rather, the child learns, by entering the Symbolic Order through language, to accept the rules and laws of society. This is what Lacan calls the Name of the Father (or sometimes the "no" of the father). The fundamental "no" of the father is the incest taboo, the law that forces the child to look beyond the mother for the satisfaction of desire.

If Physis represents nature, then Keith represents *nomos*, or law. Keith's function is to mediate between human and the laws or *nomos* imposed by the Grand Mother. In spite of the Grand Mother's attempts to control human society completely, the humans are always in danger of going astray by embracing *physis* (nature), represented by the Mu. The Mu are not only an external threat (the Mu army led by Jomy Marcus Shin) but also an internal threat—humans like Seki Ray Shiroe and many other characters who appear to be human at first but later display Mu psychic abilities, always tied to an ability to recall their childhoods. The computer relies on Keith to enforce the laws for the humans, and to wipe out the rebellious Mu who do not accept those laws.

The Grand Mother as the Big Other

The Grand Mother computer represents what Lacan calls the Other. Lacan makes a distinction between the other and the Other (with a small or a big o, although in French the word is *autre*, and many works on Lacan in English

refer to the small or *petit* a and the big A). The small other is other people, part of the realization that there are beings separate from oneself. But the big Other is what's called radical alterity (otherness), that is, the language and laws that govern the Symbolic. The mother is the first Other for the child, the source of language and commands that the child must work to understand, or at least obey even without fully understanding. Even after we mature and are no longer under our mother's care, this Other still remains as a symbolic authority. For the humans in *To Terra*, the Grand Mother is the big Other, separate from them but still regulating every facet of their lives, sometimes in incomprehensible ways.

Keith Anyan, created by the Grand Mother to enforce the law, is less a fully functioning human than a representation of what Lacan calls the Ego-Ideal. Again, Lacan is refining Freud's writing on the ego, which in this context simply means the self (not to be confused with popular use of the term ego, indicating pride or boastfulness). Lacan describes the ideal ego (notice the small letters) as the idealized image of the self, the image we project in order to impress other people (the small other). But the Ego-Ideal is directed at the big Other. Like Keith, who mediates between the Grand Mother and the humans, the Ego-Ideal is the self we create to impress the Other, the ideal we aspire to in following the rules of the Symbolic Order.

Terra as the Unobtainable Object of Desire

Terra itself is what Lacan calls the *objet a*. Remember that because we are all in a castrated state, trapped by language in the Symbolic Order, we are separated from and unable to reach the Real, or to obtain the phallus, that is, the thing we desire. Instead, the thing (*objet* in French) that we desire becomes distorted—we become fixated on something, the *objet a*, which we think will fulfill our desires, but because we can never obtain the phallus, only substitutes for it, we will always be frustrated.

Terra is that unobtainable object of desire for both the humans and the Mu. The Grand Mother has implanted images of Terra in the minds of both Keith and Physis, who transmit this desire to their followers, like the way the idea of the phallus is imprinted in the mind of the child. But for this reason, the story can't end with a joyful homecoming to Terra. Even though both the humans and the Mu eventually return to Terra, things don't work out they way they had hoped.

At the end of the story, the humans attempt to settle on Terra, although it's still polluted. The Mu army, with their superior psychic strength, force the humans to allow them to land on Terra as well, and begin to negotiate a peace treaty. For a short time it seems that humans and Mu will find a way to co-exist.

But Tony, the uncontrollable Mu child, violently disrupts the negotiations. This leads to a final confrontation between Jomy and Keith in the heart of the Grand Mother computer complex, which ends with them destroying each other, the computer itself, and Terra.

In the end, both the humans and the Mu are forced back into space. Although the entire story is about a return to Terra, in the end the return is impossible. Lacan would say, this is because the thing they desired, the *objet a*, can never be attained, because all desire is illusory. This may seem like a bleak ending. It's never pleasant to realize the things we desire don't really have the power to make us happy. Lacan is not interested in making us feel better about ourselves, but in showing that all desire is mediated, and complete fulfillment is impossible.

The Journey to Adulthood

The final chapter not only deals with frustrated desires, but also the fantasy of rebellion against parental authority, through the character of Keith Anyan. Once Tony disrupts the peace talks, Jomy attacks the central computer bank of the Grand Mother, but Keith, as always acting under the control of the Grand Mother, shoots Jomy and kills him. At this moment, the Grand Mother praises Keith, but Keith for the first time resists her, yelling, "Never warp my will again!" (Volume 3, p. 286).

As the waves of explosions that Jomy triggered continue, Keith falls down into a deeper, hidden bank of computers. There he discovers an older computer, a higher authority that we might call the Grand Father. The Father solves the mystery that has haunted Keith throughout the story: if the Grand Mother has supreme control over human reproduction, why does she allow children with the aberrant Mu genes to be born? The Grand Father answers: the scientists who built the Superior Dominion and the computers to control society believed the Mu were an evolutionary leap that would save humanity, and would not allow them to be wiped out. The Grand Father was put in place to prepare Terra for human habitation again, when humanity was ready, as it says, "to be awakened when humanity sought something higher than mother" (Volume 3, p. 301). The Grand Father gives Keith a choice: turn on the program that will make Terra habitable again for humans, or turn it off forever. Not wanting to give the humans victory over the Mu, Keith chooses to destroy the Grand Father, which leads to the destruction of Terra and his own death.

This final scene acts out the Oedipal conflict. Keith rebels against the authority of the Father, and kills him. Although Keith himself dies, he acts on behalf of humanity which is now freed from authoritarian control. Without

the Grand Mother, humans regain control over their own bodies and memories. In real life, the successful resolution of the Oedipal conflict means accepting the authority of the symbolic father, although fantasies of violence are often a part of this traumatic process. Lacan would argue that although we may free ourselves from the immediate authority of our parents, in a larger sense we are never free of the Name of the Father. Because we all exist in the Symbolic Order, we can't go back to that infantile state, before language. And yet somewhere beyond the Symbolic is the Real, a realm we can only approximate but never attain. Like Terra, the Real is forever beyond our grasp.

Terra, then, represents the desire to grow up and become an independent individual. But Terra itself is an illusory goal. Humanity can't grow up by returning to its place of origin; in fact, humanity is far better off once Terra is destroyed, and they are free to live in small self-governing units. In a post-script, we see space-dwelling people many centuries in the future. It seems that after the destruction of the Grand Mother, humans and Mu no longer are enemies, but have integrated. Instead of the artificial world of test tube babies and maturity checks, people now live in nuclear families and reproduce biologically again. Although they live in space ships, these natural families seem much more stable and fulfilling than the artificial Superior Dominion.

In the post-script, two families meet by chance, and the parents speak about their continued longing for Terra, now a dead planet they have never seen. Their children, a boy and a girl, share an instant psychic bond. Freed from the control of the Grand Mother and the Grand Father, and having developed through normal childhoods, these two are able at last to form real human connections. The *objet a* may never be attainable, but the successful resolution of the Oedipal conflict allows a person to form meaningful bonds with another person. In other words, like the infant who matures from dependence on the mother to learning to look elsewhere for the fulfillment of desires, humanity has grown from needing the control of the Grand Mother to being able to control itself. And when that happens, for the first time in the story we see two characters meet and fall in love, indicating a sustainable human society has at last developed.

Manga and Lacan

You may be wondering why there is so much of Lacan in a science-fiction manga. One answer is that Lacan wrote about common human experience, and in describing how we form our identities and how we relate to the world, he described functions that can be found anywhere, from the densest novel to the lightest pop culture magazine, whether the author intended to put it there or not.

In *How to Read Lacan*, for instance, philosopher Slavoj Žižek uses Lacan to analyze everything from Shakespeare to *Alien* to the Iraq War. As Žižek writes, "For Lacan, psychoanalysis at its most fundamental is not a theory and technique of treating psychic disturbances, but a theory and practice that confronts individuals with the most radical dimension of human experience. It does not show an individual the way to accommodate him- or herself to the demands of social reality; instead it explains how something like 'reality' constitutes itself in the first place" (p. 3).

However, if you're familiar with the history of manga in Japan, it may not be so surprising to find psychoanalytic ideas in *To Terra*. Manga in the 1970s, when *To Terra* was first published, were wildly experimental, and as the target demographic increased from high school to college age, writers developed more and more ambitious, psychologically complex plots. Keiko Takemiya got her start in shōjo manga, or romance comics for teenage girls. Most shōjo manga artists were young women, like Keiko Takemiya, who began publishing comics as a teenager, and who wrote *To Terra* when she was in her twenties.

As these women struggled with sexism in their real lives, they expressed their frustrations with gender inequalities in romance by creating fantasy worlds where the rules of romance and even biological reproduction were altered. *To Terra* was published in a boys' comics magazine, and was marketed to both male and female readers, so technically it's not part of the shōjo manga genre. But it's very similar to a lot of shōjo manga in that it's about growing up and features fantasies of alternate forms of reproduction. Most shōjo manga were heavily influenced by Freudian and Lacanian ideas. (For instance, see Midori Matsui's essay in *Feminism and the Politics of Difference*).

To Terra is what literary critics call an open text. There are many possible interpretations of *To Terra*, and many more loose threads to the story than can be covered in this chapter. For instance, the Greek names of the planets suggest that the manga could be read in terms of Greek philosophy, such as that of Plato. Because Takemiya wrote the manga in installments over a period of three years, there are places where the story seems to stop and start again, and where background information on the characters and the world they inhabit is revised or unclear. The manga was also adapted into an anime movie in 1980 and later to a twenty-four episode anime TV show in 2007,[2] both of which alter the story in their own ways.

The big issues *To Terra* raises, about individuality, maturation, and desires, resist simple answers, so it seems fitting that the manga itself does not provide a single reading of them. The Imaginary, as Lacan would say, is not something we can talk about directly, but only in mediated, incomplete ways. Lacan's ideas,

---

[2] DVDs of the movie and TV show have been released in the US with English subtitles, although the title is translated as *Towards the Terra*.

that language (the Symbolic) separates us from the Imaginary and the Real, that we are all incomplete (castrated) and that our desires can never be fulfilled may seem depressing, especially since we tend to think of psychoanalysis as a way to feel better about ourselves.

The ending of *To Terra*, with all the main characters dead and Terra destroyed, may seem equally depressing. But the maturation process is always fraught with frustration and loss. Rather than passively submitting to fantasies of maternal attachment, *To Terra* urges its readers to grow up.

12

Operation La Famiglia

SARA LIVINGSTON

Social Welfare Agency, Section 2
Classified

This confidential dossier contains documents
connected with the ongoing investigation of
the terrorist known by the code name, Franca.

[surveillance photo of subject]

The documents were collected between March
2009 and February 2010 as part of a deep cover
operation dubbed LA FAMIGLIA. Our purpose is
to capture her alive and gain intel about her
freelance work with the paramilitary group,
Padania. Our ultimate goal is to turn her
into an asset so that she cooperatively joins
our "Family." This is a delicate operation
so we've dispatched our most engaging and
sympathetic agent to make this happen.

The enclosed documents reveal a morally
complex individual who is intelligent,
empathetic, and committed to understanding the
meaning of her actions. We still consider her
hostile but we also see that she is struggling

to understand her actions and trying to decide whether or not they constitute terrorism and whether or not she should be considered a terrorist. She is equally curious about why our operatives appear to engage in the same actions as she does and are considered heroic.

As this is an ongoing operation, the contents herein should be considered TOP SECRET and may be declassified at a later date. The documents include selected inter-agency memos, transcribed phone conversations, selected posts from her blog, intercepted email messages, private letters, and other miscellaneous notes and surveillance photos.

Document #1
http://codenamefranca Blog Post 7/29/09

Born Again

I was dead for three minutes. Cold dark water filled the car, I stopped struggling with my seat belt, and my mind drifted away. The three bullet wounds I sustained during the failed rescue attempt stopped hurting, and Franco's shouts warning me to slow down before the curve faded into echoes.

I hate to admit it, but all the clichéd visions that go along with near-death experiences are true. You know—lights, colors, and flash frames of experiences. Films sometimes depict near death victims reliving their pasts, but that's just fiction. What you really see is the future you will never have. I saw flash frames of myself at a graduation ceremony receiving my law degree; I stood in parliament testifying against corrupt leaders; I tasted the first vintage of wine with my name on the bottle; I sat in a nursery rocking my newborn child. All these images came in a one second flash and I glimpsed a future worth living.

Wanting a future means I need to re-examine my identity and see if it is possible to recover Caterina. I can do that only if the Franca mark is not too indelible.

A few years ago a sudden event changed me from a university student to a political activist / freedom fighter almost overnight. Before long, I was being called a terrorist and was on wanted posters at police stations.

Now, in another sudden turn of events, I've driven off a cliff and fortunately the authorities think I'm dead. I now have an opportunity that few are given. I have the luxury of pressing the restart button and living the life I was meant to live.

I was inspired to do this by reading Jose's blog. Jose was a black ops agent working for the Social Welfare Agency. We were enemies working on opposite sides but after reading his blog, I see that he and I have a lot in common. So following his lead, I will use my own blog to evaluate my past and chart my future.

NOTE: In the previous post, Franca seems to be referring to http://jose-meaculpa.blogspot.com/ -- we can only assume that when Franca says "this," she means that these recovered files from the hard drive confiscated at ████████ formed the original content at the infamous http://codenamefranca. blogspot.com/ though we have been unable to trace an originating IP address, and Franca's whereabouts remain a mystery.

Document #1a.
Photo 7/29/09

Document #2
Personal Letter to Jose 7/31/09

Dear Jose,

I know about the family tragedy that compelled you to join the Agency and I want you to know my story so that you will understand what turned me into Franca the bomber.

I was an affluent university student—the beneficiary of generations of peaceful, effortless prosperity. My father was an intellectual and aristocrat who split his time between teaching at the university and overseeing the estate and vineyard that had belonged to our family for centuries. My name was Caterina then, and I was the only-child and heir not only to his property but also to his social position and legacy. I was young, good-looking, smart, and about to finish my law degree at the university. My world was secure; my future set.

Life was tranquil for me, but it was a socially chaotic time in Italy. In this volatile atmosphere where the government suspected everyone, my father bravely criticized a local magistrate. Before he had a chance to explain himself, he was framed for a mysterious and unsubstantiated crime, arrested, imprisoned, and then he mysteriously "died" in his cell before he could stand trial. My father had been mistaken for an enemy of the state and was eliminated. Within the time frame of one week, my world crumbled and my trust in the government was reduced to dust. For the first time, I saw institutions that I had trusted in a different light. The government and its legal system were not benevolent democratic partners dedicated to serving and protecting their people. Their benevolence was a lie. In reality, they were petty tyrants who labeled anyone who spoke out as a potential terrorist. Through its fear of dissent and its failure to follow due process, the government succeeded in creating a real enemy: ME.

Ciao,
Franca

**BACKGROUND
REC.8-1-09**

Document #3
http://codenamefranca Blog Post 1/11/10

A Little Light Reading

I've been reading a variety of writing about terrorism looking for a rationale to explain my behavior and I believe Albert Bandura's work is the most applicable to my situation. He is a well-known psychology professor at Stanford University who has written extensively about the tactics people use to morally disengage. In *Understanding Terrorism* he wrote about the role of selective moral disengagement in terrorism AND counterterrorism so the techniques he describes are as relevant for Padania and me as they are for Jose and the Agency.

One technique of moral disengagement is called moral justification. I was able to use this to examine my bomb building activities—acts I would normally define as morally reprehensible—and redefine them as personally and socially acceptable. I invested my training and bomb building apprenticeship with high moral purpose. I told myself that I was not just working toward destroying the government that killed my father, I was going to destroy a regime that had trampled on the constitution and defiled the justice system. Padania added their political goals, which involved upholding our Northern sovereignty and I suddenly felt I was protecting all of Italy from a corrupt murderous government. Moral justification sanctifies violent means.

Another technique Bandura described that helped me morally disengage was the use of euphemistic terms. Padania was fond of using "sanitized" language so that even killing a human being lost some of its repugnancy when we called it "wasting" or "a hit" rather than killing. Agency assassinations and bombing missions could be referred to as "clean surgical attacks" and if civilians were killed, they could be referred to as "collateral damage." (Terrorists are prohibited from using the term Collateral Damage—more on that later.)

Padania (and the Agency) used the language of legitimate enterprise to give an aura of respectability to their illegitimate one.

They used terms like "game plans" to describe our deadly missions, and they and urged me to be a "team player." They used euphemistic names to disguise distasteful activity. We had a guy they called "Bruno the Fixer," who would be summoned after a "hit." His job was to dispose of the corpse by dissolving it with acid, cutting it into pieces he would feed to his pigs, or burning it into ash. Calling him Bruno the Fixer made him sound like a helpful repairman rather than a corpse disposal service.

Blaming one's adversaries is another one of Bandura's techniques I used to morally disengage. I believed the government was to blame because "they started it." I viewed my father and myself as faultless victims driven to extreme means by government provocation. I felt I had a legitimate right to respond to their act of violence and which meant I could be violent too. Tit-for-tat conflict transactions like these escalate because each party does not just respond in kind, they hit back harder and the war escalates into a never-ending spiral.

I wasn't mature enough at the time to see that fixing the blame on the government not only gave me a good excuse to commit violent acts, it also let me feel a little self righteous about fighting them. So I joined Franco, learned to make bombs, and morally disengaged myself from blame. That would change over time but for the moment it was:

Good-bye Caterina . . . Hello Franca.

Document #4
http://codenamefranca Blog Post 5/1/09

What's in a Name?

New recruits in the French Foreign Legion adopt *noms de guerre* or pseudonyms to emphasize the break with their past lives. Resistance fighters adopted them for security reasons: hiding their identity and protecting their families from reprisal. People who choose to function outside the law like graffiti artists, computer hackers, and terrorists hide their real identities by using Codenames. This way they can engage in questionable activities while keeping their civilian identities secret and separate. This way they can live in both worlds, and that's what I did.

Caterina is a traditional Italian name that means "pure." It sounds soft and feminine, and it seemed to suit the "establishment" me. As Caterina, my ideals were pure, and I was untainted by my hatred for the government. Caterina could visit the vineyard, hang out in a café, and go to mass.

Franca is a harder sounding name that carries a potent meaning. It was the name of a fierce Germanic tribe, the Franks, who took their tribal name from the type of spear that they used. So my code name actually means "weapon," and that is just what I had become.

If I'm honest with myself I think that taking this name was another tool that helped me to morally disengage from what I (Caterina) knew was right. It reminds me a bit of Dr. Jekyll and Mr. Hyde. Though not a perfect analogy, in a way Franca was my Mr. Hyde and Caterina, my Dr. Jekyll. Franca was able to commit acts that Caterina would never have been capable of doing. But in my case the two personalities knew about each other and often tempered each other.

The moral disengagement techniques worked on me mostly in the planning and training stages when missions were still theoretical. But in the field, when the time came to actually kill, I stepped back from the edge. I could not injure innocent people so instead of continuing

my psychological disengagement, I started to disengage literally and physically from Padania. I stopped being a good soldier and became a freelancer taking only jobs I that I controlled. When you read about the Piazza di Spagna, you'll see that Caterina's influence was evident.

Document #4a.
http://codenamefranca Blog
Followup Post 5/09

Comment Post from Jose:

Caterina, you once commented on one of my posts and referred me to Hannah Arendt's writing on the Banality of Evil. That passage was relevant and helped me see my behavior in a different light so I want to return the favor and suggest a reading to you.

Excuse me for using the "T" word but John Horgan is the director of the International Center for the Study of Terrorism at Pennsylvania State University and pulling away from Padania and becoming a freelancer is what he calls the "internal limits" of terrorists.

In his book *Walking Away from Terrorism*, published last year, Dr. Horgan collected the accounts of twenty-nine former terrorists, many of them defectors from groups like the Irish Republican Army and Al Qaeda. He found that terrorists must inherently believe that violence against the enemy is not immoral (the moral disengagement you described in your post), BUT he found that that they also have internal limits, which they often do not learn until they are deeply embedded in a group. This is what happened to you and I applaud you for reaching your internal limit early.

Document #5
http://codenamefranca Blog Post 5/1/09

Piazza di Spagna

Today I want to talk about my disenchantment with Padania. Their political ideals seem to take second place to their economic impulses. Sometimes I wonder why I agreed to work with them.

Franco and I were asked to make a powerful bomb with a delayed fuse that they told us was for a factory being built in the countryside south of Rome. The night before our delivery date we got a call at our hotel from the Padania crew asking us to deliver the bomb there—in Rome—that night. When I asked why, the flunky on the other end slipped up and told me that the target wasn't a factory at all, the target was the Piazza di Spagna or the Spanish Steps.

If you've ever been to Rome, you know that the Piazza is one of the most beautiful and most popular monuments in the city. Both

tourists and natives use it as a meeting and leisure place. When I discovered that this culturally, historically important place was the target for one of my bombs, I had a decision to make. I believed that we should keep pressure on the government and that we should inflict damage in order to accomplish our goals, but at what price?

I decided right away that I would give them a fake bomb rather than let this happen. After this job, my relationship with Padania was damaged. The feelings of mutual distrust were growing. On a sliding scale, this decision moved me a few degrees closer to the non-terrorist side because I refused to harm innocents . . . and a few degrees closer to a hero because I saved an architectural and cultural treasure.

Document #6
email to Loretta Napoleoni 1/9/10

Dear Ms. Napoleoni,

I saw your TED talk and I felt an instant connection to you. I have since picked up your books and I have to say that you really understand what I discovered slowly—that the life of a terrorist is not ruled by politics or ideology, but by economics.

When you spoke of your childhood friend who was a member of the Red Brigades you said something about the psychological profile of a terrorist that was personally meaningful to me.

> I wanted to know what had turned my best friend into a terrorist, and why she'd never tried to recruit me. (Laughter) (Applause) . . . I found the answer very quickly. I actually had failed the psychological profiling of a terrorist. The central committee of the Red Brigades had judged me too single-minded and too opinionated to become a good terrorist. My friend, on the other hand, she was a good terrorist because she was very good at following orders. She also embraced violence. <http://www.ted.com/talks/lang/eng/loretta_napoleoni_the_intricate_economics_of_terrorism.html>

I'm writing to you to say that I'm like you—too single minded and opinionated to be a good terrorist—and I'm not really sure that I embrace violence either. I've been trying to make some decisions about my future and you have helped me. Thank You.

Yours truly,
Caterina

Document #7
email to Law Professor ██████████
8/13/09

Dear Dr. ████████████

I need your expertise. I'm trying to make sense of events I have become embroiled in and it would help me if I could talk out this legal point with you. I can't visit because it will put you in danger but I feel it is safe to write. Don't worry. My IP address is encrypted.

You taught us that Law governs all military actions and naturally, lawmakers must find loopholes for those considered to be in the defensive position. Terrorist forces are usually labeled offensive, and counterterrorist responders are labeled defensive. The offensive forces are said to destroy property and lives deliberately, so they are murderers. The defensive forces intend to kill only the offensive terrorists—if an innocent civilian gets in the way and dies, his death is not intentional, so no one is culpable for that death. In this case it is not called murder; it is called collateral damage.

If I remember correctly, the legal explanation of collateral damage is based on the Doctrine of Double Effect (DDE), first developed by Catholic casuists in the Middle Ages. Its purpose was to differentiate the intended effects of an act from those that are unintended, even if the unintended effect is likely. For example, when innocent bystanders are killed by a terrorist's bomb, we say that the terrorist intended to kill the bystanders, and we call it murder. The terrorists are morally culpable and liable for their actions because they actually target innocent people. On the other hand, responders to terror may also kill innocent bystanders, but the difference is that the bystanders were not the targets. When responders set off a bomb in a populated area, they

are committing a moral act because they intend to fight terrorists. If their bomb kills civilians it is unfortunate, but the responders are not liable or culpable for the deaths. Am I right so far?

Let's say that a government organization called the Agency is working on counter terrorism missions. Legally, the Agency would not seem to be culpable or liable when civilians die, but what if they kill an innocent deliberately and knowingly?

I can tell you about one instance where I believe the Agency committed murder. It happened in a hotel where known Padania operatives were hiding and were targeted for a quiet assassination by the Agency. Killing Padania members is no problem—it's legal and moral because they are enemies of the state. But they are not the only ones who died in this operation.

One of the young cyborg assassins, Rico, was sent in undercover to scout the situation. During her days of surveillance she met and befriended a young bellboy, Emilio. Although she was warned not to speak to anyone, she passed some time with Emilio talking and flirting. Emilio was smitten. On the day of the assassination, Rico was to dress as a maid and gain entrance to the Padania room under the pretense of delivering fresh linens. Once in the room she was to "waste" everyone there and she did.

But afterward, as Rico was escaping, she ran into Emilio in the hall. He was delighted to see her at first, but his delight turned to disbelief when she just looked at him, drew her pistol, and said, "I'm sorry."

She killed him because he was a witness. He would have been able to identify her and the Agency would have been implicated in this secret assassination. A government assassin killed Emilio, who was simply in the wrong place at the wrong time. It was considered to be an unfortunate but unintended casualty, so legally it was

considered collateral damage. I think it was murder—am I right, Professor?

Respectfully,
Caterina

Document #8
http://codenamefranca Blog Post 8/21/09

My Civilian Encounter

I wrote to my former law professor last week and gave him an example of the Agency choosing to kill an innocent young boy because he witnessed something he shouldn't have. Dr. ███████ said there have been precedents where agents or soldiers have been found guilty of murdering civilians but murder is extremely hard to prove without a WITNESS. He wanted to know if there were any that would be willing to testify. If there were any, I'm sure they've been eliminated by now. I want to write today about how I handled an accidental witness in a similar situation.

Franco and I took on a big job that would take us all the way to Sicily. We were hired to build a powerful bomb to stop the construction of the Straits of Messina Bridge. This bridge was a political hot potato because its construction would mean that Sicily would be connected to the mainland by road for the first time. The construction had implications for merchant vessels that would go out of business, trucking unions, and a huge national investment in a public works project that would benefit the south. Of course Padania, with its northern sympathies and economic motivation, decided that the bridge should be blown up before it could be finished, so they devised an intricate plot involving a kidnapping and one of our special bombs.

Pinocchio, a fifteen-year-old Padania hit man, was sent to protect Franco and me as we worked. We met Pino at an apartment where he had been staying for the past few months. A little girl, Aurora, had made friends with Pino and wandered into the apartment looking for him. I knew the Agency was rumored to be using little girls as assassins so when I saw her, I pulled a gun and started asking questions. She started to cry and told us that she was no one dangerous and would never tell anyone about us if we let her go. Pinocchio voted to kill her right away because he was taught to never leave a witness who

might identify him later. I stepped in and told Pino that Padania was not my boss and that "I choose who I kill." I protected Aurora and Pinocchio backed off.

At this point, I was not acting as a terrorist. Yes, I was going to carry out an anti-government plot to destroy property and was able to morally disengage by blaming the government for their economic aggression—but I was not about to murder a young civilian. This example of mercy was not lost on Pinocchio because later that day, he chose to spare the life of Triella, a young Agency cyborg. So my altruistic behavior not only saved Aurora, it saved Triella, and who knows how many more it saved down the line.

Document #8a.

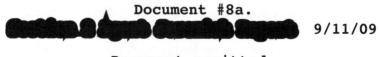 **9/11/09**

Document ommitted.

Document #9
Section 2 Agent Jeremiah Report   4/1/09

At 1:00 pm we spotted the suspect driving toward Tuscolano. After confirming her identity, we set a trap to capture Franca, the wanted terrorist. Agents Irma and Fredo pulled off the freeway and pretended to be in need of assistance. When Franca got out of her car to help, the agents overpowered her and brought her to the safe house for questioning. It is now 4:30 pm. I will proceed with the interrogation and finish the report as soon as she regains consciousness.

[The report ends here. Irma, Fredo and Jeremiah were found dead at the safe house. Franca escaped.]

Document #10
Transcribed cell phone call 4:02 pm 4/1/09

Franco: Pinocchio, Franca missed her check in.

Pino: So?

Franco: Her car hasn't moved for four hours—I'm worried—We better go find her.

Pino: I'm beat. I don't feel like going anywhere.

Franco: I don't care how you feel, get your knives.

Pino: Uhmmm . . . Okay.

Document #11
http://codenamefranca Blog Post 2/1/10

Enhanced Interrogation

The secret operations that the agency carries out are not subject to the same rules and the same public scrutiny that the official military and regular law enforcement agencies must live by. So here is another example of the Agency behaving as if they were rogue terrorists. And this time I was the victim.

I had taken a drive to Rome to check in with Uncle Marinov see what was happening internally with Padania. On my way back to the vineyard, I was spotted by an Agency operative who set a trap for me, and I fell right in. A desperate looking man flagged down my car just outside the city limits. When I pulled over he told me his pregnant wife was having labor pains in the back seat and would I help them. A "terrorist" would never have stopped in the first place. When I tried to help, they knocked me out me and took me to an abandoned farmhouse for questioning.

The man who "interrogated" me was clearly unfamiliar with the rules that govern the humane questioning of a suspect, because he beat me badly while his government colleagues looked the other way. Between punches, he told me that last year he had been injured by a terrorist bomb and had lost two fingers and the sight in one of his eyes. A "terrorist" would have been spitting back profanities, but I found myself in a strange emotional place. I could identify with this man's pain and hatred for me. He was not just beating me—he was beating the terrorist who had injured him last year in a bomb blast that took out one of his eyes. I knew his anger and I sympathized. I remember wondering if hitting me would make him feel better. I was losing consciousness because of his blows, but I felt this was a turning point for me.

I realized that empathy is what unites us all and holds the human race together, and when we lose that, we lose everything. Anger and revenge, I realized, would never make me feel better.

Document #12
http://codenamefranca Blog Post 2/10/10

My Last Days as Franca

A few weeks after my face healed from the beating, we were all at the vineyard again as one big family. Word came that Padania had betrayed Pinocchio's guardian, Cristiano. They had given the Agency the location

of his hideout in Lombardy and the Agency was planning a raid to capture and imprison him. I knew that telling Pino about this would mean that he would hurry to Lombardy to help defend his guardian.

I had no love for Cristiano. He was a gangster masquerading as a political activist, and he was responsible for training young Pinocchio to be a stone killer. But I had developed a fondness and a motherly instinct toward Pino. The months at the vine-

yard showed me that Pinocchio could be saved and might have a normal future, but he would never get a chance to try because his loyalty to Cristiano sealed his fate. He left the vineyard to either help Cristiano or die defending him.

Again, Franco and I were conflicted. We hated Cristiano, but we had grown close to Pino and could not bear seeing him fight the Agency alone. So we fueled up the Alfa and drove north to help Pinocchio rescue Cristiano.

You can guess the rest of the story. Pinocchio died in a fight with Triella, and we swooped in and grabbed Cristiano. As we sped away with him in the back seat, we took fire, and I was shot three times. I almost got away, but I forgot about that sharp curve at the top of the hill. I was losing consciousness because of the loss of blood and the last thing I remember was Franco shouting "Caterina! Don't die on me!"

He called me Caterina...

This extreme experience, although traumatic, was actually a new beginning for me. It was an opportunity for me to let Franca die and to welcome Caterina back to life, and I have decided to return to school and use what I've learned to fight the power.

I have a new ally too. Jose and I are corresponding, and I've invited him, Henrietta, and any of the other Gunslinger Girls who want out

to come and stay with me at the vineyard. Our first meeting is tomorrow. The life here was healing for Pinocchio, and I think it can be the same for the young cyborg girls.

Fictional stories of crime and terror provide a place for people to engage with major social issues—criminal responsibility, the nature of heroism, the impact of political affiliation on legal decisions, and the nature of justice. To treat these issues storytellers rely on a formula whose main ingredients are heroes, villains and satisfying endings. But in my story I think I've shown that the good guys are bad some of the time and the bad guys are good some of the time. It's very confusing and morally ambiguous, but it does perform a great service because it forces us to question our assumptions and by doing that, we are forced to confront the real issues.

When I started this blog I wanted to take inventory and make some decisions about my future and my identity, and I think I have. I know that I want a world where euphemisms are banished and the "high moral purpose" rhetoric is not allowed to justify destructive acts. I want a world where beating someone does not make you feel better and empathy is not a liability. I can promise that I will no longer think of Padania members as freedom fighters but I want Jose and the Agency to give me some *quid pro quo*.

What kind of world do you want, Jose?

Our future begins here.

Document #13
Internal Memo 2/11/10

February 11, 2010   **Classified**

CONFIDENTIAL Memo to: Prime Minister

Memo From: Monica Petris, Director,
            Special Operations Division
            Section 2, Social Welfare Agency

RE: Operation *La Famiglia*

Operations like this are painstakingly slow
but we believe our patience is about to pay
off. We received a message from our deep cover
agent that he has made contact with his target
and has arranged a meeting.

You may remember that when we launched *La
Famiglia* last year we faked the defection of
our *fratello*, Jose/Henrietta, to try to flush
Franca out of hiding. Jose and Henrietta
"disappeared" last year in a very public
way when he apparently walked away from the
agency to "save" Henrietta. We asked him to
write a PUBLIC blog we called *Mea Culpa* where
he confessed his personal failings and the
Agency's seemingly unethical exploitation of
the cyborg girl assassins we employ.

We endured that public humiliation because
it allowed Jose and Henrietta to appear
approachable and no longer affiliated with the
Social Welfare Agency. As we hoped, his blog
drew the attention of Franca who at first only
exchanged comments with him but eventually
communicated more personally. She has now
invited him to join her at her hideout. We
are within hours of capturing her.

13

Light Shows the Way

BRANDON CANADAY

*L*ight Yagami is a high-school student who stumbles upon a notebook labeled *Death Note* one day just outside his school. The notebook looks to be a joke, but he quickly finds it to be supernatural in that anyone whose name is written in it dies soon afterwards (or at the time specified by the notebook holder). Light, a very intelligent high-school student from a good family, very quickly decides to rid the world of evil by killing all criminals.

A protagonist murdering people in the first few pages of a *Shōnen Jump* story is exceptionally rare and is the manga equivalent of *Spider-Man*'s Peter Parker drowning puppies. However, Light may not be entirely to blame for his actions. The temptation to use the notebook is extraordinarily strong and explained by Light in the first chapter:

> But the Death Note has powers that would draw any person to want to try it at least once . . . somebody whom it's alright to kill . . . even better if it's somebody who has nothing to do with me.

His story will end on a steep mountain trail, the darkness winning its battle against the light of a low crescent moon. A massive crowd, each robed and bearing a glowing candle, climbs the trail in the darkness. An old person, relying on a cane to continue walking. A child in her mother's arms, unable yet to take that first step. The eternal light of the moon, and the much more ephemeral light of the candle held by a young woman. Despondent faces of the crowd give way to the hopeful face of that young woman. It's a scene, like the morals of the story itself, punctuated by black and white, but filled with grey. It's a scene indicative of hope, but suggestive of something darker. These are the final panels of *Death Note*'s remarkable battle of wits, of good and evil.

The wildly popular manga (and anime, and movie series, and game series, and . . .) *Death Note* was originally a 108-chapter series in the weekly manga magazine *Shōnen Jump*. It's noteworthy that this series was picked up by the

very youth-oriented *Shōnen Jump*. According to *Shōnen Jyanpu no Jidai*, by Jiro Saito, *Jump*'s three editorial principles are friendship (*yuujou*), effort (*doryoku*), and victory (*shouri*). At least one of these principles must be in a story for it to be included by the editors.

The Chinese characters that make up Light Yagami's name have significance: the character for Light is "moon" and the characters for Yagami are "night" and "god."

The notebook fell to the earth because a death god named Ryuk dropped it out of boredom. Not long after Light touches the notebook the horrifically-clownish death god appears to him, resembling a gothic mix of Hades and the Grim Reaper. Ryuk is basically an amoral onlooker. He is perhaps most memorable, in addition to his freaky face, for his love of apples, which is Christian symbolism that can't be ignored given the themes of temptation and punishment that pop up throughout the story.

In an interview with writer Tsugumi Ōba and artist Takeshi Obata (*Death Note*, Volume 13, Tokyo: Jump Comics / Shueisha, 2006, p. 182), Ōba claims that apples were chosen for their size and color, but even Obata found that revelation very surprising. The basic story of Adam and Eve is common knowledge in Japan, and one Aomori prefecture apple company advertises its products as being the same type of apple as that eaten by Adam and Eve.

However, the appearance of a death god makes more sense if we take a look, not at Christianity, but at Japan's native religion, Shinto.

Why a Death God?

Shinto (literally: The way of the gods) is an immanent religion, meaning, among other things, that the realms of the living and dead and of *kami* (gods) and men are not separate. The divine, including *shinigami* or death gods, is all around us.

In a religion such as Christianity there's a clear notion of Heaven and Hell. Not so in Shinto. After people die they stick around to protect their families (and to be given worship), and eventually their souls become part of the family *kami* or collective *tama* (soul).

In *Death Note*, the rules of the notebook clearly state in Chapter 107: "All humans, without exception, will eventually die" and then "after they die, the place they go is *Mu* (nothingness)." In the same chapter Ryuk tells us, "In the afterlife, whatever you've done in your life, you will still go to the same place. Death is equal." This type of eschatology, or rather lack thereof, is quite Shintoistic: all dead people, regardless of their vice or virtue, go to the same place, *Yomi*, which is a grey and gloomy place. It is closer to the world the *shinigami* inhabit in *Death Note* than to any dualistic notion of Heaven or

Hell. However bad (or good) Light's actions were, or however virtuous Light's father appeared to be, judgment doesn't await them in the world set forth in the manga, and would not await them in the real world—according to Shinto.

Shinto is primarily a collection of animistic and shamanistic rituals, methods or "ways" supported by ancient documents such as the *Kojiki*, the *Nihonshoki*, the *Engishiki*, and the *Fudoki*. In particular, the tenth-century, fifty-volume *Engishiki* prescribes "ways" in which things should be done. Over time, and with heavy influence from imports such as Confucianism and Buddhism, these "ways" or *kata* lead to a particular method of thinking about right and wrong.

There is a right way to do things and a wrong way to do things. One might also say, tongue in cheek, that there's the Japanese way to do things and the wrong way to do things. I can imagine several efficient ways to use chopsticks but in Japan there is one (correct) way. The beginner student of the Japanese language quickly learns that a ten-stroke *kanji* (Chinese characters that were adopted by the Japanese and make up the bulk of their script) that could mathematically have millions, and for practical purposes have dozens of different possible stroke orders has one (correct) stroke order. Not only that, but the pen should move on the page in the correct direction during the execution of each stroke.

These are admittedly amoral, relatively minor, sometimes frustrating cultural bumps in the road for the student of Japanese language and culture, but the point is that the way something is done is often more important than the action itself. Hence what may be considered morally wrong in the West could be okay if it is done properly, and something that may be morally correct could be opposed on the grounds of method. One Japanese high-school student told me that he thought Light was the hero of *Death Note* because of the "way" he did things. Light's nemesis, L, while intelligent, is portrayed as a shut-in and borderline slob. In contrast, we all can appreciate that Light, at least throughout most of the story, went about his business of vigilantism in a refined manner; we all loved it when, in Chapter 17, he put the miniature television in the bag of potato chips when he discovered the police had put cameras in his room and were watching him.

So, the "way" matters and matters a lot, but what are the ethics of Shinto and how could they conflict, practically or theoretically, with "absolute" or "standard" ethics?

Yoshi and Ashi

Shinto notions of "good" (*yoshi*) and "evil" (*ashi*) don't correspond with standard ethical or dualistic philosophical notions of good and evil. In Shinto

"*yoshi*" refers to an enjoyable and healthy life. "*Ashi*" usually refers more broadly or vaguely to anything polluting or doing harm to that kind of fulfilled life. The more modern term for evil (*aku*) has the meaning of evil close to the English sense but can also refer to unhappiness, disaster, and even inferiority (*zen*, a homonym and not the Buddhist sect, is the modern word for goodness).

Things like disrupting the group (a well-known, eternal, and quintessential Japanese no-no), disturbing the natural world, and disturbing *kami* (for example, ignoring proper ancestor worship or stealing something from a shrine) would all be bad. It's often the case that unethical practices in Japan start, and especially, continue, due to fear of disrupting harmony or the group. It's well documented that environmental pollution diseases, such as Minamata, claimed hundreds, if not thousands, of unnecessary victims because of citizens' reluctance to come forward simply due to the polluting company being the primary group in the town. In these cases the "good" of maintaining group harmony outweighed the good of saving lives by overriding the conscience.

Said another way, the negative consequences of disturbing the group, ostracism, for example, outweighed the positive consequences, such as fewer pollution-related deaths. It would seem that the ideal of harmony has the ability to override the traditional virtues of the individual. This is typical of Shinto, and other shamanistic religions which are, in the end, morally relativistic.

This moral "wire crossing" that occurs under the guise of maintaining harmony is at odds with any kind of philosophy that distinguishes between objective good and evil. Shinto, having originally started at the family and village level, presupposed that all people (in the group at least) were acting in the best interest of the group and were therefore good. However, it's obvious that the members of the group in those days had little choice but to act in the interest of the group and thus be "good." Ostracism would likely have meant death.

In Japanese society, this type of "good or nothing" monistic thinking has certainly given way to more "standard" dualistic notions of good and evil over the years, but not in all areas. For example, the idea that the dead go to one place, as opposed to either the good going to Heaven or the evil going to Hell, is so strong that in a survey of one hundred Japanese Catholics, in answer to the question, "Where do you think your ancestors are?" only three people responded "*tengoku*" (Heaven). In contrast, sixty-one Catholics responded "they are near" and sixteen answered "we don't know."[1]

Light executes criminals in order to create a more harmonious society and in this narrowly-defined sense could be morally defensible under what little

---

[1] This is from an article on life after death in folk Shinto by David L. Doerner. It can be found at <www.nanzan-u.ac.jp/SHUBUKEN/publications/jjrs/pdf/59.pdf>.

Shinto proscribes. (Probably owing something to Shinto, Japan, throughout most of its history, has made use of the death penalty). If Light had stopped with criminals, his actions may have been morally, if not legally, been acceptable under Shinto. However, early on he shows that he is ready to punish a wide range of people and he even considers killing some school bullies. Before the first chapter ends, he has killed a guy on a motorcycle who is only guilty of being a jerk. By Chapter 8, Light has started killing innocent people who are simply in his way. He considers, but seems to draw the line at, killing people who don't contribute fully to society. Later, although crime rates have decreased, people are living in a state of quiet fear rather than harmony. It goes without saying, then, that Light's actions are *ashi*.

A Scene Indicating Hope . . .

A massive crowd climbs the trail in the darkness, their climb illuminated by the play of the Moon's eternal light with the much more ephemeral glow of the candles. Despondent faces of the crowd give way to the hopeful countenance of a young woman. But who is she?

One explanation is that the girl in these final panels is Light's sister, Sayu. If Light was considered divine to the new religious movement's followers, then his sister would be considered divine too. Certainly this would explain how the artwork in the final scene portrays her as the significant member in the group by their standing to the side as she walks towards the moon-lit precipice. Worshipping family members as protecting *kami* is quite natural in Shinto and has been important at least since the start of agriculture in Japan. An ancestor who had labored in the fields or paddies and subsequently died would continue to protect the family and ensure a good harvest. As a (presumably) protective older brother in the living world, Light would become a protective *kami* to the family regardless of his crimes while living. As a real-life example we can see soldiers, including war criminals enshrined at Yasukuni Shrine in Tokyo, worshipped as protecting *kami* by family members and, more controversially, by Japanese politicians. The people entombed there (most physically but some in name only) are done so as a matter of course, even though some families of the dead are against Yasukuni being the final resting place of their ancestors.

. . . but Suggesting Something Darker

Yet the woman in the final frames bears little resemblance to Light's sister and that leaves us with a much more likely explanation: Shinto was a big part of imperialist Japan and after Japan's surrender in World War II, many

people sought to avoid "State Shinto" and its negative connotations. This, combined with an urge to find a new savior in democracy and its freedoms, led to numerous new religious movements, some of which might be described as cults. In modern Japan, many of these new religious movements have caused unease, and famously, one religious movement, which morphed into an apocalyptic cult, turned out to harbor the need for a bit of the old extreme violence by releasing deadly sarin gas in the Tokyo subway system.

The new religious movement portrayed in the final panels of *Death Note* reflects the distress many Japanese people feel in the face of such groups, some of which are gaining members each year in a country with a declining population. In contrast to Shinto and its unabashed polytheism, most of the new religious movements usually preach worship of a single deity, or its living incarnation. Kofuku No Kagaku, Soka Gakkai, Yamagishi Association, and Life Space (also known as Shakti Pat) are a few examples. Given all this, it's easy to imagine in the world of *Death Note*, a religious movement dedicated to its "hero" sprouting up in the aftermath of his chaotic vigilantism. The crowd is dressed like a cross between Benedictine monks and a famous cult of the late 1990s, Panawave Laboratory, which was, incidentally, not famous for violence, but for its kooky outfits and its members being ridiculously afraid of sunlight

Then again, it's easy to see *Death Note* simply as a condemnation of hubris along the lines of a Greek myth like Icarus, Japanese folk tales like Urashima-taro, and indeed many tales of yore. Nobody likes the guy who thinks he is better than everyone else (although an international survey at www.deathnote.com.au with over 24,000 votes at the time I'm writing this, shows that 54 percent of voters support Light and 46 percent support his nemesis, L). As is often said of Japanese society, the protruding nail gets the hammer.

In *Death Note* both the protagonist and the primary antagonist, L, get the hammer in the end. According to the rules of the notebook, both have gone to a place near here, *Mu*. They await no final judgment and their sin is inconsequential.

If the effect of sin in Christianity is the estrangement of man from God, then Light may be lucky to have been born into a Shinto society. At the very worst his soul will reside in the grey gloom of *Yomi*, and even then his hubris doesn't need to be repented of: his soul will know no estrangement, and giving the final panel of the manga its due weight, the one certain conclusion is that his light will shine on.

14

Writing Wrong

GILBERT M. LUGO

*T*here are as many moral issues raised in *Death Note* as there are sudden heart attacks. The first time Light tests the shinigami's notebook and witnesses that its claims are indeed true, he is shaken, stricken with the guilt of having committed murder. But the guilt he suffers is soon outweighed by his desire to clean up the "rotten mess" he sees in the world. Thinking himself to be the only one who could accomplish such a grand scheme, Light takes the first step in a journey that will continue to change him with each death—he resolves to write the names of criminals in the death god's notebook until the world is purged of all evildoers.

Although writer Tsugumi Ohba claims that he did not intend to deal with moral issues (*Death Note 13: How to Read*, p.69), this premise alone guarantees that there will at least be a good handful. With nefarious notebook in hand, Light assumes the role of judge, jury, and executioner for all criminals in the world. Any question of what authority Light has to punish (which is none, save his own self-righteousness) gives way to what would make Light think that his aim of punishing criminals is morally justified, and his reasons are varied and contradictory.

Light the Retributivist?

When Light first decides to put the Death Note to the test, he doesn't want to choose just any random person but someone who it is "okay to kill." With no particular person in mind, Light flips on the television and catches a live newscast reporting at the scene of a hostage crisis at a nursery school. The perpetrator? One Kurou Otoharada, wanted murderer. Light decides to write Kurou's name in the Death Note, not really expecting much to happen. But in less than a minute Light gets his results: Otoharada dies of a heart attack.

The Death Note works... or maybe not. It could have been a coincidence, so Light decides to test it once more, but he has a further condition now. The person whose name he writes in the Death Note should be one not merely who it is "okay to kill," but who "ought to be killed." And while waiting for his mother one day after a prep course, he finds the perfect target, Takuo Shibuimaru, a biker harassing a girl who wants nothing to do with him. Light writes in the notebook that Takuo dies of a traffic accident and before Takuo can get the girls number, he rides off to meet the grill of a truck. It's no longer a question for Light, the Death Note actually works, and it will grant him the power to become Kira, the god of a new world created in perfect righteousness.

As can be seen from Light's test of the Death Note, it's not ordinary people he wishes to write off from the world, but criminals who deserve to be punished for the crimes that they have committed. This notion that people deserve to be punished for their crimes is a core tenet of retributivist theories of punishment. As philosopher Immanuel Kant says in *The Philosophy of Law,* "Juridical Punishment can never be administered merely as a means for promoting another Good either with regard to the Criminal himself or to Civil Society, but must in all cases be imposed only because the individual on whom it is inflicted *has committed a Crime.*" (p. 90).

If the justification for punishment lies in the beneficial consequences it has on the criminal or on society, then values such as justice and righteousness become meaningless. Add to this Kant's conception of persons as autonomous rational agents, and the right to exercise one's freedom is violated when one is used as a means to some end irrespective of one's will. Punishment must be solely in response to the guilt of the offender, and it is the moral duty for a society to enact punishment upon its criminals.

Kant suggests two central concepts to his theory of punishment: the Principle of Equality and the Right of Retaliation. According to the Principle of Equality, the scale of justice should be balanced, and crimes upset that balance. The purpose of punishment is to ensure that balance is restored. For Kant, "the undeserved evil which any one commits on another, is to be regarded as perpetrated on himself." (*Philosophy of Law*, p. 91). Thus, if one steals, it is as if one stole from oneself; if one murders, it is as if one murders oneself. An idea behind this principle is Kant's categorical imperative, one formulation of which states that we should act in accordance with a maxim that we would also accept as a universal law. In other words, when a person commits a crime, he is behaving in accordance with a maxim that he would have universalized. To punish that person would not be to do so against their will, for as Kant understands it, these persons are essentially willing their own punishment as evinced by their choice of action. To punish offenders is in complete accordance with their autonomy—it treats them as the rational agents that Kant would say

they are. It respects their dignity and their freedom. Punishment, as such, brings the scale of justice back into balance. All that's left is to figure out the kind and amount of punishment to be inflicted on a criminal.

So if we accept that the crime a criminal commits is to be considered as having been committed on himself, then he should be punished in like manner as the crime he committed. This falls under what Kant calls the Right of Retaliation, or *jus talionis*. Take murder as an example. If one were to punish a murderer by any means of punishment other than execution, justice would not be served, because no amount of punishment and suffering inflicted in life can match the crime committed. The only way to justly pay for murder is to be executed. But not all crimes are to be punished by having that crime performed against the criminal. For instance, it is not necessarily the case that a thief would have his property taken from him or that a rapist would be raped. The idea here is that the punishment ought to inflict the same amount of suffering upon the criminal that he inflicted upon his victim.

Light initially adheres to elements of retributivism in justification of his punishing evildoers. Let's go back to Light's first two victims, the murdering hostage taker and the sleazy biker. When Light realized that the Death Note worked and that he was guilty of killing two people, he considered the different status of the two criminals he killed. The murdering hostage-taker Kurou Otoharada deserved to die, according to Light. After all, he was a murderer and would probably murder the hostages he took. Even Kant would agree that Otoharada should be executed for his crimes, because the only way to justly punish murder is by capital punishment. No other punishment would balance out the scale of justice.

But when Light considers the biker Takuo Shibuimaru, he realizes that the biker didn't quite deserve to die. What crime was he guilty of committing? The most one could charge him with is sexual harassment, but to punish that crime with death would not balance the scale of justice, but further imbalance it, because the punishment doesn't meet the crime. It's not giving the criminal his just dues.

With this second situation, Light strays from his original intentions and can no longer justify his actions by a retributivist theory of punishment. Remember, when Light decided to test the Death Note a second time, he wanted to use it on someone who "ought to be killed." His choice of victim, however, betrays that he's using the Death Note for reasons other than retributivist ones. In order to purify the world as he sees fit, Light doesn't simply desire for justice to be served, but for a particular end to be met and as such, maybe Light would be better able to justify his use of the Death Note on grounds of the good consequences that follow, rather than on grounds of pure retribution.

Kira the Consequentialist!

While retributivists like Kant hold that persons are to be punished on the sole grounds of their guilt, consequentialists argue that persons are to be punished so long as the consequences are beneficial. The most well-known consequentialist theory is Utilitarianism. According to Utilitarianism, the good is equated with happiness or pleasure and the bad with unhappiness or pain; therefore, an action is right when it brings about the greatest amount of happiness—and the least amount of unhappiness—for all persons equally considered.

But punishment is a form of unhappiness, because it involves inflicting pain or depriving one of some good, so in order for punishment to be justified, it has to be such that it brings about a greater amount of happiness over unhappiness for all persons considered. There are generally three ways in which punishment may bring about the greatest happiness over unhappiness. First, by punishing offenders it is hoped that the criminal himself and others will be deterred from committing crimes in the future. Fewer crimes in society will undoubtedly make for a more happy society than more crimes. Second, a criminal may be prevented from performing more crimes by being debilitated. In such cases, a criminal may enjoy a stay at the penitentiary where society will be free from at least one menace. Finally, criminals can be rehabilitated so as to no longer be the kinds of persons that commit crimes.

Light's main goal in using the Death Note is clearly the first reason mentioned above, namely to deter others from committing crimes. By knocking off violent criminals, Light intends to send a message to the world that someone is exacting righteous judgment upon the masses, a someone (Light) the world begins to know as Kira. With this knowledge, all persons would ideally begin to behave morally to avoid Kira's wrath. But Light doesn't want to strike fear into the hearts of the masses, but rather to change the way people think. He assumes that most people agree with his methods, but that they dare not reveal such sentiments in public. People have the natural right to pursue happiness, and criminals get in the way of good people exercising this right. As Kira, Light hopes to create a world where all the citizens behave morally, not because they are scared into doing so, but because they become genuinely convinced of the rightness of his actions. Kira's ultimate goal is one of deterrence.

Regarding debilitation, incarceration is usually the means by which a criminal is prevented from offending again. But in Kira's brand of punishment, criminals don't live to be debilitated. The same goes for rehabilitation. Offenders are killed and so cannot be rehabilitated. But other criminals who have served their sentences may be rehabilitated and so not deserving of punishment for crimes they committed in the past. This becomes an important point later in the *Death Note* series, where Light, playing the role of his deceased nemesis L,

who was the world's greatest detective assigned to the Kira case, no longer has the freedom to go about and write names in the notebook on a regular basis. Light decides to recruit someone who shares his ideals and can act as a proxy for him. He eventually chooses criminal prosecutor Teru Mikami, who writes in the Death Note those names specified by Kira. But when communication between Kira and Teru is lost, it is up to Teru to decide which criminals should be eliminated. Teru then begins to delete those persons who committed crimes in the past but already met their punishment according to the law. Light disapproves of Mikami's choice, because he sees it as doing nothing but instilling fear in the masses. Light's goal is to create a morally perfect world and punishing people who have already been reformed does not succeed in achieving this end, for they are already ideal citizens for Kira's kingdom of righteousness.

The Consequences of Consequentialism

One objection to consequentialist justifications of punishment is that a person may be punished for a crime that he did not commit or punished greatly for a lesser crime not worthy of such extensive punishment. If the goal of punishment is to increase the happiness and decrease the unhappiness in society, then there will be occasions where this goal could be attained by punishing innocent persons or by punishing persons more than they deserve to be. Kant's retributivism avoids just such consequences by demanding that punishment be exacted only on the guilty and that the quantity of punishment be in proportion to the nature of the crime committed. But as we have seen, Light isn't a strict retributivist, and he will go on to bear out these objections to consequentialism by both punishing those who do not deserve it and excessively punishing many crimes.

The first example we have of Light exacting judgment upon an innocent person is when he is first confronted by his nemesis L. On live television, L, whose name is displayed as Lind L. Tailor, condemns Kira as a mass murderer and vows to capture him. Light is offended by his remarks, believing himself to be righteous and bringing peace to the world. In a fit of rage, Light writes down the name Lind L Tailor in the notebook and forty seconds later he dies of a heart attack on live television. As it turns out, this was not really L, but a criminal awaiting execution on that very day. So although Light killed a criminal, he intended to kill an innocent person, L the detective.

Eventually, Light will succeed in killing innocent people, those who committed no crime whatsoever. But this isn't exactly how Light sees it. He doesn't see himself as punishing innocent people, but evildoers, and in this category he includes all the people who would attempt to thwart Kira's goal of creating a morally perfect world. Innocent people are eliminated because doing

so allows Light to go through with his plan uninterrupted. Oddly enough, it isn't simply for consequentialist reasons that Kira eliminates the innocent. In his odd sense of retributivism, Light thinks that people who would thwart his plan deserve to die. Their punishment, then, not only brings about a greater good, the most moral world possible, but some innocents are, in Light's twisted mind, receiving their just deserts.

However, even if the innocent victims are not so innocent, there's still the objection that these persons are being excessively punished. Light evinces this same sentiment when he considered his first two victims, one a murderer and the other not, one deserving of death and the other not. Light seems to understand that what he's doing is wrong, that what he's doing may be considered evil, but he believes that he's doing it for some greater good in the end. As Light says, one day he will be looked upon as righteous and just, even though the path to godhood was one of wickedness. The world needs to be cleaned up, and Light sees only himself as morally virtuous enough to do so and the only one—as far as he knows—that has the means to bring it about, the Death Note.

A Not So Happy World

Light's goal is to shape a morally perfect world where people are free to pursue their own happiness with no interference from those who would rob them of their joy. Light is certain that if the world were rid of all evildoers, then what would be left would be a perfectly just and righteous world where everyone lives in peace and happiness. But as many dystopian tales have taught us, this purging of mankind robs the world of the humanity that made life worth living in the first place. In attempting to create a perfect world, Light will inadvertently create a world where people live in fear of being judged by Kira, something he himself does not desire to occur. Light will maximize the unhappiness in the world rather than happiness, which is contrary to any justification he could make relying on consequentialism.

Death Note spans a number of years, and we eventually get to see how far Light succeeds with his plan to rule as god over a perfect world. Towards the end of his reign, we find out that roughly seventy percent of the world's population supports Kira. Even certain countries pledge their support to Kira. This would seem to speak out against the idea that Light will create a world where people live in fear. But the numbers themselves don't tell the whole story. Many who support Kira may do so simply out of fear to do otherwise. For instance, the Vice-President of the United States goes on air to announce that the US will no longer oppose Kira and that this decision is in no way an admission of Kira's righteousness. The US simply has no means to combat an enemy with such

mysterious powers. So too, not knowing how to hide from Kira's righteous judgment, many may simply give him their support and live as though they approve of his plans, while deep down inside they're living in fear for their lives.

Another consideration regarding Kira's followers comes from an incident with Near, the true successor of L who attempts to capture Kira in the second half of the *Death Note* series. While Near is hidden in a building, working on his investigation, his location is made known to supporters of Kira, and they attempt to oust him from the building. Near comments on how the crowd is made up of people who may be different from those who genuinely believe in Kira's ideals: the crowd trying to oust Near is nothing more than a fanatical base who may just end up disobeying the values that Kira himself adheres to, or they may be sheep following blindly their shepherd, or some may be actually anti-Kira, or . . . the possibilities are endless. Kira's supporters, though many, should not all be thought of as the kind and peaceful persons that Light initially wanted to protect, the persons Light wants in his perfect world. It includes far more *interesting* persons than that.

There is another reason to suspect that the world Kira will create will not bring about the greatest happiness for the greatest number. Besides Teru Mikami's decision to rid the world of people who already paid for their crimes, he also plans to remove from the world those who have talents but do not use them to the benefit of society. Light is not pleased with this second part of the plan, but not because the principle is wrong in and of itself, but rather because Light thinks it's "too early" for that kind of punishment to be meted out. Eventually, as the world is purged of all violent criminals, there will still be some left who need to be removed and amongst them will be people who don't realize their talents to the fullest extent. There will always be some group of people that will not live up to Kira's standards. As such, there will always be a worry lurking in the hearts of many that they are not living as Kira would have them live.

The laws of life under Kira's rule will become so stringent that he will suck the humanity out of society. Happiness may abound, but only within a limited framework constructed by Kira. The joy of the world as we know it, along with all of its faults, will be a thing of the past to be replaced by a less satisfying human culture, one where people live by the dictates of another man rather than pursue their own personal happiness. And if this is the case, how can Light possibly justify his actions? Not only does he fail to justify his punishment of others on retributivist grounds, but his consequentialist intentions are self-defeating; Light will end up punishing those whom he initially wanted to live in happiness. His grand scheme is left with no moral grounds and instead becomes a means for him to obtain power and control. In the end, Light's morally perfect world will be grounded on innumerable injustices, punishing not only everyone alive, but himself as well, punishment both undeserved and unfruitful.

15

Being Good Takes Practice

JOSEF STEIFF

*E*very day, Minami Masaki pretends to be someone he's not. That's okay, because he's an actor, and like his costar Sawada Kazuomi, he's got a job to do. Minami has been cast as a typical college student who discovers that he is in fact Oreas, an ancient warrior destined to protect the goddess Air from a wicked army of monsters led by Sawada's character (Gadriel). But does playing the hero on a kids' TV show potentially make Minami a better person in real life?

And, if so, does that mean playing the show's villain makes Sawada someone to avoid?

When Makoto Tateno's three-part yaoi *Hero Heel* first appeared, much of the initial interest in, and discussion of, her manga centered on its scenario—the onscreen and backstage life of actors playing roles, one pretending to be a hero, the other pretending to be a villain. But neither actor is necessarily in real life what he seems to be on the screen. In fact, on the interior splash page to the right, each actor is placed behind his costumed opponent (Minami behind Gadriel, Sawada behind Oreas), emphasizing this ambiguity and potential

205

interchangeability. It doesn't hurt that Sawada had actually been the hero in a previous TV show, *Stone Beast Squadron Gorian*, further blurring the nature of his character in *Hero Heel*.

Readers of the manga were excited by the questions raised by this disjuncture, about what it really takes to be a hero (or a villain).

Aristotle suggested in *Nicomachean Ethics* that being good takes practice, and at first glance, Minami seems to get a lot of practice by playing the hero's role. He even seems to change as the TV series continues. But I'm not so sure Aristotle would see the simple performance of scripted dialogue and actions as really practicing being good. Aristotle would say that it's the *choosing* that we have to practice, not the results. And if being good requires a choice, what choice does Minami really have? He's simply behaving as he's directed. So while he might be playing a good person, he's not really practicing the active process of choosing to be—or do—good.

I Don't Want to Think about Anything

But maybe that's okay. Maybe being an actor on the kids' show *Transdimensional Warriors Airguard* provides Minami with several important early steps that ultimately make it possible for him to be virtuous or to make good choices in the way that Aristotle suggests. Some additional perspectives on the ways in which we become virtuous might be beneficial for thinking about how *Hero Heel* and Minami's situation could reveal what it takes to become a good person. For example, Confucius might say that before we can practice virtues, we first need to have the behavior modeled for us.

In effect, this is what Minami does for the kids who watch him as Airguard Oreas on his TV show—he serves as an example. Aristotle would approve, because he writes that people need to be trained to be virtuous, and that training needs to begin in childhood. But Minami's heroic character in *Transdimensional Warriors Airguard* is a role model for Minami as well. Each week, when he gets his script, he reads about a character who consistently acts virtuously.

The power of example has been revitalized as a topic of interest in light of recent research in the areas of cognition and mirror neurons. In experiments utilizing fMRI recordings of brain activity, evidence points to the idea that seeing an individual perform a specific action can fire the same neurons in our brains as if we were doing the action ourselves. These experiments (V. Gallese and G. Rizzolatti pioneered this field with their study of macaque monkeys; R. Mukamel, E. Ekstrom, J.T. Kaplan, M. Iacoboni, and I. Fried have recently published comparable results in human studies) suggest that seeing examples of certain behaviors or actions might be nearly as good as doing those actions ourselves, at least inside our brains. Aristotle would certainly consider one's

interior state an important component of being virtuous (more on that later), but he would see behavior and action as vitally important to any discussion of virtue: for Minami to be virtuous, it's not enough just for the neurons to fire in his brain.

But unlike those kids who passively watch *Transdimensional Warriors Airguard* on TV, Minami actually has to perform—to imitate—the hero's actions. Minami does not just witness Oreas's example in the script; he is required to emulate those behaviors for the camera, much in the way that a student might trace over Kanji ideograms before doing them free hand.

The fact that Minami grows and becomes a better person through the filming of the TV series suggests that if we're initially scripted and directed to do good—literally told what to do to be good and then do it over and over under a watchful eye—we're more likely to choose good when we actually do get a choice.

While certainly not a child, Minami is presented in *Hero Heel* as someone still young (or at least immature), someone still developing his potential as a human being. Though they are not his parents, the producer, screenwriter, and director guide Minami's development, providing Oreas as an example of the type of person to be emulated.

5 Centimeters

Example and emulation have both been considered viable methods for teaching others—and developing one's own—virtue, though it quickly becomes apparent that moral education is a complex and complicated process. One concern that John Doris raises in *Lack of Character: Personality and Moral Behavior* is that emulating an idealized good person can in some cases have disastrous results because "actual persons cannot typically attain, or closely approximate" the psychology of an ideally virtuous person (p. 150). Minami is not Oreas, no matter how much he imitates Oreas's actions, and therefore he may be in some danger if he isn't cognizant of this distinction. When Minami gets hurt doing a stunt, it's because he has gotten carried away, behaving as if he were Oreas, when in fact, he's just Minami, an actor (and a rather selfish and not particularly self-aware one at that).

However John Doris isn't thinking so much of physical risks as ethical ones, "ethically dangerous circumstances where the virtuous can tread without fear but the rest of us cannot" (p. 150). Though he may intend to act in the way that his idealized virtuous person would, Minami could be vulnerable to situational pressures that Oreas would not be. For example, at the end of Scene 3, Minami leaves the bar to confront Sawada, to reveal his feelings, a confrontation that goes completely bad, turning out far differently than Minami probably hoped

as he made his way back to the studio. Rather than becoming the moment of tenderness it could have been, the confrontation results in Minami blackmailing Sawada into having sex with him and thereby further alienating him.

Airguard Oreas could have confronted Sawada (or Gadriel for that matter) and revealed his love without having the situation devolve into sexual coercion. We can infer from Doris's concern regarding ethical risks that Minami could have avoided this disaster if, instead of acting with the confidence to handle the situation that we might expect from Oreas, he had instead considered the advice that Oreas might give (if Oreas knew that Minami is not an idealized virtuous person himself nor has he yet attained the psychological traits of his role model). The advice of our ideal virtuous person is sometimes more beneficial than emulation of that virtuous person. But while he might be an ideal, Minami's alter ego Oreas isn't a real person. There's no tangible way to ask his advice; Minami has to imagine what he would advise.[1] And that's the point.

Doris isn't really talking about a situation like Minami/Oreas or even about someone we admire when he talks about an ideally virtuous person. He's drawing from ideas that have been expressed by people like Michael A. Smith and Bernard Williams who suggest that the people we get advice from or emulate are actually inside us, idealized versions of ourselves in idealized circumstances. And because actors incorporate characteristics of themselves into their roles and their roles become a part of their life experience, we can potentially think of Oreas as something more than just a character in a script: he could also represent an idealized internalized version of Minami. Add to this the fact that as they get to know the actors, the writers of TV series often begin to tailor certain aspects of their characters to them, giving the character some of the actor's attributes, Oreas may be closer to Minami's potential than we'd first assume. But Minami doesn't imagine what Oreas would advise him to do (or for that matter, what Oreas would do himself if he were faced with Minami's dilemmas).

So who's left to consult? In the backstage world of *Hero Heel*, there's no one Minami can really ask except perhaps Sawada, but Sawada plays the villain, both onscreen and off (at least from Minami's point of view), so Minami is not about to seek out his advice. Which brings us back to the fact that all Minami has at the moment are example and emulation, and the question of whether that's enough.

Where Aristotle might find some relevance to the idea of emulation is in relation to his proposal that virtue is something learned through habit rather

---

[1]   If you thought fMRIs were just about mirror neurons, G. Ganisa, W.L. Thompson, and S.M. Kosslyn have used them to record brain activity to compare the imagining of an experience with the actual experience. They found little difference. But in those cases, the subject is imagining something a bit more tangible than someone's advice.

than through reasoning, emphasizing the *doing* as a way to develop virtue. Minami can read his script over and over, thinking about how he'll perform his stunts, but that's not the same thing as actually doing them. In fact, once he physically tries to do the stunts, he will gain different insights and different knowledge than he could get from just reading about the stunts or reasoning his way through them.

One of the ways to make something a habit is to do it over and over again, so that it becomes what we call "second nature." In this case, what we're trying to create is something analogous to muscle memory. Perhaps that is what Minami is exercising each time he performs as Oreas on the TV show: a moral and ethical muscle.

Stop Playing Games

Muscle memory is a form of procedural memory and is sometimes called motor memory. We most often hear of this concept in relationship to athletics, though it applies to any endeavor that involves the need for precise and efficient motor skills, such as a musician's fingerings on a clarinet to produce different notes.

By repeating a muscle movement over and over through repetitive exercises or drills, we create a long-term muscle memory specifically for that task, allowing us to perform the task without conscious effort. Research suggests that the relationship of physical muscle activities to psychological or emotional states is much closer than we might have thought—if sad people just pretend to be happy, their moods actually do improve. Forcing ourselves to smile can actually make us feel happier! So when we're depressed, we can benefit from tapping into our own muscle memory of smiling—smile and pretend to be happy and you're happy (or at least, happier). Maybe we're all just actors, like the people who star in *Transdimensional Warriors Airguard,* and becoming a better person is as simple as acting like one.

Minami's day-in and day-out emulation of Oreas's virtuous actions by way of his performing the role are in effect a drill. The question is whether this drill would create a moral or ethical equivalent of "muscle memory" that would result in Minami ultimately making virtuous decisions when he's confronted with unscripted situations. This isn't so different from the US military's concept of "moral code memory." Warzones and battle can be morally ambiguous circumstances, and training soldiers in ways that cause moral and ethical decision-making to become habitual increases the chances that the soldiers will act ethically.

We're talking about a type of conditioned response much like the psychological conditioning law enforcement officers (like soldiers) go through

in training. Think of those police shows where we see our hero at the firing range—she's not shooting at a bulls-eye target, but rather a human-shaped silhouette. The next step is to put the officer in more dynamic situations or role-plays where she has to confront (and shoot) pop-up silhouettes. This conditioning makes the procedure a muscle memory—see a human-shaped target and shoot. Why? In order to overcome any ingrained disposition to not kill a fellow human. In our everyday life, we might assume that killing another human is not good, but in a shootout or on the battlefield, this assumption could get *us* killed. So repetitive drilling of what to do can be as much about quashing our natural hesitation to kill (or do something we've been raised to believe is unethical) as it is to do what we think is good. Minami's alter ego Airguard Oreas cannot hesitate to defeat the enemy.

So the weekly episodes of *Transdimensional Warriors Airguard* operate as a series of drills: Minami keeps practicing the same type of action over and over, that of being a hero, because it's in the script. Moral code memory and other psychological equivalents to muscle memory would suggest that doing the "right" thing becomes so ingrained as a result that when it comes time for him to confront an unscripted situation, Minami is more likely to act heroically, without even having to think about it.

Aristotle would be troubled by at least one aspect of this, though—the idea that the goal here is for moral or ethical action to become unthinking. If doing good has become so ingrained that Minami doesn't have to think about it, he's not really a good person, he's simply been conditioned to do what someone (a writer, a director) has told him is good. In fact, when Minami decides to not think about what he's doing in a scene, he's no longer mindful of the fight choreography (which is designed to look fierce without injuring the actors) and actually hits Sawada. To simply perform an act of being good without thinking doesn't make us good and in fact can result in something bad or someone getting hurt. It's the difference between result and process, and Aristotle would say that it's the process that we have to pay attention to.

All the Rage with Housewives and Young Girls

Aristotle believed that all of us, even Minami, are born with the potential to become virtuous. Even the modern criminal justice systems in Greece, Japan, and the USA are based on similar ideas that we're responsible for our choices and our actions, and therefore bad behavior can be rehabilitated—we can change. While it's been debated for centuries and considered from a number of different viewpoints, there's no consensus on whether we are born inherently good or bad or alternatively, whether we're a blank slate—a *tabula rasa*—

influenced by our context and upon which we write the choices and actions (or the world writes the circumstances) that make us good or bad. According to Greek mythology, the Fates actually determine at our birth the amount of good and evil in us; each person is different.

But Aristotle didn't see our state at birth as the stopping point but rather the beginning point. After all, if being good or bad is something innate and fixed within us, then no matter how much Minami might mimic the actions of a hero, a good person, those actions won't have any impact on his core nature. He's either born good or born bad, and any choices he makes are simply a reflection of the person he already is. Christianity sees mankind as basically and innately evil, a result of Original Sin, but we are encouraged to view Jesus's time on Earth as an example to be emulated (though we remain as marked as Sawada's lovers). Eastern religions and philosophies are a bit more optimistic about the nature of man, and while Confucius would believe in the general goodness within us all, he would also believe that regardless of that fact, an important aspect of living is to improve, to become better than we are. It's what we do with our goodness that's important, and Buddha and Confucius both lay out particular paths and practices to guide our development.

However, these questions of biology versus choice, fixed versus mutable, inherent versus situational, and nature versus nurture in relation to virtue make the fact that *Hero Heel* is a yaoi story even more resonant. Minami and Sawada are the perfect protagonists to struggle with these questions about goodness, because these are the very same questions that are debated about sexuality. Our feelings about one potentially make us consider the other in a different light, raising even more questions.

Aristotle—like Confucius—assumes that we can become better. While our degree of good or bad might be inherent, it's not fixed or unchangeable. Aristotle is not so much concerned with whether we're born good or born bad as with what we do once we're born, the decisions we make, and the actions we take—what we make of our potential to become virtuous.

Virtue is important to Aristotle because he sees it as the path to happiness, which he equates with living well, doing things well (virtue), and having family, friends, and community. Aristotle identifies three criteria that have to be met for someone to be truly virtuous. Applying these to Minami, they are:

1. that he must act knowingly or know that what he is doing is right;

2. that he has to choose these actions for their own sakes, to be virtuous;

3. that his actions cannot be the result of whim: Minami will have to act from a firm, fixed, and stable internal state or disposition.

When Minami realizes that he has met a gay person (Sawada) for the first time, he worries about his responses, feeling like he's "doing nothing but taking in what everyone tells me" (p. 71). Minami is beginning to get frustrated with the script society has handed him, and this is the first step that will help him move past examples (with their implication of telling him what to do), simple emulation, or unthinking muscle memory towards what Aristotle would consider the self-awareness and deliberation necessary to consciously do what is right for the sake of being virtuous. But it takes a while.

I'm Willing to Wait

When we first meet Minami, he's a spoiled brat who talks too much and sees a children's TV show as beneath him, even though he's been offered the lead. He dismisses the show as simple entertainment and its audience of girls and housewives (much like the readers of yaoi) as not worthy of his talent. The fact that it's the only acting job he can get doesn't make him any more appreciative or humble.

As he begins rehearsals and filming, he begins to realize that being a hero is harder than he thought. He fears something is missing and wonders if he'd be more of a hero if he liked his female costar Yuki-Chan—one of our first indicators that he's beginning to take his role seriously and wanting to be a better actor, though it's also an indicator of how far he has yet to go in understanding his own desires.

Despite having Oreas as an example and someone to emulate, Minami's actions are less consistent than his ideal, and he has yet to develop the stability of disposition to be truly virtuous. His first few attempts at trying to do the right thing in his unscripted life, such as lecturing Sawada on professionalism after catching him kissing a guy at work, are actually more rooted in his personal emotions than virtue, a fact not lost on Sawada, who

calls Minami a Peeping Tom since he wouldn't have seen the kiss if he hadn't been spying. Throughout this period of Minami's development, his actions fluctuate between what we might consider good and what are appallingly bad (such as coercing Sawada to have sex with him).

Being good does not come easy, and that's part of Aristotle's point—and the reason why we need to practice. Oreas's example may have helped Minami be able to recognize what actions are right, and his pretending to be Oreas on the TV screen may have allowed him to develop

certain habits through emulation, but he is now struggling to not just know the right thing to do but to do it knowingly. In this way, he begins to fulfill Aristotle's first criteria on the path to being virtuous.

Months later, when Minami lectures Sawada a second time, this time to treat his boyfriend better (in the panels above and to the left), Minami is acting solely from his knowledge of what's right and because it is right (Aristotle's second criteria).

Further evidence of Minami's growth is his awareness that he has been using his own boyfriend, Katagiri, to forget his feelings for Sawada. Instead of hiding or denying his actions, he chooses to be honest about them and to use his insight and awareness of them to forge a more loving relationship with Katagiri.

He is no longer the Minami we met on page 1, the self-absorbed actor wanting Sawada to notice him, to see him as an equal even though he didn't take the role seriously and was in no way (nor willing to work to be) Sawada's equal. His goals have changed through the course of his time on *Transdimensional Warriors Airguard*, till he wants only to work alongside Sawada as a fellow actor, accepting that they won't be lovers, and taking pride in the show by working to be a better actor. When he begins to better understand the consequences of his actions and take other people's feelings into account, we see just how far he has come. By the end, this journey has led him to a better understanding of himself, realizing that by being with Sawada, he has "the pain that he has wanted more than any other kind."

Minami is now a young man who is aware of others and makes active choices to do what's right, thereby fulfilling Aristotle's first two criteria—to do what he knows is right and to do it because it is right. The fact that he is more consistent, more constant in his disposition, signals that meeting the third criterion is within his reach.

The World's Not as Simple as It Seemed

If Minami has become a better person because he has played the role of a hero, what does that mean for Sawada? By reading his script each week, seeing Gadriel do bad things, and then emulating those through his performance, Sawada should be doomed—or at least predisposed—to become a villain in real life.

The problem is . . . that doesn't happen. What Minami interprets as Sawada's villainous behavior is more often an issue of context or perspective, of not understanding his intention or motivations.

As the reader, we know more about Sawada than Minami does, sometimes

maybe even more than Sawada does. Minami's initial assessment of Sawada as cold-hearted and hardly ever kind is pretty quickly dispelled when we see Sawada's generosity in performing a filmed fight sequence in such a way as to make an ill-prepared Minami look good on camera. When Sawada seems abrupt or harsh with Minami on set or about the show, it ultimately has the result of making Minami take his role more seriously, to become a better actor (and to become a better person).

Even one of Sawada's more problematic actions, his response to Minami's sexual coercion (part of which is seen in the excerpt on the previous page), seems in hindsight

to be about holding a mirror up to Minami's behavior, allowing him to fully experience the re-percussions of his threatened blackmail. This exchange is not about love, and Sawada makes sure Minami knows it. As a result, in the panels on this page, Minami realizes that he is not a good person, and his deeds are not those of a hero.

The show's producer, Aoki, points out early on that Minami is like Sawada was when he was younger, and this is our first

hint that Sawada is perhaps simply further along the journey that Minami is just embarking upon. When Minami compliments Sawada by saying he was great in his previous TV show, *Stone Beast Squadron Gorian*, Sawada has trouble taking the compliment, which could be modesty but could also be that he now recognizes some of his faults in his youth.

Though Minami might balk at this, at least at first, maybe Sawada is the example to be emulated: aware, self-assured, no-nonsense, and honest, open about his homosexuality in a way that surprises Minami and unwilling to put up with the immaturity and lack of focus that Minami initially succumbs to.

Sawada does confide in his boyfriend that he loves Minami but isn't going to tell him. He even tells Minami that he's not his type, but we later learn that Minami looks very much like Sawada's costar in *Gorian*, the man who broke Sawada's heart. Though in both of these cases it's not entirely clear whether he's doing this to protect his own feelings, it seems quite possible that he makes these decisions because he thinks it's what's best for Minami and the situation.

There's no question that Sawada's motivations can appear enigmatic, but it seems completely likely that by the end, we could interpret this story in such a way (as Tateno suggests in Scene 11) that Minami is indeed the villain who has made off with the hero's (Sawada's) heart.

The fact that Sawada was the hero in a previous TV show but is now the villain suggests that he may represent a fallen hero or an experienced and more complex hero. But going back to the idea that Sawada may be further along a similar journey of growth, perhaps Sawada is something like a sage, someone more practiced who is looking out for, guiding, and waiting for Minami to catch up to him. This is supported not just from Sawada's more confident and calm stillness at the opening press conference (when Minami just babbles) and his ability to see Minami's true self even better than he can, but also in Scene 1 when Sawada says to Minami: "I'm willing to wait for you to grow."

If we assume that being on *Transdimensional Warriors Airguard* has had a profound affect on Minami, why does Sawada seem basically unchanged? Perhaps it's because of this very point—Sawada's further along the journey, already well immersed in all three of Aristotle's criteria, particularly the third of a fixed and stable disposition. Minami's feelings and actions fluctuate rather wildly in *Hero Heel*, but Sawada's ultimately do not. He seems to operate from a pretty constant sense of himself and what actions he needs to take. That's not to say he's perfect—after all, Aristotle doesn't say "practice it until you get it right and then stop." He suggests that practice is life-long and that it takes work to maintain an unwavering and settled disposition wherein choosing to do what's right is deliberate and conscious.

Minami's change may seem so dramatic to us because he has the most distance to travel, tackling all three of Aristotle's criteria through the course of

the manga by learning what it means to be—and how to be—good through example, then emulation, and finally through action. Because he's someone who hasn't yet developed his potential for virtuous actions at the beginning of *Hero Heel*, maybe Minami is more susceptible to the influences of the role he plays.

In contrast, Sawada can play a villain and not become a worse person because he already knows what is right and chooses what's right for its own sake but more importantly because he has developed that firm, steady disposition that Aristotle says is necessary to be truly good. As a result, playing a bad guy doesn't make him one.

See, It's Not All That Special

Minami and Sawada are not the only people who act virtuously in *Hero Heel*, but it's their story that lies at its center. *Transdimensional Warriors Airguard* gives Minami plenty of opportunities to perform good actions, but it's also his interactions and relationship with Sawada that teach him about behaving virtuously, and for Aristotle, that's what's important. Minami has developed good habits through emulation and practice, but what makes him a better person, someone of character, is that he chooses good, he makes conscious choices, and by so doing, Aristotle would say that he is well on his way to finding happiness.

Traditional western storytelling, which in no small coincidence has one of Aristotle's other works (*Poetics*) as a touchstone, is built around notions of cause and effect, that our actions—our choices—have consequences, and that by making the right choices, the characters in stories can achieve their goals, be happy, and make their lives better. This is the heart of what some people refer to as redemptive drama—we can change; we can go against our nature as well as our past patterns of behavior.

"Happily ever after" takes on new meaning when we consider Aristotle's idea of happiness as the highest good, by which he means happiness as the fulfillment of one's human potentialities through the activity of the rational soul in accordance with virtue or excellence. Whether the result of advice, example, emulation, habit, conscious choice, or some combination of all of the above, if Minami can become a better person, then there's hope for all of us.

Aristotle would say that reading this chapter is no more likely to make you a better person than Minami reading his script each week. Learning to be virtuous is not something that we can figure out through reasoning, but only through experience. When *Transdimensional Warriors Airguard* ends, that's the important part. There are no more scripts. No director to tell Minami what to do. He's on his own, to make his own decisions.

I think he's ready. By doing the hard work of knowing what's right and choosing what's right from a developed and maintained stable disposition, Minami is better equipped and better able at the end of the series to live virtuously, to live happily through thoughtful habit and conscious choice. And in *Hero Heel*, he serves as our illustration of a journey that we could be taking towards such a happy life as well, showing us what's possible by example.

Now all that's left is to go practice.

16

Kenshin Is Not An Emo Pansy

DAISUKE MATSUURA

Ruroni Kenshin (Kenshin the drifter, widely known in the US as *Samurai X*) was an unusual success in *jidaigeki* or the historical-themed type of manga. Nearly fifty million copies had been sold in Japan by 2007.

When the series was first introduced to the United States in 2003, I constantly heard its title mentioned among American manga fans. In every *otaku* community I encountered, someone owned the *sakabatō* (reversed-edge sword). Every set of pictures from anime conventions included someone dressed like the main hero character, Kenshin. My personal experience with hardcore comic fans convinced me of their fascination with the comic series and demonstrated the significance of the show. Its historical backdrop—the time when a traditional Asian culture was radically merging with foreign cultures—stimulates readers' imaginations. Also, the main character's androgynous physique (a brown-haired *Gackt* look-alike with a weird sword) seems to attract and keep audiences.

Despite the attraction, *Ruroni Kenshin* is often disapproved of by some serious comic readers. They don't complain so much about the historic theme and androgynous look of the characters as they do about the main character's anti-heroic personality. Kenshin is often referred as "too naïve" to be a hero. One of the common criticisms of the series is that Kenshin is what might be called an "emo pansy." According to this argument, during the entire series Kenshin runs away from any form of commitment with others. Readers may notice that he thinks his own feelings, thoughts, and emotions are insignificant and worthless. Kenshin is regarded as a coward who cannot face his past and refuses to make any future decisions for himself. He's depressed about the loss of his first wife, Tomoe. Lastly, many fans seem to get annoyed by Kenshin's avoidance of Kaoru (whom later becomes his second wife) since he desperately believes that he is the source of all misfortune for everybody around him.

These characteristics reveal a main character who is perhaps more flawed and "real" than many characters in manga, which tends to foreground exceptional individuals. Is Kenshin really an "emo pansy" as many hardcore comic readers think? Or is there more to Kenshin? In order to answer these questions, we need to revisit the comic, analyzing Kenshin's personality in order to better understand what might lead others to see him as an emo pansy, and to offer a more complete way to think about his character by discussing two core facets of what is called the sense-making mechanism.

Are You Man Enough?

According to Encyclopedia Britannica, the word "emo" appeared first as a music subgenre of the 1980s punk rock scene, when some fans began listening to groups who favored lyrical themes dealing with personal pain and suffering. Dubbed "hard-core emotional" music, or simply "emocore," the lyrics in this genre often deal with topics such as the loss of loved ones or failed romances. Though eventually the word "emo" has come to indicate particular fashions and attitudes rather than music, the word still carries the connotation of this preoccupation with one's own torment.

When the word "pansy" is used in reference to a man, it is an insult to his masculinity. "You're a pansy" and "You're not *man* enough" are used synonymously, reflecting a severe patriarchal sexist way of thinking.

Put them together, and you get "emo pansy," a phrase generally applied to a person who wallows in self-pity by clinging to his traumatic memories, making him seem to be a weak coward or at the very least, an overly emotional—and therefore effeminate—man.

Despite what some fans think, Kenshin's personality does not fit either of these definitions—he is neither "emo" nor "pansy." Identified as one of the main characteristics of emo music, self-pity is not apologetic and does not seek redemption, is apathetic to the situations of others, neglects to accept others' helping hands since one desperately believes nothing can change the situation, and denies others' opinions.

This doesn't sound like Kenshin at all. He's a person who torments himself with feelings of guilt and laments about the sins he has committed. By going through these events and interacting with others, he integrates the concept of strength with a sense of service to others. He may carry trauma and guilt, but he always seeks redemption through his actions. He never rejects help from others when he's in trouble. And though he may have avoided staying in one place and developing intimate relationships, he never makes excuses for his personal problems.

A person who faces his issues and finds redemption cannot be considered a "pansy." Kenshin is not a weak person. He has traditional male strength demonstrated by the fact that he is a trained swordsman, and he continuously puts himself under pressure to subdue his personal issues. Dismissing Kenshin as an emo pansy seems to be hasty. Kenshin's character is determined by contemporary stereotypes, and the assumption that he is an emo pansy is biased by sexism.

Making Sense of Kenshin

For more than a century, social scientists have investigated how we gain our sense of identity and external reality through something called sense-making mechanisms. According to these scholars, we go through four interrelated phases to perceive reality. First, we notice changes in our environment. Second, we select our future action from a list of possibilities as a response to the changes. Third, we make the decision to take action. And finally, we preserve the quality of the action as a part of an event. Many scholars have agreed upon two major characteristics of this human sense-making mechanism: interdependency and retrospect. These two concepts in the sense-making mechanism seem to play central roles in explaining Kenshin's personality.

Interdependency means that our sense of "self" and of external reality are intimately interrelated with others. Karl Weick writes in *Making Sense of the Organization* that the formation of identity is based on reciprocal exchanges between individuals and through the selection of punctuations and connections with a continuously changing social context. Ronald Adler and Russell Proctor further articulate this idea in *Looking Out, Looking In*, stating that the way we see ourselves is determined by how we feel about our interaction with others. Without others' involvement and reactions, we cannot decide who we are and what we are.

If you were born and raised (and possibly survived) on a desert island, you may not have the words to describe any of your own feelings or thoughts because there is no one with whom to share those thoughts and feelings. You would not have any knowledge of social norm or the social skill to find your place in a populated setting. Social norms are the rules that tell us what behaviors are desirable, or not, within a particular social context. A person with few communication skills will lack social common sense, which consequently makes it difficult for this person to relate to others and to develop a sense of identity and relational satisfaction.

After the parents of young Kenshin (who was then called Shinta) died of illness, he was sold into slavery, and the girls he traveled with were killed one

night by Ronin burglars. Immediately following this horrific event, Kenshin was adopted by a retired swordsman and raised in the forest, mastering combat skills as he grew older and stronger. During this time the nation was divided into two factions with differing political standpoints: one was an antiforeigner faction that supported the Tokugawa shogunate government (the conservatives) and the other was an anti-isolation faction that supported imperial restoration (the liberals). Samurais assembled their forces to defend their own clans' political positions, which favored reinstating the imperial government. Young Kenshin quarreled with his master, departed from the forest for the first time, and joined the *Choushuu* clan's militia that supported this imperial restoration. He became a shadow assassin who eliminated conservatives from every street corner of Kyoto. Soon, he became to known as the fierce *Battousai*, the manslayer.

From the age of ten, Kenshin lived an isolated existence with his master in the forest and after leaving, Kenshin did not adapt well to society. As a shadow assassin, he stayed away from any casual contacts with common people in order to protect himself. He only communicated with his political allies and never interacted with others who shared different political ideas in order to avoid being prosecuted. He was not allowed to walk around the city of Kyoto freely, and he was always watched by his assigned clan. Kenshin had only minimal interactions with other soldiers. Conversations were expected to be concise and brief; thus his exposure to broader elements of social context and contemporary or popular culture was quite limited. All the communication he had with other members of the clan involved either assassination instructions or updates about political and civil warfare movements in the city and the nation. This kind of communication provides an extremely limited and specific social context.

These experiences result in Kenshin having skewed experiences of interacting with others. After leaving his isolated life in the forest, he slept, ate, and killed every day for three years while in downtown Kyoto. He developed an extremely narrow and limiting sense of community through those types of relationships. Because of Kenshin's lack of social experience with people, he failed to understand common life and to know appropriate ways to express his feelings and thoughts. He did not know effective ways to reach out to others. His unusual lifestyle certainly limited his social development, and this limitation is expressed in Kenshin's own testimony:

> I learned the principles of the *Hiten Mitsurugi Ryuu*, wielded a sword, killed all for an age in which the powerless could find happiness. But to tell the truth, up till now, I didn't know what happiness was. What I've come to fight for, and what I'll fight for from now on. . . . Living these five months in the country, with you, has taught me that. (Nabuhiro Watsuki, *Rurouni Kenshin* Volume 21, Tokyo: Shueisha, 1988, p.93)

Kenshin wasn't neglecting others like an "emo" person would do. Kenshin simply minimized his communication with others since he did not know how to relate to other people and did not share a commoner's outlook on life. Throughout the series, he chooses an extraordinary lifestyle. Though he suffers from the consequences of that lifestyle, he never gives up a strong sense of service to the others nor the quest for redemption for his past actions.

The function of interdependency in the sense-making mechanism is evidence that he is not an emo pansy. "Emo" is an unapologetic person who feels self-pity and rejects any co-operation from others to resolve a problematic situation. An individual who seeks resolutions for pressing issues, listens to others' opinions, and changes his own behaviors in order to reach the resolution is unlikely to be "emo." He is also different from a weak and cowardly "pansy" character, not only because of his swordsmanship and early role as an assassin, but because he admits his faults and seeks repentance in front of others. Kenshin never escapes or avoids his post-assassin traumas; instead, he is continually struggling to find a way to help usher in a better future for everyone.

Because of his childhood trauma, Kenshin develops a strong sense of justice. He tries to fight against various malefactors from street mobs to criminal syndicates in order to prevent the creation of another Kenshin. But he comes to realize that eliminating one criminal at a time will never wipe out the criminals in the nation. He blames society for the ultimate cause of the actions of individuals. The corruption of individuals is the product of the bad administration of the government. He develops a strong distrust for the contemporary socio-political system and believes that if the world changes, people will change. Kenshin says:

> A little more than a year ago, because I wanted to protect the happiness of the people of this country, I quarreled with my master and left him. For that reason, I wanted to end the conflict and open a new era. That's why I joined the *Choushuu*'s loyal supporter of emperor and became the manslayer. I believed that I could do this with the *Hiten Mitsurugi Ryuu*. (*Rurouni Kenshin*, Volume 21, p. 125)

The young mercenary samurai, Kenshin Himura soon becomes a fierce *Batousai*, the manslayer. However, Kenshin realizes that what he's dealing with are not the criminals, but people. He is essentially killing the believers of opposite ideas in order to make his ideas survive. Beneath the bodies and armors of enemies, his victims are human beings with ideas about the world, just as Kenshin has his own ideas. In killing his enemies and criminals, Kenshin could not stop people from having their own ideas. He becomes desperate, not knowing how to fight against ideas. In the midst of his inner struggle, the encounter with his first wife gradually changes Kenshin's notion of strength. Kenshin emotionally expresses his struggle to Tomoe:

I killed and killed, without bringing the new era one step closer. I was just a common murderer. I buried my feelings, but sometimes in my consciousness, the hazy smell of blood was never far away. That was when I met you. Your questions pierced the haze around me. My half-lost sanity returned to me. For the first time, I understood the seriousness of people's many different kinds of happiness. No matter how great the skill of the *Hiten Mitsurugi Ryuu*, no matter how I tried to raise my own skill, one man can't hope to change an era alone. And he certainly can't bear the burden of man's happiness alone. The only thing he can do is protect the happiness of the people he sees before him, one by one. (*Rurouni Kenshin*, Volume 21, pp. 126–27)

When Kenshin joined the *Choushuu* clan, he said, "If with my own dirty sword and the lives I take, I could pave the way for a new era in which all can live in peace" (*Rurouni Kenshin*, Volume 21, p. 160). Comparing this comment with Kenshin's earlier remarks, we can clearly see the conviction of his philosophy from the beginning. Through overcoming tragic events, including Tomoe's death, and through interactions with others, he has reconciled his contemporary concept of strength with his sense of service for others. Kenshin is a person who is driven to serve the people and willing to take risks to do so. He is neither an effeminate coward nor an apathetic self-centered person.

Many fans see Kenshin's feeling of guilt about his past as self-pity and, thus, evidence of Kenshin's angsty personality. Those fans claim that they didn't understand why he could not make different decisions to alter his tormented samurai life. Was Kenshin too much a coward to make life-altering decisions? Or was he just self-righteous? The answers to these questions seem to belie another core attribution of sense-making mechanism: retrospect.

Retrospect

Retrospect means that it is impossible for a human mind to live in the present moment without considering the past. In retrospect we can only see the present through the past. Let's go back to the four phases of sense-making processes. The first phase is knowing what is salient (or utterly unusual) in the surroundings. We need to rely on our memories of past events to compare. The realization of an unsettling gap between current circumstances and past experience will often make people reconsider the validity of their routine choice of responses towards certain situations, the credibility of their existing belief system, or their previous selection criteria for decision-making, and essentially their perceived identity. We consult with our past experiences to discern how we have accomplished what we have already done, and so we can determine our single best guess for future decisions. Finally, we remember the collection of incidents as our memories, and as evidence of what has happened.

Kenshin's attitudes towards his past life may seem at first to be self-pitying or focused too much on his traumas. However, according to the retrospect function of the sense-making mechanism, it's impossible for us to make decisions based on speculations other than those that grow out of our past experiences. Kenshin could not come up with ideas outside of his experience. He could *only* apply his knowledge from his own experience when faced with a variety of life situations. In order to make better decisions, he needs to go through a trial-and-error process that most people go through earlier in life.

Kenshin's comment, "But to tell the truth, up till now, I didn't know what happiness was," well represents the retrospect function of the sense-making mechanism (*Rurouni Kenshin*, Volume 21, p.93). Kenshin was traumatized from seeing the massacre of his loved ones when he was only a child. He joined the political organization and worked as a top assassin in order to make a "happy" life for people. Ironically, he never experienced "a normal happy life." His experience was limited to a life of training and killing. His experience and sense of social reference was to protect people from any physical threats, such as the traumatic incidences he experienced as a child.

You and I know that happiness is not exclusively established simply by eliminating physical threats. Kenshin could have taken other routes such as studying hard, reading books, being a local politician, or encouraging more economic equality among townsmen in order to decrease the amount of crime. But these possibilities don't occur to Kenshin because he has lived in isolation and has been exposed only to the life of a swordsman. He doesn't have the vocabulary to comprehend alternative choices to establish a common good among the people. He's not angsty; he's a product of his social environment. This argument is familiar. When we talk about "common good," some may say this means establishing social welfare, others may say tightening up national security, and some may say increasing economic activities within the market. All are aspects of "common good" for people; however, politicians primarily see the world from politicians' points of view, soldiers from soldiers', and economists from economists'. Kenshin was raised by a swordsman, pursued swordsmanship, and became a swordsman. He only could have contributed to "common good" from a swordsman's point of view.

After the civil war, Kenshin no longer wishes to be an assassin and decides to protect the citizens under the new government. He could have applied for a variety of professional security positions or worked for any national security institution as a commanding officer. However, Kenshin did not apply for any sort of newly found civil protection programs owned by the government. Here he was, a war hero who helped the liberals to take over the government and to establish the new government, and as such, he had plenty of opportunities. For instance, early in the manga, he sees one of his former allies, Yamagata, working

as a high-ranked officer in the police organization. He could have chosen a profession other than warrior in order to serve his community.

Instead, he decides to wander with his reversed-edge sword and protect the people of the community. In the community after the new era, the government strictly controls weaponry among citizens and founds police stations and military camps in each local community. The citizens are living in a safer environment than they have for a long time. Kenshin's service for the citizens is no longer necessary. Rather, a retired soldier with post-traumatic stress disorder walking around a safe environment with a sword seems to challenge the purpose of civil protection and provokes unnecessary struggles among the local community members.

Our retrospect function of the sense-making mechanism provides us insight as to why Kenshin made such an illogical choice. By the time the war ended, as it appeared in the manga, he was a front-line soldier. He did not know how the political system would be restored, nor what those political executives of the clan would decide after the bloody civil warfare ended. His association with politicians was primarily as an assassin and a warrior, limiting his experiences once again to a warrior's life. The retrospect function of the sense-making mechanism would not direct him toward a new way of thinking. He could only construct plausible visions of the future by taking into account what was "good" in his past. His assumptions of a "new good" still reside in the experiences of his past and can be heard when Kenshin notes that a new peace will arrive when the killing of individuals ceases.

Furthermore, Kenshin has no clue about systems of the new government, because he is not a politician and cannot apply any of his past experiences to speculate about future circumstances. He served as a hitman and as a soldier at the frontline; he knew he was expendable and insignificant in terms of the clan's political decisions. He was satisfied with serving for the clan and its manifesto. After the war ended, he *only* knew that through victory "peace" in the neighborhoods would be restored. Colonial American citizens after the revolutionary war knew they would be free, but they did not fully know how this concept of "freedom" would be manifested as a legal and social system. Likewise Kenshin doesn't know how "peace" will be actualized. He *only* knows that it will be different from the current situation.

The retrospect function in our sense-making mechanism suggests we cannot simply replace an old value with a new one. Instead, we can only start by seeking the similarities between the old values and the new values given our experiences, and modify the applicable old assumptions to the new system. Many soldiers who have been drafted or volunteered to serve in wars are normal civilians who gave up their jobs to fight. It is easier for them to come back and reopen their businesses after the war has ceased. Many others had to find new

jobs immediately by consulting with their possessed knowledge, skills, and the employers' needs, like college graduates.

Kenshin was originally born in the house of a farmer. As we see later in the series, Kenshin enjoyed farming while he was hiding in a village with Tomoe. He could have gone back to farming like other drafted soldiers, but he didn't. Even though he had the knowledge to be a farmer, Kenshin has been educated as an elite soldier since he was ten, and his entire social life and set of experiences were firmly anchored in a warrior's life. Retrospectively considering the amount of specialized knowledge he possessed by the end of the war, his skills as a soldier are significantly superior to his knowledge as a farmer. So, by using his experiences as a trained soldier, he decides to live as a protector of the neighborhoods.

However, when the new government introduced a different system, Kenshin did not know how to make a contribution, since he *only* knew a life based on *bushido*. He strongly disagreed with the nation governed by *bushido*; then he sought a new government system. Ironically, by destroying the system of *bushido*, he also destroyed the *only* way of living he had known, including his sense of national security and civil duty. His identity as a warrior was still tied to that system. In the new government system, Kenshin's way of living and sense of duty as a citizen are old-fashioned. Thus, he becomes a *ruroni* (drifter) and wanders around the nation as a ghost from past.

Behind the Man

In reference to the core aspects of sense-making mechanism, Kenshin's personality seems to be far from a person who has "emo pansy" traits. Such a label reduces Kenshin to a stereotype. Rather, Kenshin is a man who is a product of his society. He tries to make everyone happy by using his skill as a warrior. It seems almost humorous how the retrospect functions of the sense-making mechanism influence Kenshin's decision-making. However, he certainly shows us that what we become is heavily constituted by each choice we make in any moment of our life, and how these choices are shaped by our sense-making mechanisms.

In today's world we believe a sophisticated person should make good and fair decisions in any circumstances. However, our sense-making mechanisms, which provide the foundation for our view of the world, shape our perceptions in ways that make truly innovative decisions difficult and uncertain. We assume our present and future are based on past experiences; however, there's no guarantee of desired consequences, and in radically new circumstances these experiences may not prepare us properly for the decisions we must make. Seemingly beneficial events in one social context will not always yield

beneficial future consequences. Those who find themselves in unfamiliar social contexts may not know how to behave, and as a result, to some they may appear as emo pansies. But Kenshin demonstrates that people are more complex than the stereotypes applied to them, that how we appear to others isn't always who we are.

17

Showing the World the Right Path

GORDON HAWKES

*W*hile we don't know how many years exactly Aristotle lived before year After Colony 195, his insights might just as well have been written in the shadow of the space colonies as in the shadow of the Parthenon.

The story of *Gundam Wing* is characterized by moral struggle, by the characters trying to find the right path. To further complicate matters, the good guys aren't all goodness, and the bad guys aren't all badness. The main characters are dynamic, and they grow confused, at times, as to what the right thing to do is. Suffice to say, they aren't Adam West's Batman. As Trowa says to Quatre, after Quatre almost kills him in "Quatre vs. Heero" (Episode 25 of the anime): "We have to fight with ourselves, within our hearts, and we have to do it harshly, in order to come to the right conclusions."

But it would seem not everyone understands *Gundam Wing*. Two reviewers from separate fansites, VivisQueen and Shadowmage, accuse the series of hypocrisy. "Despite being 'anti-war'," *Gundam Wing* "hypocritically and incessantly preaches peace while resolving everything with explosions," writes Shadowmage. VivisQueen echoes this sentiment when she writes that there is an "inherent contradiction of *Gundam Wing's* pacifist theme." Three points must be taken into consideration when answering this accusation.

First, the fact that certain characters in the manga, like Relena Peacecraft, pontificate about pacifism doesn't mean that the manga itself is promoting pacifism. This point may be obvious, but it needs to be said. Characters contradict each other in the manga throughout, and it's not enough to point to one character's words and claim them as the message behind the entire work. For instance, Dorothy Dermail says at one point, "Pacifism is nothing more than an ideal, Miss Relena. Humans can only live through fighting!" Are we to suppose the writers have contradicted themselves, or are they doing what any writer does, namely, writing characters who have different, sometimes opposing, perspectives and allowing the reader to discern who is right and

who is wrong within the context of the story? It goes without saying that it is the latter. However, in all fairness, this point does not prove that pacifism is not the message of the show, although it addresses the error that the reviewers might be guilty of.

Second, one can't help but suspect that VivisQueen and Shadowmage are missing the point of *Gundam Wing*. Neither critic seems to recognize the possibility that the power-hungry warmongers *and* the pacifists are wrong within the context of the story. This would mean that the Gundam pilots are *between* the two sides, not on one side or the other. Part of the beauty of the manga is that the main characters are dynamic and develop over the course of the story. The Gundam pilots struggle through the consequences of their actions as soldiers (for example, when Heero is distraught over killing Field Marshall Noventa), a profession that is by its very nature opposed to pacifism, and they agonize at points over what is the right action to take (such as Heero deciding whether or not to self-detonate). Thus, the words of pacifists like Relena are put forward in the story, not necessarily as the overall message that the writers want to convey, but rather as part of the exploration of difficult questions surrounding warfare and the struggle for peace in human existence. If the writers meant to have a pacifist moral, then they made a terrible decision having five mobile suit warriors as the heroes of the story.

Third, to VivisQueen and Shadowmage's credit, their criticism reveals an awareness, whether explicit or not, that every story has a moral framework, within which actions are shown to be right or wrong. This moral framework provides the standard by which actions are judged, but it also allows for ideologies and beliefs to be judged from within the story as well, or from what is called an "in-universe" perspective. (VivisQueen and Shadowmage believe pacifism to be the "right" position from the *Gundam Wing* in-universe perspective.) A moral framework can be very "black-and-white," as in the old, 1950s cowboy westerns where the straight-laced, clean-cut good guys wore white hats and the dirty, rotten bad guys wore black; or it can be very ambiguous and grey, as in *Bleach*. A moral framework does not necessarily match reality, which is why we can read a manga like *Afro Samurai* and accept Afro's killings in the story but not accept this kind of thing in the real world.

The presence of moral frameworks in stories can be very subtle and we are seldom conscious of them when engrossed in the story itself. We read *Afro Samurai* and don't stop to think about whether we believe killing others to be wrong, we just accept it within the context of the story as justified, and we support the protagonist as he commits murder after murder. Likewise, VivisQueen and Shadowmage assume that in *Gundam Wing* pacifism is justified, and the writers are contradicting the "in-universe" moral framework of *Gundam Wing* by having the protagonists solve every problem with a

beam sword and buster rifle. Therefore, the criticism that *Gundam Wing* has an "inherent contradiction" in its "pacifist theme" hangs on whether or not pacifism is actually justified by *Gundam Wing's* moral framework.

If I Don't Fight, Who Will?

It is understandable that VivisQueen and Shadowmage would get the impression that *Gundam Wing* has a pacifist theme. One of the central characters, Relena Peacecraft, is shown to be a very strong character who makes a powerful pacifist stand against the Romefeller Foundation and OZ, consistently declaring both the injustice of war and the ideal of disarmament and peace. Because she is protected all throughout the story by the Gundam pilots and others, it appears she has their support. But their support doesn't necessarily translate to agreement with her ideology.

First, and most obvious of all, the protagonists of the story are five Gundam pilots who are highly specialized soldiers, whose mission is one thing and one thing only: destroy the enemy. By virtue of pursuing their mission, they tacitly disagree with the pacifist position. The very act of fighting makes them, in practice, *not* pacifists. Even within the pacifist Sanc Kingdom, the pilots, along with Lucrezia Noin, organized secretly to defend it against OZ and Romefeller with force, expressly against both Relena's orders and her pacifist position.

Second, it's not only the actions, but also the words of the pilots and other characters that reveal their disagreement with pacifist principles. Lucrezia Noin, in response to Relena's stand against Romefeller, says, "I don't believe absolute pacifism works the way Miss Relena hopes it would." Mr. Winner, Quatre's father, is depicted in the manga as a near-deranged fanatic who, no matter the cost, will not fight against OZ. He commands Quatre not to fight as well, to which the son replies, "If I don't fight, who will?" And Quatre's sister, Ilea, supports him saying, "Quatre fights for the good of the colonies, like you do, [Father]." When Relena becomes the queen of the world nation and calls for disarmament of the entire earth sphere, Heero says (after deciding not to kill her!), "Good luck. I'm off to space to *fight* the enemies of your peace [emphasis mine]."

As far as pacifism working in *Gundam Wing*, the plot distinctly shows pacifism as *not* working, or bringing about peace of the right kind. (The passive acceptance of the oppression of OZ could not be described as a good, harmonious peace.) Every time the pacifists take a stand, they are either defended by someone, or they are crushed. For example, when the pacifist Sanc Kingdom is attacked, Heero saves the day in the Epyon mobile suit;

and Mr. Winner, who had openly opposed OZ with his pacifist views, was murdered through a cunning ploy. While the manga and the anime differ over the depiction of Mr. Winner's character, both have his pacifist stand against OZ ending in his death. The implication seems to be pretty strong that a pacifist stand against a military organization willing to crush anything in its path will only result in crushed pacifists.

So it may be, as I've argued, that pacifism is not justified in the *Gundam Wing* universe. But that raises the question: What is? Furthermore, beyond the specific issue of pacifism, what's the moral framework of *Gundam Wing*?

The concept of a moral framework needs to be clarified briefly. This framework could be described as the big picture of all the smaller pieces of the moral puzzle. It's the sum of all the specific moral rights and wrongs into an overall system. Beyond that, though, it is not necessarily just a collection of individual "This is right, that is wrong" statements. It's also the system by which actions are determined to be right and wrong. A moral framework in a story is roughly equivalent to what philosophers call a system of ethics. The difference, however, is that a moral framework describes a story, or what J.R.R. Tolkien would call a "secondary reality," a created world which we look at from the outside in;[1] whereas a system of ethics seeks to describe reality, from our perspective, looking from the inside out. In seeking to describe the moral framework of *Gundam Wing* we're seeking to describe the world that Yoshiyuki Tomino and Hajime Yatate created. We can hold all three volumes of the manga in our hands, with its carefully contained universe inside the black-inked borders on each page. We don't have the same luxury with reality.

An example of a well-known ethical system would be the existentialism of Jean-Paul Sartre (1905–1980), in which we cannot know objectively what is right or wrong. While Sartre's system is more nuanced than that, the basics are evident in popular culture. Who hasn't heard the refrain, "How do *you* know what is right and what is wrong?" However, before the existentialism of Sartre and others, there were philosophers who believed that we could figure out an ethical system as a means of guiding us in how to live. We can take these ethical systems, which are philosophers' attempts to describe how we determine right and wrong in reality, and see if they accurately describe the moral framework of a story—in this case, *Gundam Wing*.

Three of the most significant moral thinkers in the history of philosophy are Aristotle (384–322 B.C.), Immanuel Kant (1724–1804), and John Stuart Mill (1806–1873). Not only did each philosopher fashion a unique ethical system, each of their systems corresponds to one of the three major approaches to ethics—virtue ethics, deontological ethics, and consequentialism.

---

[1] See J. R. R. Tolkien's essay "On Fairy-Stories" in *The Tolkien Reader* for more on this.

John Stuart Mill-iardo

John Stuart Mill inherited the basic principles of utilitarianism from Jeremy Bentham (1748–1832), his teacher and colleague. However, Mill revised and expanded the system of his teacher in the book *Utilitarianism* and created a more sophisticated and nuanced philosophy, which makes him a better representative than Bentham.

Utilitarianism has as its guiding principle, utility, or the "Greatest Happiness Principle," which "holds that actions are right in proportion as they tend to promote happiness, wrong as they tend to produce the reverse of happiness." (Happiness, for Mill, is directly equivalent to pleasure.) As a result, the emphasis of utilitarianism is on the consequences of actions, not the actions themselves. For instance, a person attempting to live by utilitarian principles, if faced with an opportunity to lie, would not think, Is lying wrong? but rather, Would lying bring happiness? In most cases it would appear that lying only creates more pain than pleasure, but there are foreseeable circumstances where the opposite might be true. It's for this reason that utilitarianism can be summarized with the phrase, "the ends justify the means."

This, however, does not allow the individual to do whatever he wants regardless of anyone else, because, according to Mill, happiness, in this context, "is not the agent's own greatest happiness, but the greatest amount of happiness altogether" (*Utilitarianism*, p. 17). This means that a serial killer who gained pleasure from killing his victims would be wrong insofar as the pleasure he gained was less than the pain he caused everyone else.

This raises the question of actions which are generally considered right but which we also know cause pain, like punishing a child. In that case, the initial pain (the punishment) could be argued to be outweighed by the pleasure later, say, of the good habits the child will develop through discipline. All actions, then, are considered based on their consequences, and a sort of calculation must be made to determine what is best. (However, unlike Bentham before him, Mill moved away from considering pleasure only in terms of quantity, and considered also quality by making a distinction between higher and lower pleasures.)

Therefore, if *Gundam Wing* has a utilitarian moral framework then there will be evidence of the ends justifying the means in the actions of characters in the story. Also, the emphasis will be on the consequences of actions, not on the actions themselves.

Only Someone from OZ Could Think Like That, Zechs

Looking at *Gundam Wing* for examples of actions done according to utilitarian principles—the end justifies the means—there seems to be one group of

characters that distinctly epitomizes the utilitarian moral approach: OZ and Romefeller. Lady Une gives a speech to the space colonies urging them to embrace OZ in place of the "oppressive" United Earth-Sphere Alliance (UESA), but her own words make it clear that she does so merely in order to gain control for OZ. She says, "The people of the colonies sure are easy to fool. Little do they realize, control will only change from UESA to OZ." Likewise, Treize is willing to send his own friend, the Lightning Count, Zechs Merquise, to his death for a political cause; he also kills General Septum, and sends Field Marshall Noventa to his death, both in order to aid OZ in its *coup d'état*.

In probably one of the most striking examples of utilitarian principles in action, Milliardo Peacecraft (Zechs Merquise), as leader of the White Fang, declares their "intent to destroy the source of war, the reason for pain and suffering in the colonies: the very earth itself!" Later, in a surprise twist, Zechs reveals that he and Treize are aiming to give the world pacifism through destroying most of the weapons of war in the epic "Final Battle." During his battle with Heero, Zechs says, "Pacifism is never possible when you still have a military force available." To which Heero significantly replies, "Only someone from OZ could think like that, Zechs." Also, Treize explains the utilitarian motivation behind starting the epic battle with White Fang to Wufei: "I had to do this in order to end the foolish cycle of war that humanity so loves." All of the above examples portray actions undertaken for which the end justified the means. Lady Une, Treize, and Milliardo are thinking only of the goal they have in mind, not the actions themselves.

But aren't all the previous examples actions which would be *wrong* according to utilitarianism? This is a fair question. In order to answer it, we must look at the situation and calculate whether the actions would bring about the most happiness or not. All of the previous examples involve a lot of pain, but remember that pain can be involved in a "right" utilitarian action, so long as the pain is outweighed by the pleasure. However, it must be allowed that from the perspective of Une, Treize, and Milliardo—especially Milliardo—they could argue that what they're doing is to bring about the greatest happiness for the greatest number. Milliardo makes his belief that this is what he is doing explicit. He seeks to "destroy . . . the reason for pain and suffering in the colonies," and says simply regarding his actions, "I know what I'm doing is right."

Another objection is that there are no examples involving the Gundam pilots. The actions of the pilots are especially relevant to the discussion as they are the heroes of the story, the characters that we are—it's safe to assume without begging the question—meant to cheer for and admire. However, this objection is easily answered. A key example of a Gundam pilot acting on utilitarian principles is Heero's attempt to kill Relena. When she first spots him washed up on the beach, he pulls out a gun to kill her because he thinks

she has compromised his mission . . . only to be thwarted by Duo Maxwell in what is arguably the funniest scene in the manga. (Duo: "Hey, wait a minute. . . . I'm the bad guy here?") Also, the Gundam pilots do things that are both admirable and praiseworthy, but not according to utilitarian principles. Heero self-detonates his Gundam in response to what he thinks are Dr. J's orders, an action which places the emphasis on duty, not consequences. And Trowa sacrifices himself to save Heero from the insane Quatre, when the zero system had taken him over. Mill tries to explain altruistic action based on utilitarian principles, but these actions demonstrate a sense of duty, not choice based on what will bring about the most happiness.

One last example should be given as evidence that Gundam Wing does not possess a utilitarian moral framework. Immediately following OZ's *coup d'état*, Lady Une thinks nothing of blowing up an entire space colony in order to get the Gundam pilots to surrender. Assuming the end justifies the means, then Lady Une's mass murder of innocent civilians could be considered acceptable, if the end were right. But it is clear that it could never be acceptable, no matter the end. There is one instant and universal reaction: what she has done is a great evil. Even Zechs, who is also part of OZ, is outraged, saying, "Lady Une, what the hell did you just do?" The implication is clear: there are some actions for which the end does not justify the means. In other words, there are actions which are wrong regardless of other considerations.

I'm Sorry, Heero, but I'm Afraid I Kant Do That

When an action is considered right or wrong regardless of any qualifications or other considerations, it's what philosophers call an objective, or universal, moral value. It's a standard which is not relative, and which is the same for all people, all cultures, at all times. It's these universal moral standards to which Kant's ethics appeal. This opens the door for the possibility, since we have seen some evidence for there being objective, universal standards in *Gundam Wing*, that Kant's ethics provide the moral framework for this manga.

The emphasis in utilitarian ethics is on the consequence of an action— an action is right if it brings about the greatest happiness. Kant's ethics are, in this way, the opposite of Mill's. Kant places all the emphasis on the action, to the point where the consequences don't matter. Kant maintains that there are objective, universal moral standards and that we can *know* these standards. "It's always wrong to torture children" is a possible example of one of these standards.

In response to the inevitable question, How do we know these standards? Kant argues that they are *a priori* knowledge, by which is meant knowledge

that we have "prior to experience." In other words, even though every person in the world has a unique cultural, religious, and family background, every person would have the same *a priori* moral knowledge.

In Kant's moral framework, then, we are able to say of actions, like that of Lady Une when she blows up the space colony, that they are objectively wrong (or right). Following this, Kant judges an action as right when it is done in accordance with the *a priori* moral knowledge, but also for the sake of duty. Duty is an important concept in Kant's ethics because the good will is that which acts for the sake of duty.

Obviously we don't know universal standards for what to do in every particular situation, like, say, when a giant, manned robot comes walking into your living room with a beam sword ("You should always scream and run away"). But Kant would not say we need to know a universal standard for every particular situation. Instead, he says that we should act in such a way that we would will our action in that particular situation to be a universal law. This is what Kant called the Categorical Imperative. For instance, Kant famously argued that lying is never right, even if it meant surrendering innocent people to be killed. But he willed that that action (telling the truth) ought to be a universal law, according to his categorical imperative.

If Kant's ethics provide the moral framework for *Gundam Wing*, we will see evidence for characters following universal maxims, and actions following the universal maxims will be right and those disobeying them will be wrong.

Kant Is Not in a Gundam Pilot's Dictionary

Heero and Trowa sacrificing themselves are good examples of actions motivated by duty. Heero may have pressed his self-detonation button thinking, "It's always right to follow the orders of a superior in combat." And Trowa may have acted on the maxim, "It's always right to protect your friends, even to the point of self-sacrifice."

However, Kant's ethics do not necessarily characterize the moral choices of the Gundam pilots. For instance, Trowa lies to Lady Une and decieves OZ in order to infiltrate the organization. The other Gundam pilots, when they realize what he is doing, support his actions, and Heero even fights alongside him for OZ, against Quatre, of all people. Trowa goes against Kant's principles, since Kant argued that lying is always wrong. But someone could say that the absolute prohibition of lying was a very particular part of Kant's personal ethics, and that the broader scope of Kant's ethics could still be the moral framework for *Gundam Wing*. Kant's ethics do indeed have a strong presence in the manga and, similar to Mill's ethics, are represented by a specific group: the pacifists.

The pacifists, who are represented by Relena and Mr. Winner, appear to follow a universal maxim that they are adamant others follow as well, which is explicitly articulated by both Heero and Relena. Just prior to the Final Battle, Relena upbraids her brother, Milliardo: "This course of action . . . your choice . . . it's wrong. Because we're both of the Peacecraft family, war is never the answer." Echoing Relena's words, Heero, subtly mocking Milliardo's utilitarian reasoning for starting the epic space conflict, says to the former Lightning Count, "Besides, what would your sister say? 'Peace should never be achieved through war,' right?" Kant's ethics are not supported by this example.

There is a strong sense that all of the Gundam pilots follow their duty, which is their mission to defeat their enemies, but following abstract standards regardless of particular contexts doesn't seem to characterize their actions. The Gundam pilots, unlike the pacifists, are more fluid.

The Nicho-MECHA-ean Ethics

Mill's ethics are concerned with the consequences of actions, and Kant's, with the actions themselves. Aristotle's ethics are concerned with character.

A "right" action, for Aristotle, is that which is conducive to man's good and a "wrong" action is that which is not conducive to man's good. Man's ultimate good, Aristotle says, is happiness, based on the fact that all men aim at happiness in all they do. But happiness for Aristotle is not just pleasure, as for Mill, but rather it's an *activity*, specifically, activity "in accordance with virtue." Virtue, for Aristotle, is to be understood as both moral and intellectual. Man starts out with a capacity for good character, but it must be developed through practice by doing virtuous acts. It's this habit of virtuous action, this virtuous character, which is essential to man's good, or happiness.

Aristotle does not exclude the idea of pleasure from happiness, but rather says that virtuous activity will naturally be accompanied by pleasure. Contrary to Mill, though, Aristotle disagrees that pleasure is man's good. Other external goods, like peace, health, money, and friends, also are necessary for happiness, because they allow for the activity to take place freely.

Aristotle's ethics are aimed at the good (which he believes to be happiness). Unlike Kant, Aristotle is not concerned with actions as right or wrong regardless of any other consideration, such as context, but unlike Mill, he still recognizes objective standards for right and wrong action. Aristotle bases these objective standards on what he believed to be universally recognized principles, discernable by intuition and reason.

If *Gundam Wing* has an Aristotelian moral framework, then actions which are to be considered right within the context of the story will be aimed at the

good; the end will not justify the means because objective standards will still be present; and instead of the emphasis being on the action being right or wrong in itself, or characters being bound by rigid rules, virtue will be emphasized.

If You're Weak, Fight to Get Stronger

In *Gundam Wing*, utilitarian ethics are represented by OZ and Romefeller, and Kant's ethics are represented by the pacifists. Both groups prove to be mistaken in their views and actions, and, by extension, their respective ethics do not provide the moral framework of the manga. This leaves only Aristotle's ethics, and the group that represents this third approach to ethics is none other than the heroes of the manga, the Gundam pilots.

The five boys from space can legitimately be the litmus test for the moral framework of *Gundam Wing* because they are the heroes. Aside from the fact that the manga draws us into supporting them, they are the group that is consistently portrayed as justified. They win in the end. Those that opposed them lose. It's their faces on the cover of every volume. So if Aristotle's ethics can be shown to characterize their actions, then Aristotle's ethics would provide the moral framework of the manga.

The Gundam pilots are always aimed at the good, which, in the context of *Gundam Wing* and given their roles as soldiers, largely means acting justly through seeking peace from the oppression of OZ and Romefeller. As Wufei defiantly exclaims, "I fight on the side of Nataku (his gundam): Justice." Dr. J explains to Relena, "Heero is fighting for peace." And Quatre's sister, Ilea, says to their pacifist father, "He's fighting for peace just like you father." Even when the colonies abandon them in their fight against the tyranny and oppression of OZ, the pilots continue to seek the good, which shows that their actions are not only dictated by orders from above, but also from a clear idea of what it is they seek after.

Unlike the utilitarian OZ and Romefeller, though, the end would not justify the means. This is clear from Quatre's statement in response to Milliardo's speech detailing White Fang's plan to destroy pain and suffering through destroying Earth. "I agree with what he wants, but his methods won't solve anything." There are objective standards behind the actions of the pilots. They speak of "justice" and "mercy." They believe killing innocent people is wrong, as evidenced by their reaction to Lady Une's destruction of a space colony, and by Heero's reaction to mistakenly killing the innocent pacifist leader, Field Marshall Noventa. And Wufei righteously declares that he "will wipe out all evil in the earth sphere."

More important, however, than any of the previous considerations, there is a repeated emphasis on virtue in the Gundam pilots. Duo Maxwell says to the unsuccessful OZ Gundam pilot, Trant, who is arrogant as to his own abilities,

"There's no way you're prepared to pilot a Gundam unless you're prepared to give your life for what you believe in." There is a strong sense that piloting the Gundam is dependent on character, or on having attained a certain level of virtue. This is further supported by Trant's own words after a failed flight attempt in Wing Zero. He asks weakly in dismay and disbelief at his failure, "Why? . . . I'm worthy . . ."

After Wufei loses to Treize in a duel, he is crushed in spirit and feels unworthy to pilot his Gundam, Nataku. He even calls himself "weak" and a "coward." (His despairing thought, "I don't deserve to pilot Nataku," further points to the idea of piloting Gundam being dependent on character.) Later, in response to Wufei's unwillingness to fight, Duo gives a very Aristotelian, albeit angry, response, which illustrates perfectly Aristotle's concept of developing virtue through doing virtuous acts. "Snap out of it, damn it! If you're weak, fight to get stronger! If you're weak, rely on the strength of others until you're strong again."

Echoing this, there is a subtle, yet poignant, example in the Final Battle action sequence of the Aristotelian concept of aiming at the good, and acting according to what you know to be right in order to achieve virtue. Heero knows Milliardo to be wrong in his utilitarian attempt to end war through (paradoxically) war, hence his screaming rebuke, "You claim to be fighting for the weak, but you're wrong!" and so he fights against him. But before he heads off to their climactic duel, Heero says, "Unless I beat him, I can't end this war . . . or the battle within myself." Heero's actions are very much motivated by their effect on his character, beyond them being right in themselves.

The five gundam pilots are more than just an example of people developing virtue, they are also an example of Aristotle's virtuous man, whose actions flow *from* virtue, because of acquired habit. In the scene where Quatre is temporarily insane due to the evil zero system in Wing Zero, he raises the buster rifle to kill Heero, but Trowa pushes Heero out of the way and is apparently killed himself. Similarly, Quatre later saves Trowa's life by pushing him out of the line of fire and taking the blow himself. Both of these examples reveal a knee-jerk reaction done without conscious thought, simply because they were the right thing to do. The man who has become virtuous would act in a like manner in all areas, acting *from* virtue without even thinking about it.

Those Boys . . . Will Show the World the Right Path

Aristotle's ethics do appear to describe accurately the moral framework of *Gundam Wing*. And a deeper understanding of Aristotle's concept of virtue gives the reader further insight into the actions of Heero, Duo, Trowa, Quatre, and Wufei.

When we think of a virtue, we think of it being opposite a corresponding vice. Courage, for instance, would be opposite cowardice. But Aristotle

argued that a virtue is not opposite *one* vice, but *two*. For instance, Wufei called himself a coward because he did not have enough courage to stay and continue fighting Treize during their first duel. But there is an instance where a mobile suit pilot had *too much* "courage." Lt. Trant, the foolish OZ Gundam pilot, rushed into battle with Wing Zero without the proper training and it ended up costing him his life. This is called rashness. Courage then is not only opposite cowardice, but rashness also. There are two extremes, one of deficiency and one of excess, and the virtue is in between them, as illustrated in the following diagram:

COWARDICE—COURAGE—RASHNESS

The Gundam pilots are a good example of this insight. In between the two extremes of war-mongering despots on one side and total pacifists on the other, the five space colony defenders must navigate their way down the middle. This seems to be alluded to, intentionally or not, by Lady Une, who says to Treize, repeating his own sentiment: "Indeed, your Excellency, those boys . . . will show the world the right path."

Aristotle said that the location of the virtue in between the two extremes is not necessarily the exact middle. The location must be determined using practical reason based on the situation. In one case it may be better to err on the side of deficiency of the virtue, in another, excess. In the case of courage, when one is piloting a Leo-model mobile suit versus a Gundam-type, it might be better to err on the side of cowardice and run away. In the case of generosity when one is rich, it might be better to err on the side of excess, and give too much away. This last point helps to clarify the solution to the "hypocrisy" dilemma which has confused some critics, or the idea that *Gundam Wing* is pacifist in its moral framework, which makes all the fighting hypocritical. The pilots are not pacifists, but it makes a lot of sense that they would err on the side of the pacifists rather than on the side of the military organizations. Yet they are still in the "middle" of the two erroneous extremes.

18

The Brink of Extinction

ASHLEY BARKMAN

"*W*hat's your sign?" is perhaps the most clichéd pick-up line in circulation—so clichéd, in fact, that this retro line is actually making a comeback. Although astrology pervades North American culture—it's a constant in any fashion or celebrity gossip magazine—skepticism is a more common reaction amongst westerners. For Koreans, however, one's zodiac sign based on Chinese astrology or personality associated with one's blood type is no laughing matter. For the young and old, friend or new acquaintance, the shamanistic question "What's your sign?" or the Daoist question "What's your blood type?" are not only standard enquiries for people getting to know one another, but are often justifications for one's disposition.

One of the ironies of the situation is that Christianity, a religion that makes exclusivist claims to the ruling out of other religions, is the dominant belief system in Korea with more than a third of its population being either Protestant or Catholic. Christianity is a fairly new religion in Korea, Catholicism having reached Korea in 1784 and Protestantism a hundred years later; nevertheless, its influence is strong: Korea, with just under fifty million people, sends the second largest number of missionaries abroad, second only to the US (which has a population six times the size of Korea). Although these statistics show that Korean Christians put their money where their mouths are, astrology, fortunetelling, palm-reading, and other occult arts are such a deeply ingrained part of Korean culture that even with the biblical admonition that such are an abomination to God (Deuteronomy 18:10–11), Korean Christians—insofar as they are still Korean—have a hard time avoiding them.

Korean culture is historically rooted in Neo-Confucianism, which is a mixture of shamanistic, Daoist, Mahayana Buddhist, and, of course, Confucian religio-philosophical beliefs. This philosophy thrives alongside Christianity in Korea, perhaps an inevitable fate of living in a postmodern global village, where peoples and beliefs meet and merge with the frequent result of diluting beliefs, softening ideas, and generating a greater tolerance of contradictions. And so

what we find is that the contemporary Korean ethos remains heavily influenced, in all its inconsistent "glory," by these five religio-philosophical traditions, all of which are successfully reflected, largely through animal conservation, in Sang-Sun Park's *manhwa* (Korean *manga*) *Ark Angels*.

Ark and Angels: A Christian Template

The title of Park's trilogy immediately conveys its Judeo-Christian influence. Playing on the homonymic "archangels," *Ark Angels* simultaneously connotes the idea of high-ranking angels, as well as evoking the story of the great biblical deluge. Park ascribes the names of Noah's three sons to her heroines, a *sentai* of angelical, magical sisters—Shem, Hamu, and Japheth ("Hamu" is a Korean transliteration of "Ham")—whose father is also named Noah.

Though limited, a few minor parallels exist between the biblical brothers and *Ark Angels'* sisters. First, there is the birth order. In the Bible, Shem, Ham and Japheth are consistently listed in that order, often misleading readers into assuming—contrary to modern scholarship—that this reflects birth order. Park appears to have followed the convention and made this misassumption as well, making Japheth the youngest sister, as well as the narrator. Second, there are the characteristics of the individuals. In the Bible, Shem and Japheth are respectful to their father and so receive his blessing, while Ham is impertinent and so is cursed. In *Ark Angels*, Shem and Japheth are described as kind and serious, while Hamu is labeled a complainer and a misandrist.

As for the story itself, the three magical sisters are sent from a parallel universe to Earth with a mission to rescue endangered species and to preserve them in a flying whale-shaped ark named "Noah's Ark." Once—or more correctly, *if*—Earth is restored to its Edenic state, the animals will then be returned.

This idea of a future Edenic Earth echoes Isaiah11:6 and 65:25, which describes the new Heaven and Earth, wherein predators and prey are released from their earthly roles and harmony exists between all creatures. In Christian terms, Christ's death and resurrection is the portal by which this New Heaven and New Earth are established, and the well-known story of Jonah and the whale is considered one of the prophetic messages of Christ's suffering that leads to his eventual victory over death. In this way, the whale-shaped ark in *Ark Angels* is likely a tribute not only to the prophet Jonah, who was saved from drowning by being swallowed by a whale and dwelling in its belly for three days, but also to Christ, whose three days in Hades is foreshadowed in the Jonah narrative (Jonah 1:17; Mat. 12:39–41). Just as Jonah's life is sustained by the whale and all people are sustained by Christ's death, so are the endangered

species in *Ark Angels* preserved in the whale, mobilizing the possibility of an Edenic future.

Despite these parallels, the similarity between *Ark Angels'* conservation message and the actual biblical flood story is superficial at best. According to the Bible, the purpose of the ark was to preserve from God's righteous destruction not only a sample of each species of animal, but also, and far more importantly, the only righteous man—Noah—and his family, who, along with the animals, were protected in the ark from a cataclysmic flood that wipes out the remainder of all land-dwelling creatures, including humans. After the flood waters subside, a new beginning in history ensues with Noah's family at the center, while the animals, being of secondary importance, are, as always, on the periphery.

In contrast, the three sisters in *Ark Angels* are sent on a mission to save Earth *from* destruction and *prevent* judgment by loading the whale-shaped ark with endangered species. Saving animals from extinction is the means by which the obliteration of the Earth, and thus humanity, is prevented. If the ark is filled halfway, the "Environment Clock" (a variation of the Doomsday Clock created in 1947 to symbolize the threat of global nuclear war, and later popularly used to symbolize other potential apocalyptic threats to humanity) will not strike midnight and "the Lord" will not destroy humanity.

While the mysterious "Lord" seems to have authority to destroy humanity if his condition isn't met, he isn't identical with God, who also appears in the *manhwa* as a ball of diffused light at a meeting where individual representatives from all the parallel dimensions are gathered in what resembles a Byzantine basilica. Because of God's appearance, the Lord concedes to the personified Earth and the three sisters, who plead to save humanity despite the enormous risk involved. The risk is that if humans continue to live their lives without giving thought to the environment, the Earth will eventually be ruined, which, because all parallel dimensions attached to Earth are connected with one another, entails the destruction of all parallel Earths.

Although Park borrows from the Noah story, she emphasizes humanity's ability to mend its ways, rather than, as the Bible does, God's righteous judgment. Park's emphasis on humanity's goodness and the biblical emphasis on righteous judgment, moreover, find parallels with another biblical narrative—the story of Sodom and Gomorrah. According to Genesis, Abraham pled with God to withhold his wrath against these two cities if ten righteous people were found within, while in the *manhwa* the three sisters plead with God to give humanity a second chance since humans have the capacity to show compassion toward fellow humans and take responsibility for their environmental mistakes. Though Abraham acknowledges the holiness of God and the existence of damnable individuals, pleading with God to spare the good, Japheth, with no

mention of thoroughly evil individuals, insists that what God has created can't be so bad that it merits annihilation.

Park's loose appropriation of the Christian stories, moreover, finds an even looser appropriation of Christian symbolism. For instance, in an episode with the ghost named Prenegue, Japheth dresses as a priest holding a cross, Shem as a nun holding holy water, and Hamu as a nurse clutching a Bible—all three bear cross motifs on their clothes as well. They attempt to perform an exorcism to stop Prenegue from haunting the turtle they are sent to rescue, but Prenegue makes a mockery of the process by imbibing the holy water, commenting on its flavor, then grabbing the cross and asking if it compliments his outfit, a moment before he attacks them. The Christian symbols, it seems, have no power to help: they are merely aesethetic, purely for show.

In sum, then, both the symbols and the stories Park uses as a template for *Ark Angels* have little of the original biblical spirit or gravitas. By and large, Christianity acts as a façade for what is actually, in terms of content, a pastiche of eastern philosophies and these various religio-philosophical traditions are successfully integrated into the text and illustrations, much as these traditions have become part of the Korean ethos. Though Christianity is today the largest religion in Korea, few would argue that the heart of Korea is Christian, as the country's roots in Neo-Confucian beliefs run deep in their long history.

Three Sisters Living the Shamanistic Four

Rows and rows of angry looking, spear-wielding *jangseung*—Korean totem poles, whose shamanistic purpose is to frighten away hostile demons—appear at the personified Earth's command as the personified Earth and the Lord attempt to impose their will on each other: to save or destroy humanity.

This scene is but a taste of Korean shamanism, which is the earliest religion found on the Korean peninsula. Like all shamanistic traditions, Korean shamanism has four basic assertions surrounding its central figure, the shaman: shamans act as intermediaries between two realms; shamans act as healers; shamans can enter the spirit realm to seek guidance; and shamans perpetuate their tradition through storytelling. In addition to scenes like the one above, *Ark Angels* explores all four aspects of shamanism in and through Shem, Hamu, and Japheth.

Firstly, shamans are often intermediaries between the human world and the all-important spirit world, which is perceived to be populated by both good and bad spirits. However, neither "good" nor "bad" are absolute or morally objective terms; they simply refer to what physically "benefits" or "harms" people. Metaphysically speaking, shamanism maintains that nothing is permanent (also a key doctrine in Daoism and Buddhism) and so

lays emphasis wholly on practical, situational ethics—good or bad decisions depend entirely on the situation and not on any absolute command of the conscience or a perfectly good God.

Moreover, since nothing in shamanism is permanent, this includes things like gender. Whereas Christianity and Confucianism, to name a few, see gender as an ontological given—gender being a preordained, unchangeable part of the soul itself—shamanism insists that gender is a social construct— something made, and therefore something that can be unmade, by people. Consequently, in a traditional shamanistic society, such as that of ancient Korea, men and women are more or less equals, meaning that either could hold the highest position in the group, that is to say, either or both could become shamans.

Although Korea's past is shamanistic, the onset of Confucianism, which introduced a systematic hierarchy of gender roles, reduced shamanism's popularity. Regardless, some argue that to this day the heart of Korea remains inescapably shamanistic.[1] Empirical evidence reveals that over fifty percent of Koreans, including some of the Christians, consult mediums and necromancers. These days, because of the Confucian turn, shamanism in Korea is usually associated with women—powerful magical females who stand as intermediaries between the seen and unseen world.

And this, of course, is what we find in *Ark Angels* as well: three females with boys' names (representing gender impermanence) taking on the role of intermediaries between Earth and its parallel dimensions. At the conference held by the Lord, where all the representatives from other parallel dimensions are gathered to decide the fate of humanity on Earth, Japheth, the youngest, speaks on behalf of her older sisters and her father (a very un-Confucian, but shamanistic, thing to do) to plead the case of humanity. She argues that because humans are "two-dimensional," having the "capacity for both good and evil," they shouldn't be destroyed. By acting as intermediaries, the sisters also act as the good or beneficial spirits who attempt to save humanity from destruction. Furthermore, the sisters also act as intermediaries between humans and animals. Just as shamans act as go-betweens between animal spirits and humans, so do the three sisters, by seeing into the spirit of each animal, convince the animals to get on the ark that will, indirectly, save humanity as well.

Shamans also have the ability, through various means, to treat illnesses. In fact, so-called Chinese or natural medicine has its roots in shamanism, and Korean medicine is an offshoot of Chinese medicine, a still popular alternative

---

[1] Simon Winchester, *Korea: A Walk through the Land of Miracles* (New York: HarperCollins, 2005), p. 186.

to western medicine. As a young girl growing up in Korea, my parents tried to get me to drink turtle's blood for its general health benefits.

In *Ark Angels*, one can see the sisters taking on the shamanistic role as healer insofar as they attempt to purge Earth of the disease brought on by human disregard for the environment. By preventing animal extinction, one species at a time, the sisters attempt to save humanity and cure the ailing Earth. It's no accident that the very first illustration in the first volume has Japheth in a T-shirt with the Korean *hangul* characters reading *"geegu sarang"*—literally, "Earth Love."

Thirdly, shamans have the power to enter the spirit realm (of gods, animal spirits and dead ancestors), in search of answers and guidance through acts of divination and fortunetelling. Shem, Hamu and Japheth have the ability to see an animal's soul in humanoid form, and thus are able to feel an enormous amount of compassion for them. And while the animal spirits don't actually give the sisters knowledge of the future, some of them, such as the lion, do teach the sisters a few important life lessons.

Finally, shamans perpetuate their tradition through myths and storytelling. Japheth, the narrator of *Ark Angels*, takes on the shamanistic role of passing on her story with the hope of preserving Earth and bringing it back to its harmonic state. The last plea she makes is to the reader himself, "Won't you all help us complete our mission? For your own good . . ." In this way, the *manhwa* itself may be seen as a shamanistic myth that attempts to transmit its message to posterity.

The four fundamental characteristics of the shaman are entwined within the plot of *Ark Angels*, which in turn may be seen as an indicator of the depth to which Korean culture is steeped in this ancient religion.

Flowing through the Daoist River, Tapping into the Daoist Magic

Central to Daoism is the Dao, which is a bland, neutral, pure, all-powerful energy force (think "the Force" in *Star Wars*), which is perceived by humans as Yin-Yang, or opposites in harmony with one another. In Daoism, everything that flows from the Dao is nature, and the aim of the Daoist is both to flow with (and not against) nature and to realize that all are one with it.

In *Ark Angels*, Park makes natural harmony between Earth and its parallel dimensions, between Earth and humanity and between humanity and animals her ultimate goal. By rescuing animals on the brink of extinction, the sisters act with nature and hence flow with the Dao. As Hamu states, "Nature looks best in its original form," and Shem relays that the human desire to possess

nature winds up draining it of its beauty. The Daoist would agree that nature at its best is nature free from human meddling.

Furthermore, at the meeting called to order by the Lord, the Lord states that the Earths are reflections of each other and the destruction of one will mean the destruction of all others. This notion is a clever application of the Yin-Yang principle, wherein harmony between opposites—including reflections—is fundamental to natural existence. Additionally, true to the spirit of harmony between opposites, Park has representatives from *every* species—even species traditionally opposed to each other—attend the meeting.

Yet understanding the Dao (which, by its nature, can't actually be understood) isn't the extent of Daoism. Possibly more than any religion, Daoism puts emphasis on magic or the Daoist master's ability to tap into the *De* (or power) of the Dao in order to achieve superhuman feats.

In *Ark Angels*, this Daoist aspect is quite clear insofar as Park has the three sisters utilizing magic or the *De* by traveling through parallel dimensions to perform magic spells to elude, or stop, their enemies: Shem is able to channel an enormous amount of strength when she is angry or annoyed, Hamu is able to hypnotize men (and anything with a masculine soul) with her beauty; and Japheth has the power to stop time but only "once a day and for no more than five minutes." Indeed, together—as a true harmony of opposites—the sisters can also summon the ark, into which they put the animals.

Nevertheless, it must be admitted that unlike the Daoist, who believes that the way by which one becomes in tune with the universe is through *wu wei* or "inaction," the sisters are clearly focused on *acting* quickly before their window of opportunity for rescuing endangered species closes. Yet this very failure to be philosophically consistent again reinforces my thesis in this chapter—that Korean culture, as it can be seen reflected in *Ark Angels*, is a mix, and not necessarily a logically consistent mix, of a number of contradictory ideas.

Confucian Confusion?

Although some have argued that shamanism represents the true heart of Korea, others, perhaps paradoxically, have argued nearly the opposite—that Korea embodies the most perfect Confucian society.

While shamanism emphasizes subjectivity and impermanence, Confucianism stresses objectivity and rational stability. While shamanism says morality and social structures are fluid, Confucianism says that both are, at their base, fixed by the decree of Heaven—not quite the Heaven of Christianity, but still imagined to be the highest, greatest place, the dwelling

of all the good gods and spirits, who speak in a unified voice in support of certain absolutes in morality.

Nevertheless, the divide between shamanism and Confucianism isn't completely insurmountable: Confucius called himself a "lover of the ancients" (the ancients being his shamanistic forefathers), and most agree that Confucianism should be seen as making more deliberate and rational (as opposed to completely disregarding) the shamanistic tradition. In this way, it's possible—though again we shouldn't try too hard to artificially reconcile all contradictions—to understand Confucianism as completing shamanism through five key concepts: *jen, chun-tzu, li, de* and *wen*, all of which, I want to argue, can be clearly seen in *Ark Angels*.

Firstly, *jen*, meaning "man" and "two," has to do with general benevolence toward all people. The person of *jen* treats all people with dignity as all "men are brothers." Although it might be a slight stretch, this attitude of *jen* can be seen in the three sisters' general benevolence toward all sentient life-forms: as Japheth says, "We don't just see an animal's physical form, but we look inside to its soul. That's why . . . we believe every life is equal and precious." Clearly insofar as we accept the shamanistic, Daoist, and Buddhist idea that animals and humans have souls, the sisters can be seen as Confucian practitioners of *jen*.

Secondly, flowing from the general principle of *jen* is the principle of *chun-tzu*. That is, the person of *chun-tzu* is the gentleman-host to his friends; such a person is concerned about what he can give, rather than what he can get; he is not overly talkative and never boasts. Needless to say, nearly all the world's heroes have something of the nature of *chun-tzu*, and the sisters are no exception: they work to promote a greater cause, even at the cost of their lives; they are selfless in their mission, and don't believe they should be treated specially because they are endowed with power. In fact, when they are not on a mission, Shem runs a humble flower shop and acts as a guardian to her younger siblings, who attend a high school in a small, unassuming town. Yet even there, their *chun-tzu* natures come into play: Hamu chastises Japheth when she suggests they ignore the bullies who are harassing another student since they can't "turn [their] back[s] on the injustice in [their] new home."

Thirdly, we have *li*, which focuses on propriety or the way things should be done given the set or Heaven-ordained nature of each thing. It's from the principle of *li* that we get the famous Five Relationships of Confucianism, which have to do with the five proper relationships in society between 1. father and son, 2. elder brother and younger brother, 3. husband and wife, 4. elder friend and younger friend, and 5. ruler and subject. Confucianism strongly advocates for gender and age hierarchy. And although *Ark Angels* subverts masculine authority via its shamanistic impulses, the fundamentals of some

of these key relationships are still maintained. For instance, Noah, the sisters' father, is unable to attend the conference that will determine the fate of Earth because he must attend a cooking class—a seemingly shamanistic undermining of Confucian gender roles; however, because the sisters do actually obey their father and attend the conference on his behalf, they exemplify the Confucian principle of children obeying their parents—a variation of the first of the Five Relationships. In this way, we again have a clear instance of the tension between the various religions—in this case, shamanism and Confucianism—within Korean culture.

Fourthly, there is the Confucian *de*, which, unlike the magical power of Daoism, refers to the power an individual—in particular, a person of authority on Earth—needs in order to enforce the socio-political ideology dictated by Heaven; indeed, for this reason, the Chinese emperor, who was thought to be the most powerful man on Earth, was called the "Son of Heaven"—not only in that he has *de* as Heaven does, but also in that he is expected to use this *de* to enforce the morality of Heaven on Earth. Though not an explicitly political *manhwa*, *Ark Angels* does show the sisters to be people of *de* in that they are charged by God himself with the task of saving humanity and since they are given the *de* to achieve their task by one of God's people, namely, Noah.

Lastly, the person of *wen* is one who appreciates "the arts of peace," such as music, calligraphy, sword dance, poetry and so on. This is to say that the ideal Confucian is not only moral (*jen, chun-tzu* and *li*) and powerful (*de*) but also aesthetically sensitive (*wen*). Of course, because Confucianism makes such a strong link between morality and aesthetics, it's no wonder that this philosophy teaches that art should largely be in praise of morality and Heaven; moreover, one of the most important jobs of art is didactics—to teach people about how to act correctly. And in this sense, it's also possible to see *Ark Angels* (in addition to a shamanistic myth) as a Confucian work of art—a text that reminds its readers about their moral obligations to Heaven, to themselves and to the Earth as a whole.

WWBD: What Would Buddha Do?

Buddhism, in its Mahayana (or more liberal) form, came to Korea in the fourth century A.D., and though its impact on Korea was not immediate, it now claims about a third of all Koreans as its followers.

The goal of all Buddhism is "extinction" (which is in vivid contrast to the goal of the three sisters in *Ark Angels*). The enlightened Buddhist aims to reach *Nirvana*, a state of nothingness, by escaping from *Samsara*, the cycle of death and rebirth, which is itself hierarchically arranged as six states of existence wherein the lowest is a dweller of hell, and the highest, a deva, a godlike individual

residing in the heavenly realms. However, even the deva is considered ensnared by the *Samsara*, as the truest state of being isn't being at all.

As we can see, then, the Buddhist tenet is paradoxical. On the one hand, individuals appear to have souls, which, based on their moral or immoral actions, which are judged by the law of *Karma*, can move up and down the levels of *Samsara*. On the other hand, the true Buddhist—the truly enlightened individual—realizes that he has no soul, and, indeed, that all things are transient and are, in fact, nothing. Although Mahayana Buddhists, which may include all Korean Buddhists, attempt to overcome this paradox by stressing—thanks to incorporating certain shamanistic elements—the highest level of *Samsara* or heaven over and against *Nirvana*, this paradox, for the serious Buddhist, is never very far away.

Now the Mahayana Buddhist emphasis on Samsaric heavens and hells can be seen clearly in the Prenegue/turtle episode in *Ark Angels*. Prenegue is a villainous ghost bent on making his host re-live the "most painful time [he] can remember." Although some might see this episode as a Christian reference to Purgatory (especially since the sisters wear the garbs of Catholic exorcists), they would be mistaken for according to the Catholic tradition, those in Purgatory have died in a state of grace (which isn't the case with Prenegue) and must remain there until their sins have been purged. Furthermore, this episode is more likely a reference to Mahayana Buddhism since it, and not Christianity, makes room for the souls of the miserable dead wandering the Earth (as we see Prenegue doing). Therefore, Mahayana Buddhism has a better explanation for Prenegue: he is a hungry ghost, a being in the second lowest state of existence in the *Samsara*, and indeed because of his continued evil on Earth, he eventually is dragged down to hell, the lowest level of existence.

Yet *Ark Angels* embraces many different religio-philosophical traditions and so has many internal inconsistencies. On the one hand, the Buddhist (Samsaric) teaching that both animals and humans are equals insofar as they have souls is clearly shown in Park's *manhwa*. On the other hand, this Buddhist idea is subverted by showing the sisters eating meat products (Hamu mentions how delicious *tonkatsu*—deep-fried breaded pork cutlet—is and the sisters are depicted on one occasion breakfasting on bacon and eggs). And this contradiction, in turn, is very reflective of Korean culture as a whole in that vegetarianism is not a common practice in Korea, even amongst Buddhists.

Hermit Kingdom? I Think Not

Throughout this chapter, I have argued that Park illustrates a microcosmic view of the Korean religio-philosophical ethos through her fantasy *manhwa*, *Ark Angels*. In differing degrees, the five key religions in Korea—shamanism,

Daoism, Confucianism, Mahayana Buddhism, and Christianity—can be found peacefully co-existing side by side, and, indeed, often under the same roof in Korea, which has erroneously been called the Hermit Kingdom, a country deemed to have been cut off from all external influences. And while inconsistencies abound—such as Christianity's prohibition against shamanistic fortunetelling and Confucianism's rejection of Daoism's relativism—Koreans (not all, of course, but many) aren't as disturbed by this as some might expect or, as in my case, hope.

19

Down the Abyss

STEVE ODIN

*I*n the various works of Hayao Miyazaki focusing on environmentalism, the landscape is often populated by the sacred presence of Shinto gods and spirits (known as *kami*), who live in a parallel world separated by a thin membrane within the multi-dimensional continuum of nature, itself connected to our familiar physical dimension through the opening of a tunnel, vortex, hole, or abyss.

My Neighbor Totoro is an enchanted tale of two young girls who fall down a hole under a sacred camphor tree decorated as a Shinto shrine, descending to the bottom of a tunnel, thereby to encounter a magical tree-dwelling nature spirit named Totoro. This is reminiscent of Alice's descent down the rabbit hole into to a fantastic Wonderland, but the Shinto animistic vision of nature as a sacred habitat or place filled with divine spirits and gods is just the starting point for a rich Japanese history and tradition of environmental thought.

Japanese Buddhism depicts nature as an aesthetic continuum of interrelated events having the intrinsic value of beauty. The Zen concept of nature includes a Buddhist metaphysics of harmonious interpenetration between the many and the one. This Zen metaphysic of nature as a continuum of interpenetrating dimensions and events is illustrated by the organismic metaphor of "Indra's Net," whereby all events in nature are visualized as brilliant jewels in a dynamic network of relationships, so that each gem mirrors the whole universe as a microcosm of the macrocosm.

The Japanese Buddhist view of nature has many points of convergence with the environmental ethics and aesthetics of Aldo Leopold, whose 1949 book *A Sand County Almanac* is often cited as one of the primary works on environmental ethics in the Western philosophical tradition. For both the environmental philosophy of Aldo Leopold and Japanese Buddhism, nature is similarly viewed as a "web" of interrelationships wherein the individual organisms and their surrounding environments are mutually dependent in a symbiotic ecosystem.

The modern Japanese philosopher Tetsurō Watsuji (*Watsuji Tetsurō's Rinrigaku*) develops an ethics based on a Zen concept of the person (*ningen*) as an individual-society interaction, which exists not in an isolated ego, but in the "betweenness" (*aida*) or relatedness of persons. Moreover, for Watsuji's Japanese ethics the person is a spatial field of relationships, including not only relations to others in society, but also to the surrounding "climate" (*fūdo*) or environment of living nature. Watsuji, like Leopold, thereby suggests that his Japanese Buddhist ethics must be expanded beyond inter-human relations, to an environmental ethics that includes relationships between humans and nature. According to Leopold's environmental ethics, it is the intrinsic value of beauty in nature which commands both an aesthetic appreciation and moral respect for nature. Likewise, just as Leopold's land ethics is itself based on a land aesthetics, Watsuji underscores the profoundly aesthetic character of ethical relationships both to other humans and to the environment.

Engaging Nature

Miyazaki's *Nausicaä*, like both the environmental ethics of Leopold and the traditional Japanese Shinto-Buddhist concept of living nature, represents a paradigm-shift from an anthropo-centric (human centered) to an *eco*-centric model of the environment.

In his autobiographical work *Starting Point: 1979–1996*, Miyazaki describes the environmental motif focusing on the human-nature relationship in his original manga version of *Nausicaä*, stating: "A major theme of this work is the manner in which people engage with nature surrounding them" (p. 251). Miyazaki describes his deep interest in the environmental themes of *Nausicaä* as in part having been inspired by reading various books on ecology such as *A Green History of the World: The Environment and the Collapse of Great Civilizations* by Clive Pointing.

Elsewhere Miyazaki describes being influenced by Frederic Back's 1987 animated film *The Man Who Planted Trees*, a film that promotes the sense of place and conservation of nature by replanting trees. Miyazaki writes: "The old man in this film has the face of a philosopher . . . Back wanted to draw someone with a far-reaching gaze, someone overlooking the planting of trees, someone watching them grow and become forests and homes to the honeybees" (p. 146). From these and other references, it becomes clear that Miyazaki's environmental theme in *Nausicaä* and other works is informed not only by his own love of nature, but also his research into ecology as well as his interest in activist movements for sustainable green living dedicated to the protection of the wilderness.

In *Nausicaä*, the atomic and biochemical war known as the Seven Days of Fire was a catastrophic holocaust of near-total destruction leveled by giant

high-tech robotic Gods of War. The story begins a thousand years in the future, when medieval tribes attempt to survive in a post-apocalyptic world, including an ever-spreading Sea of Corruption (Fukai) emanating from a polluted jungle of toxic spores, acid lakes, and giant mutated insects named the Ohmu. In this nuclear wasteland of radioactive and biochemical pollution, humans must wear gas masks in order to survive the toxic poisons in the air, soil, water, and plants.

Apocalypse, the Abyss, and Overcoming Nihilism

Miyazaki's *Nausicaä* is an apocalyptic vision of the future, which uses imagery similar to "the Abyss" in Nietzsche's existentialism. For Nietzsche, the central problem of existence is "nihilism," or loss of all absolute values through the death of God, which is like an earthquake that opens up a dark abyss. Influenced by Nietzsche's existentialism, the modern Japanese philosopher Keiji Nishitani, in his book *Religion and Nothingness,* develops Zen Buddhism as a method of overcoming nihilism *through* nihilism, thereby shifting from the life-denying standpoint of nihilism, to the life-affirming standpoint of positive nothingness. For Nishitani, Zen overcomes nihilism by a descent to the bottom of a nihilistic abyss of negative nothingness, which itself nullifies all substantial being, resulting in a breakthrough to the field of positive nothingness wherein emptiness is fullness and fullness is emptiness, so that all life is affirmed as it is in suchness.

In *Beyond Good and Evil*, Nietzsche proclaims: "And when you look long into an abyss, the abyss also looks into you" (p. 89). In a monochrome picture frame displaying Nausicaä surrounded by a dark void or abyss of nihilistic nothingness, the narrative description echoes the words of Nietzsche, saying:

> The mind of a fragile person would be destroyed by the sight of that abyss. Because the one who looks into that darkness must endure the gaze returned by the darkness itself. This girl had the unprecedented power to reach the shore of that abyss. (Volume 6, p. 32)

However, just as for Nietzsche's existentialism the task is to overcome nihilism through a joyful Dionysian affirmation of existence, so Nausicaä descends to the bottom of a dark abyss, only to defiantly resist nihilism by affirming the positive value of all life. As clarified by Hiroshi Yamanaka ("The Utopian 'Power to Live': The Significance of the Miyazaki Phenomena"), just as Nietzsche strives to overturn the life-denying moral values of nihilism through the life-affirming moral values of Will-to-Power, so Miyazaki explains how Nausicaä resists nihilism by the *power to live.* Hence, Nausicaä herself proclaims: "Life survives by the power of life" (Volume 7, p. 198). According to Yamanaka, a recurrent motif in Miyazaki's Nausicaä is that of overcoming nihilism by going *down to*

the bottom. Thus, for Yamanaka, Nietzsche's existential theme of countering nihilism by the power of life-affirmation through descent to the bottom of an abyss, is seen in Nausicaä's descent through a vortex to the bottom of the Sea of Corruption, thereby to discover a purified green forest in the process of renewal.

Susan Napier analyzes Miyazaki's *Nausicaä* as being characterized by elements such as "apocalypse," or a vision of the end of the world, and "elegy," an elegiac sense of nostalgia and grief over loss. This apocalyptic destruction of the environment is an element in Japanese literature partly due to historical events such as the nuclear holocaust of Hiroshima and Nagasaki during World War II, along with natural disasters throughout Japan's history, including devastating earthquakes, tsunamis, and volcanic eruptions. Again, an apocalyptic element is contained in the Japanese Buddhist idea of *mappō* or the age of decline in the last days of the law. Yet Miyazaki's dystopian apocalyptic vision of a future nuclear wasteland in *Nausicaä* is not the total pessimism that characterizes that other great apocalyptic narrative of neo-Tokyo, Katsuhiro Otomo's *Akira* (1988), another groundbreaking animated film originally based on a manga. Whereas Otomo's *Akira* is a celebration of the nihilism of apocalyptic destruction, Miyazaki's *Nausicaä* is an apocalyptic story that instead ends with an optimistic hope of rebirth and renewal, guided by a prophetic vision of a world reborn into the Buddhist Pure Land of peace and joy through the saving activity of Nausicaä, likened to a savior, messiah, or compassionate bodhisattva.

This life-affirming attitude in the face of an abyss of nihility is seen when Nausicaä enters an ancient temple, and a Buddhist monk proclaims the advent of an apocalypse (Daikaisho), whereupon the polluted forest will boil over to destroy the entire world. Although the monk tells Nausicaä that apocalypse is inevitable, Nausicaä declares:

> Is there no way to stop the Daikaisho? . . . So many will die. . . . No! Our God of the Valley of the Wind tells us to live! I love life! The light, the sky, the people, insects, I love them all! (Volume 4, p. 85)

Nausicaä thus overturns an existential attitude of angst or despair in the face of apocalypse as a dark abyss of nihilistic nothingness, into a joyful affirmation of all life, existence and nature.

Compassionate Savior

From the perspective of *eco-feminism*, it's significant that Nausicaä, like nearly all of Miyazaki's main protagonists, is a female. Nausicaä, as a young woman, is also the embodiment and personification of Mother Nature. Hence, Nausicaä becomes a paradigmatic eco-feminist, who protests against the domination, violation, and oppression of women as well as the correlate destruction of nature.

Miyazaki explains in *Starting Point* that Nausicaä is the name of a compassionate Phaeacian princess who saves the shipwrecked Odysseus in Homer's *Odyssey*. Her character is further based on an ancient Japanese tale *The Princess Who Loved Insects*. As the heroine of Miyazaki's *Nausicaä,* Princess Nausicaä is a feminine, gentle, and peaceful young girl, who is at the same time a fearless warrior, skillful aviator, and pilot of a wind glider, a charismatic leader of her people, as well as a compassionate savior prophesied to lead all humankind to the Pure Land of peace and joy described by the teachings of Pure Land Buddhism in Japan.

The two main women protagonists are oppositional forces—the warlike Kushana of the Torumekians, and the angelic Princess Nausicaä of the Valley of the Wind. Yet Miyazaki does not have a rigid black-and-white view of morality, but instead suggests an *ambiguity* between good and evil. Both Kushana and Nausicaä share a common aim to stop the spreading Sea of Corruption with its deadly toxic spores and army of giant insects, but their methods are completely different. While Kushana leads her people into war for the purpose of gaining control over the Earth's limited natural resources, Nausicaä adopts compassion, nonviolence, and acceptance to establish peace between the warring tribes. Against Kushana's path of war and violence, Nausicaä teaches compassion and peace: "That path leads only to hatred and an endless cycle of revenge. . . . Choose love over hatred" (Volume 6, p. 129).

In an effort to save the planet, Kushana seeks to destroy the toxic jungle with its giant mutated insects by reactivating an ancient robotic God of War. It is the very same technology of warfare using weapons that created the deadly toxic jungle. Moreover, Kushana uses the primitive emotions of hatred, violence, and revenge that led to the creation of the high-tech weapons of destruction resulting in the present biochemichal and nuclear wasteland. By contrast, Nausicaä seeks to stop the spread of the toxic forest with its giant tank-like Ohmu insects, not by destroying them with robotic war machines, but through

sympathy, gentleness, and compassion. Nausicaä has a sympathetic intuitive bond not only with people, but with all the plants, trees, and animals of the forest, even insects such as giant Ohmu. When the Ohmu become angry, their eyes turn burning hot red; yet when they encounter Nausicaä, their eyes soon turn to cool blue. Her oneness with the forest is so deep that at one point we are told she is a divine personification of nature: "This honored person is the forest in human form, she stands at the center of both worlds.... We shall make her the guardian deity of our people" (Volume 6, p. 29).

Nausicaä's mystical power to telepathically communicate with all living beings in nature is reminiscent of Shinto *miko* priestesses or psychic female shamans of Japan's animistic nature religion depicted by the "magical girl" archetype in many Japanese manga and anime. Miyazaki explains his own vision of Nausicaä as a *miko* or magical shamanic priestess functioning as an intermediary between the physical, natural, and spiritual worlds, stating: "While creating the story, I realized that the role of Nausicaä herself was not to become an actual leader or even a guide for her people. Rather, it was to act as a type of *miko,* a shaman-maiden who works at a Shinto shrine" (*Starting Point*, p. 407). Her sympathy for all humans, plants, and animals also represents the compassionate bodhisattvas of Japanese Buddhism such as Kannon the goddess of mercy. Nausicaä is thus said to be the fulfillment of ancient prophecies of a blue-clad princess riding across a field of golden light who will become the messiah guiding all people to the Pure Land of peace and joy at the twilight of human civilization.

Insect Life

Nausicaä's compassion for all living beings in nature, including humans, plants, and animals, results in her moral stand on "animal rights." Describing Nausicaä's equal regard for the welfare of both humans and animals, even insects, Miyazaki writes: "She seems to regard the lives of insects and humans in the same way" (*Starting Point*, p. 334).

The foremost ethical philosopher in the area of animal rights is Peter Singer. According to Singer, the case for animal rights rests partly on the basis of Jeremy Bentham's Utilitarian principle of moral equality, which states that one should have equal consideration for the interests of others. Moreover, Singer, following Bentham's Utilitarian ethics, holds that the principle of moral equality should be extended to *all* animals, both human and nonhuman.

Singer points out that in the Utilitarian ethics of Bentham, it is the capacity for *suffering* which gives a being the moral right to equal consideration, whether human or animal. In Bentham's words: "The day may come when the rest of

the animal creation may acquire those rights . . . The question is not, Can they reason? nor Can they talk? but Can they *suffer?*" (as cited by Singer, *Animal Liberation*, p. 7). Likewise, in Japanese Buddhist ethics, compassion for the suffering of all sentient beings in nature is also a fundamental principle. The *Nirvana Sutra* proclaims: "All sentient beings have (or are) Buddha-nature." All sentient beings in nature have equal moral standing and intrinsic value by virtue of their ability to suffer, as well as their potential for enlightenment. Nausicaä thus inquires: "Why must the plants and the birds and the insects suffer as well? So many will die. Who will atone for the pain and sadness of the Ohmu?" (Volume 4, p. 89). For Nausicaä it is an ethical axiom that *no unnecessary suffering or pain should be inflicted on any living creature,* so that all animals, even insects, have an equal right to live.

Nausicaä's method is reminiscent of the "nature study" (*shizengaku*) of Kinji Imanishi in *A Japanese View of Nature*. His Japanese "nature study" is influenced by the modern Zen philosophy of Kitarō Nishida (1870–1945). According to Nishida, founder of the Kyoto school of modern Japanese philosophy, there is a nondual continuity between humans and nature in a Field (*basho*) or "place" of nothingness. Imanishi's nature study combines the Zen feeling of oneness with nature with a study of environmental sciences, including evolutionary biology, ecology, zoology, botany, primatology, and entomology.

Nausicaä likewise attempts to understand the ecosystem, not only through a Zen-like sympathy with all living nature, but also by a study of environmental sciences. Throughout the story there are many scenes of Nausicaä as a scientist in her laboratory conducting experiments with flora and fauna specimens collected from the toxic jungle. Her scientific research is aimed at solving the problem of pollution in the ecosphere, to discover medical cures for illnesses caused by the poisoning of the environment, and to find a method for cleaning up the Sea of Corruption so as to restore the purity of nature by sustainable green lifestyles.

Through scientific experiments conducted in her secret underground laboratory, Nausicaä discovers that plants collected from the Sea of Corruption are not themselves poisonous, but have absorbed toxins from the soil polluted by humans (Volume 1, p. 76). However, at the conclusion of Volume 1, Nausicaä discovers the real secret of the Sea of Corruption (Volume 1, pp. 112–128). Nausicaä descends into a hole down through a spiraling tunnel-like vortex of quicksand, to the bottom of the Sea of Corruption. Here she takes a shamanic journey down a tunnel into a dreamlike underworld, followed by an upward ascent to share her revelations with others. By her descent to the bottom of a nihilistic abyss, she discovers that the water, air, and soil are pure underneath the Sea of Corruption, and there is no need to wear a mask. She

realizes that the huge trees filter out the poison from the toxic jungle: the trees turn to stone, the stone to sand, the sand to dunes, so that nature dies, followed by rebirth as a green Pure Land of abundant life:

> But the day shall come when the Sea of Corruption ceases to be, and a green, Pure Land is reborn. (Volume 7, p. 195)

The giant tank-like Ohmu evolved to protect the ecosystem that is functioning to purify the toxic jungle. When Nausicaa discovers an ancient place in the poison forest that has undergone the one-thousand-year filtering process of purification, she rejects staying in this paradise in order to return to the suffering world, thus to become a compassionate bodhisattva who descends from the transcendent realm of Nirvana to save all suffering beings in the realm of samsara.

Miyazaki's efforts to create a new ecosystem called the Sea of Corruption, which is a toxic jungle functioning to purify nature by filtering all poisons to renew the forests and sustain the environment, is an animistic concept of nature reminiscent of the "Gaia hypothesis" in James Lovelock's environmental philosophy. Lovelock's Gaia hypothesis does not suggest that the planet Earth is a sentient creature, goddess or spirit; rather, it holds that the Earth is an organismic, holistic, interrelated, self-regulating system, that maintains climatic, atmospheric, and environmental conditions optimal for life in nature (*The Revenge of Gaia*).

In his latest work, Lovelock speaks of the "revenge" of Gaia as the planet Earth attempts to purge itself of any source of over-population, pollution, and industrial waste, which like a cancerous tumor, needs to be removed in order for the ecosystem to survive. Miyazaki discusses his idea of an ecosystem as a "forest on the attack" functioning to restore a sustainable environment. In this context he expresses his effort "to overturn the concept of defenseless plants always being destroyed and instead create a forest that was offensive" (*Starting Point*, p. 418). Miyazaki's animistic concept of nature, thus converges with Lovelock's Gaia hypothesis, whereby the planet Earth is itself a living organism, in the sense of a holistic *self-regulating* system that functions to maintain an optimal environment to sustain life.

The Web of Living Nature

In the environmental ethics of Aldo Leopold, moral respect for nature is itself grounded in an appreciation for the intrinsic value of beauty in nature. Likewise, in the tradition of Zen Buddhism, spiritual reverence and moral respect for nature are inseparable from insight into the beauty of nature,

such as the pervasive aesthetic value qualities of *mono no aware* (pathos of things) or the sad beauty of perishability, and *yûgen* or the sublime beauty of profound mystery. Moreover, for the environmentalism of both Leopold and Zen, the aesthetic, moral, and spiritual values of nature are rooted in a deep metaphysical insight into the interrelatedness of everything in the web of living nature. According to Napier, the Japanese aesthetic philosophy of transiency as the *mono no aware* or sad beauty of evanescence itself adds to the apocalyptic and elegiac vision of *Nausicaä* with its expression of grief for what has been lost in the passage of time (*Anime from Akira to Howl's Moving Castle*).

Throughout Miyazaki's graphic novel, the stunning beauty of the surreal landscapes in the toxic jungle is breathtaking. The most astonishing visual characteristic of Miyazaki's *Nausicaä* is its imaginative vision of an entirely new eco-system of a toxic jungle with poisonous fungi and their deadly bacterial spores infested by a newly evolved species of giant insects. At the very outset of the story, Nausicaä is under the transparent eye lens from the exoskeleton of an empty Ohmu shell, watching the deadly spores from the giant fungi in

the toxic jungle fall like snowflakes, expressing sheer aesthetic delight in their delicate beauty. Moreover, from an ethical standpoint, Nausicaä's view of the toxic jungle through the lens of an empty Ohmu shell, itself reveals her ability to arrive at moral decisions by seeing nature from the multiple perspectives of others, including the perspective of insects.

Nausicaä describes a Japanese Buddhist view of the ever-changing impermanence of all life: "To live is to change. . . . We will all go on changing" (Volume 7, p. 198). As pointed out by Charles Shir Inouye in his book *Evanescence and Form*, the Japanese aesthetics of evanescence, with its underlying metaphysics of impermanence, has its origins in the early Japanese poetic tradition, wherein perishability of life was first symbolized by the image *of utsusemi,* or an "empty Chicada shell" (pp. 17–26). He further clarifies how there is a contemporary return to the ancient Japanese aesthetics of evanescence symbolized by an "empty Chicada shell" in Miyazaki's *Nausicaä,* wherein the heroine enters the Sea of Corruption to discover the empty insect shell of a giant Ohmu (pp. 195–97).

Mysterious Beauty

The new edition of the English version of Miyazaki's *Nausicaä* is now available in its original Japanese manga format, reading top to bottom and right to left, with splendid monochrome line drawings that include all the original Japanese onomatopoeia sound effects written in katakana script, with an English glossary of equivalent meanings at the rear of each volume. As the reader quickly scans the extended page layouts in this lengthy work, it gives the manga a "cinematic" quality. All the onomatopoeia with sound effects written in the katakana script accompanying the pictorial frames adds a kind of audio-visual "synaesthesia," or intersensory fusion of sights and sounds into the juxtaposed montage of a unified aesthetic impression.

The first page of each volume begins with a foldout color poster of Nausicaä, a map of the Valley of the Wind and surrounding regions, while other color foldouts contain a diagram explaining the new ecosystem that evolved within the Sea of Corruption. However, each manga volume of *Nausicaä* is otherwise drawn in black-and-white monochromatic style. Miyazaki develops a graphic style of monochrome line drawing influenced by traditional Zen brush painting techniques used to depict the pervasive atmospheric beauty of nature as an undivided aesthetic continuum. Indeed the very source of Japanese manga is traced by some to the satirical Zen monochrome line drawings featuring comic parodies of Zen monastic life known as "The Animal Scrolls" (*Chōjûgiga*) attributed to the Buddhist artist-priest Toba Sōjō (1053–1140). In contrast to American comic books

drawn in vivid color, Miyazaki's manga consists of traditional Japanese-style monochrome line drawing with surrounding blank spaces resembling the dark voids of a Zen inkwash landscape painting.

The Zenlike monochrome line drawings of Miyazaki's manga includes not only blank spaces of voidness, emptiness, or nothingness, but are often also devoid of any dialogue so as to have prolonged intervals of silence and stillness. In traditional Japanese aesthetics developed under the aegis of Zen, these empty voids and intervals of silence that characterize the monochrome backgrounds of Zen poetry, painting, and other arts, is known as *ma* or the beauty of negative space. This use of Zenlike voids in the monochrome landscapes functions to capture the pervasive aesthetic quality, mood, feeling-tone, or atmosphere suffusing transitory events throughout the continuum of nature. These monochrome line drawings of Miyazaki's graphic novel, similar to Zen black-ink landscape brush paintings, depict not only the aesthetic quality of *aware* or sad beauty of this empty insect-shell world of evanescent phenomena arising and perishing in the flow of nature, but also the aesthetic

quality of *yūgen* or the beauty of darkness and shadows that pervades the horizon of nothingness, thereby to suggest the profound beauty of mystery and depth of all things in nature.

A special feature of Zen monochrome landscape paintings is that they disclose the interrelatedness of all phenomena in the environment as each part shades into the whole as well as into all the other parts within the undivided aesthetic continuum of nature. Frederik Schodt describes the minimalist style of traditional Zen monochrome brush painting and its influence on the monochrome line drawings of Japanese manga when he writes:

> Unlike mainstream American and European comics, which are richly colored, most manga are monochrome except for the cover and a few inside pages. . . . some manga artists have elevated line drawing to new aesthetic heights and developed new conventions to convey depth and speed with lines and shading. Using the "less-is-more" philosophy of traditional Japanese brush painting many artists have learned to convey subtle emotions with a minimum of effort. (*Dreamland Japan: Writings on Modern Manga*, pp. 23–24)

Hence, the beautiful and sublime landscapes of Miyazaki's manga *Nausicaä* involves not only an environmental ethics, but also an environmental aesthetics, including both a philosophy of the beauty of nature as an undivided aesthetic continuum, along with a correlate mode of graphic artwork used to depict the mysterious atmospheric beauty of darkness evoked by the continuity, fusion, and wholeness of nature.

Green Living

Nausicaä has become widely recognized as a visionary anti-war, anti-industrial, anti-pollution, pro-ecological manga and anime that has inspired a new green movement in Japan devoted to conservation of nature. The environmental issue of sustainability through green lifestyle movements using alternate energy sources is addressed throughout Miyazaki's narrative. *Nausicaä* is a cautionary environmental tale with a strong anti-war message that alerts the reader of the dangers of warfare using biochemical and nuclear weapons capable of apocalyptic destruction of both nature and human civilization.

Moreover, *Nausicaä* contains an anti-industrial theme criticizing all technology misused to destroy the environment, while at the same time exploring alternative energy sources, especially natural wind power. To begin with, Nausicaä lives in the Valley of the Wind, wherein the wind itself protects the village from the poison miasma falling from the toxic Sea of Corruption. The ever-spinning windmills providing a sustainable alternate energy supply further help to blow away the poison spores from the toxic forest to keep

the Valley free of pollution. Nausicaä at first rides on her *mehve* plane using an engine, but later rides the wind using her elegant wind glider. While at first she uses mechanical energy, later she uses natural and sustainable energy of the wind. Likewise, she uses the sustainable wind power of windmills to pump up the pure water from deep beneath the polluted soil to conduct her scientific experiments for cleaning up the toxic jungle and restoring the natural environment.

Miyazaki's profound lifelong interest in environmentalism, ecology, and green living is recorded in his autobiography *Starting Point: 1979–1996*. Here he describes how his creation of *Nausicaä* was itself inspired by several events, starting with the pollution of Japan's Minamata Bay with mercury so that the fish and other seafood became inedible, thereby destroying the fishing industry in the region. Furthermore, Miyazaki explains how the Yanase River near his own home became so polluted that no fish or plants could live within it:

> The Yanase River runs near my house, and all it takes for me to feel really good is to see a few minnows swimming about in it. Twenty-five years ago, when I moved to the area, the river was more like a polluted ditch. . . . Twenty-five years ago, the river was so filthy people felt helpless. . . . Around ten years ago, I think it was, we started seeing duckweed growing in the river. We were thrilled to see something green thriving in such a barren wasteland. (pp. 166–67)

He adds that now The Totoro Forest Project—inspired by his works— has become active in cleaning up the Tanase River and the woodlands at its source in the Sayama hills. The Totoro Forest in the Sayama hills was purchased by the National Trust movement known as The Totoro Home Fund. Miyazaki has himself participated in community projects for cleaning the river and forest region while also donating large sums of money for The Totoro Home Fund. It is this immersion in the natural science of ecology which has led Miyazaki to create not only manga and anime focusing on environmental themes, but also to have inspired as well as participated in the development of green movements directed toward environmental activism that aim to protect nature through developing principles of conservationism and sustainability through green living.

Art Imitating Life

Beginning with both the manga and anime versions of *Nausicaä*, Miyazaki's art depicts an astonishing vision of the evolving human-nature conflict and growing environmental crisis, leading toward a possible apocalyptic destruction of the world as it develops throughout the ages, from the ancient past, to the

present, to a prophesied Armageddon doomsday event in the distant future. The value of Miyazaki's vision—and more importantly, its impact—is perhaps best expressed by Tetsuji Yamamoto:

> Recently, Miyazaki-san finished drawing [his manga] *Nausicaä of the Valley of the Wind*. I was moved to tears. This makes me want to ask Miyazaki-san about his views on the environment. People find it very difficult to understand environmental problems from discussions about the ways in which the environment is being destroyed or the fact that the earth is facing these sorts of changes. But when these issues are depicted as in *Nausicaä of the Valley of the Wind*, they are forced to think about them in a symbolic manner. I am now urging my students to read *Nausicaä* because by reading it we are made to think and feel much more deeply than we do when we listen to what scholars say. (*Starting Point*, p. 414)

Nausicaä is speaking. The question is, will we listen? Perhaps because of Miyazaki, we shall.

20

Drawing the Self

SALLY JANE THOMPSON

*T*he scene is quiet and anxious. The young man's friends stand to the side looking on. Perhaps a light rain begins to fall. He stands silently gripping the sort of wound that would generally kill a person on the spot, feeling defeated. An internal struggle will now play out (possibly with a flashback or two thrown in for good measure) until eventually, he looks up again with determination in his eyes, having pushed himself further emotionally than ever before and thus, now able to do the same physically ... and resume his fight!

Anyone familiar with manga will recognize this immediately—the classic *shōnen* manga storyline of increasing challenges to be overcome by the young, male protagonist on his way to achieving both some actual goal and the accompanying self-realization. It could be physical fighting (of a variety of forms), or any other sort of "fight" or challenge—a sport, an art form, even a board game! Anything that a character could strive to be the best in. These manga, like other types of fiction, depict the formation of the self.

Take other manga genres—*shōjo* for example, *shōnen*'s young-female-targeted counterpart. Its stories often focus on the resolution of a romantic situation as the ultimate goal, and because of this emotional focus, tend to dwell on the internal experiences and reactions of the main character—one could say a very self-focussed approach. *Josei* is aimed at older young women in their teens and twenties, and tends to deal more with its main characters' postmodern disaffection, and a certain level of self-resolution. So here, not only does the story-telling focus on the internal as in *shōjo*, but the ultimate resolution may be existential rather than, say, the fulfilment of a romance (as it might be in *shōjo*).

These approaches are, of course, just dipping into the many ways manga approaches the self. But they are also all story elements, and manga is not just a textual medium, but a visual one. A major strength of graphic literature is its multiple concurrent forms of communication, and the interplay between these

elements. How the self is *drawn* in manga is a part of how the self is presented, whether as a clear complement to the story in question, or simply one more jumping-in point to the philosophical environment the story was created in.

The Self and Environment

In Western philosophy, the idea of the individual self has been central in how both life and theory are approached. Defining this self has been a primary metaphysical pursuit, and the main question has generally been "What am I?" rather than "What is humanity?" or "What is the world?" Numerous influential Western thinkers have seen the stripping away of environmental factors and societal influences as bringing the self to a purer, truer state. In Descartes's *Meditations*, he approaches his examination of the self by "assuming" (as a reasoning technique) that all the physical things he perceives around him do not really exist. This leaves an isolated "self" considering its existence.

Western thought has not denied the obvious fact that an individual self does interact with, experience, and relate to external factors. Descartes reminds his reader that "there are two facts about the human soul on which there depends any knowledge we may have as to its nature: first, that it is conscious; secondly, that, being united to a body, it is able to act and suffer along with it" (*Philosophical Writings*, p. 275). Descartes divides reality into two realms, mental and physical, and sees the mental realm as more trustworthy than the physical. Materialism is a reaction against that kind of thinking. Materialism insists that there is just one reality, the physical, with the intangible self being either an illusion or just an aspect of the physical.

Environment and Harmony

Japanese philosophy's history, from Shinto's initial phases and through its integration of Buddhist philosophies in the Nara and Heian periods, has tended to see the self as far more intrinsically connected to both the body and the rest of the world (like materialism, lacking the tension between mind and matter).

The influential Buddhist philosopher Kūkai (774–835 A.D.) espoused the idea that "The entire cosmos is no more than the thoughts, words and deeds of the Buddha called Dainichi . . . In a perpetual state of enlightened meditation, Dainichi performs the three great practices of esoteric Buddhism: the chanting of sacred syllables (*mantras*), the visualization of geometrical arrays of symbols (*mandalas*) and the performance of sacred postures or hand gestures (*mudras*). These three activities define the nature of the universe" (Thomas P. Kasulis, "Japanese Philosophy," *Routledge Encyclopedia of Philosophy*).

The spiritual or essential nature of the universe and the self is connected to physical action and being, which are considered illusory anyway. Thus Japanese philosophy saw the self and the body as more intrinsically connected than did its Western counterpart, and this connection with physicality allows for more connectedness with the surrounding world as well.

This may be partly why a sense of place is often seen as one of the main visual approaches that distinguishes manga from western comics. In *Making Comics*, Scott McCloud refers to manga's "strong sense of place. Environmental details that triggered sensory memories . . . Frequent uses of wordless panels, combined with aspect to aspect transitions between panels; prompting readers to assemble scenes from fragmentary visual information. . . Small real world details. An appreciation for the beauty of the mundane, and its value for connecting with readers' everyday experiences" (p. 216). A new scene might be introduced with an impressive double-page spread, with a long shot of the location, and smaller panels showing small-scale environmental details . . . a teapot lightly steaming, drops of rain falling off the edge of a roof, birds in trees overhead, rats scurrying past a garbage can. . . .

These environments are often shown in a resting state rather than with action occurring within them, placing the focus truly on the environments themselves. This visual focus on creating a strong sense of environment and a sense of unity with it (in keeping with Japanese Buddhist philosophy) could in fact be seen as a whole genre of comics in and of itself. Comics like Kozue Amano's *Aria*, Ashinano Hitoshi's long-running *Yokohama Kaidashi Kikou,* and Jiro Taniguchi's acclaimed *The Walking Man* all focus on the characters having positive, harmonious experiences in their surroundings.

Visually, these works tend to share some common approaches. A large amount of space and detail is allotted to backgrounds and environments. These environments tend to be hand-drawn, with a looser, more "drawn" style than one often sees in the very linear backgrounds of much contemporary manga. Many in this background-heavy type tend to show some stylistic influence from European comics, with fine inking, few ruler-drawn lines, and hatching and short strokes building up rich environmental detail.

We also see another important element in the visualization of this harmony, and that is the visual sympathy between the representation of the characters and their environment. The drawing style between backgrounds and characters is similar in line quality, texture, and stylization, thus allowing us to feel that these characters do in fact inhabit this environment, naturally and unconsciously.

An effective example of this visual sympathy is Iou Kuroda's *Sexy Voice and Robo.* The environment is not natural; it is the city of Tokyo—or perhaps an alternate Tokyo. It is presented as vibrant and pulsating with a hum of humanity—sometimes seedy, but full of accumulated life and personal histories.

This *life* is a central theme. Its main character, Nico Hayashi, is a teenage girl who professes a desire to be a spy or a fortune teller. In one scene she says of the city, "So many buildings . . . all full of people . . . strangers. They might be sad, or lonely . . . maybe they want to share their happiness . . . or things they don't know how to say" (p. 323). A theme communicated by both the textual *and* visual elements is that the city *all* has meaning, not just the main character who exists within it, interacting with other people who, also and equally, exist within it.

Iou Kuroda, *Sexy Voice and Robo*, p. 16; © 2002 VIZ Media, LLC.

This depth of environment would simply not communicate as strongly as it does without the total visual sympathy between the way the character and environment are presented. Both are drawn with exactly the same loose, inky brushwork, and the same level of attention. Backgrounds receive a healthy allotment of page space. Background crowds are made up of individual people, and the details of movement and daily life both go on around, and interact with, the main character.

Environment and Discord

However not all—perhaps not even most!—manga use the environment and surroundings to portray a sense of connectedness. Environments are rendered in a variety of ways, some of which imply the opposite of a sense of harmony.

One common approach is a certain unconscious connectedness, wherein backgrounds are present and are drawn in a convincingly sympathetic style, but without the focus on environment, integration, and immersion of the previously mentioned titles. These often tend to be action-based *shōnen* manga, so the focus is on the action and plot, and the environment exists to support a confident representation of these. We see in this a level of comfort and integration, which reflects the philosophical approach of integration with the physical world, but develops it to a lesser extent.

Kouyu Shurei, *Alichino*, Volume 1, p. 66; © 1998 TokyoPop.

Equally common is a purely informational approach to a character's environment, seen especially in *shōjo* manga, which focuses on the emotions of its characters in relation to their interactions with other characters. In these cases, a "sense of place" establishing shot may be used at the beginnings of a scene, but once the location has been established, backgrounds are dispensed with almost entirely. All visual focus turns to the characters, with the majority of frames being medium to close-up shots of their facial expressions. In the example from *Alichino* on the previous page, environmental detail is almost entirely absent, as is common in *shōjo*—even in fantasy comics such as this one, where one might expect a focus on the unique environment (for both the visual enjoyment of its unusual elements and to create a believable world for the reader). This isn't the same as a noticeable disconnect, but it does start to lean towards a more Western focus on self.

Shin Takahashi, *Saikano*, Volume 1, p. 55; © 2000 VIZ Media.

Due to Japan's Closed Country policy during the Edo period, Western thought did not have any major impact on Japan until the mid-1800s. "The process of modernization forced Japanese philosophers to reconsider fundamental issues . . . As it has assimilated Asian traditions of thought in the past—absorbing, modifying, and incorporating aspects into its culture—so Japan has been consciously assimilating Western thought since the early twentieth century. The process continues today" ("Japanese Philosophy"). Thus Western "individualism has never taken hold in Japan as a basis for social, ethical or political theory," but it is not surprising that, as part of a global economy (both

financially and culturally), ideas of disconnection and postmodern fragmentation may be seen in many contemporary manga. In some manga the way environments are used gives a feeling of an inbuilt struggle between self and environment, reminiscent of Western thought.

The panels from *Saikano* on the previous page illustrate the common background technique of using filtered photographs. Shin Takahashi's sketchy, soft, and rounded drawing style contrasts with the more crisp photographic background and can create a sense of distance or disconnect, especially when compared to the integration of the previously illustrated examples. As well as the *style* of background visual information, the *quantity* of it is also a strong tool in communicating how the character is interacting with their environment. One example already mentioned is the lack of backgrounds often used in *shōjo* manga, simply as a reflection of the characters' internally-directed focus. However, manga that do use some level of background fairly regularly may employ panels without backgrounds to communicate a shift to this internal state—that is, when characters are temporarily *taken out of their environment*—whether through receiving shocking news, experiencing feelings of love, or any other strong internal emotional response.

The panels from *FLCL* directly below feature both a style and reduction-based approach to showing a disconnect between the characters and the world around them, as the background crowds are drawn with no detail, morphing

Gainax and Hajime Ueda, *FLCL*, Volume 1, p. 112; © 2000 TokyoPop.

into a mass of populace of which the characters are not part. One thing to note here is the predominant process of professional manga creation in Japan. Many creators are employed by a weekly serial publication, and thus work under extremely tight deadlines. The system for making this possible includes the use of assistants, who fulfil numerous tasks for the main creator, often including the provision of backgrounds (which may be revealing in terms of their level of priority). Backgrounds may (especially in real-world settings which require buildings, cities, skies, and trees) be stock images or filtered photographs. The texture of a photograph, filtered or otherwise, will not be the same as the line quality of a drawn image. However this doesn't mean that all such manga is hurt by its schedules and multi-person approach, or that the use of photographs is wholly unsympathetic with the drawn images. The effect on how the self is expressed within its surroundings may differ from one comic to another.

The Self and Others

In a 1643 letter to Princess Elizabeth, Descartes mentions, as not contradicting "the arguments proving the distinction of soul and body," the "notion of their union which everybody always has in himself without doing philosophy— viz. That there is one single person who has at once body and consciousness" (*Philosophical Writings*, p. 281).

However, this idea of the one, unified, whole self has often been challenged and examined in philosophy as numerous thinkers have tried to get to grips with consciousness, and how a consciousness relates to itself and others. As it is often from the interactions between characters that stories are woven, it's worth looking at manga's visual approach to this.

Western philosophy's initial definitions of the self generally do not involve others at all. Going back to Descartes's *Meditations*, we see an example of the Western focus on "I" rather than "we" ("I... must conclude that this proposition 'I am', 'I exist', whenever I utter it or conceive it in my mind, is necessarily true," p. 67). After being philosophically satisfied of his own existence, the next question he asks is "What am I?" ("I want to know what is this 'I' of which I am aware," p. 70). "What then am I?" he asks, "A conscious being.... What is that? A being that doubts, understands, asserts, denies, is willing, is unwilling; further, that has sense and imagination" (p. 70). These are all individual mental actions that bear no relation to others or one's environment (although they may be prompted by them).

By contrast, traditional Japanese thinking sees the individual self as already containing the natural world and other people, so that "looking inward" finds these entities already there.

Mirrored Selves

Going back to manga with this in mind, one common kind of imagery is that of multiples. In fact, this is common as a plot device as well. By way of example, a thread on an online manga discussion forum about favorite anime and manga twins received seven pages' worth of replies, with over thirty sets of twins (and the occasional triplets or octuplets) from various manga mentioned. Visually, the idea of twinning is a very popular theme, particularly in illustrations (such as for posters, artbooks or splash pages). This is often emphasized by matching outfits or identical or mirrored poses.

CLAMP is a well-known and successful collaborative group of manga creators (working largely in shōjo) who frequently use this sort of plot element in their manga, and favour mirrored, dual and connected imagery. The examples to the left are from *Tsubasa Reservoir Chronicle* which show both literal and figurative use within the same comic. Here, we see examples of literal duplicate selves. They would be recognizable as such through character design alone, but still tend to often be drawn in mirrored poses, to strengthen the implication of connection, comparison and duality.

The images on the next page demonstrate a similar symmetry of pose and point-of-view used in panels that feature two separate characters. Such symmetry's use is already established within the story in images of literal duplicates or other selves. This allows it greater impact as a visual device to show a particular closeness or connection

CLAMP, *Tsubasa Reservoir Chronicle*, Volume 12, p129, and Volume 13 p. 5, 6; © 2005 TokyoPop.

CLAMP, *Tsubasa Reservoir Chronicle*, Volume 12, p. 168, and Volume 13, p. 10; © 2005 TokyoPop.

between characters, as well as simply extending a visual theme. Additionally, dozens of illustrated cover pages for chapters of the comic (and other CLAMP works) features two or more characters in exotic or elaborate outfits which match/complement each other in design as a pair or set.

These specially linked but separate characters are interesting in terms of the previously-mentioned philosophical approaches to the self's relation to others. The implication of a special connection could be seen to combine elements of both, as it goes beyond the self as a single, totally self-reliant ego, yet the link between two particular characters implies a strong individual nature to each of these characters for them to be able to find this 'specialness' in each other. Although it is unwise to read too much into what may simply be a visual choice or plot devise, the popularity of this sort of imagery may imply a foundation of multiple philosophical approaches underlying the manga being created in Japan today.

Haunting, Possession, and Split Personalities

Another common plot device in manga is that of characters who are haunted or possessed, or hold other selves within them.

In the "Continuous Identity" chapter of Lewis's *The Elusive Self*, he discusses the idea of multiple consciousnesses, and while he sums up his approach as "one body one person," he goes on to say that "evidence strongly

suggests that some paranormal events do happen" (p. 82), as he touches briefly on the possibility of telepathy and clairvoyance. He goes on to discuss schizophrenia, and the self in dreams. The "Internal Dialogue" chapter of Wiley's *The Semiotic Self* examines our relation to ourselves and the complexity brought about by the fact that thought can be argued to occur as "dialogue"—whether unconsciously or with various internalized "visitors."

This argument of Wiley's that our thoughts may occur as "dialogue," and the idea of inner "visitors" with whom we have these dialogues (as thought processes) may relate to Kasulis's model of relations in Japanese Philosophy (that "when I look inward to myself . . . I find also part of the relatents with which I am in internal relations" p. 338). However, this is not generally the sort of conflict or plot addressed in manga which feature haunting or possession . . . these are usually a completely different "self"—another individual in the Western mold—inhabiting the character's body. In Masashi Kishimoto's *Naruto*, some characters are "possessed" by demons, but the possession here means "serves as a vessel to hold" rather than "is taken over by." The demons are external entities who have wound up inhabiting them, and with whom the characters in question can at times have discussions, as separate entities. In Hotta Yumi and Obata Takeshi's *Hikaru no Go*, the main character is haunted by the ghost of a long-deceased person. However, the ghost is not even an internal presence but an external one who is simply attached to, and thus always present around the character. They converse as two separate people would.

Even comics which deal with Multiple Personality Disorder, dark internal selves, or differences between public behaviour and private thoughts do not often feature a subtle scale with a lot of uncertainty. Generally the separate personalities are extremely distinct. This exaggeration may be due to sheer plot effectiveness, or it may indicate perhaps a higher comfort level, due to Japan's philosophical history, with the more shaded internal 'conversations' and 'persons' that Wiley discusses. Perhaps something less than the extremes that are presented would not be as striking or disturbing as it would be to the Western viewpoint of an absolute self.

Examples in this area include Satomi Ikezawa's *Othello*, the main character in which has two completely binary personalities, which emerge one at a time (one of which is not even initially aware of the other). Kubo Tite's *Bleach* features a character with a dark inner self whose visual representation is an inversion of the character's (e.g. the whites of his eyes are black, and the irises white—as the manga is in black and white, the inversion comes across very effectively). A character in *Naruto* also has a visually represented, different internal self, but this is a comedic thread used to indicate that she acts falsely

to make others like her—a subplot used in other manga, but simply related to the character's feelings and choices rather than any genuine multiplicity of personality.

The characters in these manga certainly do react in a variety of ways, and some certainly do suffer existential crises of identity ("Who am I?"), for example the central character in *Othello*. However, many manga, especially involving possession or haunting, feature characters who express unease with the ramifications or general strangeness of their situation, but do not seem to have any existential confusion in their own sense of self because of it. This may relate to the target age group (as with *josei* manga's older audience relating to its more existential bent), but may also indicate that the question "Who am I?" is not as central as it might be in similar Western works, perhaps due to more comfort in Japanese thought with a less absolute self, or less focus *on* this self.

However, examples of split personalities like *Othello* do imply a self that is fractured in its multiplicity rather than whole. This contrast implies that at the other end of the scale there *is* a wholeness to the self, and, at least in extremes, this multiplicity is a problem. Thus, these manga may be coming from a hybrid view, that the selves portrayed have a need to be one whole self, but that the threat to this need comes only from an exaggerated multiplicity rather than the shades of others that are seen as part of self-identity in Japanese philosophy.

Naruto, *Bleach*, and *Hikaru no Go* are all examples of the *shōnen* manga *bildungsroman*; but *shōjo* (and occasionally *josei*) manga also uses similar themes, with more of a tendency towards duplication, contrasts, and gender. The enormously popular *Nana* (Ai Yazawa) features two characters of the same name, with often contrasting personalities but also a particular bond. Many *shōjo* manga have plots based around gender inversion or confusion, such as a girl passing as a boy to attend a particular school (Hisaya Nakajo's *Hana-Kimi*), or even just being mistaken as one (Bisco Hatori's *Ouran High School Host Club*), as well as the reverse—"gender-bender" or cross-dressing manga could be considered a genre in and of itself. This can be seen as another example of the multiple, fractured, or altered selves around which so many manga plots are based.

The way in which a character is shown to deal with a fracturing or multiplication of self may communicate something about the social and philosophical environment of the character or author. A fragmented, unclear or multiplied self may be seen as a more disturbing prospect to the Western view of the "whole" self. The reactions of characters in these stories certainly relates to the age and gender of their target audience. However, the range of reactions—from unperturbed to existentially panicked—may also, like the depictions of characters and environments, point to an originating milieu that includes both Western and traditional Japanese views of the self.

An Ongoing Discussion

Manga's visual structure and style are forms of communication that are parallel and equal to its narrative. The coexistence of text and image is, after all, what makes comics unique and exciting. As manga-influenced comics develop further worldwide, we may see this form being pushed in new ways to use its structure and visuals to maximum impact, with an awareness of the paradigms they may point to.

In stories with plots that relate directly to the journey of the self, the visual elements can serve as a means of subtly strengthening themes. Even in stories not explicitly about the journey of the self, the visual representations give us information about the cultural milieu in which they were conceived . . . in this case, a contemporary Japan where Western philosophy of the self coexists in ongoing discussion with traditional Japanese philosophy.

HAMON

21

Why Do They Look White?

JASON DAVIS, CHRISTIE BARBER, AND MIO BRYCE

So why do manga and anime characters look white? It's probably the question that most manga fans dread hearing. It can be harmlessly asked, prompted by a "third party" seeing a friend of a friend's manga or anime collection. It can also be casually overheard when browsing in libraries or chain bookstores as a response that goes no further than the cover of the graphic novel or DVD cover that prompted its verbal release. Why do characters from Japanese comics and animations look white?

For those with only a passing familiarity with manga as originating from Japan it's the most obvious question to ask. And if you frequent chain bookstores stocking an international range of well-browsed graphic novels, manga translations, film adaptations and TV spin-offs, it's not very hard to come up with more specific variations of this question that recognize the other visual media manga and anime compete with in book and comic stores. Why is Sailor Moon as white and as blonde as Ms. Marvel or Power Girl? Why is Naruto as blond and blue-eyed as Luke Skywalker? Why is Makino Tsukushi from *Boys Over Flowers* as wide-eyed as Princess Ariel from *The Little Mermaid*?

A flippant answer might be to raise one eyebrow and do a quick impersonation of Mr. Spock speaking to Captain Kirk on the discovery of a new life form: "They're Japanese Jim, but not as we know them."[1]

It might be a lame joke, but it does help point out a few of the key issues about why people would find manga and anime characters looking unmistakably white. It highlights the expectation that physical racial differences should be visible in a comic book from Japan. Those unfamiliar with Japanese visual culture are outsiders expecting recognizable Asian-looking faces, just as they recognize Asian-looking faces or African-American faces in North American

---

[1] A special thank you to Michael Martignago for clarifying with the speed of a librarian Spock's famous words.

or European comics and animation. Our joke also highlights what we don't know about Japanese visual culture.

Since the end of World War II, manga and anime have been influenced by American comics, film and animation, and these influences have shaped visual styles used in manga, especially as character designs rather than as drawings aimed at likeness of their Japanese creators. For decades now, these designs have been accepted, experimented with or challenged as conventional ways for representing faces, eyes and bodies in the print medium of manga or the film and video medium of animation. So much of what is first seen and accepted as appearing as white faces and bodies in anime and manga needs to be rethought as being the product of visual conventions or accepted ways of representing identifiable characters.

So are we saying manga and anime characters are accepted by Japanese readers as Japanese looking? Yes. And we're most certainly not the first authors to do so. Frederik L. Schodt, recognized in the English-speaking world and in Japan for his decades-long contribution to intercultural promotion of manga through his writings and English translations of manga series such as *Astro Boy, Ghost in the Shell,* and *Pluto,* argues for recognising anime and manga characters as Japanese "self-perceptions" or "self images" (*Dreamland Japan: Writings of Modern Manga,* p. 58).

Schodt reminds us that Disney animation such as *Snow White and the Seven Dwarfs* and *Bambi* had a strong influence on Osamu Tezuka's manga character designs, especially the use of large eyes for communicating emotions. With the incredible popularity of post-War manga characters created by Tezuka, these hybrid creations of Japanese and Western character designs become an industry-defining stylization that manga readers experienced as startlingly novel, and in time accepted as familiar as well as expected. And that's a cue to return to our helpful Star Trek reference.

If we return to our imaginary browsing of the graphic novel shelves in the bookstore we started with, what if during the perusal of the shelves of new manga releases the following title appeared: *Star Trek Ultimate Edition: The Manga* published by Tokyopop in 2009. Seeing this manga version of the original TV series, written by Chris Dows and drawn by Makoto Nakatsuka, helps raise some interesting issues. Not only is each member of the famous crew of the Enterprise individually recognizable, there is also a distinctly recognizable manga style to all of the characters. And the same can be said for the manga version of *Star Wars: A New Hope* by Hisao Tamaki, although character exaggeration, even deformation, is much more pronounced and dramatically stylized (as shown in the panel at the top of the next page).

But that's the point. Non-Japanese manga fans are aware of these overlapping visual elements—the recognizable character designs and the manga

stylization—because of their familiarity with and acceptance of the striking Japanese artwork as representations for character creation and sequential story-telling. And this acceptance is being expanded on within the graphic novel market. The manga universe of manga-like visual styles has gotten bigger with Marvel Comics releasing the Marvel Mangaverse, a series of manga versions of Marvel characters.

So these manga hybrids, like those created by Tezuka, which now compete with *Naruto* and *One Piece* can be seen as presenting a challenge to those unfamiliar with manga styles: if they do represent another of way of visualising the whiteness of already existing white characters, then what is it about the familiarity of the whiteness of non-manga characters in the first place?

From *Star Wars: A New Hope*; © 1998 Dark Horse Comics.

Race-ing Faces

One way we can think differently about the whiteness attributed to manga or anime characters is to ask if seeing the faces of such characters as white actually involves selectively focussing on or privileging some facial features over others. What if people are selectively "reading" character's faces as white? When we focus on some features and leave out others, we do end up with the same faces reflecting back something very different, something that isn't as non-Japanese.

You can see this for yourself when you flick through any books published on manga and look at the reproductions of some of the famous examples of female characters from shōjo manga. Looking back at you from the pages might be the "saucer eyes" belonging to Princess Sapphire from Osamu Tezuka's *Princess Knight*, or the large dark eyes of Chi from CLAMP's *Chobits* or the large glassy blue eyes dotted with starry points of light owned by Marie-Antoinette in Riyoko Ikeda's *The Rose of Versailles*. These examples are typical of shōjo manga characters from the last thirty years, but to say they look white because of their

non-Japanese eyes ignores what they have in common—smallish noses, small mouths and rounded faces.

These repeated facial features in manga character faces are hard to associate with what is regarded as stereotypical for whiteness. This presents some problems for anyone claiming that these characters are obviously white.

Firstly, to see such faces with small mouths and noses as white is to ignore the longer history of Japanese depictions of white people as foreigners and outsiders with long noses, from caricatures of Commodore Mathew C. Perry in the 1850s to American soldiers in war manga of the 1960s. A much more recent example can be found in the 2009 science fictional manga series *Pluto* by Naoki Urasawa and Osamu Tezuka in which European characters—humans and robots—are depicted with having large curved noses. In this scene from the first volume, the robot detective Gesicht and the bespectacled Professor Hoffman are in a robotics laboratory in Düsseldorf, discussing the benefits of travelling to Japan.

From *Pluto. Urasawa X Tezuka, 001*; © 2009 VIZ Media, LLC.

Secondly, to see only large blue eyes and blond(e) hair as unambiguously non-Japanese, and even as indications of a desire for white features, is to project an idea of what Japanese faces are supposed to look like. Not only does this projection of what Japanese facial features must conform to ignore the occurrence of rounded eyes in Japanese people. But to view the alterations of Japanese eyes ranging from make-up to surgical modification as practices aimed at denying "natural" Japanese identity for a face with features that are more visibly white

is to fail to see desirable aesthetic ideals as reflective of contemporary Japanese trends in beauty, which female manga characters both mirror and promote.

The Marked and the Unmarked:
And We Don't Mean Piles of Students' Essays on Manga

If the previous arguments help to question and even challenge people's reactions to manga and anime and show how perceptions of whiteness are the result of misrecognized or mistakenly projected ideas, then the next question worth asking is why do such ideas stay unexamined? One way to tackle these questions is to draw on some of the analytical tools developed by the Russian-born linguist Roman Jakobson, in particular Jakobson's concept of markedness, which is an approach that's been applied to manga by Matt Thorn ("The Face of the Other," 2004, available at <http://www.matt-thorn.com/mangagaku/faceoftheother.html>).

Although Jakobson originally explored this idea in relation to his study of the linguistic units of language in the 1930s, it has also been adapted for studying literature as well as wider cultural forms involving language or visual signs such art or advertising. Jakobson's idea is that within a language system there are some terms which communicate what they mean in a general way. They're taken as obvious, and so are unmarked.

On the other hand, there are terms which communicate more specific meanings. This is achieved by using a term that's derived or departs from the unmarked term, and this term is marked. A quick way of getting at Jakobson's idea about markedness can be demonstrated with some traditional linguistic examples. The word "prince" as in the title of the manga series *The Prince of Tennis* by Takeshi Konomi is unmarked while the word "princess" as in *Princess Knight* by Osamu Tezuka is marked as feminine. Similarly, the manga title *Lone Wolf and Cub* by Kazuo Koike and Goseki Kojima contains both unmarked and marked terms. Wolf is unmarked whereas cub is marked as a young wolf; all wolf cubs are wolves, but not all wolves are cubs.

Now, you might be thinking: How can this help with thinking about whiteness? It looks as if markedness and unmarkedness relate only to the signs we communicate with, like the words you're reading here, rather than what somebody thinks they see on the cover of a manga.

Jakobson's work on markedness goes further than linguistic signs. Looking at the terms or categories we use to understand and communicate about the world as marked and unmarked can help with seeing how they involve and reproduce dominant social and cultural realities. This is because the unmarked term or category is privileged over the marked, so much so that it is accepted as naturally reflecting the ways things are. To explain this

we need to return to our word examples of unmarked and marked. When the word "man" is used to refer to all of humanity as in the term "mankind", the word is being used to communicate a non-sex specific meaning. It has an unmarked relation to the human species it collectively refers to. The extra meaning "man" communicates is achieved without the need to mark or make a different sign in relation to it.

On the other hand, woman is a *marked* term, with the extra mark or sign *wo*man referring specifically to adult *fe*males. Even *fe*male is the marked addition or sign added to the word male to communicate a sex-specific term. And if you find that last example is just a word that can't have any relation to how gender differences between men and women have been understood, think about marked expressions like *female* doctor or *male* nurse. Such terms speak volumes about the traditional exclusivity of gendered professions as unmarked, as naturally male or female only domains. Jakobson's investigation of language as sign systems showed that unmarked and marked pairings, like man and woman, are in an oppositional relation that is culturally weighted in favour of the unmarked over the marked. This is because the unmarked (man) is accepted as that which comes first, and is privileged as reflecting reality and as naturally standing in for members of both sexes, whereas the marked (woman) will always be thought of and experienced as secondary or dependent on and subordinate to the unmarked.

To get back to our anime and manga examples, think about titles such as *Samurai Champloo, Samurai Deeper Kyo* and *Samurai Executioner*. They all invoke and rely on general ideas and associations we might have about the historical subject of the samurai. But titles like *Samurai Girl Real Bout High School* and *Afro Samuari* are marked with extra terms or signs that invoke the specific gender identity and non-Japanese racial identity of their characters against the traditional and natural identity of the unmarked Japanese male samurai. Put simply, a samurai can be female or black and not just a Japanese man. Moreover, it might be their non-male and non-Japanese identities that will challenge the privileged traditional status of the Japanese male samurai.

And that's the point of looking at the unmarked in relation to the marked. When people unfamiliar with manga and anime characters see only white characters, they're doing two things. They're taking their experiences of predominantly white-faced characters in comics and animation they've seen in a predominantly white society such as the United States, the United Kingdom or Australia as *unmarked*, as reflecting how comic and cartoon faces naturally look. Looking at anime and manga characters' faces and learning they're from Japan, there's the expectation that the faces need to be visually marked as Japanese, that they need to look like Japanese faces. The stark contrast between unmarked and marked images that comes out in this visual encounter

is also revealing of the way unmarked signs are passed over or accepted without further thought. It isn't just that manga and anime characters are not marked as Japanese, but as manga expert Frederik L. Schodt reminds us (*Dreamland Japan*, pp. 60–62) there's the added invisibility of the social and cultural assumptions at work when we recognize a cartoon or comic face as naturally being a white face in a pre-dominantly white society. Comic and cartoon faces are taken as reflecting back the creator as well as the viewer as "self-images." But they are recognized as "self-images" because of the visual conventions that have been culturally shared and reproduced by the creators and readers.

If They're Not White, then What Are They?

For some, it might be the case that the concept of markedness we've introduced hasn't done much to raise doubts about what they think they're seeing when they look at manga or anime characters. I know they're not white, but still, it's asking a lot not to think of the characters as white. Our discussion might have even provoked even more questioning responses that put the burden of what we're hoping to get you to think about manga back onto us: If they're not white, then what are they? But such questioning is very revealing. As much as what we've looked at so far can be acknowledged and accepted as the case, to still think that there's some truth about manga characters being white opens up more issues about how people understand race as something real in the world. In fact, examining how whiteness involves an unexamined expectation of other races needing marked identifiers of non-whiteness exemplifies some of the ways race can be explored as a socially shaped reality.

Is There Race in Manga and Anime, then?

There's two ways of approaching this question. On the one hand (and that's the unmarked right hand), if you mean the storyline identification or graphic depiction of race by identifiable racial markers, then yes, such characters do exist. For example the character of Kenneth Yamaoka, a Japanese-American New York senator and presidential candidate, in *Eagle: The Making of an Asian-American President* by Kaiji Kawaguchi. Another example is the manga *World Apartment Horror* created by Satoshi Kon and Katsuhiro Ōtomo which depicts the plight of illegal Chinese, Filipino, Pakistani and Indian immigrant workers in Japan. Other examples represent the sub-cultural consumption of blackness that is part of the circulation of African American cultural identities in contemporary Japanese visual culture. Such images include the *Afro Samurai* franchise created by Takashi Okazaki, the black sprinter Dan Davis attempting to escape the Matrix in Yoshiaki Kawajiri and Takeshi Koike's short film "World Record" from *The Animatrix* anime, to the Japanese character of Tomomi Nomiya copying his hair style

from Kobe Bryant from the Los Angeles Lakers in *Real,* Takehiko Inoue's manga series on wheelchair basketball.

But there have also been racist stereotypes and caricatures used in manga such as Osamu Tezuka's 1950s depiction of African "natives" in his manga series *Jungle Taitei* [Jungle Emperor]. In the early 1990s Guy Jeans and Hiramitsu Minoru's manga series *Reggie* about an African American baseball player, Reggie Foster, portrayed the character as a stereotypical black athlete requiring control and guidance from his white agent. And more recently, "Sambo" caricatures of black Africans in the published English translation of a 2006 volume of Riichirō Inagaki and Yūsuke Murata's manga series *Eyeshield 21.*

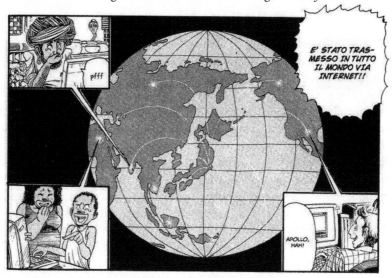

From *Eyeshield 21*, Volume 7; © 2006 VIZ Media LLC.

On the other hand, what does it mean for race to be "in" a manga or an anime? Obviously, it means to include depictions of characters that are racially or ethnically marked and therefore recognizable as one race or another. And this has been the driving force for creation and publication of comics and graphic novels that have provided and continue to offer readers positive representations or depictions of non-white characters, such as the African-American superhero comics published by US-based Milestone Media in the 1990s and the Muslim manga characters created by the Libyan-born UK manga artist Asia Alfasi. Recognizing that US and UK comics and manga are being created to reflect diverse racial and ethnic identities as positive alternatives to mainstream media is something that manga scholar Matt Thorn highlights as informing the cultural expectation that Japanese manga characters reflect their racial difference from non-Japanese.

But this brings us back to the question we posed at the start. What is it about race as a category or quality that is being referred to with a manga or anime image as well as the cultural need for images that affirm difference? What we've looked at so far with manga and anime does suggest a number of ways in which we come to know what is race is: it's a visible, bodily aspect of individuals; it involves recognition of an individual's family line as in the case of the Japanese-American character Kenneth Yamaoka; it can involve having particular experiences of unmarked privilege or daily reminders of stereotypes and racist images or even being made invisible by mainstream media; and it can involve defining oneself through and having reflected back shared images or representations affirming difference and having it recognized in a white, Christian dominated society.

What we've highlighted here are a number of different ways of understanding what race is. It's something visible and physical. And at the same time, individually defined and experienced as well as involving shared understandings across individuals at a larger social level. So, the next question might be whether one of those qualities or categories, namely the physicality or biological reality of race, is common to all of them, and so can be said to be more deeply defining of what race is. Or should we think of race as a socially shaped reality more than anything else?

How Is Race Real?

Philosophical investigation of what race is, as well as ways in which we can critically question and challenge such understanding, involves engaging with the following: what kind of thing is race and how can we have valid knowledge about it? This involves questioning how we think about race as a category that is used to classify or divide humans into racial groups or kinds based on shared characteristics that define the essential differences of one race from another.

Asking how race is real might sound like an unnecessary question for philosophy. Philosophical engagement with race and racial issues has been mostly in terms of applied ethics, human rights, equality, and affirmative action. And the reality of what makes an individual belong to a certain racial group is philosophically accepted and taken as a given kind or category, as something unmistakably real out there in the world, as something that can and does affect, and has historically affected, an individual's employment, education, and housing opportunities.

Yet philosophical questioning of how race is understood as real can involve looking at how race is a historically and socially constructed category or kind as opposed to being a natural kind. For contemporary philosophers such as Charles W. Mill, Lucius Outlaw, and Sally Haslanger critically thinking about

race starts by accepting that race is not a category reflecting natural properties that have an independent reality existing outside of the influences of belief shaping human history and social life. This means that the objectivity of what can be said about race doesn't come from the independent existence of biological properties that determine racial characteristics, or what Charles W. Mills refers to as "racial realism" (*Blackness Visible: Essays on Philosophy and Race*, p. 47). Rather, the objective nature of race as something real comes from the social basis for what can be said and thought about race in a particular society, and that's everything from individual beliefs, shared ideas and understanding to larger institutional forms such as laws and political policies. This means that the properties that define a racial category are more social than natural, so we should focus on the reasons for thinking this way about race and how such thinking is philosophically formulated.

Arguments for the social reality of race stem from the historical and social differences in racial classification as well as changes in the genetic understanding of race as a biological reality. Historically, racial classifications have changed. Before the United Sates Civil War, the US Census collected data on people by dividing them into three categories: native born, foreign and Irish. Italian immigrants to the US were once racially recognized as neither white nor black.

Similarly, racial categorization can be country or regional-specific. A person regarded as black in the US can also be considered half-black or "brown" or even white in Latin America and the Caribbean. In terms of the genetic discoveries resulting from exploring the genetic makeup of humans, the scientific support for biological reality of humans being divided into discretely defined racial groups has been seriously challenged. Of the entire genetic material comprising human DNA, only 0.1 percent of human genetic sequences vary from one person to another. And of that small percentage, a very tiny fraction, only 3 to 10 percent of that variation in human genetic diversity relates to racial differences or traits. Moreover, genetic variation is greater within genetically identified racial groups or populations than between them. This means that there isn't a genetic essence to biologically support the racial groupings we've inherited that have been based partly on physically visible differences.

To translate these challenges to how we understand what race is into philosophical terms, it's necessary to turn to traditional areas of philosophical questioning such as metaphysics and the "-ologies" that accompany most text book definitions of metaphysics; ontology and epistemology. Metaphysics is concerned with the deeper nature of reality, of what really exists. Ontology is a part of metaphysical questioning as it refers to the philosophical entities that are foundational for what we think is real, and epistemology involves questioning

and thinking about how we come to understand and have knowledge about ourselves and things in the world.

To think about race metaphysically is to think about the ontology of race, to think about the foundational basis of what constitutes racial identity. And as we've already noted, the idea of race having a biological essence or an ontological character shaped by genetics doesn't support the kind of everyday understanding of gaining knowledge about racial categories based on the physical visibility of race or what we know about our ancestors. In fact, as Charles W. Mills points out the ontological status of race involves three "nots":

> Race is not foundational: in different systems, race could have been constructed differently or indeed never have come into existence in the first place. Race is not essentialist: the same individuals would be differently raced in different systems. Race is not 'metaphysical' in the deep sense of being eternal, unchanging, necessary, part of the basic furniture of the universe. (*Blackness Visible*, p. 48)

What Mills argues for is the social ontology of race, of race being "a contingently deep reality" which means that what we might think as naturally metaphysical about race actually reflects the everyday social reality of a community or a country at a particular point in time.

To help us think further through the social ontology of race, Mills explores this social metaphysics via an analysis of everyday criteria for racial membership. These categories include bodily appearance, ancestry, self-awareness of ancestry, public awareness of ancestry, culture, experience, and self-identification (*Blackness Visible*, p. 50). As categories that are part of everyday, ordinary understanding of racial membership, Mills highlights how these have changed overtime, as well as how they inform the knowledge people have of themselves and of others as racially identifiable.

Some of these categories relate to what we've looked at so far with manga and anime, which seems to suggest that manga and anime are becoming part of the everyday, ordinary ways in which our understanding of racial membership is being reproduced. The projection of "whiteness" onto manga characters reflects how we can have knowledge about racial categories via the visible, bodily aspects of individuals, while the supposed whiteness that those unfamiliar with manga see reflects privileged experiences of white folk.

In the case of individual and public awareness of ancestry as a way of understanding racial membership, this is clearly reflected in the Japanese-American character Kenneth Yamaoka in the manga series *Eagle: The Making of an Asian-American President*. And in the case of the international manga of Asia Alfasi, her work contributes to the cultural process of Muslim self-identification.

Living with Robots

Saying that the reality of race is more social than natural doesn't mean that there's only a subjective or individual aspect to race. That's to say, it's mutually shared and recognized at a socially, wider collective level. It isn't just the case that individuals experience racial difference at an individual level. What gives meaning to an experience of or identification with racial identity is an intersubjective or shared meaning, not an individually created one. Recognition of racial identity as well as implementing changes that affect and eradicate racism involves intersubjective recognition through laws, political and governmental institutions and public policy.

Urasawa and Tezuka's treatment of robots in *Pluto* reflects this discussion of the social ontology of race, suggesting with its images race and race relations. In *Pluto* robots and humans, although physically different, co-exist in meaningful ways. What is fundamental to this shared existence is an intersubjective dimension shaping the ways humans socially recognize the existence of robots as individuals. This is evident in a number places in the series, notably in the way it uses the historical dimensions of US race relations to depict the social world of humans and robots. Civil rights and international rights ratified by the United Nations have been granted to robots, protecting them against discrimination. And the more human looking robots such as Uran, Atom, and Gesicht the Europol detective repeatedly "pass" for being human, a direct reference to the history of the social recognition or misrecognition of non-white peoples as white. There are also reminders of racist organizations as well as violence perpetuated by racists to terrorize those promoting the rights of the socially excluded. A robot hate group wanting robot laws abolished models itself on the Ku Klux Klan, and prominent human campaigners for robots' legal rights are murdered. But there's also another aspect of the series that's race-related.

Although it's not apparent when reading *Pluto*, its focus on robots, like the focus on cyborgs in the manga and anime versions of *Ghost in the Shell*, tells us something about the socially constructed nature of the relationship of Japanese society to technology. Why is it that robots are immensely popular in Japan while artificial intelligence is the big research area for US scientists? It might be that robots offer solutions to Japan's future of an ageing population that can be cared for by tireless workers. These futuristic workers may also provide possibilities for solving Japan's increasing dependence on immigrant workers. Should we read into the civil rights and legal protections for robots in *Pluto* a fictional way of avoiding the existing social reality of race in Japan? Or does the series exploration of such issues represent the possibility of a step towards social recognition at a wider social level?

To some extent, the philosophical approach arguing for the social ontology of race fits with how manga is a part of the social reality of race. Remember the unexamined assumption about seeing whiteness? That's an example of the intersubjective nature of racial identity, of the shared meaning shaping the expectation that non-white races need to make their popular culture more racially marked. And this is part of how manga, although for different reasons, is a part of the individual experience of race, in both positive and negative ways. But manga is also becoming part of the social recognition of different racial and ethnic identities. We hope manga can go further as a metaphysical companion for engaging philosophically with how such mutual recognition needs to take place in racially and ethnically diverse societies.

Manga, *metaphysical*? No way!

Only if you're still seeing only white people.

22

Never Really There

ELIZABETH A. MARKS

*F*or many American fans, Japan has come to represent something similar to what Gotham City, Metropolis, or the modified New York City of Marvel's series are for comics audiences. Japan is deployed as a remote alternate universe, of which the fan has no direct experience and of which she is unlikely to acquire firsthand impressions.

Images of Japan in manga (illustrations juxtaposed with "screen tones," or manipulated photographs) are conceptually similar to old photographs. When presented with an image of a place and time that we have not directly experienced or can recall, we must rely on secondary sources to impose meaning. In the case of a photograph of ourselves as an infant, this is a process of studying an image of a baby and being told: "Look, *this is you.*" We then respond with recognition—"Ah, this is how I once was."

Encountering images that show places we have never been is a similar process: we're dependent on outside sources—captions or instructions in the case of manga—to interpret the contents. There is a kind of faith inherent in believing in illustrated visions of Japan, an uneasiness that may be assuaged by accumulating supplementary facts about the place, by studying Japan as a means to uncover the meaning of manga's images.

The Armchair Traveler

In order to fully understand manga, we must consider it as a mass-market commodity. Walter Benjamin referred to the difference between original artwork and globally circulating reproductions as one of *aura*—that intangible feeling one gets from standing in front of a painting in a gallery versus holding a printed image of the same painting. But what do we ultimately substitute for this absent aura to make the experience of reading manga one of enjoyment rather than a nagging feeling of absence?

American fans may compensate by educating themselves about manga's point of origin (Japan), just as fans of comics have historically been inclined to accumulate knowledge about the fantasy space of their favorite series. In other words, while manga's status as a commodity has eradicated a kind of cultural presence from it, it has also accumulated a different kind of cultural "odor" (to borrow Koichi Iwabuchi's term from *Recentering Globalization: Popular Culture and Japanese Transnationalism*, p. 24), one that will evolve during its passage between national borders, and yet remain indebted to its original creators' ethnic and social origins.

Smart American publishers cater to this drive by hyping their products' connection to Japan. Manga in the US signifies Japan by retaining original page orientation and sound *kana* (sound effects, represented by Japanese characters) in the background of panels, and by no longer electing to translate numerous Japanese cultural references, such as food names. It's assumed that American fans, like fans in general, will relish the experience of recognizing *mochi* or a *kotatsu* table within the context of a story. Accordingly, manga and anime fans dominate Japanese-language classes in the US, and frequently express their desire to learn the language in terms of cultural references from the entertainment they consume. Such classes mediate between the remoteness of Japan as a place, and the proximity of its cultural exports; they ideally train the American fan to bypass the intervention of an instructive authority—the one who tells them what they are seeing and filters the aura of the original Japanese product.

Fans accustomed to this marketed illusion of authenticity react with indignation when the converse is revealed to be true. When Tokyopop revealed that it had been editing one of its most successful series, *Initial D*, to be more palatable to an American audience, fans responded as though they had been betrayed, accurately pointing to the discrepancy between marketing and production practice.

Such revelations seemingly validate practices like fansubbing (fan subtitling of anime series) and scanlating (scanning manga pages and translating them), if the fan is to ensure greater proximity to the Japanese original, and facilitate the retention of cultural aura. Moreover, Tokyopop's striving to conceal its editorial practices reveals both an awareness of the value its products have as authentically Japanese, and a curious sense of proprietary protectiveness towards what is less a straightforward process of importing and selling a product, and more about grooming a commodity for maximum profit.

That fans sense this conflict of interest is to their credit, though their attempt to move closer to manga's creation-space (the moment, when the photograph is taken, or when the drawn page still possesses the aura of an original object) is somewhat like grasping at smoke.

Manga in Japan is so ubiquitous as to be a kind of historical record; however, once imported to the US, it becomes a medium requiring excavation. Those who are able to visit Japan encounter the country itself as if it were evidence; it's only with concerted effort that fans are able to dissociate the reality of Japan from the mediated and commoditized version they have acquired via manga or its animated facsimile, anime (let alone from the many other mediated forms in which Japan is delivered to us). The spark of recognition an American fan experiences upon encountering Japan, or even many Japanese goods for the first time, is of equating the reality back to the manga, rather than the converse. Susan Sontag addressed this process in her discussion of the way most Americans experienced 9/11—by retreating into comparisons of events to filmic moments (saying, for example, that "it was like a movie") and highlighting the process by which most of us experience episodes of international conflict through photojournalism. Indeed, the comprehensive intercession of media in our lives suggests that the interpretation of Japan via manga scarcely registers to us as an atypical way of conversing with the foreign.

Drawing (for) the Machine

So then, do American comics have a more potent aura than manga because of the greater proximity to their "source?" Probably not since mainstream domestic comics reference worlds that are scarcely closer to an American audience than Japan is. And aura is largely lost to the process of production common to comics and manga.

In both countries, this means there is often only a tenuous connection between the individual page and the artist given credit for it, and that we are far removed from the original artwork by the time we buy a copy.

In Japan, it's common for *manga-ka* (manga artists) to hire staff in order to meet their deadlines, and manga is often created in a process resembling an assembly line. The nature of manga production is linked to exigencies such as low pay per page for most artists, which forces them to work on many serializations at a time and mandates the use of assistants. However, when *manga-ka* become famous they may also elect to decrease their involvement in their own series.

In one extreme case, Saito Takao (*Golgo 13*) essentially ran a factory, with fifteen full-time staff members and seven or eight people at a time supplying story scripts! (According to Frederik Schodt in *Manga! Manga! The World of Japanese Comics*, Saito sometimes only penciled in the faces of leading characters.) In this case, aura becomes speculative, as even original copies hold only marginal traces of an individual artist's aura; it's merely an abstract, imaginary notion of a moment of creation that never existed.

Economic constraints inspired a similar approach to comics production in the United States. Before publishing *The Fantastic Four* in the early 1960s, Marvel Comics relied on the imitation of successful formulas created by fellow publishers—a practice common in the manga industry where competition between publishers such as Kodansha, Shōgakukan, and Shuiesha is intense. The quality of comics at this time suffered by the familiar constraints of low pay per page, and in the US, feelings that staff were creating stories for an audience of undiscriminating children.

Although American comics are highly diverse if one looks beyond the most high-profile series released by Marvel and DC, manga's more prominent diversity creates a misperception that its publishers are more willing to take risks, and are therefore as devoted to the medium as an art form as they are a commodity. Accusations of greed and profiteering are therefore consistently made by American fans against American comics publishers and distributors of Japanese manga, but less commonly by Americans against the Japanese manga industry itself.

Nonetheless, the profit-mindedness of both countries' industries can be inferred by their tendency to engage in mass merchandizing of characters, and the successful passage of comics or manga series into cartoons or anime and feature-length films. Successful manga and comics series often become radio dramas, audio recordings, novels, plays, and of course, the ubiquitous paperbacks of compiled stories. And although the Internet has enabled non-traditional American comics to gain broader audiences in a way that used to be impossible, the non-superhero graphic story has yet to attain comprehensive mainstream appeal to the same degree as manga has in the US and Japan.

Aura Meets Collaborative Media?

So has comics further fractured its aura by allowing its most famous series to pass between artists, therefore complicating the connection between art and artist? Although this practice has generally been limited to the major superhero franchises, it's predominantly these series that are identified by manga fans as their motivation for disliking comics. As I've pointed out, these products belong to an industry wherein a single author rarely works alone from start to finish. Further, it's possible that rotating casts of authors and illustrators have lent the superheroes themselves an aura that somehow supersedes that of any particular artist: Spider-Man is more potent than the staff that brings him to life, and embodies a historical tradition rather than a particular moment. (This may also be why he has been resurrected several times by popular culture.) And although the "many artists––one series" phenomenon is rare outside of the superhero franchises, it's worth pointing out the extent to which this

practice has benefitted comics, producing some of the most critically acclaimed American comics, from Frank Miller's *Daredevil* (1979) and The *Dark Knight Returns* (1986)[1] to Neil Gaiman's *The Sandman* (1989), Chris Claremont and John Byrne's's *(Uncanny) X-men* (1975), John Broome and Gil Kane's *Green Lantern* (1959), Neil Adams and Dennis O'Neil's *Green Arrow / Green Lantern* (1970), *Captain America* (the 1964 revival) and *The Flash* (1956 revival).

The tendency for comic-book publishers to get rich while artists remained poor, which most notoriously affected *Superman*'s creators, Jerry Siegel and Joe Shuster, has largely been replaced since the 1980s by a manga-esque cult of the artist, and a predictably large pay gap between average artists and superstars. It has been common since then for fans to know the names of their favorite artists and the 'big names' just as it is in Japan. Chris Claremont and John Byrne of *X-Men* fame are one such writer-artist team, whose salaries outstripped those of their peers. This struggle to map an individual to a particular series is an intriguing means of returning personality to a mass medium, of imposing the aura of an artist on his or her globally circulating work. Where the texture of ink on paper can no longer be detected, aura is assigned to the *style* of a particular artist in order to facilitate the product's passage from mass produced commodity to the realm of unique objects.

Loving the Company

This process has been assisted by several practices used commonly in manga and historically employed by Marvel Comics as well. Stan Lee understood the financial benefit from cultivating the aura of artists, and of signifying place in his commodity-series, and broke with comic-book tradition in acknowledging the full staff of each comic book to his readers instead of just the writer (usually himself). He nicknamed his staff "The Bullpen" and gave them each affectionate alliterative nicknames (Jolly Jack Kirby, Sturdy Steve Ditko, Jazzy Johnny Romita). By emphasizing the human in the realm of mass production, Lee constructed Marvel itself as a place worthy of identification, re-envisioning the company as a fantasy world not unlike the space of Japan for many contemporary American fans.

In addition to making Marvel appear small and friendly via the foregrounding of its staff, the company cultivated a community of fans with a

---

[1] *The Dark Knight Returns* sold out and was later reissued as a graphic novel. It was the first original superhero work to be reviewed seriously and favorably in the mainstream press. Its release sparked a resurgence in Batman's popularity and led to the release of the Batman movies in 1989, throughout the 1990s, 2005, and 2008. This series would not have been possible under the mid-twentieth-century Comics Code because of its complex handling of human motivation and its iconoclastic approach to authority.

perceived stake in maintaining its 'universe'. It encouraged and reprinted fan letters, and solicited participation in the Marvel Universe by its issuance of "no-prizes"—that is, recognition alone—to fans who were able to point out continuity flaws in its storylines and explain them away.

Apparently, the Marvel Universe held similar use-value for 1960s-1970s-era comics fans that Japan does for manga fans, and this exclusive 'insider' knowledge has been manipulated in both cases for profit. Publishers of manga and comics monetize the enjoyment that fans take in being able to identify references missed by more casual readers. In the case of manga, this means locating the behavior and environment of characters in Japan's cultural history, while for comics fans the same practice applies to the history of characters and worlds that, while invented, are frequently no less accessible. However, this practice has frequently been interpreted as indicating something unique about the relationship between Japan and the US or of the meaning of Japan to American fans, rather than as signifying the common currency of fandom.

I Was Here

A similar means of bridging the gap between moment-of-consumption (reading) and moment-of-creation can be found in the tendency of *manga-ka* to break the "fourth wall," that is, to employ self-mocking jokes and overt acknowledgement of the reader (see top of next page for an example).

Tezuka is perhaps the most prominent and respected *manga-ka* to employ this technique. In *Phoenix*, Volume 1 (p. 231), for example, Masato tries to amuse a clone of his beloved Tamami by drawing cartoons, but finding his technique lacking, he wishes that Tezuka himself were there to help.

Tezuka's series, like those of Marvel, also frequently employed cross-references and plot continuity, though the connection established by this process circumvented his publisher.

Further facilitating this connection is a tendency of *shōjo* manga series to incorporate diary entries and personal tidbits by and about artists into their paperback compilations, depositing an invaluable relic of the series' creator within the manga collection and enhancing its appeal as a commodity—seemingly a requirement of

Osamu Tezuka, *Phoenix*, Volume 1, p. 231; © 2003 VIZ Media LLC.

Ai Yazawa, *Nana*, Volume 4, p. 55; © 2006 VIZ Media LLC.

the marketplace considering the likelihood, at least in Japan, that the consumer will have already read the actual story in serialized magazine format.

(Not) Made in Japan

In recognition of the value Japan has to the American 'culture industry', publishers have played with the cultivation and attachment of a free-floating Japanese aura to domestically produced products, as indicated by the number of series authored by Americans, that borrow the dominant aesthetic of manga or otherwise employ Japanese cultural cues. Tokyopop's editorial director Jeremy Ross claims that the ease with which a codified manga aesthetic and formula can be attached to content created in any country indicates that manga has become an international *style*. The company's founder and CEO Stuart Levy refines this position to suggest that the "Japanese spirit of manga" may be applied to local culture in order to produce a hybrid medium (Roland Kelts, *Japanamerica: How Japanese Pop Culture Has Invaded the US*, p. 173), while Viz's Vice President of publishing, Alvin Lu, envisions an outright convergence between manga and comics (as reported in *Publishers Weekly* by Heidi MacDonald in 2005 and Kai-Ming Cha in 2007).

Manga series authored by Americans are thus easily able to merge local culture with signifiers of Japaneseness. Although the practice of adopting Japan or Japaneseness into comics is actually nothing new (see Frank Miller's work, or *X-Men*), American-authored manga series go a step further in attempting to capitalize upon a market whose appeal transcends subject matter and visual signifiers in appealing to transnational space as the realm of experts conversant in its conventions.

This, Too, Is a Copy

The process by which Japan became a lucrative product saleable to (mostly young) Americans is a dense topic in its own right. Publishers first cautiously tested US consumers' willingness to engage with content deemed excessively foreign, and later frenetically embraced this alleged foreignness as part of their sales pitch. Essentially manga has always been just another commodity; already transnational by the time it arrived in the US thanks to the influences of American and European art on its origins, and possessing a consistent aesthetic that enhanced its value to the American marketplace. In other words, the space in which manga's stories generally unfold could be fictional (and often is) as much as it is Japanese. Manga informs us of a place called Japan as much because we are told it does, overtly and by certain signifiers that we have learned 'mean' Japan (big eyes, colorful hair, and even the format of manga books) as by any historical and local manifestations within its content.

Therefore, it's important to identify how American manga fans come to understand Japan, and to consider this as a potential instance of fan relation to what is essentially a fantasy-space. In examining the process by which manga and comics are created and how capitalistic concerns inform this process, we increase our understanding of what is lost between moments of artistic creation and of fan reception, and can better infer the benefit to fans of specialized knowledge about creation-spaces and authors.

For Japanese fans of manga, like American fans of comics, this loss is simply the supposed aura of the artist. However, American manga fans often lack the ability to identify what they see with any substantive cultural reality, and teach themselves about Japan as a means of beginning to bridge the gap.[2]

---

[2] My opening description of how fans who have never been to Japan view images of that culture in manga draws from Siegfried Kracauer's philosophical treatise on old photographs in *The Mass Ornament: Weimar Essays*.

23

Being Cute and Being Cool

THORSTEN BOTZ-BORNSTEIN

A young black man strolls down the street in Oakland, California's African American community. He is wearing a Chicago Bulls athletic suit with expensive matching sneakers. The sneakers are untied and he walks with a light limp, leaning just a bit to one side. His arms take turns trailing behind him as he ambles on his way. He knows he is cool and looks good. He follows the popular rap groups and knows all the latest dance steps. Since he lost his job as a stock clerk six months ago, he has been unable to contribute to the support of his two children who live with his former girlfriend and her mother. Halfway down the block, he runs into a good friend who is similarly dressed. They exchange a variety of low-five and high-five handshakes. Using a combination of Black speech patterns and street terminology, they discuss the latest happenings and exchange ideas about generating some income.

—JOSEPH L. WHITE AND JAMES H. CONES, *Black Man Emerging: Facing the Past and Seizing the Future*

Shinjuku, Tokyo. A group of extremely high-heeled Japanese girls wobble towards a group of Japanese young men who are sitting at a restaurant table. The girls' faces are made up with thick layers of cream foundation and powder and all of them wear sparkly things in their hair. As they listen to the men, their outlined mouths are permanently smiling. Their shaded eyes, emerging under heavy fake eyelashes, adopt the shape of golf balls and convey the impression of astonishment as well as the vague feeling that whatever the males are saying will not be fully understood. The perpetual look of embarrassment, an effect of a sophisticated application of rouge, contributes to this impression. While they clap their hands whenever one of the males makes a joke, the few words that the girls occasionally breathe into the conversation come across as squeaky, high-pitched singsong sounds modeled on "cute" anime voices. Finally, one girl takes out her cell phone from which six plush animals dangle and shows off a recently added glittery toy. In unison the other girls scream: *kawaii*!

—Observed in Tokyo, June 2007

What do these two examples—the one African American cool, the other Japanese cute or *kawaii*—have in common? At first glance not much. One is masculine and preoccupied with the dissimulation of emotion; the other is feminine and engaged in the ostentatious display of sentimentality, and vaguely inspired by manga or anime behavior. Cool produces an aesthetic of the emotionally restrained and the detached, while *kawaii* excels in attachment to creations with resonances in childhood. Cool appears as an aesthetic used by the leader of the gang while *kawaii* seems to remain the option of women who have decided to remain children.

Still, in spite of these exterior oppositions, both phenomena have some things in common. Both are social expressions that invite interaction and involve the spectator's imagination. Both "hold back," are *potentially* sexually fecund, and operate within the realm of possibilities rather than appearing as openly threatening and aggressive behaviors.

Cool and *kawaii* are antidotes to stereotypes of their respective "official" societies, which are the blandness of a plain, barren, vague, and featureless white American monoculture, and the uniformity of postwar Japanese group-oriented society determined by the corporate worker's lifestyle, entrance examination prep schools, and the domestic boredom of housewives. It's within these modern environments that cool and *kawaii* attempt to establish personal identities.

In a more global context, cool and *kawaii* are even linked, as they combat, each in its own way, the American "uncool" aesthetics of Disney by introducing values of communities, cultural heritages, and histories. This becomes particularly obvious through the wide spectrum of fields covered by manga. The African American philosopher Cornel West sees "black-based hip-hop culture of youth around the world" as a grand example of the "shattering of male, WASP cultural homogeneity" (*Keeping Faith: Philosophy and Race in America*, p. 15). *Kawaii* culture engages in a similar fight against an "official" modernity attempting to replace it with a subtler mode of what West calls "New World Modernity."

Conquering the World

The new millennium is characterized by an international youth culture that is mainly dominated by two types of aesthetics: the Afro-American cool, which, propelled by Hip-Hop music, has become "the world's favorite youth culture,"[1] and the Japanese aesthetics of *kawaii* or cute, which is distributed

---

[1] National Geographic Worldmusic website <http://worldmusic.nationalgeographic.com/worldmusic/>.

internationally by Japan's powerful anime and manga industry. Hip-Hop has become "the center of a mega music and fashion industry around the world"[2] and "Black aesthetics," whose stylistic, cognitive, and behavioral outfits are to a large extent based on cool, has arguably become "the only distinctive American artistic creation" (*Black Man Emerging*, p. 60).

The 'got to be cool' rhetoric of global brands is, according to Nick Southgate's essay "Coolhunting, Account Planning and the Ancient Cool of Aristotle," "more often than not, an indirect way of saying 'got to be black.' For many of the superbrands, coolhunting simply means black-culture hunting" (*Marketing Intelligence and Planning*, p. 457). While, as writes Roland Kelts in *Japanamerica: How Japanese Pop Culture has Invaded the US*, "several recent studies have shown that American brand names have dramatically slipped in their cool quotients worldwide" (p. 211), what remains exportable are symbols of *black* coolness.

However, Japan has also managed to massively export cool products bearing traits of its own culture. Japan is no longer a faceless economic superpower. Sixty percent of the world's cartoon series are made in Japan and Japanese games running on PlayStation 2 and Nintendo are as popular. Recently, Asian cartoons like *Akira* have been bought by Hollywood producers and new schemes—like that of hit-producing music stars exclusively known as animated characters—have become acceptable for the American mainstream. Since the release of Ôtomo Katsuhiro's popular animation film *Akira* (1999), "Japanimation" continues to invade the world. Super Mario seems to be a better-known character among American children than Mickey Mouse.

While the world may not have been penetrated by a realistic appreciation of concrete Japanese lifestyles, young people are fascinated by a more or less abstract concept of *kawaii*. At present, the world is impressed by what Kelts has called the "third wave of Japanophilia" (*Japanamerica*, p. 5), the first one having taken place in the eighteenth and nineteenth centuries when European artists discovered a uniquely Japanese aesthetics and the second one in the 1960s when hippies and beatnik writers were drawn to Asian spiritual traditions. This time Japanese culture finds an ally in the form of an American subculture with which it can fuse: (black) American cool culture. Cool and *kawaii* are soft powers that consistently penetrate the cultural fabric of international youth culture. The situation is similar to what Benjamin Barber has said about the 1960s, when American music invaded the Caribbean. The Caribbean reacted with enormous music production of its own, of which reggae is only one well-known example (*Jihad vs. McWorld*, p. 12).

---

[2] US info State Government website <http://montevideo.usembassy.gov/usaweb/paginas/2006/ 06-190EN.shtml>.

The 1999 *Newsweek* article "Cute power!" which reported that "Western-style cool is out, everything Japanese is in" (*Newsweek Asia*, 8th November 1999) misinterpreted the situation. Cool and *kawaii* are interdependent. Even more, as a compact amalgam they develop a sort of "New World Modernity" often alluded to, directly or indirectly, in works by Roland Barthes, Cornel West, and other specialists of Japanese and African American culture.

Normally *kawaii* or cute are terms immediately related to that which is warm, as opposed to "cooler" temperatures. However, the relationships and interactions between cuteness and coolness are complex. While in "white" European and American culture, cool and cute were, most of the time, defined as opposites, the "New World Modernity" created by this Afro-Japanese aesthetics is able to unite both by following its intrinsic ironical patterns. This is the reason why the *Washington Post* has called Japan, which is the country of *kawaii*, "the coolest nation on Earth" (*Washington Post Foreign Service*, December 27th, 2003, p. A01). "J-cool" becomes a new global concept that needs to be analyzed by going back to the roots of coolness.

There are other indicators of this new fusion. Together with France, Japan—in spite of (or simply *because* of) its dominant *kawaii* culture—is the country outside of the US where Hip-Hop music has developed authentic roots and has almost been established as a local culture. Though Ian Condry affirms the contrary, in Japan Hip-Hop is *not* "a veritable macho island in a sea of cute stars" (*Hip-Hop Japan: Rap and the Paths of Cultural Globalization*, p. 164), but tends more and more towards a fusion of both poles.

The American pop artist Prince, who was in 1996 presented by *Esquire* as "both imposing rock star and diminutive dress-up doll," symbolizes this sort of aesthetics because as Rhonda Garelick has found, he radiates "snarling virility commingled with doe-eyed femininity" (*Rising Star: Dandyism, Gender, and the Performance in the Fin de Siècle*, pp. 155 and 158). The same kind of flexibility is present in Japanese manga culture which produces an aesthetics of ambiguity, of fluent transformation, and an "in-between" that cannot be found, for example, in the rigid moral dualism of Disney culture. Cool and *kawaii*, especially when they are used as intercultural concepts, help to reveal underlying patterns that are obvious since Marshal McLuhan's reflections on the hot and the cool in the 1960s. The present article addresses these questions by drawing an outline of a New World Modernity in which manga play an important role and which represents an alternative to "Western" mainstream modern culture.

Cool, Kawaii, and Decadence

In the two examples at the beginning of this chapter, cool and *kawaii* don't appear as approved aspects of displays of masculinity or femininity, but rather

as symptoms of anomie, confusion, anxiety, self-gratification, and escapism that many people would also link to the world of manga. As a matter of fact, both cool and *kawaii* have repeatedly been criticized as manifestations of a celebration of vapidity that should rather be combated. Miller reports that the term *burikko*, as a kind of "reified cute aesthetic" is closely linked to *kawaii* behavior. Though *burikko* has been one of the "most popular new coinages of the 1980s" ("You Are Doing Burikko! Censoring/Scrutinizing Artificers of Cute Femininity in Japanese," p. 149) young women who employ an apparently manga-inspired "falsetto voice" and "a glissando movement through a pitch range" (p. 148), and act childishly (especially in front of men) might be sanctioned by society for an exhibition of "feigned naïveté" (p. 151), at least "within certain age/status limits or locales" (p. 156).

Though cool and *kawaii* can and often do represent means to obtain authenticity, very often protagonists of cool and *kawaii* are content with empty stylizations and subversive liquefaction of values in which no deep belief in anything seems to subsist. Paradoxically, what once was meant to provide identity will later *deprive* people of a full-fledged personality. In other words, both cool and *kawaii* are 'good' and 'bad' at the same time.

Towards a New Afro-Japanese Culture

Why Afro-Japanese? In 1997, the Nigerian philosopher Fidelis Okafor coined the term 'Afro-Japanese' in an article entitled "In Defense of Afro-Japanese Ethnophilosophy" in which he re-evaluated ethnic characteristics that are common to Japanese and Africans and that go against the current of mainstream "Western" philosophy. Okafor's insistence on "folkness," which is highly unusual and provocative in the context of Western philosophy, suggests that "Afro-Japanese" philosophy is a cultural alternative that has become possible through globalization.

In the realm of aesthetics, Afro-Japanese culture is probably best represented by the Japanese clothing brand BAPE (A Bathing Ape) which has become the preferred brand of the arguably most popular American rapper Lil' Wayne and is also worn by Pharrell, Kanye West (who performed with the BAPE-produced Terayaki Boyzs in 2008), Mos Def, The Roots, Questlove, Faith Evans, and Pusha T. Though many American consumers still remain unaware of BAPE's Japanese identity, BAPE combines cool Hip-Hop style with particularly *kawaii* motives and offers products like the Panda Hoodie or other animal themed Hoodies that replace the aggressive and popular Shark Hoodie. The brand's character Milo, a particularly cute monkey, is printed on clothes, but appears also on the newest Nintendo DS Light Game Boy where he joins Supermario, another character that BAPE uses for fashion design.

BAPE developed within the Tokyo Ura-Harajuku movement and combined an ironical view of Japanese society with an opposition to mass-produced trends. In spite of its anti-establishment posture, BAPE has established highly visible tie-ups with global companies like Pepsi-Cola, Disney, and Nintendo. For American rapper Common, the line is "all about that next level of fashion" ("Kanye, Pharrell, Mos Def Celebrate A Designer With Sole"). BAPE also collaborates with the Japanese toy Bearbrick and releases the cute figures in typical BAPE camouflage colors.

Cool

The aesthetics of cool developed mainly in the form of a behavioral attitude practiced by black men in the United States at the time of slavery. During this time, residential segregation made necessary the cultivation of special defense mechanisms, which employed emotional detachment as well as irony. A cool attitude helped slaves and former slaves to cope with exploitation or simply made it possible to walk streets at night. In principle, to be cool means to remain calm even under stress.

The African origins of cool and its affinities with African moral concepts have been noted by several authors. Robert Farris Thompson's often-cited essay from 1966, "An Aesthetics of the Cool," in which the author makes reference to the Yoruba indigenous "philosophy of the cool" (*itutu*, "mystic coolness"), which epitomizes the ideal of patience and collectedness of the mind, has made the point clearest ("An Aesthetic of the Cool: West African Dance," p. 73). Thompson takes it for granted that "the coming of the icons of the Yoruba to the black New World accompanied an affirmation of philosophical continuities" (*Flash of the Spirit*, p. 93) that overlap more or less with our current understanding of cool. West African roots indicate a striving for an active participation in an event "while maintaining a detached attitude" because for this culture, "the symbol of one's coolness is the relaxed, smiling face" ("Lester Young and the Birth of Cool," p. 254).

Already at times of slavery, the proto-cool of black America, the cool mask's popularized trademark was not limited to a rigid irreverence as a worldview but required creativity as well as seductive power. This is what mainstream America would find so confusing. The conventional, white American understanding of cool was that of 'impartiality' most likely to be opposed to a 'hot' or heated behavior. McLuhan explained in the 1960s that "formerly a 'hot' argument meant one in which people were deeply involved. On the other hand, a 'cool attitude' used to mean one of detached objectivity and disinterestedness. In those days the world 'disinterested' meant noble quality of fair-mindedness" (*Understanding Media*, p. vii). African American cool doesn't really reverse

this scheme but offers an "elastic" aspect as it subverts conventional values and meanings but remains open towards improvisation and accommodation of external elements.

Cute

The word *kawaii* comes originally from the Chinese as *ke'ai* (可爱, roughly: "which can be loved") and is defined as cute, childlike, sweet, innocent, pure, gentle and weak. Like the English word "cute," *kawaii* is a colloquial word to whose academic examination aestheticians proceed only very hesitatingly. While 'cool' is the most popular word of approval in the US, *kawaii* appears to be the most frequently used word in Japan. Though *kawaii* is only a second-class aesthetic property, in Japan, its popular aesthetic appeal is of national importance. Like cute, *kawaii* is a predominantly visual quality: there are no *kawaii* textures, tastes, or smells and on the most basic level, there seems to be no difference between the outer appearance of *kawaii* and cute objects or persons. The ethologist Konrad Lorenz has established the main characteristics of "babyish features" which lead Morreall and Loy to define cuteness as:

> a group of features that evolved in mammalian infants as a way of making them attractive to adults. The 'releasing stimuli' for nurturant behavior, as ethologists refer to cute features, include a head large in relation to the body, eyes set low in the head, a large protruding forehead, round protruding cheeks, a plump rounded body shape, sort thick extremities, soft body surface, and clumsy behavior. ("Kitsch and Aesthetic Education," p. 68)

Kawaii objects are usually small, round, warm, soft, and fluffy, and vibrate innocence and simplicity. Like 'cute', *kawaii* can be used for objects as well as for persons; in the latter case it somehow adopts the meaning of "pretty" when used for young girls and boys. If we speak of an aesthetics of *kawaii*-ness (kawairashisa), however, we address *kawaii* as a concept, and we have to lay out the differences between cute and *kawaii*. The borderline that establishes these conceptual differences overlaps to some extent with the difference between Far-Eastern and Western culture.

Many authors have linked *kawaii* to a kind of willful immaturity or childishness and a desire to be indulged like children that the Japanese call *amae*. However, it's important not to reduce *amae* to a merely passive syndrome because its existence depends on an interplay of active and passive components. *Amae*, in the way it's performed by adults, is "staged" and controlled exactly like cool.

Japanese Kawaii Culture

Pokemon animals seem to be the most original symbols of the culture which kawaii had become by the late 1990s. The most current exterior characteristics of *kawaii* were most probably "invented" in manga in the 1970s when features of exotic Europeans and ordinary Japanese girls were superposed, creating the typical image of the *kawaii shôjo*, which immediately sparked the production of a large range of cute paraphernalia meant for female consumption. Today, *kawaii* culture is more than an aesthetic style—it appears as a full-fledged way of articulating a subjective attitude that can become manifest in design, language, bodily behavior, gender relations, and perceptions of the self. Still, *kawaii* remains linked to manga to the point that any "criticism of the immaturity and escapism of contemporary youth has been closely bound with criticism of the contemporary *manga* medium" ("Japanese Subculture," p. 292). Though manga and anime remain the center stages for visualizations of *kawaii*, these stages are so closely linked to real life that it has become impossible to establish if the girls who are using singsong voices are mimicking anime or if anime is reflecting them.

Kawaii-ness, as has said Brian McVeigh, "has become a 'standard' aesthetic of everyday life" (*Wearing Ideology: State, Schooling and Self-Presentation in Japan*, p. 135). In Japan, not only middle-aged women let dangle fluffy stuffed animals from the bottom of the cell phones, but also *salarymen* (business clerks) wear Pikachu on key chains and (male) truck drivers display Hello-Kitty figurines on their dashboards. Mary Roach describes the *kawaii* situation in Japan:

> Well-heeled city women are dropping yen by the millions on a Kansai Yamamoto couture line called Super Hello Kitty. Teenage boys tattoo themselves with Badtz-Maru, the Sanrio company's mischievous, lumpy-headed penguin. Salarymen, otherwise indistinguishable with their gray suits and cigarettes, buy novelty cell phone straps adorned with plastic charms of their favorite cute characters: Thunder Bunny, Cookie Monster, Doraemon the robot cat. ("Cute Inc.")

Though most authors would put forward the intrinsically positive and charming aspect of *kawaii*, there exists also a dark and decadent side of *kawaii*, which reaches from anomie and hypocrisy to the grotesque, erotic, and violent. In manga, *kawaii* gets quite commonly combined with a mature content like glamour or evidently grotesque elements that are definitely incompatible with cuteness in a Western sense. In "hentai manga" (pornographic mangas) *kawaii* girls are involved in pornographic content, including, rape, S/M, lesbianism and pedophilia. Moral apprehensions apart, one needs to admit that one of the most interesting features of *kawaii* is that it's able to unite contradicting tendencies and values in one single concept. This it has in common with cool.

Kawaii culture isn't restricted to Japan but occurs in all industrialized East Asian countries, transported by manga, anime, and fashion. Tzu-I Chuang remarks that in Taiwan "baby talk has become a common way of speaking among adult women" ("The Power of Cuteness: Female Infantilization in Urban Taiwan," p. 22) and Xiaoming Hao and Leng Leng Teh, in their article on the impact of Japanese culture on Singaporean youth, focus on "cutie street fashion" ("The Impact of Japanese Popular Culture on the Singaporian Youth"). *Kawaii* aesthetics is also becoming increasingly popular among youths in mainland China. Every month the Chinese magazine *Rayli* brings information about the Japanese and Korean entertainment and fashion industries to Chinese young people and publishes special issues like "Childlike 31 Days" (2006).

Cool and *Kawaii* as Aesthetics of Opposition

During slavery and long afterwards, overt aggression of black people was punishable with death; for African Americans cool represents, therefore, a paradoxical fusion of submission and subversion. In principle, provocation had to remain inoffensive and any level of seriousness had to be suppressed. Because the scope of responses to oppression was limited and open attack or rebellion were impossible, cool is a classic case of resistance to authority through creativity and innovation. Finally, cool could become a triumph of spirit as a rational reaction to an irrational situation willing to put its personal stamp on everything. On the one hand, the signifying power or message produced by cool poses fascinated the world because of its inherent ambiguity and mysteriousness. On the other hand, the stylized way of offering resistance that insisted more on *appearance* than on *being* could turn black men, not in the last instance through a sort of self-produced "romantic racialism," into untouchable objects of desire. Here they come surprisingly close to the existence of women.

The driving force of cool is the "passive resistance to the work ethic through personal style" and a "defense mechanism against the depression and anxiety induced by a highly competitive society" (*Cool Rules*, pp. 41 and 158). It's not difficult to find this driving force also behind *kawaii* culture in Japan. "Officially," the situation of the Japanese woman is one of submission. Equal opportunities were fully analyzed and transcended only in the 1980s and workplace equality is far from being achieved in Japan. Traditionally, Confucian ideology expects women to be humble and reverential in relation to men, and traditional ideals of women and marriage still dominate. Many Japanese men still wish women to stay at home, and many observers will affirm that Japanese corporate culture sees "women as a source of 'comfort' for the 'company warrior'" (*Consuming Bodies: Sex and Contemporary Japanese Art,*

p. 14). At first sight it looks as if traditional male-centered Japanese culture has kept women dependent, immature, simpering, and also *kawaii*. However, though this might be true to some extent, *kawaii* cannot be reduced to a mere strategy of submission but must also be seen as a matter of protest against traditional society. Tzu-I Chuang believes that, generally, in Confucian society "acting cute is considered 'modern'" ("The Power of Cuteness," p. 25). This means that *kawaii* as a liberation project is supposed to have an effect on the real world and that it has real value connotations. "Cute is a virtue and, in an oddly paradoxical way," it is "strength," says Shiokawa ("Cute but Deadly: Women and Violence in Japanese Comics," p. 107). Like cool, which reunites within one frozen, imperturbable state antagonistic qualities like submission and subversion, or participation and non-participation, *kawaii* is by definition a contradiction in terms because here "a child and a woman are frozen in an ambiguous spot" ("The Social Production of Gender as Reflected in two Japanese Culture Industry Products: *Sailormoon* and *Crayon Shin-Chan*," p. 205). This is why in manga and anime, as they put forward women and children as active heroes, female power is contained in the fragile. "The cute is no longer the powerless in need of subversion by lesbian groups but instead a type of enfant terrible that could complicate, as much as lubricate, social relations," writes Hjorth ("Pop and *Ma*: The Landscape of Japanese Commodity Characters and Subjectivity," p. 160). Even more, *kawaii* can be understood as a female empowerment similar to that provided by fashion, eroticism or, more recently, tattoos.

In other words, *kawaii* shouldn't be understood as a method of escaping reality only but as a means of establishing a new kind of reality, which is, as for cool, the reality of a "New World Modernism." *Kawaii* (just like cool, *torendi* in Japanese) doesn't simply elude the work ethics of its society but girls "can make themselves 'cute' by working hard at it" ("Cute but Deadly," p. 107), which isn't possible with regard to beautiful (*kirei, utsukushi*).

How to Create a "New World Modernity"

Similar to Japanese, African Americans, when being first confronted with white American culture, "proceeded in an *assimilationist manner* that set out to show that black people were really like white people—thereby eliding differences (in history, culture)" (*Keeping Faith*, p. 17). Today, however, most people would agree with the first dean of African American philosophy, W.E.B. Du Bois, who believed that "there is no true American music but the wild sweet melodies of the Negro slave; the American fairy tales and folk-lore are Indian and African" (*The Souls of Black Folk*, p. 43). Today African American culture is generally conceived as a fusion of American modernity and Africanisms.

The conception of a modernity based on or influenced by non-Western cultural experiences is contrary to the classical Western philosophical system of civilizational evolution most emphatically developed by Hegel. For Hegel, the New World was very clearly an expansion of white dominance as he was convinced that "America is . . . the land of the future, where, in the ages that lie before us, the importance of the World's History shall reveal itself—perhaps in a contest between North and South America. It is a land of desire for all those who are weary of the historical lumber-room of old Europe" (*The Philosophy of History*, p. 86).

In the New World, white Americans built a civilization, which was formalist, demystifying, objectifying, and, in the words of Kochman, impregnated by an "impersonal mode of expression that whites use" and which, "along with the absence of affect and dynamic opposition, establishes the detached character of proceedings in which white cultural norms dominate" (*Black and White Styles in Conflict*, p. 21). In a word: Western modernity is uncool.

African American culture explored new possibilities without harking back to a concrete tradition. Accordingly, Cornel West, who uses the model of "New World Modernity" as a principal concept for grasping the spirit of black American civilization, draws upon ideas of modernity based upon complex appropriations of the idea of willful alienation in accordance with the profound belief in a "decadent American civilization at the end of the twentieth century" (*The Cornel West Reader*, p. 89). Black American culture is modern because it's located in the New World though it's simultaneously "timed" in an eccentric fashion. For West, "New World Modernism" resides in "the timing of our voices in ritual and everyday practices (the syncopation and repetition in speech, song sermon and prayer)—in short, the timing of our communal efforts to preserve our sanity and humanity in Euro-American modernity" (*Keeping Faith*, p. 17). West evokes the image of a modernism in which coolness retrieves human values—paradoxically—by applying a principle of a willful alienation from technocratic, "uncool," white America.

We can say similar things about *kawaii*, which achieves a sort of New World Modernity by relying on acts of delay, displacement, oblique representation, and stylization, all of which are visible in manga culture. Both cool and *kawaii* overcome a passive techno-future determined by coldness. The active cool-*kawaii* values of the New World Modernity help us to move around in the contemporary world in a more authentic and less alienated fashion. In Japan, *kawaii* images are used for the personalization of new technologies or for customizing cyberspace. From the beginning, *kawaii* has been supposed to *humanize* the modern Japanese world, in which life had become formalized and static, even for children. *Kawaii* stands in opposition to industrial alienation, affirms naturalness, intimacy, innocence, and simplicity—all of which are

positive attributes. *Kawaii* things can be touched, they provide an authenticity that is getting lost in industrial societies, *kawaii* effectuates a personalization and familiarization of impersonal, mass-produced phenomena like cell-phones or cyberspace. For many Japanese—adult or child—the Hello Kitty image on the fridge vibrates an atmosphere of security and companionship that seems to be needed in the anonymous environment of highly unsophisticated apartment blocks and flyovers. *Kawaii* is also able to "soften" power relations occurring in those impersonal, rigid vertical hierarchies common in Japan.

At the same time *kawaii* isn't *against* modernity; on the contrary, it functions as its catalyst. This represents a further parallel with cool. In the 1970s when self-centered consumption was seen as an escape from traditional Japanese culture, *kawaii*-ness signified freedom: "The cute look that dominated young Japanese's fashion in the late 1970s was adopted explicitly as a rejection of a typically Japanese style," reports Lise Skov ("Fashion Trends, Japonisme, and Postmodernism, or 'What is so Japanese about Comme Des Garçons,'" p. 145). As a matter of fact, *kawaii* doesn't at all refer to traditional Japanese cultural patterns but is partly foreign in its origin.

Both cool and *kawaii* must be perceived as modern values able to embrace antagonistic terms such as liberation, fragmentation, and alienation. As Roland Kelts has pointed out, the world appreciates Japanese aesthetics not as a derivation of the traditional culture of an old civilization but—rather on the contrary—because of the eminently modern and futuristic ambiance it offers. For many Westerners, the "eccentricities, spastic zaniness," and "libertarian fearlessness" (*Japanamerica*, p. 6) of contemporary manga and anime culture represent "a vision of the future, a fresh way of telling stories and of reproducing the world" (p. 7). The futuristic vision of a postcolonial Japan that develops an autonomous culture able to invade a world whose culture it had once been supposed to passively consume and to imitate, is indeed reminiscent of West's definition of African Americans as "New World African Moderns," who "constitute a homebound quest in offbeat temporality" (*Keeping Faith*, p. xiii).

This is why sociologists like Alan Liu see in cool writing styles of Hip-Hop lyrics a "future literary" representing the mix of knowledge work and artistic practice that will rejuvenate the humanities (*The Laws of Cool: Knowledge Work and the Culture of Information*, p. 9); and Rebecca Black believes that manga "can be held up as novel in terms of the chronological development of 'new literacies'" (*Adolescents and Online Fan Fiction*, p. 3). According to Napier, the "empowered" *shôjo* Nausicaä from Hayao Miyazaki's manga can function as "an impressive feminine role model" ("Vampires, Psychic Girls, Flying Women and Sailor Scouts: Four Faces of the Young Female in Japanese Popular Culture," p. 101). Finally, the realistic genre of "information manga" dealing with business studies or serious cultural themes has promoted manga to the status

of high quality culture. Most probably, in the end, all this will work towards an institutionalization of *kawaii* culture.

Towards a Cool-*Kawaii* Modernity

Cool and *kawaii* don't refer us back to a pre-modern ethnic past. Just like the cool African American man has almost no relationship with traditional African ideas about masculinity, the *kawaii shôjo*, especially as she appears in manga, isn't the personification of the traditional Japanese ideal of the feminine but signifies an ideological institution of women based on Japanese modernity in the Meiji period—a feminine image based on westernization. Nor do cool and *kawaii* transport us into a futuristic, impersonal world of hypermodernity based on assumptions of constant modernization. Cool and *kawaii* stand for another type of modernity, which is not the technocratic one but the one closely related to the search for human dignity and liberation. New World Modernity attempts to "time" modern civilization in an eccentric fashion and manga and anime are expressions of this modernity. Cool and *kawaii* are modern if modern means to have "the courage to use one's critical intelligence to question and challenge the prevailing authorities, powers and hierarchies of the world" (*The Cornel West Reader*, p. xvii). In this way, New World Modernity acts against both traditionalism and anti-traditionalist modernism.

Being "Cool" in Japan

Kenzaburō Ōe has designed for himself a "habit of being," as described in *Japan, the Ambiguous, and Myself,* and on page 122, he illustrates this idea with the help of a few lines from "The Novelist," a poem by W. H. Auden:

> among the Just be just
> among the filthy be filthy too
> And in his own weak person, if he can,
> Must suffer dully all the wrongs of Man,

This poem captures a lot of the qualities of cool. Ōe feels a deep concern about the ambiguity to which he has to submit as a Japanese writer in a modernized Japan (which he considers to be a "disaster") and announces that for him the highest ideal for a life in an alienated world is to remain "decent." He wants the word "decent" to be understood in the sense of "humanist." He is referring to a sort of "coolness" that is necessary when attempting to maintain human dignity within a modern world.

Ōe's insistence on "ambiguity" in several of his writings show that his experiences have much to do with Japan's ambiguous status as a country able to articulate both first-worldliness and third-worldliness. Japan's national identity is determined by a duality, or even a "triality" composed of Asia, the West and Japan. Koichi Iwabuchi explains that "Japan is unequivocally located in a geographical area called 'Asia', but it no less exists outside a cultural imaginary of 'Asia' in Japanese mental maps" (*Recentering Globalization: Popular Culture and Japanese Transnationalism*, p. 7). A further ambiguous input is produced by Japan's relationship with modernity. Though Japan has responded very quickly to the challenges posed by the prior development of science and technology in the Western world, Japanese culture still has, in Iwabuchi's words, a "curious quasi-Third World status" (p. 2). Ōe recognizes that "the modernization of Japan was oriented toward learning from and imitating the West, yet the country is situated in Asia and has firmly maintained its traditional culture" (*Japan, the Ambiguous,* p. 117). I believe that expressions of *kawaii* need to be understood within this non-linear context: they are ambiguous forms of resistance within a world that is profoundly ambiguous. This is why they so often overlap with African American cool procedures.

Cool-Kawaii Modernity Is Not South Park

Cornel West finds that in Western culture, even avant-gardist devices have become merely fashionable and faddish (*Keeping Faith*, p. 50). A typical white American escape route from impersonal modes of expression is *cynicism* that accepts the blandness of reality by putting on a sour face. American animation series like *The Simpsons* and *South Park* are results of this strategy.

For Kelts, who is tackling the problem from the Japanese side, the problem with many American animated films is that "the characters are so sarcastic and hip, they don't even seem to believe in the story they're in" (*Japanamerica*, p. 29). Kelts points out that *The Simpsons* and *South Park* distinguish themselves from Japanese animation culture, where "you don't find that sarcasm" (p. 29). The main characters' straightforward belief in the good that is so striking in anime and manga contrasts with *The Simpsons* and *South Park*, often even leading to obscenity through "an implosion of the traditional dynamics of taboo and transgression" (Larsen in "*South Park*'s Solar Anus, or, Rabelais Returns: Cultures of Consumption and the Contemporary Aesthetics of Obscenity," p. 66). In manga and anime, criticism exists but it's more global as it addresses more fundamental distinctions between 'good' and 'bad.' Therefore, it's also more philosophical, elliptic, and metaphorical.

This leads to a surprising conclusion: though the American cartoons are direct, always say what they mean, and criticize specific people, their aesthetics

of literalness doesn't produce a feeling of realism. Anime and manga, on the other hand, evoke "really" sad feelings that are fractured only by an overall aesthetic device of irony. According to Kelts, among the more complex aspects of anime and manga are the "acceptability of the illogical and the ambiguous, the hero's sense of duty above all else, the concepts of child as hero and unending quest, the undependability of a happy ending and the fact that no individual episode ever satisfactorily ties up the various and addictive narrative threads" (*Japanamerica*, p. 91).

The Matrix and New World Modernity

Cornel West's Afro-futurist vision of a New World Modernity could be best observed in the film trilogy *The Matrix*, in which West himself had the role of Counselor West. In these films, there are references to slavery and bondage as well as to race as an unalterable entity. However, because the futurist techno-dictators are white while the city of Zion predominantly populated by black people, *The Matrix* engages in a racial presentation of New World Modernity.

Claudia Springer interprets the appearance of white people in *The Matrix* as the "literal incarnation of the kind of bloodless society of drones that [1950s] hipsters loathed" ("Playing it Cool in the Matrix," p. 92) and goes as far as crystallizing a "racist paradigm associating black people with authenticity and life and white people with artifice and death" (p. 94). While in *The Matrix* "whiteness represents the soullessness and seeming transparency of modern interface culture," and race adopts the quality of being 'real,' these films break a new ground in depicting black men in relation to computers (p. 126). This is a clear indication of the existence of a New World Modernity.

One of the aesthetic sources of these patterns is the Wachowski brothers' love for, and indebtedness to, manga and anime (the brothers wrote some of the *Animatrix* anime scripts themselves). Kelts conceives of *The Matrix* as a sort of Western manga. It's not only the style in general, but also the "naïve" and straightforward depiction of a New World Modernity, which turns the Matrix films into icons of "sarcasm free, slightly befuddled search for truth and identity found in so many anime titles" (*Japanamerica*, p. 29).

A World of Floating Signifiers

It's obvious that this development announces what Roland Barthes has called, fifty years ago in his work on Japan, the "coming of the civilization of the signifier" ("Japon: l'art de vivre, l'art des signes," p. 531). Barthes attempted to see Japanese culture as a system of unrelated and empty signs, which don't

strive towards transcendence, fullness or a central sense and defined the sign in Japan as "a break that opens itself only onto the face of another sign" (*Empire of Signs*, p. 781).

Did Barthes anticipate the world of manga and anime? Barthes's vision of Japan as half-real and half-unreal is indeed more contemporary than ever since the image of Japan as a society of endless floating signs, of simulation and pastiche has been reinstated through electronic revolutions and the development of virtual reality. Barthes's vision of Japan as an empire of floating signs can also be described in terms of decentralized Hip Hop "breaks and flows" that ignore the "superb plenitude of reality" (*Empire*, p. 767). Barthes described haikus as generated by a "breach" of meaning (p. 794). The important point is that these are *only* signs of an empire without natural referential meaning.

Not surprisingly, contemporary authors use Barthes's same argument for an analysis of American cool culture. Jeff Rice finds Barthes's concepts most suitable when it comes to grasping the floating type of cool rhetoric because here signifiers can be exchanged without concern for referentiality (*The Rhetoric of Cool: Composition Studies and New Media*, p. 93). For Cornel West this is the reason why African American culture represents the ideal model of New World Modernity. Descriptions of culture in terms of exoticism or "the other" do always happen by referring to some natural, traditional, historic truth. New World Modernism, on the other hand, is able to overcome the "binary oppositions of natural, primitive, rules, and peoples of color" (*Keeping Faith*, p. 52). The world of manga, together with the naïve and straightforward mechanics through which it expresses the values of kawaii, is part of the same project. "Holding back," being subversive, operating within the realm of possibilities, and in attempting to aestheticize rather than referring to cynicism or threats, both cool and kawaii combat the uncool and bland culture of old modernity.

24

The Flaming Metaphysical Lips of Manga

GEORGE A. REISCH

*W*ayne Coyne, leader of The Flaming Lips, must be a fan of comics and manga—and not just because *Yoshimi Battles the Pink Robots* puts the fate of the universe in the hands of a Japanese schoolgirl. Every Lips album since the band's 1999 critical breakthrough *The Soft Bulletin*, through *Yoshimi*, 2006's *At War With the Mystics,* and 2009's *Embryonic* reveals a musical sensibility drenched in comics and visual arts.

For starters, the covers of these albums depict stylized, cartoonish figures struggling against themselves, the forces of the universe, or both. *The Soft Bulletin* shows a posterized image of a teenager, bathed in yellow light, pausing as if he's suddenly struck or alarmed by his shadow.

Yoshimi shows a classic sci-fi confrontation between man and machine—in this case, between Yoshimi and the evil robots who are "programmed to destroy us." And *Mystics* shows an explosion of light and color sending someone back on their heels, blown off the ground by a mysterious, tremendous force they've wandered too close to.

And superheroes make several appearances in Lips' songs though, as we will see, their powers are not so super. There's "Waitin' for a Superman" on *The Soft Bulletin*, "Captain America Splits the Audience" on the *UFO's at the Zoo* concert film. And in "The W.A.N.D." on *Mystics*, Luke Skywalker's "baton of light" saves us from the sinister fanatics who want to "rule all the world." These struggles usually take place in outer space, where most of the Lips music is set. Titles like "Approaching Pavonis Mons by Balloon (Utopia Panitia)," "Vein of Stars," "Watching the Planets," and "Aquarius Sabotage" point to far-away worlds and mind-bending, logic-defying experiences—none of which will be surprising if you've followed The Flaming Lips.

The Fearless Freaks

Since 1983, Wayne and his bandmates have been unconventional and independent. Working from Oklahoma, they've created their music and art that has been called punk, prog, psychedelic, or just weird. The same goes for

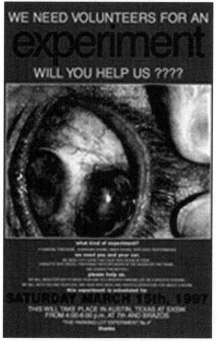

their performances, some of which they publicized not as concerts but as "experiments" in which audience members were collaborators. Their "parking lot experiments" of the 1990s had band members conducting parking lots full of cars in which fans play various tapes, created by the band, at various times and at various volumes. (If you signed up, your car stereo needed to be a good one—"the louder the better," the concert poster requested.) Other concerts had fans playing tapes on boomboxes or wearing headphones. When the band plays on stage, it's typically filled with dancing bunnies and space aliens—again, loyal fans in costume—confetti canons, bus-sized balloons, and whatever odd props The Lips have cooked up for the occasion. Brad Beesley's 2006 film about the band called them affectionately, but accurately, "Fearless Freaks."

What role does Wayne's interest in manga and sci-fi play in all this? It would be easy to argue that Wayne borrows their ideas, images, and themes

when he and his bandmates write music. But in fact the connection is deeper, for Wayne's music embodies a theory of art and iconic representation that can also be found at the heart of comics. It's nearly identical to the one Scott McCloud lays out in his *Understanding Comics*, and it goes a long way toward making sense of The Lips' freakiness as well as explaining one avenue by which manga, anime, and graphic novels are making their way into popular culture. If Wayne were master of the universe, this philosophy of art would be expanded and generalize to become a philosophy of life itself. For him, it's powerful, liberating, and lets us make the best of the life we've been given. If you've seen the Lips in concert, you may already agree that he's right.

Half-Human, Half-Lighthouse

I first began to understand this distinctive, cartoonish approach to art when I saw the Flaming Lips tour with Beck in 2006. The moment was Beck's performance of "Round the Bend," an excruciatingly sad, slow lament from his 2002 Interscope album, *Sea Change*. It's about (ironically) the blinding speed of life. Beck sounds like he's at death's door when he sings:

> We don't have to worry
> Life goes where it does
> Faster than any bullet
> From an empty gun
> . . .
> Round round round the bend
> Round round round the bend.

As Beck sang on a dark stage and slowly strummed his acoustic guitar, Wayne appeared behind him carrying a wooden chair and something with a power cord attached to it. It was an electric light, a worklight, I think, with a blue light bulb in it. He turned it on, climbed up on the chair, and began to swing the light around above his head, like a lasso. He let the cord out gradually, so by the time Beck got to the second verse, the light was making large, graceful circles, etching the darkness as he sang.

The moment was sublime, but not just because of the beauty of Beck's song, and the sinister, enigmatic quality of Wayne's effect—was the light a siren? an alarm of some kind? or a nod to the "around the bend" lyric? It was sublime because Wayne created all this beauty in such a simple, unlikely way. No computer-controlled lights or projectors or expensive devices were required— just a chair, a fifteen-dollar trip to a hardware store, and a guy, Wayne himself, willing to get up and do the work. It's an idea Wayne comes back to again and again in his art and in interviews: there is immense and amazing beauty in the

most ordinary things and circumstances. But to bring it out, and appreciate the happiness it can bring us, you have to see things and interact with them the right way.

Duct Tape and Glue

Lips concerts are festivals of this kind of on-the-spot, self-created fun and amazement. Dressed in one of his trademark suits, usually white, Wayne runs his shows like a circus impresario, sometimes singing into a megaphone, sometimes dripping with fake blood, and sometimes using hand-held spotlights or fog machines. At some point, he climbs inside his man-sized hamster ball (they call it "the space bubble") and walks (or rolls) out over the audience's outstretched hands.

In videos and movies, things get twice as weird. An early scene in *Christmas on Mars,* the band's feature film, as well as the video for *Embryonic's* "Watching the Planets," feature people squirming and climbing their way out of huge, inflatable balls through vagina-like openings. This is not as shocking or pornographic as it may sound, for these props are plainly homemade and artificial (although the naked people in the "Watching the Planets" video are obviously not artificial). There is plenty of duct tape, hot melt glue, building materials, and junk-store discoveries in these and other Flaming Lips videos.

These less than convincing special effects point again to the band's affinity with manga and comics. Metaphysically speaking, The Flaming Lips and manga artists are in the same department: they create nonrealistic art. It is not supposed or intended to represent or copy real, existing objects or events at some other place or time. That's no surprise if you're reading this book. No sane fan of Astro Boy, for example, will assume for a second that somewhere in the universe lives a young guy with black, pointy hair and jet engines in his red boots.

Most artists, though, strive for realism of one sort or another. Michelangelo wanted his David not only to stand forth as a beautiful statue; he wanted it to represent things outside the stone, like humanity, human courage, and the historical David famous for slaying the giant Goliath with his slingshot. Even inside the unreal world of Spinal Tap the quest for realism is on display when the replica of Stonehenge they commissioned turned out to be only eighteen inches, instead of eighteen feet, high. Their first performance of "Stonehenge" with the new prop was a disaster because it exposed the artifice and trickery of their art. Fans could see that the band wasn't channeling the otherworldy, mystical druids of Stonehenge with their song; but they merely were trying (and failing) to make it *appear* that they were. Between the silly eighteen-inch prop on the stage and the mysterious and otherwordly reality the prop

obviously did not represent very well, the band got caught with their spandex pants down.

The Face Value of Reality

That could never happen to the Flaming Lips because they've abandoned aesthetic realism altogether. They do not want to fool their fans into believing that those are real bears or mutant, human-sized bunnies dancing on stage, or that the opening scene of *Christmas on Mars* really captures a humanoid being emerging from some cosmic interstellar vagina that exists next to some white dwarf that you can see in a telescope. For their purposes, having fans dress up as bunnies or birth themselves from inflatable props in a video is *more* interesting and fun than

any attempt to fool their audiences with life-like special effects.

According to Scott McCloud, nonrealism is a key to understanding comics and explaining, in particular, how comics emotionally engage us. In his *Understanding Comics* (Harper Collins, 1993) he discusses an icon consisting of an oval, two dots, and a line. You would instantly recognize the figure as a face, however, proving McCloud's point

THUS, WHEN YOU LOOK AT A PHOTO OR REALISTIC DRAWING OF A FACE--

--YOU SEE IT AS THE FACE OF *ANOTHER*.

BUT WHEN YOU ENTER THE WORLD OF THE *CARTOON*--

-- YOU SEE *YOURSELF.*

From McCloud's *Understanding Comics*, p. 36.

that comic drawings engage us not in spite of appearing unrealistic, but *because* they are unrealistic. The lack of realism hooks us the moment we actively supply the missing information and decide for ourselves that this figure, which doesn't look anything like a real person's face, is nonetheless a face. "Icons demand our participation to make them work," he explains. Though the process he calls "closure," the replacement of the parts and aspects given on the page with the whole that is perceived, the reader breathes life into what is really lifeless ink. The only life in that crude face is "that which you give to it" (p. 59).

Compare this face to the realistic face McCloud provides. You can't help but perceive and react to this other face quite differently. You might find the person attractive or unattractive; they might remind you of some real person that you have particular feelings about. Whatever the

details mean to you, you more or less automatically perceive them and the associations they bring. And you probably won't be able to shake them and see the figure as a generic face. The figure itself, in other words, has taken interpretive control away from you and away from the comic artist.

The less realistic the icon, the more power the artist (and reader) have to realize a compelling story or message. Cartooning, McCloud says, is "amplification through simplification." "By stripping down an image to its essential 'meaning,'"—a generic human face, in this case—"an artist can amplify that meaning in a way that realistic art can't"(p. 30).

There's no better soundtrack to McCloud's claim than "Do You Realize?," one of the Lips' most popular songs. It's also about a face, and a few other little things:

> Do you realize that you have the most beautiful face?
> Do you realize that we're floating in space?
> Do you realize that happiness makes you cry?
> Do you realize that everyone you know someday will die?

The song is not about any particular face or about any particular people that are going to die. Wayne knows, however, that his audience will invest their own feelings and associations in the song and make the lyrics real and specific in the way they hear them. To use McCloud's term, listeners will provide their own closure and make the song point to what they care about. This works *so* well, "Do You Realize?" is now Oklahoma's state song (take *that* Rogers and Hammerstein).

Of course some of the song's popularity comes from hometown pride—it's the band's biggest hit to date. But it's also because of this unique power of nonrealistic iconography: because the symbols and ideas involved do not refer to far-away realities, they can better lead us toward truths and realities about ourselves and our own experiences that really matter.

Truth, Happiness, and Bobby Brady

In an interview with *Dusted* magazine, Wayne acknowledged the distinctive, often childish sound of his voice—"it always sounds a little bit like Bobby Brady or something." But this quality works with the lack of realism in his music to get at the things Wayne cares about:

> **DUSTED:** The things you talk about in your songs, especially with *The Soft Bulletin* and even with [*Yoshimi*], they seem like really deep concepts, but the style strikes

me as if they were the observations of a little boy looking at these things that maybe a little boy wouldn't understand.

> WAYNE COYNE: Well, yeah, I think in some ways, it is that sort of fairytale, storybook format that we kind of set a lot of it in. You know, it's meant to seem like these things that I'm in awe of, or these things that I think are wondrous things, I try to sing about them like I'm seeing them for the first time and maybe that enthusiasm and me being in awe will make the listener kind of feel like, "gosh, you're right". . . .

By creating art that *fails* to correspond to the real world we see and touch every day, he lures his audience away from their ordinary experiences, memories, and expectations of adulthood. Without our usual been-there-done-that sophistication and familiarity, that is, Wayne becomes more like a kid whose wonder and enthusiasm is infectious. "Do You Realize?" Wayne told Mog.com, is like

> a guy waking up from a coma, you know, seeing things for the first time. Which when I am around kids when they are fascinated by bugs or farting or whatever, you again are like 'yeah you're right; we really do live in an endlessly interesting world'. (http://mog.com/indiepixie/blog/243754)

Now we know what Wayne is doing with all those enormous, inflatable vaginas. By making them so cartoonish and fake, he breaks the ordinary associations they would have with pornography or anatomy in order to make the strangeness of the underlying biological facts shine forth in all their bizarreness. In the language of "Do You Realize?" his point seems to be "Do you realize that everyone you know came out of someone else?"

Trouble in Bizarro World

This "endlessly interesting world" Wayne portrays in "Do You Realize?" is a kind of Bizarro world. We think we walk around on solid, motionless ground, but in fact "we're floating in space." We think the sun rises and sets, but in fact that's "just an illusion caused by the world spinning round." We all like to be happy, but sometimes "happiness makes you cry." And we each enter this world through another person (traditionally called "mother") who's already here. And then we die.

Along the way, however, there's an endless procession of oddities and amazements—many of them catalogued in the Lips' many albums and videos—that make it all worthwhile. There are girls that color their hair with tangerines and eat vaseline for breakfast. There are zoos and strange creatures

called "giraffes." There are clouds that taste metallic, and regularly scheduled rituals—Wayne's favorites appear to be the ones bizarros called "Halloween" and "Christmas"—during which the bizarro humans exchange gifts and food while dressing up in all kinds of costumes.

But not everything is okay. Many bizarros don't realize where they are and, as a result, they are often unhappy and unamused with life. Some people, in fact, seek to hide the truth about how amazing and interesting this world is because they can profit when most believe we are condemned to live out our years on a drab, dull planet. Wayne's anger about this political circumstance is palpable on 2006's *At War with the Mystics*, on which his interest in bugs, vaginas, evil robots, and science experiments gives way to a focus on ideas *themselves* and how we too often let ideas, revelations, and sudden realizations—and those who claim to speak for them—control our lives and our happiness.

The shift is illustrated on the cover. What is this ferocious, exploding, dangerous and startling thing our puny human has stumbled into on the cover of *Mystics*? Being blown off his feet, he almost surely takes it to be a game-changing encounter that will transform his experience of life and the world.[1] But we know that it is in fact an explosion of iconographic nonrealism. It's not a thing, depicted in paint or ink, that is blowing apart; it's not a depiction of the earth opening and unleashing cosmic forces. It's nothing but paint and ink itself, exploding all over the CD cover.

The album nods to the semantic puzzle that sent the art world swooning in the 1940s and 1950s when nonrealist painters like Mark Rothko and, especially, Jackson Pollock were all the rage: What would a painting of spilled paint look like? How should it be interpreted? Would it be a representation,

---

[1] The cover is a visual representation of "The Spark that Bled," on *The Soft Bulletin*, in which Wayne compares a seemingly momentous, life-changing realization to a bullet ("the softest bullet ever shot") that makes his head bleed. For a while, it seems that this realization was going to rock his world ("it was all the rage, it was all the fashion"). But in the end it was a false hope for all those who had joined the bandwagon ("the out-reached hands had resigned themselves to holdin' on to something that they never had, and that's too bad.") For it turned out to be just an idea that, like the paint blobs on the cover of Mystics, did not necessarily refer to or represent any objective truth.

created on a canvas, of what you would see *were you to see some spilled paint* at some other time in some other place? Or, would the painting itself be a bunch of paint spilled onto the canvas before you? In the first case, the painting would be a representation of something else. In the second, it would not be a representation at all—just a canvas with paint spilled on it.

As a champion of nonrealism, Wayne would obviously choose answer number two. And judging from the songs on *Mystics*, he means it. The war he wages is against fanatacism and fanatics—that is, people who instead choose answer number one and presume that the ideas or beliefs they champion refer to important truths about reality that affect everyone. For fanatics, their causes and concerns can seem bigger than anything or anyone else. And that can be dangerous for the rest of us. "Free Radicals" goes,

> And you think you're a radical
> But you're not so radical
> In fact, you're fanatical
> Fanatical!
> I'll tell you right now
> You oughta change your mind

In "The W.A.N.D," Wayne uses a Luke Skywalker defense against "fanatical minds" who seek "to rule all the world." But he knows what to do:

> I got a plan and it's here in my hand
> A baton made of light
> We're the enforcers,
> The sorcerer's orphans,
> And we know why we fight.

Throughout the album, he attacks those who seek to control others by "tricking" them into accepting ideas and interpretations of life's meaning that we need not necessarily accept. In "My Cosmic Autumn Rebellion," for instance, he revisits "Do You Realize?" and urges a friend to resist nihilists for whom the fact that we will all someday die is the game-changer that explodes all the value and meaning of life. "So don't you believe them," he warns. "They'll destroy you with their lies / They only see the obvious."

Ideaman! We Need You!

But in light of Wayne's and McCloud's nonrealistic theory of icons, we have to ask whether any idea or realization should really have that kind of control over us. The explosion on the cover of *Mystics* is, after all, an explosion of meaningless, nonrepresentational paint. Like McCloud's stick-figure face,

what it means for us—the life and importance this event or realization will have—is up to us to determine.

What's at stake, Wayne believes, is our happiness and the very quality of our lives. In this regard, he's nothing less than a philosopher of happiness. He told *Dusted* that there is this "built in Flaming Lips philosophy" and its core idea is "that we create our own happiness":

> This idea that we wait for some great savior to come along and make our lives good ... if you are lucky, maybe that does happen. For the most part that doesn't happen to people. What happens is you say "Well this is the life I have these are my friends this is the world I am in. Let's make this work. Let's make this the thing that makes me believe in myself and be happy." And I think that's a real thing.[2]

He said the same thing in his installment of NPR's feature "This I Believe":

> I believe we have the power to create our own happiness.
> I believe the real magic in the world is done by humans.
> I believe normal life is extraordinary.

In Bizarro World, as you might have predicted, we are our own superheroes responsible for protecting ourselves and getting by we well as we can.

Flaming Lips fans must agree that the best expression of this is *The Soft Bulletin*'s "Waitin' for a Superman," in which Wayne himself wrestles with a potentially life-changing explosion, namely the death of his father from cancer. For the first time, it seems, while visiting his father and talking about his chemotherapy ("Is it overwhelming to use a crane to crush a fly?"), Wayne fully realized the gravity and sadness of the situation.

Things were "as heavy as they could be," so it was "a good time for Superman to lift the sun into the sky" and bring some light and happiness. But Wayne knew that that would not happen. By the time the chorus rolls around, the song grows into a message for all who have put their trust in Superman:

> Tell everybody waitin' for Superman
> That they should try to hold on best they can
> He hasn't dropped them, forgot them, or anything.
> It's just too heavy for Superman to lift.

Superheroes are fictions and there are limits on what they can do for us. We might even think of them as ordinary people, like the little boy who wears

---

[2] Wayne's view of life as embedded essentially among one's friends and, presumably also family, points to another element of manga likely at work here—the dominance of Confucian society-based ethics (as opposed to western, idea- or duty-based ethics) that is discussed by Andrew Terjesen in Chapter 4 of this volume.

Superman's cape in the song's video, who can only lift so much. Our best bet, therefore, is take matters into our own hands, realize clearly the facts of the world we live in (however bizarre they may be), and find some way to get by without any Superman's help. It may require us to take a fresh look around us; and it may require us to think of our lives as comics that require our intellectual and emotional participation to make sense and to have a good ending. In our bizarro world, like being at a Flaming Lips concert, you're never just along for the ride.

Half-Lighthouse, Half-Human

Wayne has complete confidence in his philosophy. Perhaps this reveals the best meaning behind his enigmatic human lighthouse: He's warning us away from dangerous metaphysical waters where we may be drowned by fears and insecurities that are merely our own ideas, fanatically blown out of proportion; and he's guiding us to a safer, happier place where we can begin to understand that the same conceptual dynamics that make comics and manga go—amplification through simplification, clarity about realism and nonrealism, and the active role of readers in providing closure—translate into a transformative philosophy of life.

So when you see the festival of dancing bunnies, aliens, ghosts, and Santa Clauses on stage, when thousands of colored balloons fall from the ceiling, when Wayne sings wearing four-foot rubber hands or cruises out over the audience in his space bubble, you will be watching people collectively create an alternate universe of happiness.

In comics, McCloud says, "creator and readers are partners in the invisible creating something out of nothing time and time again" (p. 205). But when The Flaming Lips play, musicians and fans become partners in creating this universe, song after song, out of nothing but guitars, drums, duct tape, and imagination.

It may even be a game-changing, explosive realization for you (perhaps as Wayne asks, "Do You Realize?") that not only can you shape your experience the same way . . .

. . . but that you already are.

"Round the Bend"
Lyrics by Beck Hansen
Published by Cyanide Breathmint Music/BMG Songs. ASCAP.

"Do You Realize?"
"Free Radicals"
"W.A.N.D."
"My Cosmic Autumn Rebellion"
"Waitin' for a Superman"
Lyrics by The Flaming Lips
Published by Lovely Sorts of Death Music, EMI Blackwood Music, Inc. BMI.

Select Your Warrior

CHRISTIE BARBER developed an interest in manga while living in Japan. She was fascinated by the evocative stories, and was driven to lug piles of these books—hard to find in Australia at the time—home with her after every subsequent trip to Japan. This interest in manga led her to her current research at Macquarie University, where she also teaches Japanese language, culture, and history.

ADAM BARKMAN is Assistant Professor of Philosophy at Redeemer University College. He is the author of *C. S. Lewis and Philosophy as a Way of Life* and *Through Common Things*. Besides the countless afternoons spent scouring Toronto's Chinatown looking for *otaku* goods with his brother, Adam fondly remembers his wife—fresh from reciting her wedding vows—attempting (and failing) to appreciate *Berserk*, his daughter, Heather, distracting him from the latest episode of *Gundam*, and hearing he was going to have another child, his son, while engrossed in *Macross*. There's also the time that his mother came with him to a manga and anime conference, but both of them are still trying to block large parts of that out . . .

For the past few decades, **ASHLEY BARKMAN** has been holding her birth year and blood type accountable for all her imperfections and blunders in the hopes of escaping crushing guilt. Unfortunately, she discovered that she's being inconsistent in her beliefs as free will plays a significant role in what she is and is to become. Hopefully, she'll continue to be enlightened as she lectures at Yonsei University. Ashley holds MAs in English and Theology, both from the University of Toronto. As a pop culture junkie, her recent publications include contributions to *30 Rock and Philosophy*, *Mad Men and Philosophy*, and the cover design for *Through Common Things: Philosophical Reflections on Global Popular Culture*.

ELIZABETH BIRMINGHAM didn't know manga existed until her then five-year-old son Griffin discovered Pokemon comics at the public library, and she first asked, "What on earth is this stuff?" Because she's an English professor, her question soon became, "What does this mean?" She lives in Fargo, North Dakota, and has long winters to read lots of shōjo manga and way more Plato than anyone ought to.

THORSTEN BOTZ-BORNSTEIN is a German philosopher trying to be slightly funnier than Kant. Being attracted by everything that is virtual, stylish, playful, and dreamlike, he has been drawn towards things Japanese ever since infancy. He has found

much of the desired dreamlike atmosphere in classical Japanese philosophy but has also elaborated on profound parallels between the design of the new Mini Cooper and traditional Japanese pottery or provided philosophical reasons why some Japanese subjects tend to use the English language as a "linguistic air-guitar." The continuation of his research takes place in a setting not less unreal than Japan: Kuwait.

MIO BRYCE is the Head of Japanese Studies at Macquarie University. She has a love of stories and is intrigued by the varied and complex representations of human nature she finds in fiction, especially manga. Freedom is very important to her, and when she sees it, she's sad about Japanese insularity. She wants to always be herself, and be with others. She also has a love of old buildings. One day, she'll be a wanderer with only a shoulder bag.

BRANDON CANADAY has never actually seen a death god but has been contemplating right and wrong since studying ethics under Richard T. De George at the University of Kansas. A light, possibly of divine origin, has led him to study, work, and travel extensively from India to Japan, and it is those two cultures in particular, one the home of Buddhism, the other the home of Shinto, that have kept him "on the road" for well over a decade. He currently resides in Japan, perhaps not far from *Yomi*, where he teaches, translates, and takes in as much of the local literature (especially manga) as possible.

JONATHAN CLEMENTS is often found with his arms sunk in soapsuds at the kitchen sink, weeping softly and remembering that all things must pass, for like the colors of the summer camelia, prosperity is ever followed by decline. With a BA in Japanese, and an MPhil. in Publishing Studies, he was formerly editor of *Manga Max* magazine and a contributing editor to *Newtype USA*. He is the author of *Schoolgirl Milky Crisis: Adventures in the Anime and Manga Trade*, and co-author of both the *Anime Encyclopedia* and the *Dorama Encyclopedia: A Guide to Japanese TV Drama Since 1953*. He is a PhD candidate at the School of Digital Media, Faculty of Applied Design and Engineering, Swansea Metropolitan University, researching an industrial history of Japanese animation.

Working at Macquarie University, **JASON DAVIS** can safely say that a decade-long English-language passion for Japanese popular culture has had a very noticeable impact for Librarians: Michael Manga, the geology professor, is turning up in less and less search results for articles on Japanese manga every year. Jason is also a member of an exclusive group of mangaphiles who have been escorted from Kinokuniya bookstores on two continents for overly encouraging customers to "breathe in" the finely textured examples of ramen noodles and sashimi pictured in the manga cooking series, *Oishinbo*. Jason's petitioning to have scratch-and-sniff applications included in books on manga featuring cooking has yet to convince publishers and editors of their olfactory potential, but his "lone wolf"-like devotion to the cause continues. Need more convincing of Jason's catchy ideas for books on manga? What about a manga on planetary and geophysical sciences by Professor Michael Manga . . .?

GORDON HAWKES has yet to gain a fandom of his own, but hopes that his chapter in this book will be the start. At the moment, his most obsessive and devoted fan is his wife, Sarah, who reads everything he writes. Gordon originally toyed with the idea of becoming a mobile suit pilot, but gave up that career path when he discovered the high mortality rate. Instead, he decided to devote his life to the significantly more safe (but dramatically less glorious) pursuit of truth: philosophy. He has completed a bachelor's degree from Prairie Bible Institute in Alberta, Canada, and hopes to one day get both his PhD and a job as a professor of philosophy.

NANCY KANG teaches in a private correctional facility (also known as a major research university) in New York where she apprehends criminal grammar issues amongst the juvenile population. Her specialty is prosecuting perverse pronoun placements, deviant or delinquent diction, recidivistic redundancy, and aggravated adverbial abuse. While her charges are usually raised on a strict regimen of reading, writing, and ego-deflation, she imagines integrating manga into the syllabus some day. Since learning is not supposed to be fun, this dream may not occur until after tenure or receipt of the Nobel Prize, whichever arrives sooner. Accessing lolicon and hentai for non-educational purposes in her classroom usually incurs a severe penalty; past offenders have pleaded down to a. memorizing a list of 110 useful literary terms like *Künstlerroman* and *aubade* and setting them to a techno beat; or b. naked jumping jacks while reciting Anglo-Saxon heroic poetry. When not discussing manga or feigning intellectual prowess, Kang researches race and other riot-worthy topics of enduring cultural significance.

This Section 2 Agent is currently under deep cover using the codename **SARA LIVINGSTON**. Could there be a better cover for Security Specialist than being a female Associate Professor at a small mid-western college? Nope. Serving as a faculty member in the School of Media Arts at Columbia College Chicago is the perfect cover. While she awaits her next mission she does what regular faculty members do—she teaches writing courses and consults with organizations that want to use new media and blogging to advance their institutional goals. In her spare time she writes about popular culture, contributing chapters to the likes of *Anime and Philosophy: Wide Eyed Wonder* and *Battlestar Galactica and Philosophy: Mission Accomplished or Mission Frakked Up?* It's been years since Section 2 last sent her on assignment, and many more may pass before she is called on to be an Agent again, but she accepts that fact. In her business, patience is a virtue and identity is transient.

When **GILBERT M. LUGO** isn't pushing papers for the New York State Division of Housing, he studies philosophy at Hunter College of the City University of New York. As a child, Gil (as he prefers to be called) was drawn to anime and manga because of their splendor, but now enjoys them, in addition to that, because of the rich characters and the many moral dilemmas they find themselves in. He's often quiet and keeps to himself in order to avoid the attention of any shinigami or Death Note owners. And if he ever comes across a Death Note, he promises to never use it and hide it where it can never be found. Seriously.

If **ELIZABETH A. MARKS** were a manga character, she would likely belong to the idiom of 'nerd hero'—perpetually flustered and blushing, with a drop of sweat hovering just to the side of her brow, head buried in a book as she tries to look inconspicuous. When not reading back-to-front, she is a PhD student in anthropology at Rice University in Houston, where she allegedly studies Japanese media, and tries to find time to practice her Japanese. She holds a master's in anthropology from the University of Chicago and one in media studies from The New School. In a previous life she taught art and design, and encouraged her students to invent manga characters of their own. She'd love to be drawn by Yazawa Ai.

DAISUKE MATSUURA is a graduate assistant in the Department of Communication and Journalism at the University of Wyoming. His research interests include the socio-cultural effects of comics and films both in the US and Japan. He was born in Tokushima, Japan. Ever since he was young, he's been amused by Japanese manga and anime. In his school years, he was in love with American comics and films. A small town Japanese boy came to America to study comics and films. Now he is married to an attractive web journal enthusiast.

NICOLAS MICHAUD, who is known by his students as "The Dark Alchemist" because he always wears black, teaches philosophy at the University of North Florida. He spends his time trying to create Chimeras by combining or transmuting his students with squirrels, but he has not succeeded, as of yet, though he has managed to annoy many squirrels—and a few students. I suppose he might eventually get around to actually teaching class, someday. . . .

STEVE ODIN teaches in the Department of Philosophy at the University of Hawaii. He's the author of *Artistic Detachment in Japan and West*, and regularly travels to the Land of the Rising Sun to research Japanese aesthetics, including literature, art, crafts, and cinema. He has now evolved into the cyberspace Otaku dimension of Manga and Anime, where—inspired by Azuma Hiroki—he develops *otaku tetsugaku* (Otaku philosophy), such as the chapter in this book. Concerned that the Toxic Jungle will soon boil over as the biosphere collapses and rushes into Apocalypse, he has now joined Nausicaä the Pure Land Messiah in the study of nature, ecology, and environmental philosophy.

ADA PALMER is usually a scholar or researcher, comparable to Saruta, but with more literary interests than Tezuka's typical mad scientists. She frequently plays a professor of European Intellectual History at Texas A&M University, researching the history of science, religion and atheism, and the Renaissance reception of classical philosophy. Her other reincarnations study Japanese popular culture, especially gender and folklore in manga and anime, and above all on Osamu Tezuka himself and his "Star System." Her most technologically-oriented incarnation runs TezukaInEnglish.com. She also appears in several brief incarnations at anime and sci-fi conventions, and, in an unusually non-scholarly role, as a composer of Norse mythology-themed music for the a cappella group *Sassafrass*.

GEORGE A. REISCH is the series editor for Open Court's Popular Culture and Philosophy Series and editor of *Pink Floyd and Philosophy*. He also coedited *Monty Python and Philosophy*, *Bullshit and Philosophy*, and *Radiohead and Philosophy* and writes a regular column, "Pop Goes Philosophy," on popmatters.com. Someday, he hopes, the world will realize that bizarro world is the real world, that Wayne Coyne is humanity's most insightful philosopher, and that this will all be made clear in a future book titled *The Flaming Lips and Philosophy* (with a foreword by Astro Boy).

DEBORAH SHAMOON has been a fan of manga and anime since long before the Internet, when small clubs gathered to watch unsubbed VHS tapes for an entire weekend and the only communication was by poorly photocopied newsletters. She later parlayed this interest into a PhD in modern Japanese literature and film, and a position as Assistant Professor at the University of Notre Dame, where she constantly reminds her students how much easier they have it now. She has published widely on Japanese film and music as well as on manga and anime in various academic journals, and she is the author of a forthcoming book on the history of shōjo manga.

In his pupal phase **BRUCE SHERIDAN** was a musician with philosophical tendencies who discovered upon emerging from the chrysalis that he had grown film-making wings. Unable to resist the whims of nature, he has directed, produced, and written for the screen for thirty years. Since 2001 somebody (he's not sure who) has let him run the world's largest film school at Columbia College Chicago. He often sneaked away from film shoots and various places of employment to study philosophy at the University of Auckland (New Zealand) where somebody (he's not sure who) gave him a Philosophy Prize and a graduate degree with first-class honors. He is currently a PhD candidate in philosophy researching the imagination and its relationship to creativity and artistic development.

CARL SOBOCINSKI is currently Assistant Professor of History at Yonsei University, Korea. Any students who have endured his classes learn very quickly his appreciation for films, cartoons, and, in the course of writing his chapter for this volume, manga. Several years ago his students at Kent State University presented him with their original edition of "Dr. Sobocinski's Guide to Films and Cartoons," which listed every film and cartoon he mentioned in class through the entire semester . . . each of them with some

connection to the course. Yes, Carl enjoys historically-themed films and stories, but he can be insufferable when they have serious (or even minor) historic inaccuracies. Hence, his participation in this volume.

JOSEF STEIFF is *not* an adolescent Japanese girl, though a glance at his bookshelves might make you think otherwise. Sure, he loves *Black Jack*, *Bastard!!*, and *Fullmetal Alchemist* as much as the next guy, and his prized possession is Otomo's single-issue *Memories* (which served as inspiration for the anime film "Magnetic Rose"), but he harbors a weakness for the likes of *Fake*, *Hero Heel*, *Last Hope*, *Negima!*, and *Revolutionary Girl Utena*. When he's not teaching film, he works on his house, reads about space, and eagerly awaits new scanlations of *Zipang* online, further proving that he's nothing if not a walking set of contradictions. Despite all that (or maybe because of it), he tries really really hard to be good.

TRISTAN D. TAMPLIN took a career guidance exam in high school that indicated that he should become either a religious leader or a test pilot. Instead, he got a PhD in philosophy, which he quickly parlayed into a career as a designer and photographer. An avid soccer player and fan, he currently lives in Manchester, England. Once the veil is lifted, he hopes to turn out to be an exceptionally kind person, who also happens to be embarrassingly rich.

ANDREW TERJESEN is currently a visiting Assistant Professor of Philosophy at Rhodes College in Memphis. His interests include moral psychology and comparative ethics with a strong emphasis on what it means to be a good person, although this may just be a way to rationalize spending a significant amount of money and time reading comic books. The results of his "research" can be found in *Supervillains and Philosophy* and *Anime and Philosophy*, among other places. Unlike some connoisseurs of visual narrative, he is not ashamed to admit that he reads and enjoys the superhero genre (though he wishes mainstream American comics publishers followed those in Europe and Japan in not relying too much on one genre or a "shared universe") and dreams of the day that he will see Kazuo Koike's version of the Hulk in English (or the even more obscure Superman stories produced in Japan).

SALLY JANE THOMPSON is, as far as she knows, a unified self with no doubles, twins or doppelgangers—at least in her immediate social circle. She's an illustrator and comicker working towards an MA in art and design, thus spending her time both making and writing about comics—in fact they've consumed more of her life every year ever since she picked up that first copy of Rumiko Takahashi's *Ranma ½* as a teenager. She is a member of UK and Ireland comic circle IndieManga as well as working with a variety of publications, and she is involved in workshops, events, and conferences around (and outside) the UK related to comics. On second thought, perhaps she could use one of those doubles.

"Okay, I can handle the library being gone (but there's no Häagen-Dazs, Mr. Donuts or Denny's here!)"

Adler, Ronald B., and Russell F. Proctor. 2007. *Looking Out, Looking In.* Twelfth edition. Belmont: Wadsworth.

Allison, Anne. 2000. *Permitted and Prohibited Desires: Mothers, Comics, and Censorship in Japan.* Berkeley: University of California Press.

Andreasen, Robin O. 2000. Race: Biological Reality or Social Construct? *Philosophy of Science* 67.

Appiah, Kwame Anthony. 1995. The Uncompleted Argument: DuBois and the Illusion of Race. In *Overcoming Racism and Sexism,* edited by Linda A. Bell and David Blumenfield (Lanham: Rowman and Littlefield).

Aristotle. *Nicomachean Ethics.*

Aurelius, Marcus. *Meditations.*

Azuma Hiroki. 2007. The Animalization of Otaku Culture. In *Mechademia 2: Networks of Desire,* edited by Frenchy Lunning (Minneapolis: University of Minnesota Press).

———. 2009. *Otaku: Japan's Database Animals.* Translated by J.E. Abel and Shion Kono. Minneapolis: University of Minnesota Press.

Ban Toshio. *Tezuka Osamu Monogatari.* 1992. Tokyo: Tezuka Productions. Smithsonian Freer Gallery of Art and Arthur M. Sackler Gallery <http://www.asia.si.edu/film/tezuka>.

Bandura, Albert. 2002. Selective Moral Disengagement in the Exercise of Moral Agency. *Journal of Moral Education* 31:2.

———. 2004. The Role of Selective Moral Disengagement in Terrorism and Counterterrorism. In *Understanding Terrorism: Psychological Roots, Consequences, and Interventions,* edited by F.M. Moghadda and A.J. Marsella (Washington, DC: American Psychological Association Press).

Barber, Benjamin R. 1995. *Jihad vs. McWorld.* New York: Times Books.

Barthes, Roland. 1982 [1970]. *Empire of Signs.* New York: Hill and Wang.

———. 1994 [1968]. Japon: l'art de vivre, l'art des signes. *Œuvres completes II, 1966-1973.* Paris: Seuil.

Benjamin, Walter. 2006. *Selected Writings: Volume 3, 1935–1938.* Cambridge: Belknap Press.

Bentham, Jeremy. 1988. *The Principles of Morals and Legislation.* Amherst: Prometheus.

Black, Rebecca W. 2008. *Adolescents and Online Fan Fiction.* New York: Peter Lang.

Blocker, H. Gene, and Christopher I. Starling. 2001. *Japanese Philosophy.* Albany: SUNY Press.

Bolton, Christopher, Istvan Csicsery-Ronay Jr., and Takayuki Tatsumi, eds. 2007. *Robot Ghosts and Wired Dreams: Japanese Science Fiction from Origins to Anime*. Minneapolis: University of Minnesota Press.

Bosse, Joanna. 2007. Whiteness and the Performance of Race in American Ballroom Dancing. *Journal of American Folklore* 120:475.

Brann, Eva T.H. 1991. *The World of the Imagination: Sum and Substance*. Savage: Rowman and Littlefield.

Brown, Jeffrey A. 2001. *Black Superheroes, Milestone Comics, and Their Fans*. Jackson: University Press of Mississippi.

Bryce, Mio, Jason Davis, and Christie Barber. 2008. The Cultural Biographies and Social Lives of Manga: Lessons from the Mangaverse. *Scan: Journal of Media Arts Culture* 5:2 <http://scan.net.au/scan/journal/display.php?journal_id=114>.

Byrne, Ruth M.J. 2007. *The Rational Imagination: How People Create Alternatives to Reality*. Cambridge: MIT Press.

Carter, Robert E. 2000. *Encounter with Enlightenment: A Study of Japanese Ethics*. Albany: SUNY Press.

Chuang, Tzu-I. 2005. The Power of Cuteness: Female Infantilization in Urban Taiwan. *Stanford Journal of East Asian Affairs* 5:2.

Cixous, Hélène. 1974. The Character of 'Character'. *New Literary History* 5:2. In *Changing Views of Character*, translated by Keith Cohen (Baltimore: Johns Hopkins University Press).

Clements, Jonathan. 2009. *Schoolgirl Milky Crisis: Adventures in the Anime and Manga Trade*. London: Titan.

Clements, Jonathan, and Motoko Tamamuro. 2003. *The Dorama Encyclopedia: A Guide to Japanese TV Drama Since 1953*. San Francisco: Stone Bridge.

ComiPress. 2007. Discrimination in Japanese Manga. *ComiPress: Manga News and Information* (January 25th) <http://comipress.com/article/2007/01/25/1399>.

Condry, Ian. 2006. *Hip-Hop Japan: Rap and the Paths of Cultural Globalization*. Durham: Duke University Press.

———. 2007. Yellow B-boys, Black Culture, and Hip Hop in Japan: Toward a Transnational Cultural Politics of Race. *Positions: East Asia Cultures Critique* 15:3.

Confucius. *Analects*.

Coogan, Peter. 2006. *Superhero: The Secret Origin of a Genre*. Austin: MonkeyBrain Books.

Cornyetz, Nina. 1994. Fetishized Blackness: Hip Hop and Racial Desire in Contemporary Japan. *Social Text* 41.

Cowie, Elizabeth. 1992. Pornography and Fantasy: Psychoanalytical Perspectives. In *Sex Exposed: Sexuality and the Pornography Debate*, edited by Lynne Segal and Mary McIntosh (London: Virago).

Currie, Gregory. 2005. Imagination and Make-Believe. In *The Routledge Companion to Aesthetics*, edited by Berys Gaut and Dominic McIver Lopes (London: Routledge).

Currie, Gregory, and Ian Ravenscroft. 2002. *Recreative Minds*. Oxford: Oxford University Press.

Daniels, Norman. 1994. Principles for National Health Care Reform. *The Hastings Center Report* 24:3 (May–June).

De Mente, Boye Lafayette. 1993. *Behind the Japanese Bow*. Chicago: NTC/Contemporary.

Descartes, René. 1972 (1954). *Philosophical Writings*. London: Nelson's University Paperbacks for The Open University.

Dinerstein, Joel. 1999 [1998]. Lester Young and the Birth of Cool. In Gena Dagel Caponi, ed., *Signifyin(g), Sanctifyin', and Slam Dunking: A Reader in African American Expressive Culture* (Amherst: University of Massachusetts Press).

Dittmer, Jason. 2007. The Tyranny of the Serial: Popular Geopolitics, the Nation, and Comic Book Discourse. *Antipode* 39:2 (March).

Doris, John M. 2005. *Lack of Character: Personality and Moral Behavior*. Cambridge: Cambridge University Press.

Du Bois, W.E.B. 1997. *The Souls of Black Folk*. Boston: Bedford.

Dupré, John. 2008. What Genes Are and Why There Are No Genes for Race. In *Revisiting Race in a Genomic Age*, edited by Barbara Koenig, Sandra Soo-Jin Lee, and Sarah Richardson (New Brunswick: Rutgers University Press).

Epictetus. *Handbook*.

Erino, Miya. 1993. *Ladies' Comic no Joseigaku: Dare ga Sodateru, Naze Teishaku shita? [Gender Studies in Ladies' Comics: Who Raises (the children), and Why So?]* Tokyo: Kōsaido.

Faiola, Anthony. 2003. Japan's Empire of Cool Country's Culture Becomes Its Biggest Export. In *Washington Post Foreign Service* (December 27th), p. A01.

Figal, Sara Eigen, and Mark J. Larrimore. 2006. *The German Invention of Race*. Albany: SUNY Press.

Fujikawa, Takao. 2007. Whiteness Studies in Japan: Visible and Invisible Types of Whiteness. In *Historicising Whiteness: Transnational Perspectives on the Construction of an Identity*, edited by Leigh Boucher, Jane Carey, and Katherine Ellinghaus (Melbourne: RMIT/School of Historical Studies, University of Melbourne).

Galbraith, Patrick W. 2009. The Otaku Encyclopedia. Tokyo: Kodansha International.

Gardner, Richard. 2008. Aum Shinrikyō and a Panic about Manga and Anime. In *Japanese Visual Culture: Explorations in the World of Manga and Anime*, edited by Mark MacWilliams (Armonk: Sharpe).

Garelick, Rhonda K. 1998. *Rising Star: Dandyism, Gender, and Performance in the Fin de Siècle*. Princeton: Princeton University Press.

Graf, Fritz. 1997. *Magic in the Ancient World*. Cambridge: Harvard University Press.

Gravett, Paul. 2004. *Manga: Sixty Years of Japanese Comics*. New York: Harper.

Griffis, William Elliot. 1905. Introduction. In Inazo Nitobe, *Bushido: The Soul of Japan* (New York: Putnam's).

Hadot, Pierre. 2004. *What Is Ancient Philosophy?* Cambridge: Harvard University Press.

Hall, Rashaun. 2005. Kanye, Pharrell, Mos Def Celebrate A Designer With Sole. In *MTV News Articles* (January 12th) <www.mtv.com/news/articles/1495796/20050112/story.jhtml?headlines=true>.

Hankins, James, ed. *The Cambridge Companion to Renaissance Philosophy*. Cambridge: Cambridge University Press.

Hao, Xiaoming, and Leng Leng The. 2004. The Impact of Japanese Popular Culture on the Singaporian Youth. *Keio Communication Review* 26.

Haslanger, Sally. 2000. Gender and Race: (What) Are They? (What) Do We Want Them to Be?. *Noûs* 34:1.

———. 2005. You Mixed? Racial Identity without Racial Biology. In *Adoption Matters: Philosophical and Feminist Essays*, edited by Sally Haslanger and Charlotte Witt (Ithaca: Cornell University Press).

———. 2005. What Are We Talking About? The Semantics and Politics of Social Kinds. *Hypatia* 20:4.

———. 2008. A Social Constructionist Analysis of Race. In *Revisiting Race in a Genomic Age*, edited by Barbara Koenig, Sandra Soo-Jin Lee, and Sarah Richardson (New Brunswick: Rutgers University Press).

Heal, Jane. 2003. *Mind, Reason, and Imagination: Selected Essays in the Philosophy of Mind and Language*. Cambridge: Cambridge University Press.

Hegel, G.W.F. 1900. *The Philosophy of History*. London: The Colonial Press.

Hjorth, Larissa. 2003. Pop and *Ma*: The Landscape of Japanese Commodity Characters and Subjectivity. In *Mobile Cultures: New Media in Queer Asia*, edited by Chris Berry, Fran Martin and Audrey Yue (Durham: Duke University Press).

Honderich, Ted. 2006. *Punishment: The Supposed Justifications Revisited*. Revised Edition. Ann Arbor: Pluto.

Honey, Maureen, and Jean Lee Cole, eds. 2002. *John Luther Long's* Madame Butterfly *and Onoto Watanna's* A Japanese Nightingale: *Two Orientalist Texts*. New Brunswick, NJ: Rutgers University Press.

Horgan, John. 2009. *Walking Away from Terrorism: Accounts of Disengagement from Radical and Extremist Movements*. New York: Routledge.

Hughes, Sherick A. 2003. The Convenient Scapegoating of Blacks in Postwar Japan: Shaping the Black Experience Abroad. *Journal of Black Studies* 33:3.

Hume, David. 1974. An Enquiry Concerning Human Understanding. In *The Empiricists*. New York: Doubleday.

———. 1985. *A Treatise of Human Nature*. London: Penguin.

Hwang, David Henry. 1986. *M. Butterfly*. New York: Plume.

Ienaga Saburo. 1978. *The Pacific War*. New York: Pantheon.

Imanishi Kinji. 2002. *A Japanese View of Nature*. Translated by P.J. Asquith, Kawakatsu, Shusuke Yagi, and Hirouuki Takasaki. New York: Routledge.

Inouye, C.S. 2008. *Evanescence and Form*. New York: Palgrave Macmillan.

Inwood, Brad, ed. 2003. *The Cambridge Companion to the Stoics*. Cambridge: Cambridge University Press.

Israel, Jonathan. 2002. *Radical Enlightenment*. Oxford: Oxford University Press.

Ito, Kinko. 2002. The World of Japanese Ladies' Comics: From Romantic Fantasy to Lustful Perversion. *Journal of Popular Culture* 36:1.

———. 2003. Japanese Ladies' Comics as Agents of Socialization: The Lessons They Teach. *International Journal of Comic Art* 5:2.

Iwabuchi Koichi. 2002. *Recentering Globalization: Popular Culture and Japanese Transnationalism*. Durham: Duke University Press.

Jakobson, Roman. 1990. *On Language*. Cambridge: Harvard University Press.

Jones, Gretchen. 2002. Ladies' Comics': Japan's Not-So-Underground Market in Pornography for Women. *US-Japan Women's Journal* 22.

———. 2005. Bad Girls Like to Watch: Reading and Writing Ladies' Comics. In *Bad Girls of Japan*, edited by Laura Miller and Jan Bardsley (New York: Palgrave Macmillan).

Kai-Ming Cha. 2007. Viz Media and Manga in the U.S. *Publishers Weekly* (April 3rd), <http://www.publishersweekly.com/article/CA6430330.html>.

Kant, Immanuel. 1993. *Grounding for the Metaphysics of Morals*. Indianapolis: Hackett.

———. 1997. *Critique of Pure Reason*. Cambridge: Cambridge University Press.

———. 2009. *The Philosophy of Law*. US: Dodo.

Kasulis, Thomas P. 1990. *Intimacy: A General Orientation in Japanese Religious Values*. Honolulu: University Press of Hawaii.

———. 1998. Japanese Philosophy. In *Routledge Encyclopedia of Philosophy*, edited by E. Craig (London: Routledge), <www.rep.routledge.com/article/G100SECT3>.

———. 1998. Introduction to Part Four. In *Self as Image in Asian Theory and Practice*, edited by Roger T. Ames with Wimal Dissanayake and Thomas P. Kasulis (New York: SUNY Press).

———. 2004. *Shinto: The Way Home*. Honolulu: University of Hawaii Press.

Kawashima, Terry. 2002. Seeing Faces, Making Races: Challenging Visual Tropes of Racial Difference. *Meridians: Feminism, Race, Transnationalism* 3:1.

Kelts, Roland. 2007. *Japanamerica: How Japanese Pop Culture Has Invaded the US*. New York: Palgrave Macmillan.

Kershaw, Sarah. 2010. The Terrorist Mind: An Update. *New York Times* (January 9th), <www.nytimes.com/2010/01/10/weekinreview/10kershaw.html?pagewanted=all>.

Kidd, Chip, ed. 2008. *Bat-Manga!: The Secret History of Batman in Japan*. Art by Jiro Kuwata. Translated by Anne Ishii. New York: Pantheon.

Kieran, Matthew and Dominic McIver Lopes, eds. 2003. *Imagination, Philosophy, and the Arts*. London: Routledge.

Kinsella, Sharon. 1998. Japanese Subculture in the 1990s: Otaku and the Amateur Manga Movement. *Journal of Japanese Studies* 24:2.

———. 2000. *Adult Manga: Culture and Power*. Honolulu: University of Hawaii Press.

Kochman, Thomas. 1981. *Black and White Styles in Conflict*. Chicago: University of Chicago Press.

Kors, Alan. 1998. *The Birth of the Modern Mind: An Intellectual History of 17th & 18th Centuries*. Video lecture series. Chantilly VA, the Teaching Company.

Kracauer, Siegfried. 2005. *The Mass Ornament: Weimar Essays*. Cambridge: Harvard University Press.

Kroopnick, Steve. 2005. *Comic Book Superheroes Unmasked* (DVD). Time Machine, A&E Home Video.

Lacan, Jacques. 1977. *The Seminar XI: The Four Fundamental Concepts of Psychoanalysis*. New York: Norton.

———. 1997. Jacques Lacan from 'The Mirror Stage' (1949). In *A Critical and Cultural Theory Reader*, edited by Anthony Easthope and Kate McGowan (Toronto: University of Toronto Press).

Larsen, David. 2001. *South Park*'s Solar Anus, or, Rabelais Returns: Cultures of Consumption and the Contemporary Aesthetics of Obscenity. *Theory, Culture, and Society* 18.

Leader, Darian, and Judy Groves. 2006. *Introducing Lacan*. London: Icon.

Leavitt, G.C. 1990. Sociobiological Explanations of Incest Avoidance: A Critical Claim of Evidential Claims. *American Anthropologist* 92.

Leder, Jane Mersky. 1993. Adult Sibling Rivalry: Sibling Rivalry Often Lingers through Adulthood. *Psychology Today* (January–February), <www.psychologytoday.com/articles/199301/adult-sibling-rivalry>.

Lewis, C.S. 1999. *An Experiment in Criticism*. Cambridge: Cambridge University Press.

Lewis, Hywel D. 1982. *The Elusive Self*. London: Macmillan.

Liu, Alan. 2004. *The Laws of Cool: Knowledge Work and the Culture of Information*. Chicago: University of Chicago Press.

Lloyd, Fran, ed. 2002. *Consuming Bodies: Sex and Contemporary Japanese Art*. London: Reaktion.

Loti, Pierre. 1895. *Madame Chrysanthème*. Paris: Calman Lévy.

Lovelock, James. 2006. *The Revenge of Gaia*. New York: Basic Books.

Lu, Amy Shirong. 2009. What Race Do They Represent and Does Mine Have Anything to Do with It? Perceived Racial Categories of Anime Characters. *Animation* 4:2.

Lui, Meizhu, and United for a Fair Economy. 2006. *The Color of Wealth: The Story Behind the US Racial Wealth Divide*. New York: New Press.

Lynn, Cheryl. Sambo, I Am?. In *Digital Femme*, <www.digitalfemme.com/journal/index.php?itemid=222>.

MacDonald, Heidi. 2005. More from Tokyopop's Jeremy Ross on OEL Manga and Contracts. *Publishers Weekly* (October 18th), <www.publishersweekly.com/article/CA6275188.html>.

Machery, Edouard, and Luc Faucher. 2005. Social Construction and the Concept of Race. *Philosophy of Science* 72.

Mallon, Ron. 2007. A Field Guide to Social Construction. *Philosophy Compass* 2:1.

———. 2006. 'Race': Normative, Not Metaphysical or Semantic. *Ethics* 116:3.

Manes, Kimiko. 2005. US Culture: Lessons from the Classroom. *The Daily Yomiuri* (April 26th).

Marks, Elizabeth. 2005. Reading Right to Left: Anime, Manga, and the Japanese and American Cultural Exchange. MA Thesis, The New School.

Matsui Midori. 1993. Little Girls Were Little Boys: Displaced Femininity in the Representation of Homosexuality in Japanese Girls' Comics. In *Feminism and the Politics of Difference*, edited by Sneja Gunew and Anna Yeatman (New South Wales: Allen and Utwin).

May, William F. 1994. The Ethical Foundations of Health Care Reform. *The Christian Century* (June 1st–8th).

McCarthy, Helen. 2009. *The Art of Osamu Tezuka*. New York: Abrams ComicArts.

McCloud, Scott. 1994. *Understanding Comics: The Invisible Art*. New York: Harper.

———. 2006. *Making Comics: Storytelling Secrets of Comics, Manga, and Graphic Novels*. New York: Harper.

McLuhan, Marshall. 1964. *Understanding Media: The Extensions of Man*. New York: McGraw Hill.

McVeigh, Brian. 2000a. *Wearing Ideology: State, Schooling and Self-Presentation in Japan*. New York: Berg.

McWilliams, Mark W., ed. 2008. *Japanese Visual Culture: Explorations in the World of Manga and Anime*. Armonk: Sharpe.

Mengzi. 2008. *Mengzi*. Indianapolis: Hackett.

Mill, John Stuart. 1861. *Utilitarianism*.

Miller, Laura. 2004. You Are Doing Burikko! Censoring/Scrutinizing Artificers of Cute Femininity in Japanese. In *Japanese Language, Gender, and Ideology: Cultural Models and Real People*, edited by S. Okamoto and J.S. Shibamoto Smith (Oxford: Oxford University Press).

Mills, Charles W. 1998. *Blackness Visible: Essays on Philosophy and Race*. Ithaca: Cornell University Press.

Miyazaki Hayao. 1996. *Starting Point: 1979–1996*, translated by Beth Cary and Frederik L. Schodt. San Francisco: Viz.

Mizunashi Akari. 2010. Every Incest Manga, Ever. In *Baka-Updates Manga* (January 13th), <www.mangaupdates.com/showtopic.php?tid=16039andpage=1#post348888>.

Morreall, John, and Jessica Loy. 1989. Kitsch and Aesthetic Education. *Journal of Aesthetic Education* 23:4.

Mukhopadhyay, Carol Chapnick, Rosemary C. Henze, and Yolanda T. Moses. 2007. *How Real Is Race?: A Sourcebook on Race, Culture, and Biology?* Lanham: Rowman and Littlefield.

Nabokov, Vladimir. 1997 (1955). *Lolita.* 2nd edition. New York: Vintage.

Nagel, Thomas. 1974. What Is It Like to Be a Bat? *The Philosophical Review* 83:4.

Nakar, Eldad. 2003. Nosing Around: Visual Representation of the Other in Japanese Society. *Anthropological Forum* 13:1.

Napier, Susan J. 2005. *Anime from Akira to Howl's Moving Castle.* New York: Palgrave Macmillan.

———. 2007. *From Impressionism to Anime: Japan as Fantasy and Fan Cult in the Mind of the West.* New York: Palgrave Macmillan.

———. 2008 [1998]. Vampires, Psychic Girls, Plying Women and Sailor Scouts: Four Faces of the Young Female in Japanese Popular Culture. In *The Worlds of Popular Culture,* edited by D.P. Martinez (Cambridge: Cambridge University Press).

Napoleoni, Loretta. 2009. The Intricate Economics of Terrorism, TED Talk. <www.ted.com/talks/lang/eng/loretta_napoleoni_the_intricate_economics_of_terrorism.html>.

Nietzsche, Friedrich. 1989. *Beyond Good and Evil.* New York: Vintage.

Nishitani Keiji. 1982. *Religion and Nothingness.* Berkeley: University of California Press.

Nozick, Robert. 1974. *Anarchy, State, and Utopia.* New York: Basic Books.

Odin, Steve. 1997. The Japanese Concept of Nature in Relation to the Environmental Ethics and Conservation Aesthetics of Aldo Leopold. In *Buddhism and Ecology,* edited by Mary Evelyn Tucker and Duncan Williams (Cambridge: Harvard University Press).

Ōe Kenzaburō. 1995. *Japan, the Ambiguous, and Myself.* Tokyo: Kodansha.

Okafor, Fidelis U. 1997. In Defense of Afro-Japanese Ethnophilosophy. *Philosophy East and West* 43:3.

Outlaw, Lucius T. 1990. Toward a Critical Theory of 'Race'. In *Anatomy of Racism,* edited by David Theo Goldberg (Minneapolis: University of Minnesota Press).

Palmer, Ada. 2006. Rock Holmes: Transformation (Parts 1–4). In *Tezuka in English,* <www.tezukainenglish.com>.

———. 2009. Film Is Alive: The Manga Roots of Osamu Tezuka's Animation Obsession. Smithsonian Freer Gallery of Art and Arthur M. Sackler Gallery, <http://www.asia.si.edu/film/tezuka>.

Patten, Fred. 2004. *Watching Anime, Reading Manga.* Berkeley: Stone Bridge Press.

Plato. *Phaedrus.*

Power, Natsu Onoda. 2009. *God of Comics: Osamu Tezuka and the Creation of Post World War II Manga.* Jackson: University Press of Mississippi.

Prough, Jennifer. 2006. *Mediating Ningen Kankei: Gender, Intimacy, and Consumption in the Production of Shōjo Manga.* Dissertation, Duke University <www.proquest.com.proxy.uchicago.edu>.

Pugliese, Joseph. 2002 "Race as category crisis: whiteness and the topical assignation of race." Social Semiotics 12, no. 2: 149-168.

Rau, Petra. 2002. Bildungsroman. In *The Literary Encyclopedia* (November 13th), <www.litencyc.com/php/stopics.php?rec=trueandUID=119>.

Rawls, John. 1971. *A Theory of Justice.* Cambridge: Harvard University Press.

———. 1993, *Political Liberalism.* New York: Columbia University Press.

Raz, Aviad E. 1999. Riding the Black Ship: Japan and Tokyo Disneyland. Cambridge, Mass. : Harvard University Asia Center

Russell, John. 1991. Race and Reflexivity: The Black Other in Contemporary Japanese Mass Culture. *Cultural Anthropology* 6:1.

Ryle, Gilbert. 2000 [1949]. *The Concept of Mind*. Chicago: University of Chicago Press.

Satō Kenji. 1997. More Animated than Life: A Critical Overview of Japanese Animated Films. *Japan Echo* 24:5.

Schodt, Frederik L. 1983. *Manga! Manga! The World of Japanese Comics*. Tokyo: Kodansha.

———. 1996. *Dreamland Japan: Writings on Modern Manga*. Berkeley: Stone Bridge.

———. 2007. *The Astro Boy Essays: Osamu Tezuka, Mighty Atom, and the Manga/Anime Revolution*. Berkeley: Stone Bridge.

Seneca. *On Anger*.

Singer, Peter. 2002. *Animal Liberation*. New York: HarperCollins.

Skov, Lise. 1996. Fashion Trends, Japonisme and Postmodernism, or 'What Is So Japanese about Comme Des Garçons.' In *Contemporary Japan and Popular Culture*, edited by J. Whittier Treat (Honolulu: University of Hawaii Press).

Solomon, William David. 2001. Double Effect. *The Encyclopedia of Ethics*, edited by Lawrence C. Becker <www.saintmarys.edu/~incandel/doubleeffect.html>.

Sontag, Susan. 2004. *Regarding the Pain of Others*. New York: Picador.

Southgate, Nick. 2003. Coolhunting, Account Planning, and the Ancient Cool of Aristotle. In *Marketing Intelligence and Planning* 21:7.

Springer, Claudia. 2005. Playing It Cool in the Matrix. In *The Matrix Trilogy: Cyberpunk Reloaded*, edited by S. Gillis (London: Wallflower).

Stromberg, Fredrik. 2003. *Black Images in the Comics: A Visual History*. Seattle: Fantagraphics.

Sundstrom, Ronald R. 2002. Race as a Human Kind. *Philosophy and Social Criticism* 28:1.

Takemitsu Makoto. 2003. *Nihonjin Nara Shitte Okitai Shinto*. Tokyo: Kawade.

Takeuchi Osamu, et al. 2006. *The Encyclopedia of Contemporary Manga / Gendai Manga Hakubutsukan 1945–2006*. Tokyo: Shōgakukan.

Tezuka Osamu Monogatari. 1992. Tezuka Productions. (French edition *Osamu Tezuka Biographie*, Casterman ; Italian edition *Osamu Tezuka: Una Biographia Manga*, Coconino Press).

Thompson, Jason. 2007. *Manga: The Complete Guide*. New York: Ballantine.

Thompson, Robert Farris. 1999. An Aesthetic of the Cool: West African Dance. In *The Theatre of Black Americans*, edited by Erroll Hill (New York: Applause).

———. 1983. *Flash of the Spirit*. New York: Vintage.

Thorn, Matt. 2001. Shōjo Manga: Something For the Girls. *The Japan Quarterly* 48:3), <http://matt-thorn.com/shoujo_manga/japan_quarterly/index.php>.

———. 2004. The Face of the Other. *matt-thorn.com* <www.mattthorn.com/mangagaku/faceoftheother.html>.

Tolkien, J.R.R. 1975. On Fairy-Stories. In *The Tolkien Reader* (New York: Ballantine).

Toku, Masami. 2007. Shōjo Manga! Girls' Comics! A Mirror of Girls' Dreams. *Mechademia* 2.

Volaire. *Zadig*.

———. *Story of a Good Brahmin*.

———. *Candide*.

———. *Poem on the Lisbon Earthquake*.

Watson, Gerard. 1988. *Phantasia in Classical Thought*. Galway: Galway University Press.

Watsuji Tetsurô. 1996. *Watsuji Tetsurô's Rinrigaku: Ethics in Japan*. New York: SUNY Press.

Weick, Karl E. 2001. *Making Sense of the Organization*. Malden: Blackwell.

West, Cornel. 1993. *Keeping Faith: Philosophy and Race in America*. New York: Routledge.
——. 1999. *The Cornel West Reader*. New York: Basic Civitas Books.
White, Joseph L., and James H. Cones. 1999. *Black Man Emerging: Facing the Past and Seizing the Future*. London: Routledge.
Wiley, Norbert. 1994. *The Semiotic Self*. Cambridge: Polity.
Winchester, Simon. 2005. *Korea: A Walk through the Land of Miracles*. New York: HarperCollins.
Wood, Joe. 1997. The Yellow Negro. *Transition* 73.
Wright, Bradford. 2003. *Comic Book Nation: The Transformation of Youth Culture in America*. Baltimore: Johns Hopkins University Press.
Yadao, Jason S. 2009. The Rough Guide to Manga. London: Rough Guides Ltd.
Yamanaka, Hiroshi. 2008. The Utopian 'Power to Live': The Significance of the Miyazaki Phenomena. In *Japanese Visual Culture: Explorations in the World of Manga and Anime,* edited by Mark MacWilliams. New York: M.E. Sharpe.
Zack, Naomi. 2002. *Philosophy of Science and Race*. New York: Routledge.
Žižek, Slavoj. 2007. *How to Read Lacan*. New York: Norton.

Manga

Aida Yu. 2005. *Gunslinger Girl* Volume 3, (English text). Texas: ADV Manga.

———. 2007. *Gunslinger Girl* Volume 5, (English text). Texas: ADV Manga.

Amakawa Sumiko. 2005. *Cross*. Volume 1. Los Angeles: TokyoPop.

Amano Kozue. 2004. *Aria*. Volume 2. 2003, translated by Kay Bertrand. Texas: ADV Manga.

Arakawa Hiromu. 2005-10. *Fullmetal Alchemist*. San Francisco: VIZ Media, LLC.

Ashinano Hitoshi. 1997. *Yokohama Kaidashi Kikou*. Volume 4. Tokyo: Kodansha.

CLAMP. 2003. *Magic Knight Rayearth*. Volume 1. 1993, translated by Anita Sengupta. Los Angeles: TokyoPop.

———. 2007. *Tsubasa Reservoir Chronicle*. Volume 12. 2005, translated by William Flanagan. London: Tanoshimi.

———. 2007. *Tsubasa Reservoir Chronicle*. Volume 13. 2006, translated by William Flanagan. London: Tanoshimi.

Fujishima Kosuke. 2007. *Oh My Goddess!* Volume 1. Milwaukee: Dark Horse Comics.

Gainax, and Hajime Ueda, *FLCL*. 2004. Volume 1. 2000, translated by Roy Yoshimoto. Los Angeles: TokyoPop.

Hashiguchi Takahashi. 2009. *Yakitate!! Japan*. Volume 15. San Francisco: VIZ Media, LLC.

Hatori Bisco. 2005. *Ouran High School Host Club*. Volume 1. San Francisco: Shōjo Beat Manga (VIZ Media, LLC).

Hotta Yumi, and Takeshi Obata. 2004. *Hikaru no Go*. Volume 1. San Francisco: VIZ Media, LLC.

Inagaki Riichiro, and Yusuke Murata. 2005-10. *Eyeshield 21*. San Francisco: VIZ Media, LLC.

Ikezawa Satomi. 2004. *Othello*. Volume1. New York: Del Ray Manga.

Ishinomori, Shotaro. 2003-04. *Cyborg 009*. Los Angeles: TokyoPop.

Kaori Yuki. 2004. *Angel Sanctuary*. Volume 1. San Francisco: VIZ Media, LLC.

———. 2004. *Angel Sanctuary*. Volume 2. San Francisco: VIZ Media, LLC.

———. 2004. *Angel Sanctuary*. Volume 3. San Francisco: VIZ Media, LLC.

———. 2007. *Angel Sanctuary*. Volume 20. San Francisco: VIZ Media, LLC.

Katsura Masakazu. 2002. *Zetman*. Tokyo: Shueisha, Inc.

Kawaguchi Kaiji. 2000. *Eagle : the making of an Asian-American president*. Translated by Yuji Oniki. Volume 1. San Francisco: VIZ Media, LLC.

———. 2001. *Zipang*. AnimeA, Manga On-Line, <manga.animea.net/zipang.html >

Kishimoto Masashi. 2003. *Naruto*. Vo. 1. San Francisco: VIZ Media, LLC.

Kubo Tite. 2008. *Bleach*. Volume 25. San Francisco: VIZ Media, LLC.

Kuroda Iou. 2002. *Sexy Voice and Robo*. English Adaptation Kelly Sue DeConnick, Trans. Yuji Oniki. San Francisco: VIZ Media, LLC.

Kurumada Masami. 2005. *Knights of the Zodiac (Saint Seiya)*. Volume 1. San Francisco: VIZ Media, LLC.

Masamune Shirow. 2007. *Appleseed*. Vols. 1-4. Milwaukee: Dark Horse Comics.

Matsori Hino. 2007. *Vampire Knight*. Volume 1. San Francisco: VIZ Media, LLC.

———. 2007. *Vampire Knight*. Volume 2. San Francisco: VIZ Media, LLC.

———. 2007. *Vampire Knight*. Volume 3. San Francisco: VIZ Media, LLC.

———. 2008. *Vampire Knight*. Volume 7. San Francisco: VIZ Media, LLC.

Matsumoto Leiji. 1987. *Cosmoship Yamato*. Tokyo: Akita Shoten Comics.

Miyazaki Hayao. 1982-94. *Kaze no tani no Nausicaä*, 7 volumes. Tokyo: Tokuma shoten.

———. 2004 *Nausicaä of the Valley of the Wind,* 7 volumes.Translated by David Lewis and Toren Smith. San Francisco, California: VIZ Media, LLC.

Moriyama Daisuke. 2004. *Chrno Crusade.* Volume 1. Los Angeles: San Val.

Nakajo Hisaya. 2004. *Hana-Kimi: For You in Full Blossom.* Volume 1. San Fransisco: VIZ Media, LLC.

Nakazawa Keiji. 2004. *Barefoot Gen. A Cartoon Story of Hiroshima.* Volumes 1-10. San Francisco: Last Gasp Publishers.

Ohba Tsugumi, and Obata Takeshi. 2006. *Death Note.* Volume 12. Tokyo: Shueisha, Inc.

———. 2006. *Death Note.* Volume 13. Tokyo: Shueisha, Inc.

Ohba Tsugumi. 2005. *Death Note.* Volume 1. San Francisco: VIZ Media, LLC.

———. 2007. *Death Note.* Volume 9. San Francisco: VIZ Media, LLC.

———. 2007. *Death Note.* Volume 10. San Francisco: VIZ Media, LLC.

———. 2007. *Death Note.* Volume 12. San Francisco: VIZ Media, LLC.

———. 2008. *Death Note: How to Read.* Volume 13. VIZ Media, LLC.

Park Sang Sun. 2005. *Ark Angels.* Volume 1. English Adaptation Jamie S. Rich, Trans. Monica Seya. Los Angeles: TokyoPop.

———. 2006. *Ark Angels.* Volume 2. English Adaptation Jamie S. Rich, Trans. Jennifer Hahm. Los Angeles: TokyoPop.

———. 2007. *Ark Angels.* Volume 3. English Adaptation Jamie S. Rich, Trans. Jennifer Hahm. Los Angeles: TokyoPop.

Shurei Kouyu. 2005. *Alichino.* Volume 1. 1998. English Adaptation Paul Morrissey, Trans. Amy Forsyth. Los Angeles: TokyoPop.

Tachikawa Megumi. 2001. *Saint Tail.* Volume 1. Los Angeles: TokyoPop.

Takahashi Shin. 2004. *Saikano.* Volume 1. 2000. English Adaptation Lance Caselman. Trans. Yuko Sawada. San Francisco: VIZ Media, LLC.

Takei Hiroyuki (concept: Stan Lee). 2010. *Ultimo.* San Francisco: VIZ Media, LLC.

Takemiya Keiko. 2007. *To Terra* (Tera e). 3 Vols. Trans. Dawn T. Laabs. New York: Vertical.

Tamaki Hisao, and George Lucas. 1998-99. *Star Wars: A New Hope.* Milwaukee: Dark Horse Comics.

Taniguchi Jiro. 2005. *The Walking Man.* Wisbech, UK: Ponent Mon, S.L., 2004.

Tateno Makoto. 2005. *Hero Heel.* Volume 1. Gardena, CA: Digital Manga Publishing.

———. 2006. *Hero Heel.* Volume 2. Gardena, CA: Digital Manga Publishing.

———. 2007. *Hero Heel.* Volume 3. Gardena, CA: Digital Manga Publishing.

Tezuka Osamu. 2004. *Phoenix:* "The Future" Volume 2. Translated by Dadakai: Jared Cook, Shinji Sakamoto, & Frederik L. Schodt. San Fransisco: VIZ Signature, VIZ Media, LLC.

———. 2008-10. *Black Jack.* New York: Vertical.

———. 2006-07. *Buddha.* New York: Vertical.

Urasawa Naoki, and Osamu Tezuka. 2009. *Pluto. Urasawa X Tezuka, 001.* Translated by Jared Cook and Frederik L. Schodt. Volume 1. San Francisco: VIZ Media, LLC.

———. *Pluto. Urasawa X Tezuka, 002.* 2009. Translated by Frederik L. Schodt and Jared Cook. Volume 2. San Francisco: VIZ Media, LLC.

Watsuki Nabuhiro. 1998. *Rurouni Kenshin* a.k.a. *Rurō ni Kenshin* a.k.a. *Samurai X* (Volume 21). Tokyo, Japan: Shueisha Inc.

Yamanaka Akira. 2004-05. *Spider-man J.* Tokyo: Kodansha; New York: Marvel Comics.

Yatate Hajime. 2000. *Gundam Wing.* Volume 1. Los Angeles: Mixx Entertainment.

———. 2000. *Gundam Wing.* Volume 2. Los Angeles: Mixx Entertainment.

———. 2000. *Gundam Wing.* Volume 3. Los Angeles: Mixx Entertainment.

Yazawa Ai. 2005. *Nana.* Volume 1. San Francisco: Shōjo Beat Manga (VIZ Media, LLC).

Searching Yggdrasil ...